Landscapes of Accumulation

South Asia Across the Disciplines

A series edited by Muzaffar Alam, Robert Goldman, and Gauri Viswanathan
Dipesh Chakrabarty, Sheldon Pollock, and Sanjay Subrahmanyam, founding editors

Funded by a grant from the Andrew W. Mellon Foundation and jointly published by the University of California Press, the University of Chicago Press, and Columbia University Press.

South Asia Across the Disciplines is a series devoted to publishing first books across a wide range of South Asian studies, including art, history, philology or textual studies, philosophy, religion, and the interpretive social sciences. Series authors all share the goal of opening up new archives and suggesting new methods and approaches, while demonstrating that South Asian scholarship can be at once deep in expertise and broad in appeal.

Recent South Asia Across the Disciplines titles:

We Were Adivasis: Aspiration in an Indian Scheduled Tribe
By Megan Moodie (Chicago)

I Too Have Some Dreams: N. M. Rashed and Modernism in Urdu Poetry
By A. Sean Pue (California)

Wombs in Labor: Transnational Commercial Surrogacy in India
by Amrita Pande (Columbia)

Voicing Subjects: Public Intimacy and Mediation in Kathmandu
Laura Kunreuther (California)

Writing Resistance: The Rhetorical Imagination of Hindi Dalit Literature
by Laura R. Brueck (Columbia)

Democracy against Development: Lower Caste Politics and
Political Modernity in Postcolonial India
by Jeffery Witsoe (Chicago)

Landscapes of Accumulation

Real Estate and the Neoliberal Imagination in Contemporary India

LLERENA GUIU SEARLE

The University of Chicago Press
Chicago and London

Llerena Guiu Searle is assistant professor of anthropology at the University of Rochester.

The University of Chicago Press, Chicago 60637
The University of Chicago Press, Ltd., London
© 2016 by The University of Chicago
All rights reserved. Published 2016.
Printed in the United States of America

25 24 23 22 21 20 19 18 17 16   1 2 3 4 5

ISBN-13: 978-0-226-38490-0 (cloth)
ISBN-13: 978-0-226-38506-8 (paper)
ISBN-13: 978-0-226-38523-5 (e-book)
DOI: 10.7208/chicago/9780226385235.001.0001

Library of Congress Cataloging-in-Publication Data

Names: Searle, Llerena Guiu, author.
Title: Landscapes of accumulation : real estate and the neoliberal imagination in contemporary India / Llerena Guiu Searle.
Other titles: South Asia across the disciplines.
Description: Chicago ; London : The University of Chicago Press, 2016. | Series: South Asia across the disciplines
Identifiers: LCCN 2016006711 | ISBN 9780226384900 (cloth : alk. paper) | ISBN 9780226385068 (pbk. : alk. paper) | ISBN 9780226385235 (e-book)
Subjects: LCSH: Real property—India. | Economic development—India. | India—Economic conditions—21st century.
Classification: LCC HD876.5 .S437 2016 | DDC 333.30954—dc23 LC record available at http://lccn.loc.gov/2016006711

♾ This paper meets the requirements of ANSI/NISO Z39.48-1992 (Permanence of Paper).

Contents

Acknowledgments

Like buildings, this book is a joint effort. Many people have made this project possible, and I am deeply grateful for all of their insight and support. I owe a deep debt of gratitude to Jeremy and all of the people at EuroFund for sharing their expertise, frustrations, and hopes with me. In a secretive, competitive industry, Jeremy's generosity and open-mindedness stood out. In keeping with ethnographic tradition, I have given EuroFund employees and everyone I interviewed pseudonyms; I have also changed project details, locations, and company information so as disguise the identity of the firms EuroFund and BuildIndia. (Where an individual has been quoted or company information is available in a published source, I use the real name.) Many other people who I cannot name here spared precious time to answer my questions, connect me with their friends, take me on site visits, and shower me with housing brochures. This project would not have been possible without their willingness to share their work with me.

In India, this project benefited from conversations with and assistance from Anjali Alexander, Lalit Batra, Keya Dasgupta, Urvashi Deshpande, Swapna Doshi, Anjan Ghosh, Jayoti Gupta, Diya Mehra, Prasananshu, Swagato Sarkar, and Sudeshna Sengupta. I am grateful to Asher Ghertner and Preetha Mani for their friendship and guidance. Sheetal Chhabria has modeled for me careful scholarship and thoughtful living; she shaped my early experiences in India, and her family has generously welcomed me on numerous occasions. Her husband, Dean Accardi, was our patient roommate, and along with friends Caitlin Cox, James Hare, David Lunn, and Shashi Sinha, helped make language studies and fieldwork enjoyable. Aseem Shrivastava has helped me to understand the macroeconomic framework and sociopolitical stakes of the land grab. Reyaz Badaruddin introduced me to Delhi, and his continuing friendship has sustained me through the years. Jan Baker, Mark Kaplan, Dilip da Cunha, and Anuradha Mathur encouraged my delight in Indian aesthetics and enriched my early visits. Mike and Preethi Knowles made it possible for my husband to join me in Delhi. Prem and Abha gave me a place to stay during fieldwork, and Raka Gupta graciously took me in when I returned in 2014. Minu Das taught me how to cook, among so many other things, with a sharp wit and a warm heart; I miss her dearly.

My research was supported through grants from the National Science Foundation and the American Institute of Indian Studies. I would like to thank the staff of the AIIS in Delhi, Jaipur, Kolkata, and Chicago for their assistance with the logistics of my fieldwork and the AIIS teachers in Jaipur for their patient Hindi instruction. The Centre for Studies in Social Sciences, Calcutta, provided institutional support during my fieldwork. The University of Pennsylvania provided writing support through the Department of Anthropology's Zwicker Fund as well as through a Graduate School of Arts and Sciences Dean's Summer Fellowship. I would not have been able to return to India in 2014 without generous support from the Dean of Faculty Office at Williams College.

I began this project at the University of Pennsylvania, where I had the opportunity to learn from many wonderful people. Asif Agha never failed to inspire me with his wealth of theoretical insights and profoundly original way of thinking about space. Greg Urban's interest in corporations developed parallel with mine, and, when I returned from the field, we found we had much to discuss. Ritty Lukose provided constant encouragement, made perceptive interventions, and offered sage advice. Ruth Schwartz Cowan and Robert Kohler welcomed me as an honorary member of the History and Sociology of Science Department and opened up a new world of scholarship. Jay Dautcher, Clark Erickson, and Christian Novetzke were exceedingly generous with their time and feedback. Kathy Hall has continued to mentor me long after the methods class I had with her. Fellow graduate students Melanie Dean, Kerry Dunn, Luke Fleming, Andi Johnson, Abby McGowan, and Teresa Raczek provided intellectual stimulation and emotional support. Animated late-night kitchen talks with Christy Schuetze set the foundations for my fieldwork.

In Providence, Paja Faudree, Lina Fruzzetti, and Catherine Lutz helped me to work productively as an exchange scholar at Brown University. Kathy Bartholomaus and Sarah Watson gave me reading materials. My aunt Lucie Searle taught me the rudiments of real estate finance; she continues to demonstrate that these tools can be used for progressive ends. Conversations with Harris Solomon and Sohini Kar at the Coffee Exchange got me out of the house. Sohini's ideas sparked numerous collaborative conference projects, and she has read, heard, and commented on much of my work. As a mentor, colleague, and friend, Lindsay French has been an unfailing advocate for my work.

In Williamstown, Michael Brown, Antonia Foias, and Olga Shevchenko encouraged and supported me. I am also grateful to my students at Williams College, who shed fresh light on much of the theoretical ground on which this book is built. I am happy to have been hired by the University of Rochester, where I could not ask for more inspiring and nurturing colleagues: Kristin Doughty, Robert Foster, Thomas Gibson, Kathryn Mariner, John Osburg, and Daniel Reichman. Rose Marie Ferreri and Carlie Fishgold have helped me navigate my new institutional home.

Audiences at the Yale Modern South Asia Workshop, New York University, Williams College, the University of California at Irvine, Franklin & Marshall College, Brown University, the University of Pennsylvania, the University of Göttingen, and the University of Chicago have provoked rethinking and revision. Lisa Björkman, Geert de Neve, Henrike Donner, Ludovic Halbert, Lisa Mitchell, Hortense Rouanet, and Stine Simonsen Puri have enabled me to make some of these presentations. In particular I greatly appreciate the feedback I have received from Amita Baviskar, Laura Brown, Jamie Cross, Ajay Gandhi, Akhil Gupta, Mike Levien, David Ludden, William Mazzarella, Meredith McGuire, Champaka Rajagopal, Bhuvaneswari Raman, Adam Sargent, Aurelie Varrel, and Liza Weinstein. Ritu Birla urged me to return to Marx's idea of "fictitious capital," and Kaushik Sunder Rajan's question about price appreciation also got me reading Marx again. Matthew Hull thoughtfully encouraged me to rethink transparency. I was so delighted to have a chance to compare notes with Tejaswini Ganti; who knew that film and real estate were so similar?

I am deeply grateful to the many people who have engaged with the manuscript itself, helping me over the years to articulate and clarify my arguments. My editor, Priya Nelson, and her assistant, Ellen Kladky, have enthusiastically supported the project and provided editorial guidance. Susan Karani and Margaret Thurston meticulously copyedited and proofread the manuscript. Two anonymous reviewers for the press provided invaluable suggestions. Tom Gleason and Sheetal Chhabria provided generous feedback on my entire manuscript. Sarah Carr, Sohini Kar, and Christy Schuetze consulted on the introduction in its various incarnations. Corinna Schlombs provided very thoughtful and encouraging comments at the eleventh hour. Emily Pawley's insights have brought clarity and logic to my most turgid prose. Our conversations always inspire me to see my work anew. Finally, Constantine Nakassis has pushed and prodded me to think subtly about my data, and his insightful reading of the manuscript provoked, I think, a much stronger work. I am particularly grateful to him for reading multiple versions of the transparency chapters and for instigating wholesale revisions.

This project has been on my desk during some of the most momentous moments of my life, both joyful and tragic. My fieldwork and writing would not have been possible without the unflagging encouragement of my husband, Joshua Enck, who has supported me in so many ways. I could never have finished the book without the help of my in-laws, Mary and Jim Enck, who have been so generous with love, encouragement, and time spent with our young son. My parents, Colgate and Cecilia Searle, built the foundations for my research by teaching me to appreciate and critique landscapes. My mother was a voracious reader, an exacting editor, and a champion of everything I ever did. I'd like to think she'd be tickled to see a book with my name on the spine, so I dedicate this book to her memory.

Money Terms

Throughout the book I use the Indian terms *lakhs* and *crores* to discuss Indian real estate prices, as my informants did. I use the terms *billions* and *millions* when quoting international real estate sources.

1 lakh = Rs. 100,000

1 crore = 100 lakh or Rs. 10,000,000

Wherever I have calculated dollar costs for rupee amounts, I have used an exchange rate of Rs. 41.5 to the US dollar, the average exchange rate during my fieldwork period (October 2006–March 2008), according to Federal Reserve currency exchange statistics. Using this average exchange rate, 1 crore rupees is $US 241,000 or just shy of a quarter million US dollars.

Introduction: Building Stories

Familiar Stories

During the real estate boom in 2006, Delhi's satellite city Gurgaon confirmed a familiar story about India's modernization.[1] In Gurgaon, brand names—Eriksson, Nokia, Sapient, Genpact, Citibank, Dell, and Microsoft—adorned gleaming business complexes that towered over the remnants of what was, until twenty years ago, an agricultural landscape of fields and villages. The facade of the City Centre mall framed giant advertisements: oversized Samsung phones, Bata shoes, and Van Heusen dress shirts hovered over groups of Indians in jeans and T-shirts or more traditional *salwar kameez* making their way into the air-conditioned atrium. Outside, cars jostled for space in a sandy lot, and drivers waited at tea stalls amid construction debris, tarps, and exposed wires (fig. 0.1).

Nonexistent in the late 1990s, malls like the City Centre numbered in the hundreds by 2007, constructed alongside golf courses, luxury homes, and information technology campuses across India.[2] In Mumbai, high-rises housing the middle classes increasingly replaced the walk-up, multiunit *chawls* that housed generations of the working class.[3] In Kolkata, towering housing complexes sat uneasily alongside the fisheries of the Eastern Wetlands (fig. 0.2). At Hinjewadi, outside of Pune, brave glass facades housed software firms in a technology "park" reminiscent of New Jersey or California in the United States. Similar buildings have come up in Bangalore, Hyderabad, Chennai, and smaller cities too.

Journalists, scholars, and residents treat these new buildings as symbols of India's economic growth and global integration. Glitzy office buildings, five-star hotels, and gated apartment complexes seem concrete evidence of the social and cultural changes that have accompanied the opening up and flourishing of the Indian economy over the last three decades. They suggest the

FIGURE O.1. "City Centre" mall on Mehrauli-Gurgaon Road in Gurgaon, 2006.
Source: Photo by author.

emergence of a globally familiar society of nuclear families whose members shop in malls, work in the information technology sector, and travel abroad. These urban landscapes suggest that a global future—an "India of glitter and privilege" (Bhaduri 2007, 552)—has already arrived.

However, India's new high-rises are actually speculative gambles. Rather than signs that Indian society is rapidly globalizing, new buildings are predicated on *forecasted* social and economic changes. Concrete and steel obscure the stories about India's growth that fuel construction. Once completed, buildings become evidence that these stories were true. *Landscapes of Accumulation* captures the performative character of these stories and the projective nature of construction by studying building producers themselves: the developers, financiers, and consultants who move capital into real estate in the hope of accumulating more. Rather than considering buildings as containers for human activity, and thus signs of already completed social change, this book examines the communicative processes through which buildings are produced in contemporary India.

By looking beyond the facades of Gurgaon's striking buildings to examine the experiences of the people who produce them, *Landscapes* provides insight into a geographical sea change underway in India and around the world: the

FIGURE 0.2. High-rises east of Kolkata, 2005.
Source: Photo by author.

privatization of urban development and the violent resettlement of the urban poor to make way for the construction of buildings for elites. It traces these processes to new ways of producing buildings. The liberalization of the Indian economy—and, more specifically, policies allowing foreign direct investment in Indian real estate—has enabled new encounters between Indian real estate developers and foreign investors that have transformed the way that real estate is practiced. India's violent and frenzied spate of urbanization results from a process whereby Indian land and buildings are becoming pawns in an international game of capital accumulation. Investors, developers, consultants, and government officials are transforming Indian land from a local resource for agricultural or industrial production into an international financial resource. They are constructing international routes of capital accumulation by transforming Indian land and buildings into internationally tradable assets and Indian developers into internationally acceptable business partners. To do so, they are recreating in India the trappings of real estate markets that have reshaped societies and landscapes around the world: land titles, title insurance, securitized mortgages, leases, mutual funds, etc.

Landscapes of Accumulation takes as its ethnographic object the *encounter* between international investors and their Indian intermediaries as they attempt to produce an international market in Indian land and buildings. This means that, unlike many traditional ethnographies, this is not a place-based account that documents the customs, manners, and beliefs of a geographically bound community or institution.[4] I carried out ethnographic fieldwork for this book for sixteen months between October 2006 and March 2008, and during January 2014, primarily in Delhi and its environs, but also in Kolkata and Mumbai.[5] I conducted participant observation with a European real estate fund and interviews with more than one hundred and forty people involved in real estate: fund managers, analysts, developers, architects, marketers, brochure designers, brokers, bankers, high-rise housing residents, planners, journalists, magazine editors, consultants with international property firms, and others.

What I found were attempts to standardize practices. Gurgaon's new glass and steel towers are familiar, reminiscent of California, Singapore, or Dubai. How such global architecture has been self-consciously and purposefully created *in India* requires explanation. Rather than uncover a process of "glocalization" (Robertson 1994)—where local consumer tastes prompt multinational corporate adaptation—I shift focus to the agency of investors, who demanded that Indians meet international expectations. Investors worked to enroll Indian developers as local intermediaries who could negotiate local politics and regulations in order to make Indian land and buildings into standardized products that could be traded abroad.

In popular depictions foreign investment is an automatic process constrained only by government regulation. Globalization appears as "flows" of money, information, images, and culture (cf. Appadurai 1996). Instead of "flows" I highlight "frictions." Relationships between developers and financiers were not always smooth; indeed, they exemplified what Anna Tsing has called the "frictions of global connections" (Tsing 2005, 3). Studying these "frictions" demonstrates that foreign investment is a power-laden process of creating chains of intermediaries.[6] It is a hard-won accomplishment, a contingent, uncertain process of constructing authority, changing practices, and standardizing things so that they can be invested in and exchanged.

Stories were central to my informants' standardizing projects. Stories about the growth of India's economy, foreign investment, consumer demand, and cities—a collective narrative that my informants called the "India story"—recast Indian society as a rapidly globalizing frontier of capitalism and as a market for new buildings. The "India story" is future-tense: it describes India as an "emerging" nation, one soon-to-be characterized by a thriving middle class of young, educated workers who contribute to an economy larger than that of the US, who buy goods from all over the globe, and who live in cities. Stories about the growth of a new India shaped my informants' aspirations and their business plans, helping them to draw investment to India, to create partnerships, and to construct an international market in self-consciously global Indian buildings.

These stories are a vital element of neoliberal power. Using the term "neoliberal" in the title of this book, I draw on geographer Waquar Ahmed's definition of neoliberalism as "a form of power that creates congenial spaces for the extraction of revenue in countries that were, until recently, relatively less accessible to capitalist exploitation" (Ahmed 2010, 621).[7] Studying the processes through which India's high-rises, IT parks, and malls are being made into such "congenial spaces" reveals that neoliberal imaginings form landscapes of accumulation by creating frontiers of action and profit. Those frontiers are the product of value projects that differentiate along a modernizing trajectory and thus make conceptual space for progress, improvement, and profit—as well as actual spaces designed to encourage the very economic growth and social change of which they are thought to be the outcome.

Large-Scale Land Sale

The material power of the "India story" is evident all over India. A spectacular real estate boom gripped India in the early 2000s.[8] Developers built new malls, office complexes, and high-rise apartments in India's major cities and bought hundreds of thousands of acres of farmland in order to build more. Property prices skyrocketed; estimates range wildly, but the head of mortgage finance at a major Indian bank told me that property prices in North India had increased by 300 percent in 2007 alone. Developers made fortunes from these rising prices, which in turn encouraged land speculators, who pushed land values even higher as they bid for parcels.

In the wake of economic liberalization in the early 1990s, an influx of private and international capital into what had been a state-dominated urban development process precipitated this building frenzy. In turn, the function of states has changed. Indian municipal and provincial governments—like governments around the world—have used urban space as a tool to attract international investment. They have shifted from a social welfare–oriented managerial approach to an "entrepreneurial" style of governance focused on "mobiliz[ing] city space as an arena both for market-oriented economic growth and for elite consumption practices" (Brenner and Theodore 2002, 21).[9] In their quest to create "world cities" and to attract international investors, information technology companies, and middle-class consumers, Indian municipalities have poured money into highways, flyovers, and airports and provided concessions to private developers.[10] Even Marxist governments in West Bengal and Kerala have sponsored information technology parks in an effort to attract industry and investment.[11]

Middle-class activism around urban aesthetic issues has galvanized support for moving manufacturing, wholesale markets, and informal economic activities (hawking, rickshaw driving, etc.) away from city centers, just as skyrocketing land prices have provided incentives to municipal governments and private landowners anxious to profit from the new uses to which land could be put.[12] As land values outstripped manufacturing profits, industrialists sold mill land to developers, often to the detriment of former workers.[13] Various government agencies—the railroads, postal service, and Department of Telecom, for example—also made plans to auction off surplus land or to redevelop properties to capitalize on realty values, just as politicians have de-reserved public plots, opened up ecologically sensitive land to development, and auctioned off government land to private bidders.[14]

City governments have also appropriated land for real estate development by clearing slums. In the early 2000s, at least 79,000 households were evicted in slum demolitions in Delhi.[15] In Kolkata, 131,000 people were evicted to make way for the new township at Rajarhat.[16] In Mumbai, the municipal corporation demolished approximately 90,000 slum dwellings, displacing as many as 450,000 people and clearing three hundred acres of land between November 2004 and March 2005 alone.[17] Together, the airport renovation project and Dharavi slum redevelopment projects threatened another 120,000 households in Mumbai.[18]

In the countryside, too, a struggle over land has been raging. Land aggregators representing major companies have been out in villages, convincing farmers to part with their land. Real estate developers have been accumulating thousands of acres of land reserves, what they called "land banks"; Delhi Land and Finance, for example, more than doubled its land reserves between April 2006 and January 2007, from 4,265 to 10,255 acres (Dagar 2007; DLF Limited 2006, 2007).[19] Public authorities have also been taking rural land by eminent domain, invoking the Land Acquisition Act of 1894 to jumpstart highway projects, ports, mines, industrial plants, and townships.[20] The private companies, investors, and developers who will develop and operate these infrastructure projects through "private-public partnerships" benefit from the state's involvement, while landowners, farmers, and laborers are often poorly compensated.[21]

The 2005 Special Economic Zone (SEZ) policy has spurred the acquisition of land by providing considerable tax incentives to the developers and industries who build and operate SEZs, privately controlled territories established to encourage exports.[22] As of February 2008, an estimated 760 SEZs had been proposed, with a combined area of over 450,000 acres; these projects were estimated to displace ten million people currently dependent on agriculture (Citizens' Research Collective 2008; see Shrivastava and Kothari 2012, *Seminar* 2008).[23]

The current scale of land acquisition is unprecedented. Traditionally, land in India has been economically vital as a means of agrarian production, and it has been viewed as a permanent store of wealth more enduring than gold, cash, or livestock. Simultaneously, land ownership has carried prestige, associated with high caste status, political power, and wealth. In many places in South Asia, people see themselves as sharing in the substance of their land; ancestral land embodies ties of kinship, citizenship, and village belonging.[24] For these reasons, land markets in India, while existent, have been constrained; historically, Indians have sold land primarily in distress situations of extreme debt, drought, or famine.[25]

Protests indicate that the land acquisition underway is a form of dispossession. On March 14, 2007, police and Communist Party of India Marxist (CPI(M)) members opened fire on villagers protesting government acquisition of fourteen thousand acres of agricultural land for an Indonesian conglomerate's proposed SEZ in Nandigram, West Bengal.[26] They killed at least fourteen people and brutally assaulted and raped uncounted women.[27] Nandigram shocked the nation. Activists, scholars, and opposition parties condemned the CPI(M) and called for West Bengal Chief Minister Buddahdeb Bhattacharjee to resign. Yet Nandigram is merely the most dramatic flashpoint in this struggle. In Singur, farmers protested the government's appropriation of nearly one thousand acres for the Tata Group's Nano car factory;

they eventually forced Tata out, though not until after land had been acquired (see Chandra 2008).[28] Through marches, rallies, sit-ins, and violent clashes with authorities, farmers have opposed land acquisition all across India.[29]

Constructing Routes of Accumulation

India's real estate markets are being built with land expropriated through these violent confrontations. Scholars have interpreted this vast land grab as an example of "accumulation by dispossession," an idea David Harvey adapted from Karl Marx to describe how capitalists capture resources in order to profit from them (Harvey 2003).[30] While Harvey uses the term broadly, sociologist Michael Levien defines "accumulation by dispossession" narrowly as the "use of extra-economic coercion to expropriate means of production, subsistence or common social wealth for capital accumulation" (2012, 940), and he sees it as a political state-driven process (2015a).[31] In India, the government has been the primary coercive agent, assisting corporations in accessing cheap land, and so scholars have documented the experiences of people caught up in state projects, particularly those torn violently from their homes and pushed to the urban fringes through flawed slum demolition and resettlement projects,[32] as well as farmers dispossessed of their land for SEZs and other corporate projects.[33]

These studies provide important insights into the mechanics, scope, and effects of dispossession, but they leave *accumulation* under-explained. Instead of asking "How does the state dispossess people through land acquisition?" I ask the complementary but converse question, "What work are people doing to accumulate capital through Indian real estate projects?" Clearly capital accumulation is now made possible through the state's role as a land broker; but this does not fully explain why Indian capitalists suddenly demand so much land and why Indian land has become so profitable.

Demand for Indian land has increased as it has taken on new value as an international commodity. When land is expropriated, it is not necessarily already a tool for capital accumulation. Acts of dispossession alone do not transform Indian land into something from which international investors can profit; land, buildings, and companies must be transformed into fungible assets and markets must be created for trading them. This book traces that work.

Anthropologists, sociologists, and historians have shown that making objects tradable requires abstracting, simplifying, and standardizing work; commodification is a sociocultural process that "disentangles" objects from their singular histories and human attachments.[34] Such processes of abstraction do not leave commodities stripped of their human associations but entangled in new ones. Indeed, my aim in this book is not merely to assert that Indian land has become commodified, for land sales have a long and complex history in India; rather, my goal is to show the work people are doing to transform land into a new kind of commodity, structured through new social relations, practices, and values.

Donald MacKenzie calls these social relations and practices the "infrastructures of markets: the social, cultural, and technical conditions that make them possible" (MacKenzie 2006, 13); in order to emphasize the ways in which these infrastructures enable capital accumulation, I call them "routes of accumulation." They include systems of property rights, practices of extending credit, and ideologies about market behavior as well as technologies for grading, standardizing, and transporting goods and for communicating market information.[35] Efforts to create new routes of accumulation are attempts to institute new practices, technologies, and ideas in order to transform Indian land into an asset that can be traded abroad. As such, it can serve the "world city" pretensions of urban elites and the high profit expectations of developers, corporations, investors, and municipal governments.

Some scholars have assumed that real estate is *already* a global practice. For example, Neil Smith, describing gentrification as a global phenomenon, comments that "the mobilization of urban real estate markets as vehicles of capital accumulation is ubiquitous," and he cites high real estate prices in mid-1990s Mumbai as an example (Smith 2002, 446). Others do not explain the formation of the financial techniques that enable dispossession. For example, Saskia Sassen (2014) describes the "assemblages" of people and financial technologies that are excluding vast populations from social, economic, and natural resources but does not explain how they are forged.[36] By treating practices and assemblages as ready-made, such accounts make it seem as though capitalism is always the same everywhere or as though capital unfolds on its own, apart from human intervention.

Both scholars build on traditions of political economy that bracket out cultural and historical particularities in search of general laws of capital (Harvey 2013: 14–25). While the tools of political economy are powerful, general laws do not help us to understand the emergence of new capitalist formations or the social mediations through which markets expand (Kar 2013). Rather than assume that routes of accumulation assemble themselves, or that real estate is already a global practice, I seek out the work that people are doing to forge routes of accumulation. I demonstrate that international real estate practices are even now being adopted in India and that this process is contested not just by civil society groups, but by industry members themselves. Analyzing these conflicts and the work that real estate producers do to attract partners, change their behavior, and thus, construct markets reveals a range of capitalist *practices* rather than one, unitary capitalist "system" and helps us to understand the contours and limits of capitalists' power.

The Neglected Builder[37]

Asking how new routes of accumulation are formed has led me to focus on private sector building producers rather than building residents, dispossessed former residents, or the state. The private sector's role in urban development has expanded dramatically as state roles have changed. Whereas state entities dominated city building before the liberalization of the 1990s, today private sector elites—bankers, contractors, developers, architects, lawyers, brokers, international property consultants, and others—are also working to produce Indian cities alongside state actors.[38] Yet, despite the ubiquity of private-sector construction worldwide, scholars have paid little attention to these building producers. What John Logan wrote over twenty years ago is still true today: "Much is written about land-use patterns, gentrification and world cities, but little is said about land developers, real estate syndicators or insurance companies" (Logan 1993, 36; see also Haila 1997).[39]

Indeed, anthropologists are much more apt to write about building residents than producers. For example, those who have investigated high-rise housing and gated communities in India[40] and elsewhere have delineated important relationships between housing and middle-class identities.[41] However, focusing on housing consumption does not reveal why or how certain types of housing are constructed, except through the assumption that the real estate industry merely responds to consumers' desires. Such an assumption fails to take into account commodity producers' attempts to create demand for new products and their continual quest for new markets, as critical ethnographies of marketing practice have highlighted in other contexts.[42]

If we know that shaping consumer desires is a major focus of capitalists' activity, less well understood are the mechanisms through which capitalists' own desires and strategies are shaped.[43] Since developers see buildings as tools for accumulating money and prestige, not just as spaces for living, they respond to investors, as much as (or perhaps more so) than to consumers. Interactions with investors shape their strategies and aspirations.

One place those interactions occurred was the mirror-lined ballroom at the Taj Mahal Palace Hotel in Mumbai in 2006. There, eddies of men in dark business suits congregated around a glass-paneled coffee bar and bouquet-topped tables. They exchanged business cards, shook hands, and chatted. These representatives of foreign private equity firms, real estate funds, and banks from Europe, the US, and Southeast Asia had come to the Global Real

Estate Institute conference to find deals with Indian real estate developers. A scholar friend in Delhi described the real estate boom as resulting from the "perfect marriage" between foreign capital and Indian elites. And, indeed, conferences I attended resembled elaborate mating rituals between the two groups. In fact, foreign investors compared finding a local business partner to dating, and they used metaphors like "getting in bed with a partner" to describe the process of "tying up" with another firm.

Rather than witness conflict-free marriages forming, however, I saw people struggling to form fragile partnerships over difference. Foreign investors and Indian developers disagreed on critical issues like how to value land or how to hire architects. Investors confided that they found India perplexing. A developer from the UK told me pessimistically that he thought "half the guys" at a conference we attended in 2006 would go back to the United States or Europe without investing. I asked him why, and he explained,

> Well, you're a manager of five funds and you've got five hundred million dollars to spend—it's much easier, isn't it, when some guy comes to you with a mixed, balanced portfolio for New York or London? You can do the deal Monday afternoon. It would take you ten years to invest that money in India.

In part, this book investigates why investing in Indian real estate is slow by international standards and what industry members are doing to speed up the process. As I conducted my research, I came to see globalization as *work*: those engaged in expanding markets face the problems of aligning others to their interests and gaining control over work processes, business practices, labor, and materials.[44] Industry members overcome differences in practice in order to form partnerships, move money, and build markets.

The frictions between Indian real estate developers and foreign investors illuminate critical differences between Indian and foreign real estate practice, yet these differences are not necessarily those of nationality, but of business interests. What I call "foreign" investors are often men of Indian origin, educated in prestigious American business schools with experience working for American or European banks, private equity firms, or consulting firms. International firms have chosen such investors to head up their Indian operations because they assume they have local contacts and some understanding of Indian business practices. Also, many foreign funds that establish offices in India hire local staff members, as do the international property consultancies and other intermediaries working to make Indian real estate a profitable international investment. My discussions with Indian-born, locally educated staff indicate that they differentiate themselves from Indian developers and align themselves with the interests of their parent firms.

Communicative Markets   ·

I went to India to study people making markets, but I primarily encountered people making representations of markets: spreadsheets, consultancy reports, economic predictions, investor presentations, sales pitches, etc.[45] So similar were many of these representations that I began to think of a particular narrative as "the party line." Eventually, however, I recognized that this "party line," what my informants called the "India story," both mattered and required explanation. Indeed, I argue that representations are not incidental to real estate practices—they do not just stand in for something else that is more real—rather, they *constitute* attempts to construct new markets.

It is easy to see the stories that economic actors tell as fictions, dismissing them as after-the-fact rationalizations, disingenuous attempts at manipulation, or delusions. For example, David Harvey, explicating Marx, writes that

> the self-presentations, self-perceptions and ideas of the agents of finance (as well as of capitalists in general) are delusional, not in the sense that they are crazy (though, as we will see, they often are) but *necessarily* deluded in the sense that Marx described in his theory of fetishism. . . . The bankers and financiers are, in some ways, the very last people to trust, not because they are all fraudsters and liars (even though some of them patently are), but because they are likely to be prisoners of their own mystifications and fetishistic understandings. (Harvey 2013, 145–46)

Scholars on the political Left have trouble taking capitalists' worldviews seriously for fear of appearing to condone them (notice Harvey's distancing parenthetical expressions). Moreover, Harvey and Marx suggest capitalists' understandings are distorted by the structures of capitalism itself: bankers cannot "see" what's really going on behind the surface appearance of money begetting money.

However, to dismiss economic actors' stories as mere rationalizations "mistake[s] institutional *efforts* to re-make the social world for *descriptions* of the way the world is" (Agha 2011, 28). Capitalists' stories are not descriptions only to be judged right or wrong; they are "efforts to re-make the social world"—or, in this case, efforts to make an international market in Indian land and buildings. Understanding this point of view means taking very seriously the idea that people "do things" with words (Austin 1975). When people tell stories, they don't merely exchange information; they create social relationships with one another and conceptually organize the world so as to act in it.[46] Thus, instead of debating whether financiers are delusional or prescient, it is more productive to understand what their stories *do*.

Like the stories that Indian filmmakers' tell about why films succeed or fail (Ganti 2012a, 245–47) or the economic narratives that central bankers spin (Holmes 2014; Smart 1999, 2006), real estate producers use narratives to guide their actions in the face of uncertain futures. Indeed, scholars of the social studies of finance have argued that the representations through which actors know about economic activities—from the stock ticker (Preda 2008) to the computer terminal (Knorr Cetina and Bruegger 2002; Zaloom 2006) and finance theory (Callon 1998; MacKenzie 2006)—far from being neutral, actually shape economic activity. For example, Koray Çalişkan argues that cotton traders use what he calls "prosthetic prices"—indices, market reports, and rumors—in realizing the actual price of cotton through individual sales such that "the location of the global market is not geographical, but graphical. It is made up of documentary, technological, and indexical tools" (2010, 18). Even exchange is not an unmediated dyadic moment but a process that relies on a cascade of representations—contracts, bills of lading, letters of credit, etc.—and extensive networks of agents (Çalişkan 2010, 59–83). In these accounts, the "the market" is not a thing (or an abstract pricing mechanism) so much as an arena of reflexive, communicative activity; representations are not epiphenomenal to but *constitutive of* markets.

Every building is the material precipitate of millions of acts of communication between investors, developers, architects, construction workers, and others as they plan and construct (cf. Gieryn 2002). What we call "the Indian real estate market" (or even more specifically, for example, "the market for residential buildings in Mumbai") is a communicative arena in which numerous actors—from mortgage lenders to interior paint manufacturers and bureaucrats—interact with customers, clients, investors, partners, and employees. Just as language use coexists with—indeed, is fundamentally constituted by—models of language use (see Agha 2007a), so are real estate practices continually informed by reflexive models of those practices. Real estate market participants use representations of buildings, competitors, buyers, real estate practices, and "the market" itself to plan their projects, make deals, and organize construction. As they do so, they are making routes of accumulation, project by project and deal by deal.

Value Projects

The representations I collected—brochures, advertisements, consultancy reports, sales pitches, and other speech events—are instruments in real estate producers' reflexive and purposive attempts to construct value: their *value projects* (see Agha 2011; Nakassis and Searle 2013). I use the term *project* to capture the improvisational nature of their strategies; industry members pursue goals, but outcomes are by no means certain. By *value*, I mean something different than traditional Marxist, structuralist, or neoclassical accounts. *Value* does not have a unitary source, such as labor, nor does it emerge from an established structural system: it emerges from ongoing social and political processes (see Ferry 2013; Verdery 2003). Lucidly synthesizing anthropological debates on the concept, Elizabeth Ferry defines "value" as "the politics of making and ranking differences and deciding what kinds of differences are important" (Ferry 2013, 18). This way of understanding value encompasses efforts to achieve both economic and symbolic capital, both money and prestige; it enables us to analyze contexts in which the structures and institutions that might regularize value are absent or changing (see Guyer 2004); and it encourages us to look at small scales, at interactions as they unfold, and at the variety of stances people take toward one another and their activities.

Real estate producers aim to boost the value of their companies, properties, and themselves in the eyes of investors, consumers, and the general public in order to finalize the deals that bring them profits. Conveying the possibility of profit involves telling stories that position these entities well in relation to other highly regarded trends (see Tsing 2005). It also involves displaying signs that convey that they are particular kinds of people: credible, trustworthy, competent, professional, etc. To convince others of the value of their companies and properties, real estate producers also needed to distinguish them. Real estate developers and investors challenged competitors'—and even potential partners'—expertise, questioned the value of their practices, and contested their ability to forecast real estate trends. These discursive moves were attempts to "make and rank differences." Such efforts took on increased salience in a context in which real estate producers were improvising the rules of the game they were playing.[47]

Landscapes of Accumulation traces real estate producers' value projects as they unfolded in documents and speech events. Part 1 explores how real estate producers used stories about growth, or what my informants called the "India story," to draw global finance capital into Indian real estate. In order to convey the possibility of profit, producers relied heavily on predictions. Chapter 2 explores the ways in which real estate producers circulated predictions about economic growth to position India as a profitable investment. Chapter 3 demonstrates how producers use these same predictions to guide their investment and construction decisions once in India. In chapter 4, I explore one growth story in detail: industry members circulated predictions about growing numbers of young, high-earning consumer-oriented Indians to demonstrate demand for high-end real estate products and thus garner investment. These predictions, I argue, are a potent way of organizing action and creating a new market because they rely on logics of comparison that differentiate India from other places in the world only to project a profitable convergence in the future. In chapter 4, in particular, we see how creating value for Indian real estate relies on creating hierarchies of goods, people, and places. These hierarchies create the frontiers of capitalist activity and thus possibilities for action.

If part 1 (chapters 1–4) explores "the politics of making and ranking differences," part 2 (chapters 5–8) examines "the politics of . . . deciding what kinds of differences are important" (Ferry 2013, 18). Real estate producers competed with one another for funding, consumers, clients, and profits on a complex terrain at the intersection of Indian and international real estate practices, where what was valuable was up for debate. These debates over value were also debates over control, particularly as foreign investors strove to make Indian practices conform with international ones. Thus, as debates unfolded over which business practices were better, what kinds of expertise garnered profits, and what kinds of construction projects made good "gambling pieces," a new terrain for real estate practice and new means of accumulating capital were established.[48]

To understand these debates I trace two value projects in particular: investors' attempts to make their potential Indian partners "transparent," and their attempts to build "quality" buildings in India. In chapter 5 I show that by labeling Indian real estate practices nontransparent, foreign investors insisted upon changes in developers' accounting practices, valuation methods, firm organization, and interaction style. In short, they used transparency claims as tools in a bid to transform Indian real estate developers into globally familiar business partners, credible intermediaries in an emerging chain of capital accumulation. Chapter 6 explores Indian developers' attempts to achieve prestige and professional status. These value projects coincided with and conflicted with the goal of "transparency." In response to the demands of foreign financiers and Indian consumers, Indian real estate developers have attempted to transform themselves into "global professionals," but, in their profitable new role as intermediaries to global capital, they need to continue doing the "dirty" work of land agglomeration that marks them as nontransparent, not-quite global players. Together, these chapters show the structural contradictions that shaped real estate producers' value projects and their attempts to collaborate.

Finally, chapters 7 and 8 follow one international fund's attempts to profit from the difference between Indian and international fields of real estate practice through building quality buildings. In doing so, however, the fund faced a profusion of other claims to "quality" and challenges to the value of its employees' expertise. These chapters explore the fund's fraught attempts to construct authority, find partners, and transform real estate and construction work processes.

In short, real estate producers aim to create differences; to position themselves well in relation to hierarchies of goods, people, and places; and to change potential partners' practices. In tracing their value projects, I show how semiotic contests over credibility, prestige, and practice are central to real estate producers' attempts to extract capital from Indian land.

"Studying Up"

Like other anthropologists, I faced challenges applying traditional participant observation approaches to studying elites.[49] "Studying up" (Nader 1969) reverses the power dynamics of fieldwork; rather than study people with less economic and political power than myself, I was studying people with more. This created difficulties for me in meeting and interacting with industry members, gathering basic information, and delving into industry practices. Gradually, however, I began to find my moments of frustration revealing. The challenges of studying business practices revealed the contours of different business cultures and helped me to see the particularities of the Indian real estate industry in its moment of turbulent and sudden expansion.

My first moment of disconnect as an anthropologist came with my definition of my interactions with my informants. Whereas I thought of myself as "conducting interviews" in an anthropological mode, my informants saw our interactions as "meetings": bursts of time that had to fit into a schedule and compete with the other meetings that crowded the day. To achieve face-to-face interactions, I had to adapt to Indian businessmen's meeting scheduling habits. My informants were very busy; they scheduled appointments flexibly and chronically arrived late. Often, my informants would ask me to call them on a particular morning, and they would tell me then if they could fit me in, or very likely, to call back the following day. Some contacts would put me off for weeks or months and then tell me they were free that afternoon, or in an hour. I spent much of my fieldwork frantically trying to get across town and waiting in office reception areas once I had arrived. After weeks of calls, canceled meetings, and false starts, I might have half an hour with an important contact, a time shorter than the ideal interviewing conditions outlined in books on anthropological method (e.g., Weiss 1994), but consistent with business people's practices and schedules. My informants also often answered their phones, checked their e-mail, or attended to employees or clients in the middle of our interactions, as they would in other meetings.

While I found these meeting practices jarring, my informers found my motives, plans, and status mysterious. For example, they attached their own meanings to my word "research." In keeping with the discipline's history in India, many of my informants associated anthropology with the study of tribal groups or archaeology. They asked me the moment they saw "Department of Anthropology" on my business card, "What is an anthropologist doing studying real estate?" When I explained I was doing a study, my informants expected it to be an industry report, available in a few weeks. Everyone wanted a copy, and they were baffled when I said I would be in India for another year or so doing research. From their point of view, my study would be out-of-date, and therefore useless, before it was published.

Moreover, as a foreign female student, I did not fulfill my informants' expectations of the kind of person with whom they usually met. While industry members usually negotiated deals during meetings, they found that I was neither a potential investor nor a possible partner. I had no stake in a particular deal or project; I didn't bring money, land, or contacts to our interactions — only questions and dubious expertise.

As a woman, I was an anomaly in a male-dominated industry. Some, especially older informants, treated me as they might a younger female relative; others tried to flirt. As a woman, I was excluded from the informal moments of male sociality through which so much business is done. Also, my perceptions of gender norms and safety sometimes led me to limit my interactions, as when, for example, I canceled travel plans with a young investor who had offered to let me come to Bangalore to watch him close a deal when I realized it would just be the two of us traveling.

My ambiguous social position was reinforced by another problem inherent in "studying up": I could not afford the emblems that would have placed me in my informants' social world. Since my informants assumed that I lived in a fancy, expatriate neighborhood, they were surprised on the rare occasions that I admitted to living in déclassé Lajpat Nagar (a lower middle class Punjabi neighborhood). Similarly, I did not wear a fancy watch or jewelry, travel with my own car and driver, or flaunt the latest-model cell phone. Whereas many anthropologists struggle with the problems created by their comparative wealth, my research budget paled in comparison to the incomes of those I studied and the budgets of their companies, putting certain research activities out of reach. I was unable to accompany visiting architects on a last-minute Delhi–Chennai flight because the cost of the ticket was US$1,000, much more than my monthly budget. Although corporate data was often the only source of data for trends I was interested in quantifying, I could not afford it.[50] Some corporate events were also prohibitively expensive. For example, registration at the Global Real Estate Institute conferences cost US$2,475 (for single nonmembers who preregister six weeks in advance).[51] While frustrating, my encounter with these barriers and questions of status revealed crucial facts about the contours of the social world I was studying that might have remained invisible to me if my way had been smoothed by money and status.

Ultimately, I found a way into development conversations: a European real estate fund (which I call EuroFund) whose managing director saw a use for a cultural anthropologist. Where I hoped to learn about residential building, he hoped that I would be able to provide insight into Indian housing preferences so that his firm could "tap into cultural norms" when designing a new housing complex. He agreed to let me "intern" at the office in return for access to my findings from resident interviews. Even here, the managing director—otherwise quite supportive of my work—was reluctant to let me sit in on meetings. Most problematically, the first project to materialize for the fund was a commercial project (described in chapters 7 and 8). As fund employees focused energy on commercial real estate, my offer of residence preference data "lost value" in their eyes. In order to remain involved in the firm's activities, I helped to do basic research, and I took corporate visitors on tours of Delhi and Agra. In return, I gained industry contacts, learned about project finance, and interviewed the managing director and other employees. These meetings and interviews provided insights into the industry as a whole.

Even with EuroFund's help, my conversations with other industry members were initially baffling. I regularly felt that my informants were fobbing me off with pat phrases and vague explanations. Many of my informants were skittish about sharing even the most basic information with a tape recorder running.[52] In part, this is because employees of large corporations operate within a tight legal framework that regulates what they can and cannot say about projects. Many sign nondisclosure agreements about their work. As a result, foreign informants were concerned about their names or company names being used in published material. For example, one woman to whom I was introduced through a mutual friend was concerned that her job at a multinational company, or even her ability to continue working in India, would be jeopardized should she speak with me. Although I promised her that we could come up with a way of identifying her in my book that did not compromise her position, in the end, she declined to be interviewed. This experience highlighted for me what was at stake for my informants, who operated in a world where sharing information could damage the course of careers and lives.

It was not only multinational employees who were secretive. Developers' unreturned phone calls, dodged questions, and polite promises illuminated a strategy that differed from the corporate secrecy of large companies but mirrored it. Real estate developers were particularly secretive about one important aspect of the industry: its ties with politics and "black" (cash or untaxed) money. While I could not wish away cash transactions as "distortions" to an otherwise smoothly functioning market since they are central to how Indian companies buy land, construct buildings, and sell apartments, I also had difficulty studying them directly.[53] While ubiquitous, cash profits and political connections are not highlighted in glossy company brochures, and they were brought up reluctantly and euphemistically by most of my informants, who often prefaced their comments with disavowals: "I don't know if it's true, right or wrong, but every now and then I've been told that . . ." one broker began. When I expressed my frustrations about not being able to study cash transactions, Avinash, a consultant who—in contrast to many of my other informants—had just told me about asking a politician for Rs. 20 crore and about friends who could gather Rs. 100 crore by making a few phone calls, advised me, "you can't prove *shit*."

Indeed, Avinash's stories were impossible—even dangerous—to verify. The public face of the industry to which I did have access existed in tension with the world of black money and political influence that everyone knew existed but some navigated more successfully than others. Rather than study "black" exchanges directly, then, I examine the way industry members' ability to navigate those channels of accumulation played out in relationships between investors and developers in their attempts to make international real estate markets. Expertise in fostering political connections was central to Indian developers' new role as intermediaries to global capital, but it also created contradictions that highlighted the conflicting value projects at stake in their market-building activities.

Industry secrecy emerged from illegality and concerns over reputation, but the real estate boom itself also created conditions that demanded secrecy. Since information itself was a commodity in the highly volatile, competitive real estate market, industry members treated prices, profits, deal structures, and project details as highly guarded secrets. My Indian developer informants cared less about being quoted in an American book than about saying something from which I (or their competitors) might profit.

In an industry in which communication was structured by concerns about secrecy, I found it difficult to obtain financial records, projections, deal structures, construction costs, and profit margins due to this data's commodity value.[54] Of course, so did my informants. They frantically and relentlessly

sought out information and debated its worth. Indeed, they conducted research that came remarkably close to my own fieldwork practices, what some
have called "para-ethnography" (Holmes and Marcus 2005) or "research in
the wild" (Callon and Rabeharisoa 2003): they interviewed landowners and
residents, visited competitors' housing projects, kept little notebooks, collected industry reports, and met with people to ask them questions about
their business. As I struggled to differentiate my own research from theirs,
I realized that my informants' representations of Indian real estate were not
straightforward descriptions of Indian real estate markets but attempts to re-
make the very terrain on which they operated.[55]

While some forms of knowledge seemed unstable, others seemed like certainties. Real estate developers' representations of a rapidly globalizing and
westernizing Indian society were so familiar they seemed to leave me nothing to say about them.[56] This banality, however, belies their power. While investor presentations and stock prospectuses appear trite in their rehearsal of
stale claims and statistics, they are vital, for they constitute the background
against which arguments are made, properties are sold, and deals are closed.
Just as development discourses define problems so as to necessitate particular
techno-managerial interventions (Ferguson 1994; Mitchell 2002), business
discourses shape practices.

Recognizing these documents' familiarity led me to investigate their power.
Real estate images are widely circulated by powerful actors—multinational
corporations and consultancies, multilateral organizations, and newspapers—
and I trace that circulation in this book. Moreover, these images are powerful
because they cohere with our commonsense understandings of the world.
If we've already encountered the United Nations urbanization forecasts that
real estate developers circulate, for example, such statistics also reinforce
our deep-seated idea that human history is a story of progress from rural to
urban, agrarian to industrial (cf. Ferguson 1999). Understanding such seemingly unremarkable predictions, then, leads me to analyze important stories
about growth, progress, and modernity that inform all of our lives—and that
help build markets and cities.

Routes of Accumulation

Gurgaon

During my fieldwork, to get to Gurgaon, twenty kilometers southwest of central Delhi as the crow flies, you would travel south through the city's variegated urban fabric and down the Mehrauli-Gurgaon Road (fig. 1.1).[1] Its numerous lanes of traffic wind past wooded scrub, nurseries, and stone dealers; side lanes lead to villages and "farmhouses" (estates of the rich and famous). There is always at least one *pani-wala* with his umbrella-shaded metal box inscribed *machine se thanda pani* (machine-cooled water) serving the crowd at the bus stop at Andheria More, the major intersection where the traffic coming south along the Mehrauli-Gurgaon Road meets the traffic coming east from Vasant Kunj. You can also catch a ride from here in one of the SUVs that buzz up and down the road taking workers to Gurgaon's call centers. On the right side of the road, behind a line of trees now marooned in traffic, people sell hand-forged metal implements from a row of huts. Andheria More gets its name from *andheri*, darkness, and *mor*, a turn. According to a friend who used to commute along this road, even a few years ago, there was "nothing" here; it was a turn into the darkness. Now this is a bustling thoroughfare, linking Delhi to up-and-coming Gurgaon.

Near the Delhi-Haryana line, the road turns to the right and rises, crossing the Delhi Ridge, as the tail end of the Aravalli hills is called. Here you can glimpse the occasional, lumbering *nilgai* (an Indian antelope) among the scrub and trees. From the ridge, you descend into a chaos of billboards selling alcohol and real estate: Gurgaon. The road zips past Corporate Park and the Global Business Park, each with large expanses of mirrored, tinted glass. The cream-colored walls of Garden Estate, one of the earliest gated housing complexes in Gurgaon, are visible behind walls of bougainvillea to the right. The road takes a tight bend at the village of Sikandarpur, past construction supply

FIGURE 1.1. Delhi and surrounding cities of the National Capital Region.
Source: Adapted from Eicher Delhi city map, Eicher Goodearth Limited, 2006. Drawn by author. Computer graphics by Joshua Enck.

vendors and real estate brokers. Another sharp turn brings you to a strip of road where thirteen malls in different stages of construction elbow for space.

In front of the malls is a littoral zone of parking, pedestrians, and small shops with jaunty, jostling signs: plywood dealers, hardware vendors, painters, brokers, decorators, stone dealers, contractors, electricians. The city's main business seems to be self-construction. Cars are parked higgledy-piggledy, overflowing designated parking areas. Shoppers wind past water-tanker tractors and *chai* stands to reach security-guarded, manicured mall entrance areas.

Gurgaon's industrial clusters are along the National Highway-8: to the north, the Maruti automotive factory, started in the early 1980s, and to the south, Hero Honda scooters. Numerous multinational industrial suppliers have located near these plants. Since the late 1990s, alongside manufacturing, textiles, and pharmaceuticals, the information technology industry has boomed here. In 2006–7, Gurgaon accounted for 10 percent of the country's software exports and its call centers employed between 150,000 and 200,000 people (GurgaonWorkersNews; Vinayak 2006). Familiar names like Nokia and Pepsi adorn Gurgaon's Business Centers, World Trade Centers, and Info-Technology Parks.

To the north of the Mehrauli-Gurgaon Road, past the residential neighborhood DLF City Phase II (named after its developer, Delhi Land and Finance), DLF's recent corporate venture, Cyber Greens, is actually blue with tinted glass and metal siding (fig. 1.2). To the south is DLF's golf course, the American Express Building, and the concrete and rebar husks of the housing complexes coming up along Golf Course Road: the Palm Springs, the Exotica, the Pinnacle, the Belaire, La Lagune, and others. Cheap metal fencing lines Golf Course Road, supporting lush, colorful advertisements for as-yet-nonexistent places: happy families, romantic couples, swimming pools, and palms are all familiar motifs (fig. 1.3). Beyond the fencing and the sweeping entrance archways of future projects are muddy lots and dusty, wind-swept fields.

Banners advertising "world-class" real estate and "international standard" construction crowd Gurgaon's intersections. The new malls, housing complexes, and business parks being constructed in Gurgaon are not unique to

FIGURE 1.2. DLF Cyber Greens, Gurgaon, 2007.
Source: Photo by author.

FIGURE 1.3. Advertisements line Golf Course Road, Gurgaon, 2007.
Source: Photo by author.

India but familiar to cities the world over. New residential complexes offer
amenities that might seem unremarkable to Americans: gyms, swimming
pools, clubhouses, master bathrooms with his-and-hers sinks, open kitchens,
and children's rooms. However, such elements are new to Indian housing, as
evidenced by the manuals for living that developers issue to new residents.

Gurgaon's architecture is not merely self-consciously global; it is futuristic.
Taking architectural cues from Dubai, Shanghai, Singapore, and California,
Indian builders are imagining a global future and building it in Indian now.
The buildings themselves—with their spiraling atriums, space-needle towers,
and jutting prows—seem forerunners of a future age. Gurgaon's futuristic
malls, gated high-rise housing, golf courses, and five-star hotels tower over
the remnants of fields and villages. Where once farmers grew mustard, employees of transnational corporations can now sip coffee or shop for Mercedes
Benz cars. In popular media and everyday discourse, Gurgaon's glitzy buildings have come to index India's newfound prosperity and the country's new
footing on the global economic stage.

To understand how radical Gurgaon appears to many Indians, we must
understand it in the context of Delhi's existing landscapes. Gurgaon's
malls and high-rises contrast starkly with the narrow lanes of the walled

seventeenth-century city built by Mughal Emperor Shah Jahan; the grand avenues and monuments of Colonial New Delhi, built after the British moved their capital from Calcutta in 1912; the neighborhoods hastily allotted to some of the 500,000 refugees who flocked to the city after the Partition of India and Pakistan in 1947; the spacious bungalows of South Delhi; and the neighborhoods built by the Delhi Development Authority in the state's grand (but unsuccessful) bid to provide housing. Just as these landscapes tell us something about the time in which they were built, making Delhi's architecture a palimpsest of its history, so too do Gurgaon's malls and high-rises reflect the current era of liberalization.

Especially if we consider Gurgaon's striking buildings as tools for making money, then understanding the city's sudden growth requires understanding how developers—and now international fund managers—accumulate capital through the built environment. How did constructing Gurgaon come to seem profitable—and why in the 1990s and 2000s? I argue that the liberalization of the economy in the 1990s changed the structure of the real estate industry: it ushered in new roles for private-sector elites and spurred the growth of real estate–related markets such as mortgage financing and media, which precipitated the real estate boom that transformed Gurgaon into a sign of globalization.

Most importantly, accumulating capital through the built environment has entailed not just constructing buildings, but engaging with finance capital. Liberalization opened Indian real estate to new sources of finance capital from abroad, making foreign investors important new actors in the industry. In conjunction with Indian developers, consultants, lawyers, and bureaucrats, investors have attempted to transform Indian land and buildings from local resources for farmers or industrialists into international financial resources from which they can profit.

Liberalization

In India in 1970, state-run television only broadcast a couple of hours a day; a highly centralized and state-monitored film industry dominated music recording; foreign goods were hard to come by; only a few (Ambassador) cars plied the roads; and many construction companies worked exclusively for the government or for clients in the Middle East. Today, there is a proliferation of media—from satellite TV to regional-language newspapers—an influx of foreign goods and companies, and a construction boom.[2]

Many of these changes have roots in the1970s and 1980s, but the watershed moment to which scholars refer is 1991, when the Government of India repealed many of the protectionist policies of the Nehruvian state. With the aim of "making Indian industry globally competitive and increasing the extent of integration with the global economy" (Department of Economic Affairs 1996), the Government of India adopted reforms designed to tighten monetary policy; increase exports; reduce state involvement in industry, banking, and financial markets; and increase foreign investment.[3] With these reforms, India opened its markets to networks of global finance and embarked on an "externally oriented, consumption-led path to national prosperity" (Mazzarella 2003, 5).

This external orientation has changed the game of real estate. The liberalization of the Indian economy precipitated a flurry of construction as developers scrambled to construct space for foreign tenants, non-resident Indians, and an Indian nouveau riche. As they used new sources of finance to do so, they have helped develop Indian real estate as a financial instrument in its own right, a means for foreign firms and wealthy Indians to invest in Indian buildings alongside stocks and bonds. I turn now to the legal and institutional changes that have enabled Indian real estate to grow so rapidly.

Interconnected Markets and the Real Estate Developer's Role

To understand the effects of liberalization on the Indian real estate market, it helps to visualize "Indian real estate" as a series of interconnected markets for building-related products and services. These include markets in land, permits, construction materials, project finance, consulting services, mortgages, media about real estate, consumer durables, and home decorating products (fig. 1.4). Each of these interrelated markets consists of buyers and sellers, of course, but many of the buyers are real estate–related companies (construction, media, and consulting firms, for example) rather than building occupiers (home buyers or corporate tenants). Each of these interconnected markets has grown over the last twenty years, especially since liberalization.[4]

At the hub of this growing system of interconnected markets is the real estate developer. The developer buys land from farmers, politicians, or other landowners or bids on it in government auctions. He pays "speed money" to bureaucrats in planning agencies for land-use and construction permits.[5] He then purchases the services of marketers, surveyors, architects, lawyers, and construction firms and procures finance in order to transform land into buildings which he can sell or rent.[6] Like a merchant who circulates commodities rather than producing them, a developer plays a different structural role than a builder, who constructs the building (and provides the labor, materials, and equipment for doing so). In practice, in India, this division is

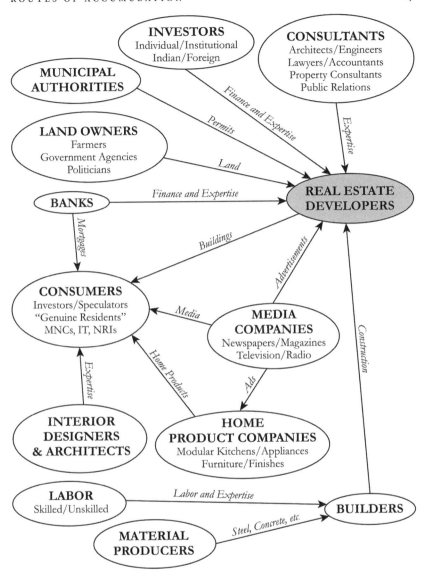

FIGURE 1.4. The Indian real estate industry consists of numerous interlinked markets. Lines in this diagram represent sales, with the buyer at the arrow end.
Source: Drawn by Joshua Enck.

not so neat: many developers started out as builders and still retain some construction capabilities within their firms (see Patel 1995, 147–48).[7] Similarly, a large development company might have its own in-house architectural, marketing, or land-surveying team. Given the large amounts of money necessary to purchase land and construct buildings, developers also rely on financing

from others (banks, individuals, international funds, etc.), thus implicating
them in flows of financial capital.

This configuration of interrelated markets, with the real estate developer
(or developer-builder) at its center, is new in India, as are many of the markets'
players and products. The role of real estate developer has existed in India at
least since Partition, in varying forms in various regions. However, developer-
led capitalist property development has coexisted with cooperative, self-built,
and government-produced systems of building development (Patel 1995).[8]
In the past, builders constructed buildings directly for government clients,
industries, cooperative housing societies, or individual landowners. Those
clients coordinated finance, land procurement, and, sometimes, construction. While these other forms of property development still exist in India, the
developer-led capitalist property model—with its subsidiary markets—has
risen to the fore, particularly in relation to government-led construction.

In the National Capital Region, for example, government agencies such as
the Ministry of Rehabilitation and the Delhi Improvement Trust developed
close to 6,000 acres of land around Delhi to house the more than 500,000
refugees that came to the city after Partition. Private developers also sold plots
of land, but the state, in an effort to control planning and ensure the provision of housing to the majority of residents who could not afford market-
rate housing, established the Delhi Development Authority (DDA) in 1957
and froze all development on vacant land in the city in 1959 (Kacker 2005).
Similar legislation in other cities gave municipal urban development authorities a monopoly on large-scale building activities. In 1976, the Government of
India passed the Urban Land (Ceiling and Regulation) Act (ULCRA), which
limited the amount of vacant land that one owner could hold and established
procedures for the state to appropriate land held by individuals and companies in excess of the limit (Acharya 1987).[9] Through such regulations, the
government aimed to curb urban land speculation and ensure housing for
the poor.

During this period, developers were restricted from large-scale private
work. Some developers worked as builders on government contracts and small
private projects. Others operated at the margins of the legal system. Some
sold plots in unauthorized developments, as demand for housing outstripped
the Delhi Development Authority's provision of new homes.[10] By 1993, more
than one thousand such colonies existed in Delhi (*Economic Survey of Delhi
2005–6*). Others became brokers in obtaining ULCRA exemptions from
politicians, and they played the high-priced market for exempt land which
developed.[11] Writing about Ahmedabad, Patel argues that developers who
learned to navigate around the ULCRA actually consolidated power during

this period: "After 1976, not only was a specialist agent, who could manage the supply of land necessary, but possibilities of making super-profits from property development also multiplied" (Patel 1995, 137).

Since the liberalization of the economy, the model of state-dominated urban development has crumbled nationally as states and municipalities, urged by the central government, have opened urban development to private corporations.[12] In the National Capital Region, this shift began a decade earlier, in the 1980s. While the Delhi government had closed off opportunities for developers to develop large projects legally, the neighboring state of Haryana invited private firms to develop townships. With the Haryana Development and Regulation of Urban Areas Act of 1975, the state established a mechanism for private companies (called "colonizers" in the Act) to obtain licenses to develop land into "colonies."[13] The state began issuing licenses in 1981, attracting developers especially to Gurgaon. There were reportedly twenty-six developers active in Gurgaon by the mid-1990s, although three companies—Delhi Land and Finance, Ansals, and Unitech—have dominated Gurgaon's development (Jamwal 2004).[14]

New Sources of Finance

While benefitting from this government policy shift toward private-sector construction, developers in India today also obtain financing from new sources. Before the late 1990s, developers had almost no access to formal, institutional financing because the government kept public sector banks from lending to them (Patel 1995, 124). Developers funded projects by attracting investments from private individuals; by having housing buyers pay for their homes in advance installments; and by partnering with landowners.[15]

Efforts to build mortgage markets brought more capital into real estate. Deepak Parekh started the first mortgage granting institution, the Housing Development Finance Corporation, in 1977 (Budhiraja, Piramal, and Ghoshal 2001). The creation of other housing finance companies beginning in the late 1980s; the entrance of commercial banks to mortgage lending in the 1990s; a sharp fall in interest rates (from 16 percent in 1989 to below 10 percent in 2004); and the introduction of tax incentives for mortgage-takers helped the market grow. The government also took an active role in developing the mortgage market by establishing the Housing and Urban Development Corporation in the late 1970s and the National Housing Bank in 1988.[16] Outstanding mortgage loans as a percentage of GDP more than doubled between 2001 and 2005, from 3.4 percent to 7.25 percent (National Housing Bank 2006).[17] Prior to the availability of mortgages, Indians purchased homes using personal savings, so this market has greatly expanded the consumer base for housing projects, particularly among the salaried "middle class."[18] (It is important to note, however, that unlike the United States, very few mortgages in India are securitized like the mortgages responsible for the American mortgage crash; most continue to be held on the originating banks' books.)[19]

In the 1990s, the government loosened restrictions, and banks began lending to developers, though it was not until 1998 that real estate was named a "priority" lending sector along with other industries.[20] Formal domestic investment funds for real estate were made legal in 2004. These changes radically expanded the capital available to developers, enabling them to develop large, speculative projects. However, in 2006, the Reserve Bank of India, fearing a real estate bubble, prohibited Indian banks from lending to developers for the purchase of land, and it raised the collateral required on real estate loans. In 2007, the banks raised interest rates for developers, from 13 to 15 percent (*Economic Times* 2007f).

Finding constrictions on formal financing in India, real estate developers sought funding through another avenue that had recently opened up. The Government of India allowed foreign investors to fund Indian construction projects beginning in 2002, and it further liberalized the policy in 2005. In order to scale-up their businesses, Indian developers eagerly turned to international private equity and other funds for capital, and many sought to "go public," that is, list on the Bombay Stock Exchange to attract investors (see chapters 5 and 6).[21]

In addition to new sources of formal "white" financing available, Indian real estate developers continued to rely on "black"—untaxed, illegally earned, or cash—money to finance their projects, tying real estate to political and criminal underworlds.[22] With much of its value officially undocumented, property has been "an ideal investment for black savings" (Kumar 2002, 23), and this has only intensified since liberalization (Weinstein 2008). Real estate assets are heterogeneous and unique, making them difficult to value and easy to undervalue in official records. Developers routinely record only 10 to 25 percent of the value of land transactions to avoid taxes. Like land, apartments and homes are often sold with part of the value transacted unofficially in cash, part officially in check.[23] Landowners, builders, developers, and property buyers have all been historically willing to take cash (to operate "in black"), making real estate fairly unique among industries in providing opportunities to earn returns on cash assets without attracting the tax authorities (Patel 1995, 116–18).

Post-liberation, as the state has transformed its role in the economy, state-private sector patronage networks have been reconfigured and decentralized, not eradicated (Chandra 2015). As the state has increasingly become central to land acquisition and conversion, politicians and bureaucrats extract bribes from developers and also speculate in land in advance of regulatory changes. Politicians use their "black" earnings from these activities to fund payments to supporters at election time (see Björkman 2014), and they reinvest cash in property, making politicians an important source of funding for developers (see Patel 1995, 116–18). Politicians and gangsters, then, remain crucial actors in real estate markets.

New Consumers and Ancillary Markets

Since liberalization, developers have built for new consumers: Non-Resident Indians (NRIs), multinational companies, and the Indian information technology industry.[24] The entrance of multinational companies and Non-Resident Indians into the Indian market after liberalization in the early 1990s spurred a spike in real estate prices in cities like Mumbai and Delhi; the sudden demand for space outstripped supply (see Brauchli 1995; Nijman 2000). In the National Capital Region, developers designed projects specifically for NRIs and recruited buyers from Dubai, Singapore, and elsewhere. Several told me that at that time, only NRIs and the wealthiest Indians could afford to buy what they were constructing.

Buildings and advertisements from the early 1990s indicate an NRI target audience. Malibu Towne, developed "by an ex-NRI Californian," claimed to offer "the ambiance of a typical lush green American housing development," while DLF's Beverly Park condominiums were modeled after properties the DLF chairman saw in Florida. Advertisements addressed NRIs or corporate employees: the "Colonial American Style Country Home" in one advertisement is "Ideal for . . . diplomatic residences, Multinational, NRIs, Exporters, etc." Similarly, Ansals marketed its Residency Studio Apartments for the "busy businessman" (fig. 1.5).[25] Today, developers continue to woo NRI clients, through advertisements (King 2002), websites, direct mailings, and offices and property fairs abroad (Varrel 2015).

As well as housing for NRIs, developers began building office space for the multinational companies expanding into India in the mid-1990s and the growing IT industry. Existing offices in Delhi did not meet these firms' specifications, as they were lacking a guaranteed power supply, air-conditioning, and large contiguous spaces. Developers responded with new designs. For one of its first office buildings for this post-liberalization target audience,

FIGURE 1.5. This Ansals Residency advertisement targets business people. The ad copy reads: "It's like owning a deluxe room in a luxury hotel. A home-away-from-home with the exclusiveness of a hotel and the facilities of a resort. FOR RS.1.99 LAKHS ONLY! . . . Now, Ansals give the busy businessman an option he had always wanted—a 'business home.' Here you can give your work undivided attention, and yet be in a home-like environment. So, you get the best of both worlds, and none of the distractions."
Source: *Hindustan Times*, 1993.

DLF flew its architects to look at a building near the Charles de Gaulle Airport in France. The result was Corporate Park, now home to Pepsi, GE, and Oracle (fig. 1.6).[26]

Multinational corporations such as McKinsey, Microsoft, the Royal Bank of Scotland, Fidelity, and IBM have worked directly with Indian developers, architects, and interior architects to construct "build-to-suit" offices in India. Architects I spoke with said they learned about international design, construction methods, and standardizing their own production through working on such projects. Many have also collaborated with multinational firms' in-house architectural teams to recreate international specifications in India. Architects can do so now increasingly with imported materials: tiles, flooring, plumbing fixtures, siding, outdoor pavers, glass for curtain walls, and other architectural materials can now be imported from around the world, in another growing ancillary real estate market.

As the real estate market has grown, so too have other related services: architecture, engineering, marketing, accounting, and law firms were scrambling to add staff or build property-specific divisions in 2006–2007.[27] Acting as intermediaries between Indian real estate developers and potential

FIGURE 1.6. DLF Corporate Park, Gurgaon, 2006.
Source: Photo by author.

foreign corporate clients, subsidiaries of international property consultancies were first established in India in the mid-1990s: CBRE in 1994 and Cushman Wakefield in 1997, followed by numerous others (DTZ, Jones Lang LaSalle Meghraj, Knight Frank, Colliers, etc.). Banks have also added property divisions. These companies publish industry reports and provide brokerage and advisory services, in effect circulating international methods for valuing, marketing, and maintaining property as they interact with Indian developers.

A market in paper has arisen alongside these markets in expertise, bricks, and finance. The *Hindustan Times*, for example, began carrying the occasional real estate related article in about 1999, in its Life and Style section. By 2001, it had a dedicated real estate section, HT Estates, which, alongside property listings, featured profiles of interior designers, residents, developers, and upcoming projects; advice on dealing with contractors; information about obtaining home loans; and tips on home decorating. Other major newspapers and magazines have followed suit, with special sections or "line extensions" devoted to real estate, and television channels have added property-focused television shows such as business news channel NDTV Profit's "Hot Property" program. Developers took out almost four thousand full-page newspaper ads in 2006; they also advertised heavily on the radio and on property websites such as Magicbricks.com and Indiaproperty.com (Bhatia and Shah 2007).

Although my informants underscored that "home decorating"—calling on the expertise of interior designers to beautify the home—was a novel concept in India, a growing number of architectural and interiors magazines, real estate magazines, and women's magazines feature advice on home decor.[28] These new media and the (imported) home products advertised in them—appliances, modular kitchens, bath tiling, fixtures, furniture, paint, etc.—have created new interest in home decorating and interior design among building consumers.

To summarize, the fifteen years since economic liberalization began have ushered in a larger role for private developers vis-à-vis the government; new avenues for financing real estate projects; new consumers; and new ancillary markets. These changes precipitated a real estate boom that involved many people—construction material importers, media conglomerates, architects, lawyers, graphic designers, bankers, politicians, builders, and developers—each working to expand these interconnected real estate markets.

Accumulation through Labor Exploitation

Real estate developers have thrived since economic liberalization. Between 2004 and 2008, real estate development companies in the National Capital Region announced increasing profits (table 1.1) and paid themselves handsomely (table 1.2).[29] Nationally, salaries for real estate executives often outpaced salaries for CEOs in sectors such as manufacturing and IT (see Hussain 2008b; Raja D. et al. 2007).[30] As firms expanded rapidly and competed to attract professionals from other industries, salaries for Indian real estate

TABLE 1.1. Selected NCR real estate developers' profit after tax (in Rs millions).

Company	2004–2005	2005–2006	2006–2007	2007–2008*
Unitech	348	876	13,055	16,692
DLF	459	961	19,337	78,558
Omaxe	50	1,190	1,381	*no data*
Parsvnath	657	1,070	2,718	4,087
Ansal API	*no data*	374	1,321	1,735

Sources: Ansal API 2007; Batlivala and Karani Securities 2006; DLF Limited 2007, 2008; Omaxe Limited 2007; Parsvnath Developers Ltd. 2008; Unitech 2007, 2009.

* These are fiscal years, ending March 31st.

TABLE 1.2. Executive salaries at selected NCR real estate development companies.

Company	Executive	Title	Fiscal Year	Salary* (Rs millions)
Unitech	Ramesh Chandra	Chairman	2006–7	11.8
DLF	T. C. Goyal	Managing Director	2006–7	45.0
Omaxe	Rohtas Goel	Chairman/Managing Dir.	2005–6	3.6[†]
Parsvnath	Pradeep Jain	Chairman	2007–8	60.0
Ansal API	Anil Kumar	CEO	2006–7	4.5

Sources: data from Hussain 2008b; Parsvnath Developers Ltd. 2008; Unitech 2007a.

* This may not include housing, health, and other allowances, nor does it take shares or share options into account.

† This is Goel's salary from the fiscal year ending in March 31, 2006. The company also paid him Rs. 13.2 crore that year for the use of the brand name "Omaxe," to which Goel owns the rights. In light of the company's forthcoming initial public offer in 2007, Goel promised to forego this royalty until 2008, with a payment of Rs. 10 lakh each subsequent financial year (Raja D. and Hussain 2007). This arrangement hints at the creative ways directors find to extract profit from their companies.

development firms' lower level employees also increased by 25 to 30 percent each year between 2006 and 2008 (Hussain 2008b).[31]

Overall, Indian real estate developers' profit margins—though variable and difficult to trace—ranged above 20 percent, making them significantly higher than margins for other Indian industries or American real estate projects.[32] DLF apparently kept a profit margin of 35 to 40 percent on mid-market residential projects and 75 percent for luxury residences (Raja D. 2008b).[33] Pankaj, a consultant, told me, "You take a typical real estate project in ah, Delhi—Gurgaon, wherever. Even at whatever land cost that land is available, I don't think any real estate developer looks at a project, which has an IRR [internal rate of return] of less than 35 percent after tax."

These returns have been made possible by the expansion of the numerous real estate–related markets outlined in the previous section. Particularly because of their central position in these interrelated networks and the availability of new sources of finance, real estate developers have increased the capital they can circulate through the built environment. By marketing new buildings as "elite" and "global," targeting new consumers such as NRIs, and creating demand for new styles of construction, they have worked to increase the prices of finished commercial and residential construction.

At the same time, they have benefited from—and perpetuated—systems that keep laborers poor and construction costs low. Construction costs are only between 20 and 40 percent of total project costs. The managing director of one of India's largest construction firms estimated that only 10 percent of construction costs are for labor, with 4 percent of that for supervisory staff. [34] David Mosse, Sanjeev Gupta, and Vidya Shah (2005) report that even government jobs squeeze labor to reduce costs. They interviewed municipal officials who admitted that "financial constraints exert pressure to keep project costs down and that given the relatively fixed costs of materials and transport, building contractors make their profits on the labour component through exploitation of cheap migrant labour recruited via mukkadams [*jamadars*]" (3030).

The results of such exploitation are hidden behind the advertisements for Technicolor luxury lives that enclose construction sites (fig. 1.7). On one such site, which I visited with a woman from a social services nonprofit, I met a woman named Aasha who was nursing her baby on the stoop of the bamboo and tin hut provided by the developer. Her face was haggard and wrinkled beyond her age. She tugged at the end of her deep green sari, making sure it covered her head as she spoke to us. A child, about four, squirmed at her side, and her daughter, maybe eight years old, lugged a plastic oil jug sloshing with water back to the hut. Aasha leaves her children here, untended, when she works on the site. Less than a month before we met, Aasha and her husband came to Gurgaon from Jhansi, Uttar Pradesh, where they had left two older children with Aasha's in-laws. Asked why she came to Gurgaon, she explained their land in the village was *sukha*, dry: "Without water, how can I feed my family? We had nothing to eat." The woman I was with asked if her husband had worked in the village. Aasha laughed at the suggestion and said, no, there was no work in the village. So her husband's *mama* (maternal uncle) suggested they come to the city to work with him on a construction site, and they came. She and her husband each earn Rs. 65 a day. [35]

Aasha's situation is not unique. Like other construction laborers, she and her husband came to Gurgaon to escape desperate rural conditions. A study of 425 construction worker households at ten sites in the National Capital Region found that workers had migrated to escape drought, debt, and unemployment in their home villages. Just over half of the migrants had come from Chattisgarh, a state where only 16 percent of the land is irrigated. [36] Families struggling to survive on small, rainfall-dependent plots in rural areas where wage labor is only sporadically available, and at reduced wages, feed their children by migrating (Mobile Crèches 2008). [37] Real estate industry profits thus accrue from agrarian distress.

The construction work to which migrants flee is no safe haven. Few construction workers make the legally mandated minimum wage. In addition, they face long hours of work; squalid living conditions; job insecurity; health problems; hazardous working conditions; and often, harassment at the hands of authorities. [38] Scattered press reports of construction worker fatalities and

FIGURE 1.7. On-site construction worker housing, Gurgaon, 2007.
Source: Photo by author.

illness hint at the hazards of hard physical labor with poor equipment and inferior materials on sites lacking warning signs, fencing, and first-aid stations.[39]
These perilous landscapes, this hard work, and this deprivation fuel real estate
sector profits, which, contrary to industry rhetoric, trickle up, not down.

Developers and construction companies wield significant power to resist
the enforcement of existing labor laws or the implementation of new ones.[40]

Certainly industry outsiders have made determined efforts. In the mid-1980s, a group of activists began pushing the government to pass comprehensive legislation for construction workers. After more than a decade of pressure, the Central Government passed the Building and Other Construction Workers (Regulation of Employment and Conditions of Service) Act (known as the BOCW) and the Building and Other Construction Workers' Welfare Cess Act in 1996.[41] This comprehensive legislation, however, remains largely unimplemented. As late as 2007, only thirteen of India's twenty-eight states and seven Union Territories had established Welfare Boards under the Act (see CWFI 2008).[42] In May 2008, the Supreme Court chided the government for passing "beautiful" but unimplemented laws (*Indian Express* 2008).[43]

The reasons for these failures are clear. While developers and contractors are politically well-connected, construction workers—especially migrants—are not a constituency for anyone (Mosse, Gupta, and Shah 2005, 3031). As a floating population, they are removed from political networks of patronage and enmeshed instead in a system of hiring that separates workers from the big-name contractors and developers who are their ultimate bosses. Just as Aasha traveled to the city with her husband's *mama*, most rural migrants use kin networks and intermediaries to find construction jobs. These intermediaries, or *jamadars*, find work, negotiate a piece rate for a particular job, and pay the laborers a wage (from which they take a cut).[44] The practice of hiring workers through chains of subcontractors and *jamadars* contributes to contractors' and developers' ability to disavow knowledge of or legal responsibility for their workforce. Laborers are left depending on their most "intimate exploiters," *jamadars* and petty bosses, for a semblance of security and sustenance (Mosse, Gupta, and Shah 2005, 3032).

Labor conditions are so appalling and workers' exploitation so egregious that it is tempting to make labor the only center of our analysis of capital accumulation. However, labor exploitation does not fully account for industry gains. Indian real estate developers have also accumulated capital by buying up farmland at a tremendous pace; some re-parceling it and selling it to other developers. Developers who bought land before about 2004 were able to construct and sell properties in 2007 or 2008 at inflated prices without incurring high land costs, achieving much higher returns than those who purchased land later. Ashish, a consultant, explained that some returns were so high as to be incalculable: "They [developers] bought land at historical levels so land is almost free. Then they get funding through development and pre-sell that, so it's like how do you calculate return when you have not even put your hand in the pocket and you have made money?" This unprecedented appreciation of land values, which makes land bought in the past ("at historical levels") seem "almost free," hints at capitalist logics that exceed Marx's labor theory of value.

Spectacular Accumulation

Like developers flipping land parcels, international investors seem to be able to divorce capital accumulation from building construction. For example, Trikona Trinity Capital PLC, an investment fund headquartered on the Isle of Man and managed from the Cayman Islands, listed on the London Stock Exchange Alternate Investment Market in April 2006 and began investing in Indian real estate projects that year. For the fiscal year 2007–8, the fund reported a gross internal rate of return ranging from 27 to 179 percent for eleven of its twelve investments (Trikona Trinity Capital PLC 2008, 14).[45] Trikona had not significantly changed the land. These investments had simply gained value since Trikona had first invested in them, seven to sixteen months previously, in part because Trikona's interest in the properties attracted other investors (Trikona Trinity Capital PLC 2008, 9).

Investors invest in order to "realize assets," that is, sell them after their value has increased. Trikona was one of the first funds to do so successfully. In November 2007, its managers sold a percentage of the fund's investment in four different projects to an affiliate of a German fund, SachsenFonds GmbH, for £32.1 million, realizing an internal rate of return of 108 percent on its investments. These gains pushed Trikona's Net Asset Valuation up 22 percent and helped the fund achieve a before-tax profit of £64 million (Trikona Trinity Capital PLC 2008, 9). In June 2008, Trikona sold £54.33 million more of its stake in several projects to SachsenFonds, realizing 115 percent on those investments (Trikona Trinity Capital PLC 2008, 4).

SachsenFonds bought into potential real estate projects, not completed construction. While images of construction workers grace almost every page of Trikona's annual report, little construction was underway by 2008: one of the projects was only at the planning stages; another had not been fully cleared of slum dwellers; an unbuilt luxury high-rise had sold 41 percent of its apartments; the site of one retail project had been excavated; and an SEZ project had received government approvals (Trikona Trinity Capital PLC 2008, 18, 22–25, 30).

How do we understand this kind of accumulation, in which construction does not seem to play a role? Describing the biotech industry, Kaushik Sunder Rajan writes about "the coexistence of at least these two simultaneous, distinct, yet mutually constitutive forms of capital, one directly dependent on the production of commodities, the other speculative and only indirectly so" (Sunder Rajan 2006, 9). Similarly, real estate combines commodity production (constructing buildings) with this second, more speculative form, what Marx has called "merchant's or trading capital" (1981, 379) and what we would call today "finance capital."[46] Merchant capitalists deal not only in commodities but in all sorts of "fictitious" forms such as money, land, and shares, which are not the product of labor, but which come to have prices.[47] Those prices, Marx warns, are "irrational" and without limit. Seemingly divorced from the material limits of labor power, interest-bearing capital appears self-generating, capable of growing "in geometric progression" (1981, 523); it is "money that creates more money" (Marx 1981, 515).[48] Thus, in future-oriented industries like biotechnology or real estate (or financial ones, like banking), accumulation can exceed the surplus value created by labor.

Trikona's "exits" are an excellent example of "money that creates more money." While, in Marx's terminology the rise in the value of Trikona's investments was "fictitious," the £86.43 million Trikona earned from the sale was not. What makes this kind of accumulation possible? Anna Tsing uses the term "spectacular accumulation" to explain how capitalists use stories to "conjure" the possibility of profit in advance of capital-intensive, uncertain endeavors like mining (Tsing 2005, 57, 75). I argue that in addition to the semiotic work of positioning entities as desirable, spectacular accumulation is made possible by transforming the social relations and practices in which commodities are embedded to make them tradable. Thus Indian developers profit when they resell a parcel of land after changing its regulatory status from agricultural to buildable land, and Trikona Capital profits when its fund managers work out how to make an Indian construction project into a set of shares that can be exchanged abroad. Both also position their investments as profitable, and they rely on the circulation of stories about growth in doing so.[49] This work is not the labor from which surplus value is extracted: it does not make buildings. Instead it creates the conditions of possibility for things to be traded: cumulatively, it makes markets.[50]

Financialization of Urban Development

Trikona Capital's exits herald the transformation of Indian land from a resource for agricultural or industrial production to an international resource for spectacular accumulation. This transformation has occurred within an international context in which finance capital has risen to prominence and capital managers have turned real estate into a financial asset. I turn briefly to these wider trends before returning to the ongoing work that investors, developers, consultants, and others are doing to financialize real estate in India.

Since the 1970s, capitalists' profits have increasingly come, not from selling goods, but from investments (Krippner 2005). Finance capital has grown
in complexity and volume since the 1970s, when the collapse of the Bretton
Woods monetary system spurred the growth of international currency markets.[51] Since then, emboldened by steady deregulation, financial institutions
have developed and aggressively sold new financial instruments upon which
corporations have increasingly relied to manage the uncertainties created by
increased monetary volatility and global production chains.[52] In the "vast
casino" (Strange 1997) that has emerged, the magnitude of currency trading has far outstripped trade in goods, and largely liquid, speculative capital
flows have precipitated international financial crises around the world (most
notably in Mexico, Brazil, Argentina, South East Asia, the US, Iceland, and
Greece).

The rise of the global finance industry and its associated producer services has contributed to the "financialization of urban redevelopment" (Rutland 2010). As financial firms cluster in the center city districts of cities like
New York and Tokyo, land prices rise out of proportion with national markets
and in line with financial districts abroad (Sassen 2001, 190–96). These same
financial firms invest in real estate in other cities, linking them together in an
international real estate market.[53]

Internationally, real estate has also become a *resource for* finance capital.
A new range of investors (the same financial industries for which the real
estate industry builds office space—i.e., banks, insurance companies, pension
funds, private equity and hedge funds) capitalize real estate projects through
increasingly complex financial mechanisms, perhaps the most well-known of
which is securitization (see Boddy 1981; Logan 1993). Real estate assets of all
kinds have been "re-engineered" so that they can be traded as fluidly as bonds
(Morris 2008, 57–58). As Donald Trump Jr. commented to an Indian newspaper during a 2007 visit,

> Real estate is a finance game today. From a banking perspective, it's no longer
> considered any different from other forms of corporate finance. In the high
> end segment in which we operate, real estate is seen as part of an individual's
> investment portfolio, along with stocks and bonds. (*Economic Times* 2007e)

The result, in places like London, has been "a long-term shift away from what
might be called 'industrial landownership' (where land is owned essentially as
a condition of other production) and towards 'financial ownership' where the
ownership of land is itself the means of extracting a profit" (Massey 2007, 48).

I argue that a similar transformation is unfolding in India, as the result of
concerted efforts of developers, investors, consultants, and the Indian gov-

ernment to reshape Indian land, buildings, and companies into globally legible vessels of finance capital and means of spectacular accumulation. Since land and buildings cannot move, they need to be transformed into types of property that can be exchanged overseas—titles and shares—by replicating the practices of international real estate in India. The profits Trikona Capital garnered from selling to the German fund were made possible by this ongoing work.

Making Indian Real Estate into an International Financial Resource

Coming from real estate markets where property is already a financial instrument that can be traded internationally, foreign investors have found that Indian land and buildings did not meet their expectations for how real estate should work. They expected that there would be groups of existing buildings that they could buy up in a "portfolio of assets"; that office buildings would be owned by one company and leased out to tenants, not owned by many different people; that office buildings would provide tenants with air-conditioning and electricity; that apartments and houses would be bought by individuals with mortgages, not cash; that it would be legal to buy land and develop it; that foreigners could get permits for land use changes; that documents would guarantee property ownership; that the government and private consultancies would keep statistics about real estate activities; that financial structures such as Real Estate Improvement Trusts and Real Estate Mutual Funds would be legal and commonplace; and that valuing a property would be a straightforward technical process, not a disputed, inconclusive one.

Industry members have fought to reproduce these practices in India and to transform Indian real estate into an internationally familiar field of practice on numerous fronts. They have pressured the central and state governments of India to make a more "efficient" market in land through repealing acts like the ULCRA which limited private developers' access to urban land parcels; to open urban infrastructure projects up to the private sector; to enable foreigners to invest in Indian real estate and infrastructure construction; to reduce stamp duties (taxes on property transactions); and to computerize land records (Raman 2012). While these efforts are often rationalized through appeals to efficiency, growth, or poverty reduction (e.g., Shastri 2007; World Bank 2007), they are also bids to make land a more easily traded asset, freed from the monopoly of state development authorities and the uncertainty of land titling systems unfamiliar to foreigners.

To do this work, foreign fund managers and Indian developers have had to partner with each other. Fund managers found they had to work with Indian developers who could use their longstanding networks with local politicians, bureaucrats, and landowners to agglomerate land and obtain permits for development. Indian developers saw these partnerships as ways to garner capital and prestige just as they were scaling up their property development plans (see chapter 6). As Halbert and Rouanet (2014) argue, such partnerships enable investment to occur by "filtering away risk"; they also created frictions and risks of their own.[54] In order to reduce these risks, investors have tried to transform how Indian real estate development companies do business by changing their internal organization and altering their business practices (see chapter 5).

Investors have devised ways to make buildings as well as companies "investable" by constructing new buildings and creating novel property formations that would enable them to trade the buildings outside of India. Although there are many buildings in India, foreign real estate investors felt that few of these buildings made good investments. A senior vice president at an American private equity firm told me that in India

> there are no portfolios to buy, there are no fixed assets to buy. There are no rental buildings yet. You can count buildings on your fingertips. If you have moved in Delhi and Bombay, tell me, how many buildings can you buy today that has a single owner? Maybe DLF has five buildings. That's it. Unitech has two buildings. Who else? Nobody else. Hiranandani might have one building. So where is that opportunity for anybody to buy these kinds of assets? Where are the portfolios? These portfolios will get built in the next ten years. But 'till that time, a private equity player has to be a developer.[55]

Investors felt that there were no readily available real estate portfolios in India the way there would be in the US or Europe, where these firms are used to investing in groups of real estate assets at a time.[56] They did not think that there were even individual buildings to buy because Indian buildings were not built to the standards that international real estate developers and their multinational corporate clients expect: they have the wrong layouts, sizes, facades, construction quality, and features. Moreover, most existing buildings have been sold in "strata" to numerous buyers, making them impossible to purchase as one asset and resell. In the absence of buildings-cum-assets that meet foreign expectations, foreign investors were acting like developers: in partnership with Indian firms, they were constructing new buildings designed to make better tools for spectacular accumulation.

Investors and developers have devised ways of structuring those buildings as financial instruments they can sell (or "exit" from) profitably. They have hired lawyers, accountants, and property consultants to figure out how to do this while meeting shifting government requirements for foreign direct investment. A foreign fund, for example, might establish a subsidiary company in a tax haven like the Cayman Islands, which in turn shares ownership of a joint venture company with an Indian developer-partner. That joint venture company (also incorporated in a tax haven) owns 100 percent of a "special purpose vehicle" (SPV) in India which constructs a new building.[57] Instead of selling the building outright, and incurring the taxes and restrictions the Indian government has put on such a sale, the foreign fund can sell shares in either the special purpose vehicle or the joint venture company to other investors (fig. 1.8).[58] As they devised these complex deal structures, foreign funds, Indian developers, and all their consultants created new buildings-as-financial-structures (here, a building as shares owned by various offshore companies).

Finally, representations were an important aspect of market-making work. Foreign investors and Indian developers have created buildings-as-commodity-images. Developers and their consultants have devised a host

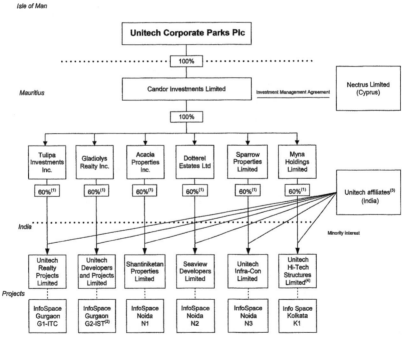

FIGURE 1.8. The Unitech Corporate Parks Plc. corporate structure.
Developers and investors devise ways of structuring their real estate investments so that shares in construction projects can be sold outside of India. (G1-ITC, G2-IST, N1-3, and K1 are construction projects/buildings.)
Source: Unitech Corporate Parks, Plc. 2006.

of image-fashioning products that range from elements of the building itself (novel architectural motifs and features, elaborate entrance gates, landscaping, the building's name, its location, etc.) to representations of the building such as brochures, model apartments, advertisements, videos, and scale models.[59] As communications for potential end users (apartment residents, tenants), these representations aimed to connect particular buildings with social imaginaries that developers hoped would lend prestige to their properties, enable them to earn a higher profit, and increase their sales. But they were also used to impress potential investors about the building capabilities, business strategy, and reputation of the developer. (Chapter 7 examines the role of this building imagery in contests over value between developers and investors.) Significantly, building-images appear before the buildings they represent exist. Because they give nonexistent commodities a desirable present form and developers without a construction track record the appearance of capability, these representations encourage property buyers and investors to part with their money. Technologies for a speculative trade in future buildings, they enable trade to flourish ahead of the slow, capital-intensive process of construction.

Members of the industry have produced representations of the Indian real estate market itself. Property and management consultants—groups like Ernst & Young or CBRE—have written market reports that developers and investors pick up at conferences, download from the web, or Xerox from one another. Journalists have summarized these reports in the financial newspapers, circulating their findings to the wider business community. By describing the Indian real estate market in the same jargon used for other markets—in terms of cap rates, yields, and asset classes—and by representing it using graphs that compare India to other markets along measures of mortgage penetration or retail space constructed, these reports have helped industry members envision Indian real estate as a market comparable to those elsewhere. They produce a narrative of industry growth and progress toward an international norm that attracts investors comforted by indicators of similarity and eager to share in the proceeds of growth (see chapters 2 and 3).

In conclusion, Gurgaon's high-rises, malls, and offices have emerged in the era of liberalization because regulatory changes have altered the structure of the real estate industry, resulting in new consumers and forms of finance as well as providing an expanded role for private sector developers. In the context of the increasing dominance of finance capital globally, the "opening up" of Indian real estate to foreign capital precipitated attempts to transform Indian land and buildings into routes of spectacular accumulation. Land, as "fictitious" commodity, was, anyways, open to this kind of accumulation, but through ongoing work, investors and others have attempted to make Indian land function like financialized property elsewhere by further altering laws and practices. The first step in this ongoing, uncertain work was attracting finance to India, for it did not just flow there. In the next chapter, I examine the semiotic work done to convince foreign fund managers that Indian real estate would make a promising investment.

PART I

Speculating on Indian Futures

The "India Story"

What was a speculator anyway, if not a storyteller, who wrote the ending before the beginning?

S C O T T A . S A N D A G E , Born Losers: A History of Failure in America

The "India Story"

Sanjeev, a broker specializing in Gurgaon and South Delhi realty had assembled some old housing brochures for me, and I stopped at his office in central Delhi to pick them up. As we sat across from each other at his desk, sipping tea, he handwrote price information on the brochures, and we chatted about various Gurgaon housing projects. He suggested, as many of my informants did, that I should personally invest in real estate. Perhaps I could even convince friends back home to join me. I protested that I should have invested four years ago, before the real estate market took off. Surely, now whatever I bought was bound to lose value. Sanjeev looked up from his writing, put his pencil down, and told me he was going to tell me a story. He motioned to my notebook and instructed me to write it down.

Sanjeev recounted that his uncle bought property in Defense Colony (an affluent neighborhood in South Delhi) in 1965. He paid 4.5 or 5 lakh for a 500-yard plot of land and the construction of a house on it. His uncle's next door neighbor sold an identical piece of land (without the house) for 6.5 or 7 lakh a few years later. That plot of land kept changing hands. In 2002, it sold to a developer for two crore. Five years later, it sold for 15 crore. Sanjeev asked,

> The question is, when was the best time to have bought that property? It may have been in the last couple of years. The highest appreciation may have happened between 2002 and 2007, or even after that, because the property may have rose from two to five crore and then maybe the prices were flat for a bit, and then it tripled to 15 crore.

He concluded his tale with a moral:

> You see, any time seems like a bad time to buy property because of the appreciation. But in the last fifty to sixty years, property on a five-year cycle has

never let anyone down. If, God bless you, you have enough money to buy property, and you invest in a decent location, real estate in India will not let you down.

Sanjeev hoped to convince me that appreciation always indicates profit to be made, and not an impending crash. In so doing, he recounted a morality tale for a booming market, a story of incredible appreciation extrapolated as faith in continued appreciation.

Sanjeev was not alone in his ability to cite real estate values from memory, nor in his insistence on their continued escalation. Informant after informant expressed faith in ever-increasing values. One real estate consultant argued that prestigious locations face no limits to appreciation, citing the sale of an apartment on Marine Drive in Mumbai at an astounding 85,000 rupees per square foot to prove his point.[1] Many unquestioningly, enthusiastically insisted that real estate would never decrease in value. Gurdeep, the marketing director for a Gurgaon-based developer, asserted:

> Real estate is something that has to appreciate. It is historically in the last thousands of years, if you see, that real estate cannot have a cycle that goes down—it only has to appreciate. Yes, within a cycle there are graphs that are going up and down, but over a period of time real estate has to appreciate. Every five years it has to go up by one hundred percent. It has to. I mean if you see historically, it has. So there is no way that it won't.

Like Sanjeev, Gurdeep transformed historical trend (however loosely interpreted) into future necessity, claiming "real estate *has* to appreciate."[2]

Many of my informants simply told dramatic, personal stories of appreciation. They recounted tales of relatives and friends who bought plots of land in Gurgaon in the early 1980s at 300 or 350 rupees per square yard; by 2006, those plots were worth about 60,000 rupees per square yard. A broker in Gurgaon bought an apartment for his family in 2002 at Rs. 1,700 per square foot; in 2007, it was worth Rs. 6,000 per square foot. A mall developer told me he paid Rs. 900 a square meter in 2003 for land on the outskirts of the National Capital Region (in Ghaziabad); he claimed that nearby land was selling for Rs. 35,000 a square meter just three years later. Another developer boasted that his plot in Saket (a posh South Delhi neighborhood) had appreciated to 1.5 crore (Rs. 15 million) in 2006 from one lakh rupees in 1985. Like Sanjeev, he concluded, "When we bought it in 1985, we said the price is very high. Today we say the price is very high. But I believe in the next ten years, this fifteen million will become thirty million."

These ubiquitous stories about price appreciation are just one example of stories about growth circulating in the Indian real estate market in 2006–

2007: stories about the growth of consumer demand, of the Indian workforce, of Gross Domestic Product (GDP), of incomes, of foreign investment, of the real estate industry, of infrastructure, of IT. These stories appeared in news-paper articles, industry reports, investor presentations, Government of India publications, brochures, and conversations. My informants have a shorthand for this collective narrative about India's growth: they called it the "India story" (fig. 2.1).

The "India story" has elaborate endings and thin beginnings. Indian devel-opers, foreign investors, consultants, and the Indian government love to talk about the future, pausing only briefly to extrapolate from the past. Members of the industry repeat predictions until they gather the patina of common sense and the persuasiveness to motivate action. As a result, high land prices precede discernable economic activities and demand; colorful brochures describe buildings which, in present form, are muddy lots; and predictions of India's glorious globally integrated future coincide with its impoverished present. Persuasive endings, told and retold, are helping to create the Indian real estate market.

I trace the circulation of these stories about India's incipient growth from Goldman Sachs reports to business magazines, the Indian press, govern-ment publications, and developers' presentations. Tracing this circulation reveals how industry members translated internationally circulating stories about economic growth into performative discourses in India.[3] Cumulatively, people used these stories to position India as profitable and to draw invest-ment into Indian real estate—necessary first steps in creating an international market in Indian land and buildings.

Certainly, India was not the only place to witness a boom in property investment in the 2000s. Looking back, we see similarities with American, Spanish, and other property markets around the world, such that surely the "India story" shared many elements with discourses circulating in those con-texts. Neither is it surprising that financiers and developers made investments based on projected future growth. But these stories and projections have be-come accepted common sense for many, and thus deserve scholarly scrutiny. Their power stems from repetition, from their broad circulation in realms outside of real estate, their intersection with other discourses about a "rising Asia," and their legitimation as a form of economic knowledge.

The fundamental difference between discourses about the future (like the "India story") and those about the present is that there is not yet a future against which to judge the former. Stories of growth do not *describe* the future, so much as open up possibilities and motivate others to orient themselves toward them; they are tools. Through the discourses that I describe here,

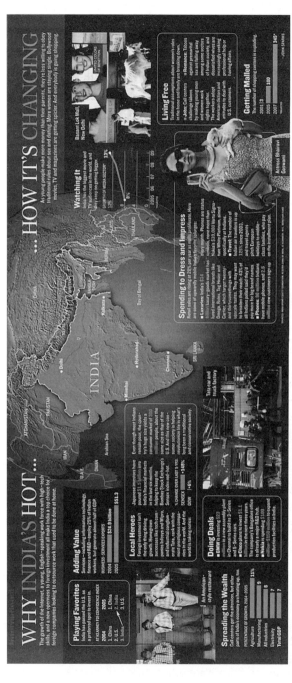

FIGURE 2.1. The "India story" has been popularized by magazines such as *Newsweek*. The diagram reads, "WHY INDIA'S HOT. . . . The growth of the Internet, a young, English-speaking work force with high-tech skills, and a new openness to foreign investment all make India a top choice for foreign companies looking to outsource work that used to be done at home. . . . HOW IT'S CHANGING. As young people make more money than their parents, they're less willing to obey traditional rules about sex and dating. More women are staying single. Bollywood movies, TV and magazines are getting spicier. And everybody is going shopping."

Source: Zakaria 2006.

various actors attempt to position particular investments as profitable by delineating their relationship to a desirable future. Such a future is possible, they claim, if you just buy our apartment, invest in our project, or partner with our firm. Discourses about the future provide models for action in the here and now. Thus, to the extent that they convince their audiences, discourses about the future are technologies for organizing action in the present.

As one strand of the "India story," my informants' stories about real estate prices worked on several levels. They constituted a major source of information in a market lacking statistical data. Neither I nor my informants had an "objective" ground from which to view the rate or geography of price appreciation. In India, there are no reliable statistical indicators or official sources of real estate data: no housing starts or completions, no residential sales statistics, no construction spending data, and, until 2007, no price indices.[4] No one could tell me how many projects were under construction, how many square feet had been completed in a given year, or what had been sold. Moreover, prices were difficult to determine. Many property transactions are unrecorded; those officially documented usually underrepresent the actual selling price to avoid taxes.[5] As one fund manager told me, one has to stay "close to the ground" to learn of transactions as they occur; one needs to be well-connected to be well-informed. On this informational level, then, stories about prices guided developers and investors as they bought, sold, and invested; acting on stories of appreciation, they hoped to position themselves and their projects for the future.

Industry members also used stories about prices for their own ends. Just as Sanjeev told a story about price appreciation in the context of asking me to buy property, brokers, developers, investment fund managers, buyers, and others told these stories to one another to prove their own success, persuade others to invest with them, sell their services, convey a lesson, or dismiss another's claim. Information about real estate in India came embedded in these interactional contexts. Given that my informants engage in buying and selling, the context was often a potential sale. Just as brokers used stories about appreciation to convince potential buyers, developers made presentations laced with predictions to entice investors, and consultancies published reports about the real estate market in order to showcase their competence and gain clients.[6]

Taken together, these stories of meteoric price appreciation chronicled massive change. They heralded the creation of new assets, the entrance of new investors, and the emergence of large-scale trading in land and buildings—in short, the expansion of global finance capital into Indian real estate. Moreover, *these stories helped fuel that expansion.* As people told stories about price appreciation, they advertised the profitability of real estate as an investment. The possibility of profit drew more investors into the market, further increasing demand, and thus escalating prices. If one could sell while this inflationary spiral was still growing, escalating prices meant high profits. Stories about growth are, and are intended to be, self-fulfilling prophesies.

Real estate industry members themselves saw these dynamics. When I asked Pankaj, a consultant with an Indian engineering, real estate, and infrastructure consultancy, why he thought the real estate market had suddenly become so "hot," he answered, "the runaway success of one or two locations in the country." He explained, "if you take a Gurgaon, for instance, prime [residential] property selling at 14, 15, 1700 rupees a square foot has moved to the region of 5,500–6,000 rupees a square foot in less than two years. What that has done—is, ah, that it's fueled a massive inflow of interest from developers of all hues and colors and across locations." The possibility of profit—broadcast through stories, rumors, and reports—drove the inflationary spiral of speculation and fueled the transformation of land into a new asset.

Perpetual growth is not inevitable. As we well know, stories of rapid appreciation can also indicate the possibility of a sudden crash. Profits can be too high and price rise too sudden to suggest long-term money-making prospects. This was the point the managing director of a European real estate investment fund (EuroFund), Jeremy, conveyed as he told me about a parcel his fund looked into buying in Hyderabad.[7] He prefaced his story with the assurance that this is "an absolute true story, no exaggeration or hyperbole." The sellers, two men, had assembled three hundred acres of land at about thirty thousand dollars per acre two years before Jeremy approached them in January 2006. As Jeremy noted, "now there'd be plenty of places in [Europe] where thirty thousand an acre would seem like a pretty healthy price for an acre of land." They offered the land to Jeremy for one million dollars per acre. While Jeremy was mulling over the offer, transactions on nearby land indicated that values were shooting upward. By October, the sellers told Jeremy that five acres adjacent to their land had sold for four million dollars an acre. Jeremy summarized:

> So here, in the course of ten months—or if you want to look at it over two years—land that two years ago was thirty thousand an acre, in the year 2006, in the course of ten months, went from one million to one-and-a-half million to two-and-a-half million to four million per acre, in the course of ten months.

He indicated his incredulity at the speed of this price escalation by repeating the time frame "in the course of ten months." Unlike Sanjeev's tale, the moral of Jeremy's story is the unjustified nature of appreciation, not faith in its continuance.

Jeremy underscored his view by using the term "speculation":

> That's approaching Dutch tulip bulb speculation in terms of the ridiculous run-up in value. There's—it's impossible I think to believe that anything is happening in India and Hyderabad that would justify prices rising at that rate.

Jeremy's analogy to the Dutch tulip bulb craze and his use of the term speculation, linked to "ridiculous" values, is pejorative. Jeremy was one of my most skeptical informants. Here he deploys his experience in international real estate to judge the Indian market as an "overheated situation." He saw little rationale for the price escalations and believed that values would soon drop.

A few of my informants classified certain markets as growing too fast. In late 2006, Pankaj, the consultant, described the situation as a "mania":

> The real estate market has started sizzling, and this sizzle is probably the only term that can describe the mania. You are talking about the appreciation rates of the order of 30–40–50 percent on an annualized basis, happening across locations. You are talking about a country where per capita incomes are still 700 odd dollars—you are talking about places like Delhi and Gurgaon offering no home, no house for less than a 250,000 dollar kind of ticket price.

For Pankaj, high appreciation rates were an indicator of a "sizzling" market, one in which prices no longer represented the underlying value of assets or matched the spending power of buyers. These disconnects could signal an impending "correction," the term my informants used to describe a downturn in prices, or more alarmingly, a "crash," a term they would use but rarely uttered.

Since stories about appreciation foretell two opposing possibilities—profit or loss—those involved in producing real estate were careful to avoid the suggestion of a "mania" or the possibility of a "crash." Many Indian developers, anxious for foreign funding, eschewed terms like "speculative," "artificial," or "overheated." In fact, almost everyone in the industry denied being "speculators"—a derogatory label—and insisted on long-term interests. In an interview with me, one developer punned, "So, that's why it is called *real* estate. It is not artificial, nothing comes down here." He added later, "demand is fundamental, solid, it will never go down." Many went beyond extrapolating from past appreciation; they told elaborate stories to justify growth. Thus the "India story" also worked to assuage the anxiety of engaging with an uncertain future. It reassured market participants by glossing over the possibility that everyone knew was there—the possibility of failure, devaluation,

"crash"—and insisting on stable growth. These strictly optimistic stories disavow the possibility of failure, and yet, at the same time, index it. To the extent
that these discourses help to buoy price appreciation, they bring everyone
closer to the possibility of price collapse.[8]

My informants believed that socioeconomic "fundamentals" would drive
demand to meet supply, avoiding an oversupply and price corrections. One
veteran consultant recounted the crash in real estate prices that coincided
with the Asian economic crisis of the late 1990s. Just before the crash, real
estate prices had risen, making Mumbai and Delhi among the most expensive
cities in the world (see Brauchli 1995; Nijman 2000). When comparing that
crash with the situation in 2007, he concluded,

> The economic fundamentals were not the same, and that's why the prices
> came down. We have come *back* to that peak now—in fact, we've gone beyond
> those prices, of course—only difference is that the economic fundamentals are
> today different: the demand is there, the consumption is there, the economy is
> doing much better than it did that time. We opened up.

"Fundamentals"—here economic indicators and consumer demand linked
to the "opening up" or liberalization of the economy—are the linchpin of
his reasoning. There may be a slight correction, he explained, but there will
be no crash this time because the fundamentals have changed. Everyone active in the real estate market elaborated on this theme of "fundamentals," key
indicators that their shared stories about India's economic and social future
would come true. In pointing to these indicators and repeating these stories,
fund managers, bankers, developers, journalists, and the Government of India guided the expansion of international capital into Indian real estate.

The Flood of Money

Indian real estate became a popular new investment in the mid-2000s in
part due to the dynamics of the global financial system, which, by 2005, was
plagued by a crisis of overaccumulation. Money had been pooling up in
Western markets: "An unprecedented wave of capital [was] flowing around the
world, with all of its owners anxiously searching for a better return" (Ip and
Whitehouse 2005). Due in part to high oil prices and low US interest rates,
the global total of fixed-income securities doubled between 2000 and 2006,
reaching 70 trillion dollars (Blumberg and Davidson 2008).[9] By 2007, pension
funds, mutual funds, and insurance companies controlled US$59.4 trillion in
financial assets; Asian central banks, hedge funds,[10] private equity funds,[11] and
oil exporters together owned another US$8.4 trillion (Wessel 2007).[12] Peter

Fisher, managing director at the New York investment company BlackRock, told the *Wall Street Journal*, "People talk about a wall of money everywhere. Bankers talk about too much money chasing deals. Private-equity funds talk of money chasing them. And buyers of corporate and asset-backed debt seem to come at the bond market from all directions" (Ip and Whitehouse 2005).

With asset prices dropping, money managers sought new, and more risky, investment opportunities.[13] They found two principal solutions which India potently combined: real estate and "emerging markets." First, investors turned to real estate assets, creating a worldwide real estate boom. In 2005, the *Economist* estimated that residential property prices in developed economies rose by $30 trillion between 2000 and 2005, "dwarfing" previous housing bubbles and the global stock market bubble of the 1990s (*Economist* 2005). In 2006, investments in commercial real estate worldwide reached a high of $645 billion, up 33 percent from the year before (Kilbinger 2007). Investors not only invested in new buildings; they found ways to trade existing assets more freely, elaborating the mortgage-backed security structures that bankers had developed in the 1980s.[14]

Second, investors turned to the so-called "emerging markets," including India, in search of returns. For example, Varun Sood of Capvent AG, a private equity firm based in Switzerland, explained why he started investing in India:

> We started looking at India because the return expectations in Europe and the U.S. were slowing down due to the huge capital over-hang. . . . Three to four years ago, there was so much capital that investors were beginning to expect very low returns. We had to look outside because we had a target of 25–30% IRR [internal rate of return] and we could only get that by looking at some of the more under-served markets. So, we set up operations in India and China. (Snighda Sengupta 2007)

Indian real estate combines the appeal of real estate and emerging markets. An employee of Hypo Real Estate, a German real estate bank, told me that "India is the land of opportunities. The margins India can offer are way ahead of what's on offer in other markets."

High returns attracted investors, but the fear of few expansion possibilities also motivated investors' interest in Indian real estate. An American investor at a roundtable discussion at a 2006 real estate conference had long-term ambitions for India: "We're running out of markets. Where would we go next? . . . In three years time, if we move out [of India] where would we go? We're in China, in Brazil, Russia, North America, Europe. So we're trying to invest into a platform in India that will produce profits year after year." The search for new markets made foreign capital managers serious about investing in India.

Money managers' and investors' interest in "emerging markets" and real estate fits the broad outlines of Marxist geographical theory, particularly the work of David Harvey. Harvey postulates that in crises of overaccumulation—when a flood of money inundates the global financial system—capital expands to find new assets, whether through commoditizing noncapitalist social arrangements or opening up new regions to accumulation (2003). By investing in Indian real estate, fund managers hoped to produce new landscapes for future production and accumulation. Investments in roads, factories, offices, airports, electricity grids, warehouses, housing, ports, schools, communication infrastructures, etc.—both absorb excess capital and lay the groundwork for the future. This "spatial fix," as David Harvey (2003, 115–116) has called it, is a "fix" in two senses: it is both a solution to overaccumulation and a "fixed" structure (a "deadweight") that will eventually be devalued and destroyed in order to accommodate future modes of accumulation.

What is important to see here, however, is that capital does not expand to produce new landscapes of its own accord; despite the way that scholars sometimes write about capital, it is not an agent. Rather, *capitalists* circulate, invest, and accumulate capital. From the point of view of fund managers, real estate developers, and consultants, moving money into Indian real estate was a risky endeavor, dependent on a leap of faith. That leap of faith is social, shaped by the "India story," borne by it, and hopefully propelling it into fruition. The manager of a European architectural hardware firm's Indian branch reminded me that when he opened the branch six years ago, India was a longer bet than was in 2007: "Now everybody's going on about the boom in India and how it is, you know, going to become one of the big superpowers, but six years ago, it was just another undeveloped country that wasn't going anywhere." How did this manager (like so many others) see a "big superpower" in what was then "just another undeveloped country"? Why did his firm open an office in Mumbai and not, say, Lagos? Stories about growth shape capital expansion and the production of new landscapes of accumulation.

India Re-Branded

An overaccumulation crisis might have prompted money managers to look for risky, unorthodox, and high-yielding assets, but enterprising fund managers and bankers directed them toward particular investments. Over the last two to three decades, fund managers have increasingly marketed Third World countries as investment opportunities, using projections of economic growth to interest investors.[15] Especially early on, this effort involved new language. Banker Antoine van Agtmael remembers coining the term "emerging markets" in 1981 as a marketing ploy. He had difficulty selling his "Third-World Equity Fund" to skeptical institutional investors and realized that he needed

> an elevator pitch that liberated these developing economies from the stigma of being labeled as "Third World" basket cases, an image rife with negative associations of flimsy polyester, cheap toys, rampant corruption, Soviet-style tractors, and flooded rice paddies.

He settled on "emerging markets" to sell the fund because it "suggested progress, uplift, and dynamism" (Agtmael 2007, 5). In order to interest investors, he felt he had to sell them something that sounded profitable, not hopeless. Numerous fund managers and bankers have similarly re-branded assets to sell growth opportunities in the developing world.

The investment bank Goldman Sachs has contributed largely to this effort, publishing a series of reports which have helped re-brand India as a profitable investment destination. Beginning in 2001, Goldman Sachs researchers grouped India with Brazil, Russia, and China (the BRICs) and announced a shift in the center of GDP growth toward these four large "emerging economies."[16] In particular, the 2003 report, "Dreaming with BRICs: The Path to 2050," gained international attention for predicting that the BRIC economies would outpace those of the developed world by 2050. The authors conclude:

> In less than 40 years, the BRICs economies together could be larger than the G6 [US, UK, Germany, France, Italy, and Japan] in US dollar terms. By 2025 they could account for over half the size of the G6. Of the current G6, only the US and Japan may be among the six largest economies in US dollar terms in 2050. (Wilson and Purushothaman 2003, 1)

The report spells out the implications of this shift for investors and companies, predicting "higher returns and increased demand for capital"; increased spending; and "significant opportunities for global companies" faced with "shrinking" markets elsewhere. In short, they suggest that moving into the BRIC markets will be an important "strategic choice" multinational firms and investors will want to make (Wilson and Purushothaman 2003, 2).

While these reports originally circulated among Goldman Sachs employees and clients, the *Financial Times*, the *Economist*, *Newsweek* and other publications summarized them, popularizing their message, and other banks and global consultancies published their own reports along similar lines.[17] Subsequent media coverage soon signaled a sea change in international opinion. One review concluded, "The growth opportunities offered by some developing countries are just too exciting to be ignored" (Coggan 2003). A commentator in the *Financial Times* wrote, "After years of being overshadowed by

China and its extraordinary record of economic growth, the world's second most populous country is making a comeback. India, it is whispered, may at last have what it takes to start catching up with its larger neighbour" (*Financial Times* 2003). The term "BRIC" quickly became accepted business-speak, and the idea that economic growth would come from the emerging economies was the new common sense.[18] The 2003 BRIC report's success surprised author Roopa Purushothaman, who commented, "We thought it would be popular but we just didn't think it would take on the form it did" (Dua 2006).

While the BRIC reports predicted economic growth over the next half century, they galvanized *short-term* interest in Brazilian, Russian, Indian, and Chinese stock markets. Morgan Stanley Capital International started an index of BRIC stock market performance in 2005, and the Dow Jones Indexes followed suit in 2006 (*Wall Street Journal* 2006).[19] HSBC Holdings began the first BRIC investment fund in 2004, followed by Franklin Templeton Investments, Deutsche Asset Management, Schroder Investment Management, and Goldman Sachs (Karmin 2006a). BRIC funds such as these attracted $4 billion in investments between January and July 2006 alone (Hudson 2006). Emerging markets' stocks began a long upturn in 2003, further interesting investors, and the Morgan Stanley Capital International BRIC Index more than tripled in value between 2003 and 2006, outperforming general emerging markets indices (Karmin 2006a and 2006b; Wilson 2007). As Craig Karmin of the *Wall Street Journal* put it, the emergence and popularity of BRIC funds "reveal how fund companies act to capitalize on new trends—even ones that have timetables stretching out to midcentury" (Karmin 2006a).

The Goldman Sachs reports may not have *caused* the BRIC stock markets to surge between 2003 and 2006, for there was certainly interest among investors in "emerging economies" prior to 2001. Indeed, investors, fund managers, pundits, consultants, and journalists took up the term "BRIC" with a gusto that indicates they already believed Goldman Sachs's claims; the BRIC reports perhaps gave name to what was already an incipient investment trend. Also, as noted above, fund managers faced pressures to find new investments. Yet the sudden popularity of BRIC funds, the rush to invest in BRIC stocks, and the surge in BRIC stock market valuations does suggest that Goldman Sachs's research team was able to guide investment—and thus the expansion of finance capital—simply by coining a catchy new acronym and a convincing story predicting growth.[20] In so doing, they helped position India as a desirable investment location, and they provided a language that Indians could use when selling companies, projects, and apartments to international and domestic investors.

My informants reiterated the stories popularized by Goldman Sachs analysts, other consultancies, and the media about India's heralded long-term growth potential to describe their firms' expansions into India. Simon, the head of the Indian office for a British real estate investment firm, described his firm's owners' interest in India:

> As the market is in the West in terms of prices being so low, umm, I think they felt that long-term growth was going to be in the, inverted commas, developing markets. So they wanted to find a country that has long-term growth opportunities.

Another of my informants, a retail consultant working with a prominent Indian real estate development firm, had himself moved to India because he felt the Indian economy—and with it the real estate market—has long-term growth prospects. He thought that places like the Middle East might be "bigger marketplaces" right now, but "when the market starts to cool, India is still going to go." The Indian economy, he explained,

> will have highs and lows like all economies; you would not be insulated whatever anybody says. But, it will have probably fifteen years of steady growth, based on domestic population changes that go on there. And that's a place that can guarantee an income.

By "domestic population changes," he was referring to India's young population, which in many consultancy reports, is used as evidence of future economic growth. He concluded, "If the rest of the marketplaces crash, everybody will try to enter India at the same time." He, however, would already be there, where growth would "guarantee an income." The senior vice president of an American private equity firm felt similarly that India was a sure-fire long-term investment: "Unless something dramatically happens to the overall region or the country, I don't see, you know, that—at least for the next fifteen years, anything can go wrong in this story." For real estate investors, the "India story" seemed like a good long-term, and even shorter-term, wager. (Note how Goldman Sachs's projected horizon of 2050 shrank to "the next fifteen years": 2006–2021.) While predicting long-term growth, then, the BRIC reports catalyzed near-term action: the movement of firms into India.

Getting in the Game

An ecstatic Indian media circulated the stories woven by Goldman Sachs and other banks and consultancies. In India, the *Economic Times*, *Indian Express*, *The Hindu*, *Business Week*, and others summarized BRIC reports with triumphant headlines like "No Kidding, by '50 India May Be No 3 Economy" and "India to Overtake US by 2050."[21] By 2006, with the Indian stock market soaring, the GDP climbing, foreign investors investing in Indian firms and real estate, and Indian companies making overseas acquisitions, the Indian media celebrated India's newfound status as a rising star:

> In the past, India has been global number one in starvation deaths, getting food aid, getting foreign aid, and—according to Transparency International—in willingness to give bribes. But suddenly, after two decades of playing second fiddle, analysts such as Credit Suisse predict that India will grow faster than China in 2007. A country once regarded as a bottomless pit for aid is competing for the number one position in the global growth league. (*Economic Times* 2006)

This is exactly the sentiment a wealthy investor expressed to me at a party I attended in Delhi: "It's about time that India saw progress."

During my fieldwork, the English-language media channeled nationalist sentiments into support for "India Inc," a synecdoche that elides India's businessmen's interests with the national interest. Tracking the rise of India Inc. through corporate takeovers and overseas acquisitions, the *Economic Times* labeled these stories with tagline "The Global Indian Takeover."[22] As one *New York Times* commentator noted, "This desire to highlight every small achievement as proof of India's unstoppable rise has become a national sport. An obsessive conviction that India is destined for international supremacy is spreading fast" (Gentleman 2006; see also Mishra 2006).

The front page of the national financial daily the *Economic Times* on September 25, 2007, provides an example of this "obsessive conviction." The *Economic Times* uses sports metaphors to suggest that India is finally making the cut, arriving to compete globally at long last. A page-width headline reads: "Superpower: India 2020. They are unstoppable, they are restless, they are tireless, they are fun, they are fantastic. ET [*Economic Times*] cheerleads a young and zippy India." Below is a picture of India's victorious Twenty20 World Cup cricket team, led by Mahendra Singh Dhoni.[23] The headline conflates India's cricket victory with its predicted rise to superpower status, punning on Twenty20 (cricket) and 2020 (date). Beside the photograph is more copy which likens athletic to economic success:

> Dhoni [India's cricket captain in 2007] and his band of boys have done it, finally. Youth has triumphed. This team symbolizes India. It has loads of aggression, tones of determination and a feisty fierceness that can crumble the strongest of opponents. India Inc has been displaying this in-your-face aggressiveness for some time now and it's only fitting that our Global Indian

Takeover campaign has now been capped by this fantastic win. At ET [*Economic Times*] we've been calling this pursuit of global dreams World at Your Feet. And this indomitable will to win comes from one of the greatest lessons taught in B-schools: teamwork. Which, dear reader, reflects the true spirit of Chak de India.[24]

To the side of the photo of the winning cricket team is a blurb about Rahul Gandhi "winning" the post of general secretary of the Congress Party. Below that, the SENSEX, India's stock market index, is shown to have reached new heights, along with the rupee. Placing these news items under the same "Superpower: India 2020" headline, the *Economic Times* editors suggest that economics, politics, and sports provide a combined arena for proving India's prowess; just as Dhoni "and his band of boys" are now the best in the world, so too will India's B-school (business school) graduates win in the arena of global capitalism.

By comparing cricket to capitalism, the Indian media narrates the "India story" within the frame of postcoloniality, as a story of colonial subjects beating their masters at their own game. This frame recasts the "India story" not as a dry economic narrative but as a story of national triumph, freedom, and glory. The Indian media applauds when Indian firms buy American companies or British brands—as when the Tata Group bought Jaguar, Land Rover, Tetley Tea, and Corus steel—reading present corporate growth as a replay of national struggle and a sign of more growth to come. Swaminathan S. Anklesaria Aiyar (a consulting editor at the *Economic Times*), for example, announced in his 2004 *Times of India* column about Indian companies' takeover of international firms, "The global system is no longer rigged by and for white men. It can be used by Indians no less than Americans to leverage their talent to create global corporate empires. The process has begun" (Aiyar 2004).

Joining the global game, Indians have had to change their rules of play. The BRIC reports (and others like them) prescribe reforms that would make India more conducive to foreign investment. The authors of the 2003 Goldman Sachs report comment, "The key assumption underlying our projections is that the BRICs maintain policies and develop institutions that are supportive of growth" (Wilson and Purushothaman 2003, 2). A 2008 Goldman Sachs report entitled "Ten Things for India to Reach its 2050 Potential" makes clear that their projections are predicated on a specific policy agenda: in short, "India needs to improve its governance, control inflation, introduce credible fiscal policy, liberalise financial markets and increase trade with its neighbours" in order to grow as predicted (O'Neill and Poddar 2008, 1).

The Goldman Sachs reports are projections with strings, predictions that prescribe the conditions necessary for their realization. These are not simple empirically based extrapolations that might encourage action performatively, but moral blueprints that mandate change in order to force a particular future into being. The authors O'Neill and Poddar suggest neoliberal solutions for the problems of corporate governance, government deficits, declining agricultural productivity, poor education, and ailing infrastructure. The report is laced with the language of citizen choice and government accountability, and it promotes private-market solutions such as public-private partnerships, further financial deregulation, more foreign participation in education and agriculture, lower government subsidies, the removal of land ceilings, etc. The kind of growth described here requires the transformation of India into a profitable ground for finance capital.

What these intertextually linked stories about India's future suggest, in short, is that "emerging markets" do not emerge on their own; they are *made* to emerge, as people coin new names ("emerging markets," "BRIC," etc.), circulate narratives couched in the language of economic prediction, and make stipulations and mandates. Such markets are inaugurated in stories and realized by actions based on those stories. Such markets are coaxed into being with the promise of spectacular growth and the threat of economic stagnation.

Infrastructure for Growth

Goldman Sachs's stories about growth and prescriptions for reform were not entirely new. In 1994, an Expert Group established by the Department of Economic Affairs used projections of growth to legitimize the shift in government policy toward the commercialization and privatization of infrastructure provision, arguing that "the kind of economic growth projected will not be possible without a substantial improvement in all areas of infrastructure" (Department of Economic Affairs 1996, 3). Conversely, growth was also needed to boost the infrastructure and real estate sectors: the Expert Group maintained that "it will also not be possible to find the necessary resources [for infrastructure provision] . . . unless the country's economic growth accelerates" (Department of Economic Affairs 1996, 3). Believing economic growth would only be possible with increased foreign investment,[25] the Expert Group recommended the continued liberalization of the financial sector and the maintenance of "an open foreign investment regime" (Department of Economic Affairs 1996, 4). According to this circular logic, growth requires infrastructure, infrastructure requires growth, and both require foreign and private sector funding. This logic spurred the regulatory changes that enabled the emergence of an international market in Indian real estate.

The 1998 Housing and Habitat Policy transformed these logics into official government policy.[26] Asserting that "the Government has to create a facilitating environment for growth of housing activity rather than itself taking on the task of building," it signaled a shift away from years of prioritizing the role of various state-run development authorities and housing boards (Ministry of Urban Affairs and Employment 1998).[27] Many states followed the national lead. In Delhi, for example, the 2021 Master Plan opened up more than 20,000 hectares for private development, breaking the Delhi Development Authority's near monopoly on large-scale development projects (MPD-2021 2007; Rai 2007). The *Wall Street Journal* called the new Master Plan a "jackpot for developers and builders" (Sabharwal 2007).

In the most comprehensive attempt to set "in motion a completely market driven urban development process," the Ministry of Urban Development established the Jawaharlal Nehru National Urban Renewal Mission (JNNURM) in 2005 (Batra 2007).[28] This initiative links Central Government funding for projects in sixty-three cities to a set of mandatory reforms which reduce developers' transaction costs, minimize uncertainties in the development process, and make more land available for development.[29] In short, the program seeks to develop "an efficient real estate market with minimum barriers on transfer of property" (JNNURM 2007, 74) and thus "catalyze investment flows in the urban infrastructure sector" so that cities will live up to their projected contribution to national economic growth (Ministry of Urban Development 2006).

The Government of India has taken additional steps to make real estate development accessible both to the Indian private sector and to foreign investors. The Securities and Exchange Board of India began allowing venture capital funds to invest in real estate in 2004, spurring the development of domestic real estate investment funds (TrammellCrowMeghraj 2007). The Government of India legalized foreign direct investment in township construction in 2002 and further liberalized the policy in 2005 (table 2.1). Now foreign direct investment in real estate could proceed without prior approval from the government or the Reserve Bank of India.[30] The 2005 Special Economic Zone (SEZ) policy has also helped to make large tracts of land available for real estate projects by providing considerable incentives to both developers and industry. The policy waives import duties, service tax, and central sales taxes for Special Economic Zone developers and gives them free reign to construct infrastructure and townships. Individual states have added their

TABLE 2.1. Regulations for foreign direct investment in Indian construction-development projects.

Minimum area developed	Serviced housing plots: 10 hectares
	Other projects: min. built-up area of 50,000 sq. meters
Minimum project capitalization	Wholly owned subsidiaries: US$10 million
	Joint ventures: US$5 million
Repatriation period	Three years from completion of minimum capitalization*
Timeline	Completion within five years of obtaining permits
Compliance	Project must comply with all local planning/zoning rules and obtain all necessary building approvals

Source: Adapted from Department of Industrial Policy & Promotion. 2005. Ministry of Commerce & Industry, Government of India. SIA (FC Division). "Press Note 2," http://www.urbanindia.nic.in/moud /programme/ud/main.htm. Accessed November 23, 2006.

* The Government of India has gone back and forth on the question of whether foreign institutional inves- tors buying shares in an Indian real estate company in advance of a public offer should be exempt from this three-year lock-in period. The Department of Industrial Policy and Promotion and the Securities and Exchange Board of India has been in favor of the exemption, and the Reserve Bank of India, anxious about foreign investment fueling a real estate bubble, has opposed it (see *Business Standard* 2007a; Sikarwar 2007; Subramaniam 2007).

own incentives in terms of rebates on land, decreased stamp duty, and vari- ous incentives for investors. With these regulatory changes in place, foreign investors were no longer "left with their noses pressed against the window" of Indian real estate development (Smith 2004); the government welcomed investors with open arms.

Making the Pitch

So did Indian real estate developers. Building on stories of growth familiar from the BRIC reports, Indian developers sought foreign investors using media such as investor presentations, industry reports, and company pro- spectuses. In Parsvnath Developers' corporate presentation, for example, everything on the Powerpoint slide describing Indian real estate is rising, ex- panding, growing, or improving: it advertises India's "consistent and sustain- able GDP growth, expanding service sector, rising purchasing power, faster urbanization, increasing impact of IT/ITes and organized retail sector, [and] improving regulatory framework" (Parsvnath Developers Ltd. 2007).

Like their counterparts in other markets, developers and fund managers use projections of high returns to attract investors.[31] They also rely on the "India story" of dramatic economic growth to sell India. Describing the inves- tor presentation he had drafted at his previous real estate investment firm in about 2004, Vivek, who now works at a private equity firm, recounted, "BRICs [the report] had just come in the market. I took a lot of the themes from the BRIC report." Indeed, his presentation begins with a triumphant statement of India's arrival in the international spotlight—"India is here to stay as an economy"—and a chart showing a projected increase in India's share of global GDP between 2000 and 2010. A graph demonstrates India's "solid GDP growth" since the economic reforms—a process of growth that the presentation claims has continued despite changing governments and coalition politics. Not only is India growing, it claims, but the process is not at risk of political derailment (Primary Real Estate Advisors).[32]

Why is GDP growth a sign of the future profitability of real estate investments? Rajesh, the vice president of an Indian real estate development firm that operates in the National Capital Region, conflated general economic growth with individual returns as he explained why he thought foreign investors saw Indian real estate as profitable:

> See, what they [foreign investors] come and observe is what I observe. It's an 8 percent GDP. So if I had 500 billion today, next year I'm going to be 500 billion into 1.08. And then that becomes the basis for another 1.08. So it's a compounded annual growth rate at a much higher rate. And as the base expands, that 8 percent becomes more and more majestic.

He reads the rate of GDP growth directly as a compound annual growth rate; high GDP growth translates into corporate growth and thus high returns. Although this may not work in practice, it reflects the general excitement about economic growth and the logic of the 2003 BRIC report, which foresaw greater returns for investors in countries (like India) that need capital to grow fast. His statement also captures the self-perpetuating nature of investment and growth: rates of increase become more "majestic" over time.

If the BRIC reports were novel back in 2003, by 2006–2007, the "India story" was industry common sense. At the Global Real Estate Institute conference in 2006, the head of India's National Housing Bank, S. Sridhar, presented the audience with a Powerpoint slide listing reasons for investing in India. The man sitting next to me in the audience, a developer from Mumbai, shifted in his seat during the presentation, grumbling that this was "stuff everyone in the room knows" before leaving to take a phone call. Several of my informants claimed that they didn't need to make a hard sell to attract investors. India was "hot," Vivek explained; it had been the "flavor of the month" for the "last fourteen to fifteen months." Whereas his twenty-three-slide 2004 presentation included eleven slides explaining "Why India," and eight "Why real estate in India," his presentations in 2007 focused on his firm's strengths and his particular investment strategy, since everyone already knew the "India story."

An executive at another real estate–focused private equity firm agreed: "India is a pretty sold-off story," he told me.

Enter Foreign Investors

Lured by the financial media, news about regulatory changes, or direct campaigning from municipalities and developers, foreign investors entered the Indian real estate market beginning in 2002 and increasingly after 2005. Like other stories about growth, reports about this investment acted as tools: by broadcasting Indian real estate's appeal to foreign funds, they made it attractive to other investors. Particularly in a context where no one knew for sure how much money was coming in, announcements of planned investment acted as advertisements for Indian real estate, encouraging the very activity they described.

Firms from Singapore, Indonesia, Malaysia, the Middle East, and Canada were among the first to take advantage of the newly liberalized real estate sector beginning in 2002, many investing in joint-venture housing projects with Indian state government housing authorities or Indian developers (Basu 2004).[33] Reports written for foreign investor audiences showcased these new entrants as indicators of India's "vibrant real estate investment market" (Ernst & Young 2006). As early as 2004 an article in the *Asian Times* proclaimed, "It's not just the stock markets in India that are being swarmed by a gush of foreign funds. The same goes for the country's property markets" (Basu 2004). This cycle of investment and advertisement recurred after the regulations were further liberalized in 2005.[34] Articles and reports published lists of the investment funds foreign firms had started, along with the amounts they planned to invest, thus calibrating world-famous financial firms' interest in Indian real estate in the billions of US dollars (table 2.2).

The firms that announced plans to invest in Indian real estate included foreign developers, property investment companies and real estate investment trusts, large banks and investment services companies, private equity firms, and hedge funds. Specialized real estate-related firms such as Israeli mall-developer Gazit Globe, hospitality firm Four Seasons Hotels and Resorts, and Singapore-based Accor Hotels also announced multimillion dollar joint venture projects. In addition, numerous small groups of Non-Resident Indians formed informal funds each investing $10 to $25 million in specific real estate projects, often in cities where the investors had relatives (Ramanathan 2007a). Indian banks (HDFC, ICICI), corporations (Tata, Dalmia), and real estate developers (Unitech) established domestic real estate funds which operate similarly to the foreign funds, attracting both Indian and foreign investors.[35]

TABLE 2.2. Anticipated investment in Indian real estate, ca. 2006–7.*

Fund	Total Planned Investment ($US)
AMC Reit	1 billion
American International Group	250–300 million
Ascendas IT Park Fund	230 million
Blackstone Group	1 billion
Carlyle Group	500–750 million
Citigroup Property Investors	125 million
Emaar Properties	4 billion
Fire Capital	50 million
GE Commercial Finance Real Estate	63 million
GE-Ascendas Fund	500 million
Goldman Sachs	1 billion
Hines	1 billion
ICICI Venture	700 million
IL&FS	530 million
JP Morgan	360 million
Lee Kim Tah Holdings	115 million
Lehman Brothers	300 million
Oak Investment Partners	5.8 billion
Pegasus Realty	150 million
Reef/DB Real Estate (Deutsche Bank)	300 million
Royal Indian Raj International	2.9 billion
Salim group	100 million
Siachen Fund	100 million
Solitaire Capital India	49 million
Stargate Capital	186 million
Sun-Apollo Ventures	630 million
Trikona Capital's Trinity Capital Fund	450 million
Walton Street Capital	300 million

Source: Compiled from figures provided in ASSOCHAM 2006; Ernst & Young 2006; Ramanathan 2007b; Soni 2007; Zachariah and Abraham 2007.

* This is not a complete list; it merely represents some of the figures the media reported.

In the midst of highly publicized investment announcements, it was difficult to discern how much foreign investors were actually investing in Indian real estate, and this uncertainty fueled buoyant predictions. The Association of Indian Chambers of Commerce and Industry of India (ASSOCHAM) published estimates in a widely cited report in November 2006 (table 2.3).[36] However, at that time, India's Department of Industrial Policy and Promotion (DIPP), which tracks foreign direct investment, did not publish disaggregated data for real estate (see DIPP 2006), so it is unclear how the ASSOCHAM arrived at its figures, which do not accord with the real estate sector figures the DIPP later published (table 2.4).[37] According to the DIPP, foreign direct investment in real estate certainly increased dramatically after 2005; however, it only accounted *cumulatively* for $2.71 billion, or 4.54 percent of the

TABLE 2.3. ASSOCHAM estimates of foreign direct investment in Indian real estate.

Year	Total FDI (billion $)	Share of real estate in FDI	FDI in real estate (billion $)
2003–4	2.70	4.5%	0.12
2004–5	3.75	10.6%	0.40
2005–6	5.54	16%	0.89
2006–7 (est.)	8.00	26%	2.08

Source: Adapted from ASSOCHAM 2006.

TABLE 2.4. DIPP estimates of foreign direct investment in Indian real estate.

Year	Total FDI (billion $)*	Share of real estate in FDI	FDI in real estate (billion $)
2004–5	3.76	—	0
2005–6	5.55	0.68%	0.038
2006–7†	15.73	3.0%	0.47
2007–08‡	24.58	8.9%	2.18

Source: Data from DIPP 2008.

* These figures represent the equity capital components of foreign direct investment only (including advances), omitting re-invested earnings and other sources of capital (see Srivastava 2003). The DIPP now includes a table estimating foreign direct investment according to the International Monetary Fund guidelines (or what it calls "international best practices") that includes reinvested earnings and other sources of capital, estimating total foreign direct investment inflows at $6,051 billion for 2004–5; $8,961 billion for 2005–6; $22,079 for 2006–7; and $29,893 billion for 2007–8. I chose to use the smaller, equity-only (not "international best practices") figures because the DIPP reports real estate foreign direct investment inflow data is in this equity-only format (see DIPP 2008).

† Provisional.

‡ Provisional.

total cumulative foreign direct investment inflows for all sectors of the Indian economy between April 2000 and March 2008 (DIPP 2008).[38]

Rather than cite DIPP estimates—which, anyways, appear only after a delay once provisional figures are reconciled with the Reserve Bank of India—consultancies made their own estimates from deals they were privy to, press releases, fund announcements, Securities and Exchange Board documents, and other industry sources. I kept a similar tally, but I only became aware that others did the same when a young analyst at Religaire, an Indian financial services company, told me about his own personal notes, meticulously recorded deal-by-deal from the newspaper reports and the rumor mill.

The lack of definitive figures—as well as the habit of reporting plans rather than committed investments—fueled widely divergent estimates and optimistic predictions.[39] For example, *Mint, Today,* and the *Economic Times* all reported in 2007 that foreign funds had raised a total of $3 billion to invest in Indian real estate; other estimates ranged from $6 to $15 billion.[40] Reports of how much funds had raised incited analysts and consultants to predict that foreign investment would grow even more in the coming years—by anywhere from $1–$4 billion annually.[41]

Such predictions peppered industry speech. An analyst with the international property consultant Trammel Crow Meghraj cited a Merrill Lynch report in a conversation with me, using its prediction that "$14 billion [in foreign investment] will hit the market in the next four years" to conclude that foreign investment "will double the size of the market" and cause Indian builders to build twice as much as they are now. Another consultant told me "I mean as a country we used to have a billion, maybe two billion dollars of foreign investment per annum, maybe two to three years ago. That's jumped up to ten-twelve billion already, and the bulk of that is happening in real estate." The director general of the real estate industry lobby group NAREDCO boasted, "In the past six months we have seen three billion dollars [of foreign direct investment]—maybe there will be 5–6 million by the end of the year."

Thus the hyperbolic language (investments "surging," "pouring," or "flocking" to Indian real estate); the habit of citing total fund amounts ("the $250 million U.S.-based Maia" fund or "Trikona Capital's USD 450 million realty fund" [Ernst & Young 2006; Gangopadhyay 2006]); and the unquestioned circulation of various consultancies' rosy forecasts established an atmosphere of perpetual overestimation, in the business papers, consultancy reports, and in developers' and consultants' own speech. Foreign investment entered Indian real estate in an environment where the wet ink on a Memorandum of Understanding (a nonbinding agreement) was taken as solid proof of money changing hands. More than tracking financial flows, then, reports about the influx of foreign investment served as a tool for attracting yet more capital. The small beginning—a few funds announcing plans to invest—was sold as a successful ending, with Indian real estate attracting billions in foreign capital.

I have argued that the possibility of profit—broadcast through stories, rumors, and reports—drove the inflationary spiral of speculation and fueled the transformation of Indian land into an international asset by attracting investors and prompting regulatory change. The "India story"—a collective narrative about Indian economic growth and social change—has served a range of value projects: showcasing a bank's economic prowess, selling newspapers, attracting investors, and justifying government policy changes. As it got taken up by people to pursue various ends, the story was told and retold and thus made available to others as a resource for their own value projects. People based their actions on these stories about the future; in particular, foreign fund managers began to see Indian real estate as a profitable investment opportunity and moved their money, offices, and personnel there. Catalyzing action, tales of price appreciation could raise the price of land and tales of foreign investment could stimulate more foreign investment. Over time, the "India story" solidified into common sense; it became something that everyone involved in Indian real estate already knew.

3

Betting on the Future

Reanalyzing Speculation

Scholars and pundits see speculation as a group psychosis, one that creates euphoric manias and devastating crashes; they describe it as "irrational exuberance" (Shiller 2000) or "the madness of crowds" (Mackay 1980).[1] However, describing speculation as psychosis, scholars downplay both the pervasiveness and the productivity of forecasting as a capitalist practice. I now underscore the uncertainties surrounding real estate investment in India in order to highlight the productive role that stories about the future play in shaping industry members' actions. These acts of imagination are not "the madness of crowds" but the logic of contemporary business practice. They have become a significant means of organizing people that is distinct from the state-imposed dictates of planning and development projects—even if they share with development discourse a deep faith in modernization.[2]

The *Oxford English Dictionary* defines the verb "to speculate" as "the buying and selling of commodities or effects in order to profit by a rise or fall in their market value; to undertake, to take part or invest in, a business enterprise or transaction of a risky nature in the expectation of considerable gain." Speculation is central to the spectacular accumulation described in chapter 1; it characterizes most Indian real estate ventures, which involve large outlays of capital, long gestation periods, high risks, and the "expectation of considerable gain." Yet "to speculate" also means the act of conjectural or theoretical thinking: speculative knowledge. The "India story" is speculative in both of these senses: it is a form of speculative knowledge that enables spectacular accumulation.

In chapter 2, I argued that the "fundamentals" that inform investors' understanding of the prospective yield of Indian real estate assets are shared stories about the future of Indian economy and society—collectively called

the "India story"—that mingle with and are supported by third-order inter-
pretations about others' belief in those stories. The "India story" worked performatively, helping to create the investor interest that it described. Here and
in the following chapter, I explore the content of the "India story" in more
detail, for it not only foretold economic growth and price appreciation; it also
helped industry members guess what shape growth might take. I examine
the ways in which the "India story" guided developers and investors as they
imagined future economic activities, thus serving as a resource for real estate
producers deciding what to build. In the next chapter, I consider expectations
about what kinds of people will inhabit real estate projects—in particular,
the assumption that a rising number of high-earning "genuine residents" will
buoy demand for new construction.

Narratives about India's progress buttressed by statistical extrapolations
and industry forecasts guide the production of landscapes designed for particular futures. These predictions rely on logics of comparison that differentiate India from other places in the world only to project convergence in
the future. Estimations of the future state of the market do not rest on the
assumption that "the existing affairs will continue indefinitely" as Keynes assumes (1936, 152), but rather on the assumption that they will change, that
economic growth will transform Indian society and economy. And yet,
growth is expected to occur along a fixed trajectory of progress; by traversing the developmental path of other nations, India is expected to "catch up"
with them. The kind of change that real estate producers expect—and for
which they construct—is based so heavily in this repurposed development
discourse that the India of the future is expected to resemble the more "developed" places today. Developers thus construct buildings for a future that
looks like Dubai, Singapore, or London today.

Foretelling the Future

On one of my first days at EuroFund, (a European real estate investment
fund with an office in the National Capital Region where I conducted participant observation in 2007 and 2008), I spoke with Ravi, a director at the
fund. When I stopped by his office, he was pouring over the latest Gurgaon
master plan, trying to read the future in the acres of land the development
authority had just opened for construction. He pointed out the parcels of land
EuroFund was considering developing and spoke anxiously about placing a
hundred million dollar "bet," as he put it, on any one of them. He wondered,
what will this place look like in five years? Where will people want to live?
He considered whether a prestigious Delhi address would remain desirable

even as the city became more congested. Would the "current urban centers sustain themselves?"—or would they become "unlivable"? Gurgaon troubled him too. He worried that the heterogeneity of projects coming up next to each other might compromise his project's future value. "I have no clue who my neighbors will be," he complained. Uncertainty threatened his firm's value project.

Ravi's colleague Samiksha thought other areas in the National Capital Region would prove better bets than Gurgaon, which she felt was "fast on its way to becoming an urban slum" due to poor planning, a lack of open space, and congestion. She complained about Gurgaon's reliance on Delhi for its infrastructure, and she wondered what would happen to it once the airport, in need of expansion and hemmed in by government land, moves. If, as she feared, Gurgaon becomes a "ghost town" or a "mess" in fifteen years, Euro-Fund's project might lose value.

When I asked Jeremy, the managing director, about the high-stakes location decisions he faced, he answered with an analogy from the United States, for my benefit:

> In Manhattan, for office space, I'd say the best address is 47th, 48th, up to 50th on Park Avenue. But it's impossible to say in Gurgaon. What is the Park Avenue of Gurgaon? That's a little like asking, what's the Park Avenue of Houston? It's all built helter-skelter, seemingly without a master plan. Even on this new master plan, nothing jumps out to say they're really trying to organize it; it's more like retroactively fitting what's there.

He found deciphering the future of Gurgaon's development difficult, even from the planning documents, because the city does not correspond well to his understanding of the relationship between urban form and real estate values. Presented with such a "helter-skelter" place, how could he determine what would make the best (i.e., most remunerative) location for a commercial building?

The fact that both investment funds like EuroFund and Indian real estate development companies must construct the assets they invest in exacerbates a problem in real estate: the need to predict what a market will be like in the future. Investors could not observe occupancy rates in an existing building before buying it, as they might if they bought a building in another country. They had to make predictions about what Indian markets would be like in three to four years, as the uncertain process of buying land, rezoning it, and then designing, constructing, marketing, and selling or leasing a building is lengthy. Investors and developers faced the problem of investing large sums of money in projects that would likely not earn a return for a long period of time.

Jeremy worried that land prices, "having gone up so dramatically in the last few years," might have outstripped the future profitability of any investment his fund might make. The "proof" of whether a parcel of land is "really worth" its current selling price, he told me,

> will only come once somebody has built a building and leased it up and then held it for at least three years to see if those rents are holding for that period of time. . . . You have to be able to look down the road and have some confidence about what's going to happen over the next, you know, three, five, seven years, that in truth in our business you never can ultimately know for sure.

In choosing where to build, real estate producers had to guess what the future urban landscape would look like and how it would affect rents or sale prices. Developers and investors ran the risk of creating a project devalued by future events: a collapse in land prices, an oversupply of similar buildings, a change in technology or design, an undesirable adjacent use, or a lack of demand caused by any number of factors. Perhaps this is the reason so many used the language of gambling to describe the business. My informants spoke of developers taking "positions in land" or investors "taking calls" on a particular market. With each project, members of the industry were "betting" on the future.

Creating Speculative Knowledge

While my informants' language sometimes reflected their anxieties, speculation is a dirty word in the real estate business as it is in academic scholarship. Real estate developers did not explain skyrocketing land and real estate prices as the result of their own spectacular accumulation; rather, they took them as proof that the "India story" was true. My informants' denial of their own acts of speculation was a central component of their attempt to attract investment: they created the appearance of profitability by avoiding the appearance of "irrational exuberance" even as they engaged with risk.

Similarly, rather than describe their knowledge as "speculative" or conjectural, my informants used the term "market research," perhaps because it gave their knowledge production a scientific air. They often proclaimed industry predictions as certainties, hiding and disavowing their own anxieties. Yet, the unprecedented nature of real estate development in India highlighted the conjectural nature of real estate knowledge.

My informants did sometimes pejoratively describe others as operating by "gut feel"—at once conjuring the tacit knowledge necessary to navigate the future and denigrating it. As part of their characterization of Indian developers as inexpert and unprofessional (see chapter 6), consultants, investors, and brokers described them as operating on "raw touch and feel" alone. One consultant complained, "Very few [developers] do market research. Otherwise, it's just a world of copycats. They just look at what their neighbor is doing and launch for two hundred rupees less."

Despite this stereotype of unthinking greedy builders, developers and investors had a range of strategies for parsing the present to gamble on the future. Some developers hired marketing agencies to conduct focus groups to determine if a new housing type or mall would be well-received. Others commissioned international property consultants (CBRE, Jones Lang LaSalle Meghraj, Knight Frank, Cushman Wakefield, DTZ, etc.), Indian consultants (IL&FS Property Management and Services Ltd, Feedback Ventures, Technopak, etc.) or the property service division of Indian banks (ICICI, HDFC, etc.) to conduct market studies. These consultants performed property valuations, produced financial models, estimated the demand for real estate in a particular locality, and recommended a "product mix" for a particular piece of land (i.e., a mixture of hotels, shopping, offices, and housing).

Many developers and investors, however, expressed doubt about the timeliness and accuracy of these formal reports. Ajay, an analyst with a New York–based real estate investment fund, complained that the information in consultants' reports was "common knowledge" and that commissioning research often took longer than the window he had for deciding on a deal. One developer I asked about hiring property consultants, answered rhetorically, "Who knows our country more than we do?" Another launched into a rant about how surveys ask "foolish" questions and produce equally "foolish" replies. He concluded, "If somebody tells you he does a market research, he is telling a lie. Nothing can be done there."

Ashish, a consultant, expressed a similar skepticism:

> A lot of it [research] is rubbish, these so-called experts don't know. You can't predict the market. You can forecast in the US . . . they have 20 to 30 years of historical data. So they can predict, in the third quarter X will go up by Y percentage points. But this is a completely different market. Whatever is happening is unprecedented.

According to Ashish, a lack of historical statistical data renders much research and prediction nonsense. Furthermore, Indian real estate is such a new market, its dynamics are "unprecedented"—both historically and cross-culturally. Of course, this assertion positions Ashish, as an Indian consultant, in a privileged position to understand the market; if foreign statistical models do not apply, local intuitions should gain value, he argues implicitly. By contrast to Ashish's insistence on India's exceptionalism, as we shall see, many of my informants believed that India was traversing a path already trod by more "developed" nations such that India would come to resemble them over time.

In a market so new, the formal procedures that international property consultants used to value land seemed not to work. International practice holds that when you estimate the value of a parcel of land by comparing it to the value of similar parcels nearby, that valuation should approximate one achieved by running numbers on the development of a project on the parcel. But in India, where there were more buildings planned than constructed, there were few comparables from which to benchmark value or determine what the revenue from development was likely to be. As a result, comparative and potential valuations rarely aligned. In a heated debate about valuation at the 2007 Global Real Estate Institute Conference in Delhi, one analyst expressed frustration about using the comparative method for valuing property:

> It assumes you have the data, but here there is no data. Especially in a market like Bombay. I have seen two properties on either side of a road, one selling at 25,000 rupees per square foot and the other at 14,000 rupees per square foot. . . . I can get a number [a valuation] but the developer and investor will never agree.

The market was so volatile that even when values were known, they offered little guidance.

In a context where statistical and historical information was not readily available, thought to be unreliable, or in dispute, learning about the market required creativity. Rather than hiring consultants, the developers and investors I spoke with each had their idiosyncratic method for collecting signs of market activity. They claimed to investigate everything from the amount of competing space "coming up" nearby, the state of the roads, and proposed government projects, to the literacy rate and age distribution of a locality. At EuroFund, an employee combed the business papers every morning for news, accumulating binders and binders of articles on real estate trends, regulations, deals, and companies that other employees could mine for information. A developer I spoke with in Kolkata made inferences from data on demand for other consumer products (cars, appliances, etc.), assuming that "it's the same consumer" buying houses and cars.

Most of my informants swore by personal site visits as their primary tool of market research and cultivated their own speculative knowledge through carefully cultivated social networks.[3] Ajay, the analyst, collected data through what he called "informal" checking:

> You pick up the phone, you get on the net, you pull up broker numbers, you start calling brokers randomly. You talk to five, ten brokers. With three, you talk about the possibility of buying land in a location that you know about, the rest you talk about selling land. You get differentials, you get an idea, right.

In order to "get an idea" about land prices in a particular location, Ajay informally polled a number of brokers, using the "differentials" between their answers to approximate prevailing prices. A shopping mall developer told me he polled relatives living in whatever city in which he was planning a mall. He also visited the main shopping districts and watched shoppers. Another developer said he relied on mortgage lenders (rather than brokers) to find the prevailing prices for apartments and the number of homes selling.

Beyond rumor and hearsay, information on land transactions (many of which are unrecorded or occur partially in cash) was scarce. In the absence of hard data, developers reported relying on networks of informants to piece together a picture of real estate markets in different locales. Their methods resembled those of the US Federal Reserve Bank, which calls on bankers, manufacturers, retailers, and others to report on economic conditions in real time. According to Douglas Holmes, the Fed has "developed an intellectual apparatus operating in vivo, a performative apparatus composed of interlocutors who are not merely representing economic conditions: they are actively participating the creation of those conditions" (Holmes 2014, 51). Real estate industry members similarly rely on other market participants' reports to assemble a picture of market activity, though one much more fractured and partial than that of the US Federal Reserve Bank.

However, Ajay does not just get reports from other market participants in vivo; he steps into the market himself as someone other than himself. When "checking out the site," Ajay asks local business owners in the vicinity of a possible project about rents, land prices, and their customers. His method resembled undercover sleuthing:

> I have a story to tell people so that they give me a quotation they would give to a potential buyer, as opposed to a potential investor. If someone was to realize that I work for a fund, a real estate fund in Delhi, he would jack up the price. But if I was a potential home buyer—and I'm dressed in jeans and *chappals*[4] and T-shirt, so I'm not wearing, you know—the watch is off, the mobile phone doesn't come out.

Ajay understands that prices are not fixed but depend on who the buyer is. In order to ferret out uninflated prices, he makes site visits in the guise of what he imagines to be an ordinary buyer, not a representative of a big city fund. To do so, he implicitly tells a story about who he is, but even by erasing the signs of city wealth (watch, mobile phone), his speech probably belies his education and white-collar employment. His ordinary potential buyer is not a famer or rural industrialist, but a member of the urban middle classes, a professional, as he is (see chapters 4 and 6).

Allocating Capital to Land

Ajay, Ravi, Samiksha, Jeremy, and others struggled to figure out where they should invest and what they should build in a market where even basic price information was difficult to obtain. Their uncertainty contradicts the image that Marxist geographic theory presents of how capitalists transform landscapes. David Harvey argues that developers need look no further than land prices as they decide how to develop land:

> The land market shapes the allocation of capital to land and thereby shapes the geographical structure of production, exchange and consumption, the technical division of labor in space, the socioeconomic spaces of reproduction, and so forth. Land prices form signals to which the various economic agents can respond (Harvey 1999, 369).

According to Harvey, by responding to signals in the land market, developers compete for better rents and thus promote the "highest and best uses"—that is, the most profitable uses—forcing out tenants who cannot pay high rents and ultimately effecting a reorganization of space. Land markets are thus a "basic co-ordinating device" for the production of capitalist landscapes.

Harvey's description of land markets as smoothly oiled price-producing machines seems ill-suited to explaining the Indian situation, in which prices were unreliable and hard to come by and participants were constructing new markets in land. Particularly in India's convulsive, tumultuous real estate markets—markets undergoing great transformation—value was in flux, and prices seemed constrained only by the imagination. Moreover, no one actor or institution understood the "overall requirements of accumulation" (Harvey 1999, 370) or the "needs" of labor and capital, much less has the capability to anticipate what they would be in the future. What would the "highest and best use" prove to be? Aquaculture? Private schools? Airports? Formula-1 race-tracks?[5] In India in 2006–8, everyone was groping in the dark, anticipating various future scenarios, working to enhance their own profits, and situating themselves (they hoped) well in the face of future trends.

If not current prices, then what guides the allocation of capital to land? The answer lies in Harvey's own discussion of land market contradictions.

Harvey sees land markets as a coordinating system that is nonetheless liable to failure as a means of producing productive landscapes for capital accumulation. Capitalist land markets are contradictory because land is a fictitious commodity: "What is bought and sold is not the land, but title of the ground-rent yielded by it. . . . The buyer acquires a claim upon anticipated future revenues" (Harvey 1999, 367). Thus, developers and investors make decisions based on *future* rents, not current ones. It is precisely because land prices are based on expectations of the future (speculative knowledge) that developers and landowners seek out higher rents (spectacular accumulation) and thus transform landscapes. Harvey writes that "the freer interest-bearing capital is to roam the land looking for titles to future ground-rents to appropriate, the better it can fulfill its co-ordinating role" (Harvey 1999, 369).

And yet, the very "fluidity and dynamism" of fictitious capital threatens to derail productive capital: "But by the same token, the more open the land market is, the more recklessly can surplus money capital build pyramids of debt claims and seek to realize its excessive hopes through the pillaging and destruction of production on the land itself" (Harvey 1999, 369). The "reck-lessness" of speculative moments is brought about by the fictitious character of land and "the anarchistic character of . . . competition" (Harvey 1999, 370)—the same competition that at other moments productively goads land-owners toward change. Thus, precisely because land prices rely on antici-pation and developers compete for better rents, land markets suffer from a tendency to dissolve "into a nightmare of incoherency and periodic orgies of speculation" (Harvey 1999, 370). Speculation is a "necessary evil" of the system by which land markets allocate capital to the production of new geo-graphical configurations—enabling both creativity and waste.

Harvey overstates the rationality of land markets, especially in situations in which they are being made. Capitalists do not merely slavishly respond to the price signals of already established markets; they create new markets. By looking instead at the "irrational" moments that he wishes were not vi-tal to capitalism, we see that perhaps the anticipatory allocation of capital to land shapes land markets, not vice versa. The process of anticipating future land uses and rents—the leap from present situation to future possibility—is guided as much by imagination, by speculative knowledge, as by current prices. Indeed, it may set prices: speculative knowledge enables spectacular accumulation.

Moreover, speculative moments are not only moments of great *competi-tion*, as Harvey suggests, but consensus. They are "astonishing moments of be-lief, moments when large numbers of people [come] to agree on a particular form of value, a particular kind of future" (Pawley 2011). Coordination among

landowners and developers producing new landscapes for capital accumulation comes not from land markets—since those are being transformed—but
from shared stories. That is, *stories provide signals for the production of land
and property markets.*

The stories that guide real estate producers' decisions and thus the construction of real estate markets are social in two senses. First, they articulate
social imaginaries: visions of a future Indian society, its composition, wealth,
and desires. Just as Ajay's impersonations are fueled by his understanding
of Indian society, the other approaches to research I have described rely on
often-unarticulated assumptions, as simple as "rich people will buy expensive apartments" or as involved as "an airport is essential infrastructure for
globalizing cities, and the possibility of its moving threatens the vitality of
this locale." Or that "access and proximity to the airport is an attractive feature for India's nouveau riche." Speculating on streams of future rents (or, for
many Indian developers, future sales prices) requires recourse to stories about
Indian society and its futures.

Second, stories themselves are social in nature. Developers' visions ad-
hered to a shared common sense about the possible and the impossible, about
what would make a good project or what would garner a high rent in the
future. The stories I heard from my informants displayed a surprising coher-
ence, even to the repetition of particular expressions, suggesting their origin
in common interactions and in the shared circulation of various media.

Development Discourses Revived

At the center of the "India story," orienting most industry predictions and
assumptions, was a unidirectional and teleological vision of social change
which placed India "behind" more "developed" nations in a race for economic prosperity and technological achievement. This vision draws on the
development discourses of the mid-twentieth century, which anchored a
global system of governance that emerged after World War II. As colonial nations gained independence, world leaders and newly formed institutions re-
inscribed international hierarchies by labeling the Third World as underdeveloped and therefore lacking (see Abrahamsen 2000, 18; Gupta 1998, 10–11).
This label "underdeveloped" came to have a range of negative meanings: "to
be a national community that is inferior, backward, subordinate, deficient in
capital and resources, an inadequate member of the international order, and
(by extension) a shabby imitation of the 'developed'" (Gupta 1998, 40). As
Akhil Gupta argues, developmental discourses drew on the colonial civilizing
mission with one central difference: postcolonial subjects represented not just

inferior races, but "the *past* of the 'developed,'" such that, through modernization, they might catch up with them (Gupta 1998, 41, original emphasis).

Here, and throughout the book, we shall see examples of development discourses repurposed for the current era of globalization. With the breakdown of Bretton Woods, the Third World debt crisis, and the dissolution of socialism, a globalization project governed by new elites and institutions has replaced the development project (McMichael 1996). The *goals* of human advancement and progress that animated the development agenda of the twentieth century remain, but the *means* have changed. Rather than achieve development through the national replication of an economic regime that stressed import substitution, development is now understood as national specialization through export-oriented industrialization (McMichael 1996, 36). While development today is supposed to come from integration with world markets through foreign investment and exports, creating those markets depends on a familiar story of transformation from backward to advanced, immature to mature.

Thus, informed by an "India story" that builds on development discourses, Indian real estate developers and investors assume that India lags behind the rest of the world. In the context of globalization, however, there are two slight differences between the "India story" and earlier discourses. First, developers and investors interpret India's inadequacies as a sign of possible profit because they assume that India will pursue development through liberalization. Second, rather than follow exactly the same modernization path as the more "developed" nations, developers and investors assume that India will advance its own specialization: information technology. Guided by these ideas, developers were building for an export-oriented information technology sector inhabited by high-income people. They looked to Shanghai, Dubai, and New York for inspiration in the expectation that India would "catch up" with those places in the future.

Global Integration

Sanjeev, the broker we met at the beginning of chapter 2, explained his enthusiasm for Gurgaon to me:

> Intrinsically, if you believe in the India story . . . then you know Gurgaon is only fifteen kilometers from the airport, you know the biggest mall is coming up here, you know that most of MNCs [multinational corporations] are relocating to Gurgaon, then where is the risk over a five year cycle? A hundred and fifty Fortune 500 companies are in the pipeline to come to Gurgaon. They are

going to move about a thousand senior Indian expats back into this country. BMW has opened its largest showroom in Asia in a mall here. So *abhi* [as of now], we have not yet scratched the surface.

Sanjeev believes that Gurgaon is poised for growth. The indicators? The possible relocation of multinational firms, the opening of a foreign luxury car showroom, and the construction of a large mall signal both that others also "believe in the India story" and that an influx of wealthy property consumers is on its way. Rumors, newspaper reports, and other bits of news about current events and those about to happen give credence to the "India story." Moreover, Sanjeev believes that Gurgaon's connections to the global economy, aided by its proximity to the airport, will grow. For Sanjeev, the predicted influx of multinational corporations is an index of future prosperity, a likelihood on which one should bet by investing in real estate.

Like many of my informants, Sanjeev's pitch for investing in real estate hinges on his belief that multinational companies will continue to move their Indian headquarters, back-office services, software development units, and retail outlets to Gurgaon, integrating Gurgaon—and India in general—more closely with the global economy over time. Reports and presentations selling Indian real estate to investors reinforce the idea that economic growth depends on India's new role in the global economy and on the further development of this role. They also suggest that as integration progresses, Indian society will converge culturally with affluent places abroad. I examine the belief in the growth of an internationally familiar, consumerist Indian society in chapter 4. Here, I argue that to bet on Indian real estate is to wager on India's continued global economic integration.

Since liberalization, India's economy has bypassed significant industrial development in favor of service-sector led growth. Services grew to around 50 percent of India's GDP by 2005, while industry's share leveled off since liberalization, and agriculture continued to decline (Banga 2005; Gordon and Gupta 2004). However, while the service sector has grown, service sector *employment* has not; in fact, services' share of employment actually fell slightly between 1990 and 2000. India's jobless service-sector growth means that the majority of Indians still work in agriculture, the sector whose share of output has dropped by 33 percent since the 1950s (Gordon and Gupta 2004, 5–8).[6]

The Indian real estate industry does not serve the majority of the population, which remains mired in rural crisis. Rather, it serves the high-profile, fast-growing, and prosperous segments of the service sector: the potential buyer in *chappals* and a T-shirt discussed above. Since the 1990s, developers have provided offices for business services, IT, communications, banking, and insurance companies, and they have constructed hotels, restaurants, and shopping malls—the landscape of assumed economic and cultural convergence.

Industry documents argue that the demand for service-sector buildings that the leading edge of economic liberalization has produced indicates plenty of future demand for similar buildings. In particular, real estate reports harp on the growth of IT, an industry closely tied to international sources of contracts, funding, and now ownership.[7] Emphasis on an "expanding service sector" and IT in industry reports' "demand driver" lists makes sense in light of the fact that the IT industry accounted for "around 75% of the total demand" for Indian commercial real estate in 2007 (JP Morgan 2007, 40). So industry reports and Indian developers' prospectuses were peppered with charts like "IT Industry: Increasing Real Estate Requirements" which match the growth of the IT sector to estimates of its continued demand for office space (Emaar MGF Land Limited 2008, 69). Industry consensus holds that the IT industry will "continue to be the primary driver behind A-Grade leasehold office space sector," joined by other sunrise industries associated with the "new economy" and international investment (e.g., financial services, biosciences, pharmaceuticals, etc.) (DTZ 2007, 4). Developers are betting that India's specialization in these fields will drive economic and real estate growth.

Developers and investors believe that India's service sector-heavy growth will lead India to improve its place in a global hierarchy of economies over time. Expected growth provides an aspirational path up what my informants called the "value chain." Various industry reports hint that the transformation from back-office services to research and development is already underway: "From a mere provider of cheap labour as seen earlier, India is now a long term investment destination," claims real estate consultancy DTZ (DTZ 2007, 4). Kamal Nath, former Minister of Commerce and Industry, asserts that "the country's journey upward from rudimentary call centers in basements" (Nath 2008, 86) will continue because growth is "implicit in the architecture of the ITES value chain that India is currently climbing. Leaving the simpler voice-based functions far behind, India has moved up to the highly complex territory of KPO [Knowledge Process Outsourcing]," off-shoring engineering, architectural, and biotech services (Nath 2008, 84). This aspirational vision of India's increasing integration with the global economy takes the IT sector—itself a small segment of the service sector and an even smaller percentage of employment—as the bellwether of "the Indian economy," (a synecdoche that ignores most of the country's economic activity and its populace). Moreover, it implicitly devalues India's economic present and near-past—its "cheap labour," "rudimentary call centers in basements," and "simpler voice-based functions"—in order to create a direction for growth, toward "the highly complex territory of KPO." Implicitly, this discourse differentiates the Indian economy from others only to posit convergence in the future, as Indian labor costs and technological sophistication increase. By discrediting the present, these discourses orient capitalists' actions up an aspirational path, a new route of capital accumulation and improvement.

Real estate industry members believe that by hitching their own value projects to the IT industry, they can move "up the value chain" as well. An executive at a private equity firm claimed that as multinational firms like GE and Microsoft established research and development centers in places like Bangalore, the incomes of the "*highly* trained people" they employed rose:

> So kind of the product now they aspired from the developers also started going up. So last four-five years in fact then you saw a shift in the kind of the real estate that started coming into the country. It was more aspirational. It was more in terms of quality, in terms of features, in terms of, you know, overall offering.

He suggests that as India's IT industry becomes more knowledge-based, providing more "value added" for foreign firms, the Indian real estate industry will also progress, offering more sophisticated products. He believes that the IT and real estate industries can climb the "value chain" together. Global economic integration will enable both national and industry development.

Convergence Logic

Based on this belief in increasing integration and growth, real estate reports and investor presentations commonly identify disparities between India and other countries, recast them as potential growth opportunities, and thus advertise for investment. Delhi-based Parsvnath's investor presentation reminds the viewer that whereas China has 800,000 hotel rooms and Manhattan alone has 100,000, there are only 105,000 hotel rooms in all of India. Rather than seeing this figure as a sign of poverty, Parsvnath uses it as evidence for a remarkable investment opportunity in the hospitality sector (Parsvnath Developers Ltd. 2007). Developers make similar arguments about other scarcities: the comparative lack of mortgage penetration, the dearth of organized retail, the meager contribution of real estate to GDP, the slow rate of urbanization, and the low number of housing units in India. Thus, by harping on growth, investor presentations and industry reports miraculously transform an infrastructure-poor country with an acute housing shortage into an attractive real estate investment opportunity. They suggest that an investment in Indian real estate is a wager that these indicators will converge on an international norm as the economy becomes more closely tied to global trends. These assumptions recall the way that development discourses defined India as inadequate and destined to tread a similar historical trajectory as Europe, but here, those inadequacies are recast as positive, as the possibility of profit.

Developers and fund managers often mention India's housing shortage, for example, citing anywhere from 19 to 30 million units needed. They estimate that new housing construction in India is only growing at 4 percent, lagging behind China's 15 percent a year (Slater 2002), and predict that the shortage will grow, from 20 million units in 2005 to 80 million units by 2012 (Unitech 2008). Industry members cite these figures to prove the industry's social relevance, as well as to advertise the need for construction. As R. R. Singh, Director General of the real estate industry lobby group NAREDCO, told me, "the demand and supply gap is huge so there is tremendous scope of investment in construction and real estate industry. We have a 22–30 million housing shortage." Developers rarely mention that what's needed is housing for the poor, since that is not seen as a profitable investment, nor that they overwhelmingly produce housing for the rich, since that would negate their claims to social relevance.[8]

Just as housing needs to be built, according to this logic, so do modern shopping malls and stores. A report on the Indian retail real estate sector by the Indian retail advisory firm Technopak and the Indian bank ICICI describes India as a "late entrant" to the "shopping mall phenomenon":

> Currently, there are 137 operational malls in India, and still expected to grow at 40–50 percent per annum. However if you consider population to mall ratio, we are way behind some of the developed economies. [The] USA, with just about 380 million inhabitants, has over 1,200 shopping malls.

The comparison leads the authors to determine that in order to "catch up" to the developed world, "India *needs* at least 1,000 modern shopping malls in over 500 towns and cities, providing high quality space options to various consumer goods and service providers to reach out to burgeoning consuming class" (ICICI Property Services and Technopak Advisors 2007, iii, my emphasis). This gap-prediction routine is a call to action: in order to keep pace with the "next wave" of service-sector growth, reports urge, invest in "organized" retail formats now (ICICI Property Services and Technopak Advisors 2007, 2). Real estate producers responded to this logic. A representative of a foreign retail developer explained to me:

And see what happens is, when you come to a market and you find something missing—like everybody says that India has only 3 percent or 4 percent of organized retail, rest everything is unorganized—but that unorganized thing is opportunity, right, actually if you look at it.

Armed with the idea of convergence, consultants convert lacks into opportunities.

This logic led to the characterization of the Indian real estate market as "immature." Ajay complained that "the markets here [in India] are very very very—not really unevolved, but they're not that mature," a claim he substantiated by citing the low mortgage-to-GDP ratio. His statement harkens back to colonial discourses which conflated individual human development with stages of civilization. Informants routinely began explanations with phrases like "Since you are from a very advanced economy . . ." to underscore their assumption that I would be used to a different level of real estate development. They also used terms like "catching up," or made comments such as "the retail industry here is still at the very early stage"—all of which indicate that they believe that India is "behind" the "developed" world but moving forward on a similar historical trajectory.

Following this logic of comparison and catch-up, the lack of the kind of assets that the global real estate industry likes to buy and sell is an indication that these assets will soon be built. For example, a real estate report by the Indian investment bank Edelweiss Capital argues that

> investable real estate assets in India are only USD 50–80 bn [billion] or 6–10% of India's GDP compared with 40–50% in most developed countries. As the sector becomes more organised and conducive to institutional funding, we expect investable assets to increase to 20–25% of GDP over the next ten years. This implies investable asset creation of USD 480–600 bn, which at 40% equity funding, means a further market cap creation of USD 160–220 bn. (Edelweiss Securities 2006, 34)

All this predicted asset creation requires funding and promises returns. Edelweiss Capital's analysts have transformed the difference between India and "most developed countries" (what could be seen as a shortcoming) into scope for growth, which is an advertisement for investment. This logic explains why the predicted growth of the real estate sector itself is a ubiquitous selling point in industry literature.[9]

The subtext of this comparative discourse is the assumption that India will become more like other nations over time, eventually meeting the "standard" for hotel rooms, population-to-mall ratio, or urbanization levels. These reports all assume that the country is destined to follow a trajectory that leads to shopping malls, office parks, hotels, and high-rise housing bought with mortgages. Moreover, that trajectory is shared by other "emerging economies." One private equity executive told me that his bosses had done work in Mexico a few years back, and that they believed that they could "replicate the same kind of a business model maybe in India." Success in Mexico in 2001 qualified them to work in India in 2007. By applying various statistical "benchmarks," industry members find the "scope for growth" they use to advertise Indian real estate as an investment destination.

These predictions and international comparisons helped real estate developers and investors wager on uncertain futures. The repetition I have created here through these examples mirrors the circulation of these discourses from reports to meetings to interviews, creating such an overwhelming consensus that a possible future appears as a certainty for which one should prepare. Repeated often enough, predictions galvanize developers to concentrate construction in cities, encourage consumers to get mortgages, and build malls—rather than building, say, cooperative housing in villages or incubator space for small (non-IT) businesses. They encourage investors to meet benchmarks, fulfill industry projections, and build Indian real estate markets—and landscapes—that resemble those elsewhere in the world.

The Production of Inevitability

Stories about the future often translated prediction into prescription. Not only is a particular future possible—as many consultancy reports, brochures, sales pitches, and government reports argue—but *you must do X now* to make it happen. Thus, many of my informants spoke with prescriptive authority. Note, for example, the slippage between extrapolation and prescription in the following exchange with the consultant Pankaj:

PANKAJ: What needs to change obviously is the fact that you are talking about. I mean, in sheer numbers today our urban population could be about 300 to 320 million. That needs to increase to about 550 million in the next twenty-five years.

LS: When you say "needs to increase"?

PANKAJ: I mean, will increase to about 550 million, if you look at population growth and urbanization changes.

LS: So is that just looking at past trends and extrapolating forward?

PANKAJ: Absolutely, absolutely. And these are various extrapolations. You are talking about the need for urban capacity to more or less double over the next twenty-five years.

So strong is the idea that India should conform to statistical indicators from other countries that Pankaj believes that India *needs* to travel the developmental path that they assume. Pankaj's translation from projections into prescriptions reflects both the implied threat in many industry reports—the threat of economic stagnation and backward slippage—but also their normative force: that "development" is a necessary goal, not just for profits, but for national and individual self-worth.

The prescriptive tone of industry discourse encourages the expectation that the reform process will continue and thus the Indian economy will become even more globally integrated. For example, one report concludes, "Given India's apparently insatiable need for funds to drive and sustain its nascent economic growth, further financial liberalization can be expected" (Srinivas 2006, 20). The very process of liberalization kindles expectations of further reforms, especially when the press reports every possibility, hint, or prediction of further change, and when politicians encourage the belief that liberalization is an inevitable process undisturbed by politics. For example, Kamal Nath, India's Minister of Commerce and Industry from 2004–2009, wrote in his recent book *India's Century*:

> Over the past decade, almost every major national and regional party has been part of one government or another. They have had their views and differences, their own opinions on the pace and acceleration of change. Yet the broad thrust of economic policy has not been disturbed. Governments come and go; the process continues. (Nath 2008, 76)

Since many see continued reform as critical to sustaining economic growth rates, few believe the government will derail the process.

My informants were keen to see further reforms that would create demand for real estate: in particular, liberalizing education, which would enable foreign schools to establish Indian campuses, and liberalizing retail, open only to international firms investing in single-brand stores and wholesale trade units in 2006–2008. They felt they *needed* foreign investment to be relaxed; many had built malls too large to fill with the limited number of Indian chain stores. At one meeting I attended, an Indian developer planning a large mixed-use development discussed creating office space that could be transformed into shops once the regulations were relaxed. Today, he claimed, you just can't fill a million square feet of retail in India.

Despite a lack of "organized" (corporate) Indian retail and significant popular resistance to it, Indian developers and foreign investors continue to bet on its growth. Even as protests against Indian retail chains made news headlines,[10] a retail consultant I spoke with dismissed the ongoing *tamasha* as "just noise":

> This is Indian democracy at work, and in one level it is good noise to make in small towns and cities where you've got a huge vaster population, and they will make these noises, and in the big cities we will continue doing the malls. And the two won't interface with each other, so that there is lot of noise talked but no action. . . . And none of it will stop international retailers from coming in. They will come in. It's just noise. In truth it's just noise, and that noise will continue.

This consultant presents a stark view of the disconnect between small-town discontent and big-city development, as well as between citizens' concerns and the inescapability of liberalization. He claimed that politicians sometimes "play to" the "noise" of discontent, "but they won't stop that [reform] process from going on." Similarly, the marketing director for a developer in Gurgaon believed that foreign investment in retail would be further liberalized: "It has to happen, it has to. Government cannot avoid getting into this growth. . . . And each government wants to out-perform the other. So they have to bring in this growth, and we have to sustain this growth." In this view, growth is a self-fulfilling prophesy, propelled by its own momentum.

Conclusion

In the gap between the present and the future—the gap that promises spectacular accumulation—real estate developers and investors have relied on a remarkable consensus about India's economic and social future to guide their actions. Industry forecasts and other forms of speculative knowledge brought the future into the present, making particular kinds of projects seem like good gambling pieces in the game of Indian real estate.[11] Based on comparisons with other places which showed India lacking, these forecasts guided developers and investors toward filling the gaps, nurturing the economic integration and sociocultural convergence that the story predicted. If the reigning story of our times is that markets will catalyze human development, capitalists use this same story to move capital and build markets.

What is the India for which developers build? An urbanized, high-income, consumerist society with great demand for apartment complexes, shopping malls, restaurants, and resorts. An economy integrated into the global financial service-based economy through specialization in the IT industry. A retail sector open to foreign retailers and thus demanding new kinds of retail space, as well as national highways, ports, and storage facilities to support new supply chains. An India convenient to business travelers with plenty of hotel rooms, airports, spas, and golf courses.

In anticipation of this future, Indian developers are building projects like Raheja's 225-acre engineering SEZ in Gurgaon, a "duty free enclave" with its own power supply, sewage treatment facilities, and security; Delhi Land and Finance's "Emporio," a 3,000-square-foot luxury mall in South Delhi housing international retailers like Cartier, Louis Vuitton, and Swarovski in a marble-clad atrium with chandeliers and grand pianos; and "Aerotropolis," a 2,300-acre airport-based city in West Bengal.[12] Indian developers and foreign investors are gambling that the Indian economy will continue its current trajectory toward liberalization and global integration; they are betting that this future vision will come to pass, and they are building for it.

These discourses about the future create concrete realities—though not necessarily the social realities of industry rhetoric. Based on these discourses about a glorious, globally integrated Indian future, Indian governments are clearing slums and displacing their own citizens to provide land for developers. The new "infrastructure for growth" that developers are building is *not* the infrastructure that the majority of the population needs: affordable housing, water, sanitation, and transport. Rather, it is a landscape designed to enable large multinational corporations, foreign investors, and Indian elites to accumulate capital.[13] Its construction testifies to the power of speculative knowledge to present possibilities for action, to align people to them, and to generate effects in the world.

Constructing Consumer India

Nine hundred million people. Seven hundred and eighty million consumers of cooking oil. Seven hundred and six million consumers of tea. Four hundred and fifty million buyers of casual footwear. Forty million TV-owners. Two-and-a-quarter million automobile-owners. A.k.a a market called India.

Business Today 1996

What We Talk about When We Talk about Demand

By the spring of 2007, rising interest rates and inflated prices had slowed home sales in cities across India. Rumors circulated that investors were exiting markets like Gurgaon where they thought prices would fall (Hussain 2007b). Even while the business dailies published articles like "India's Realty Boom Losing Steam?" many developers remained bullish on the industry in public (Whiting 2007). Their bullishness, as I discuss here, depended on claims about a certain kind of person, the "genuine resident."

One informant, an older Sikh man who personally invests in property in the National Capital Region, worried about depreciation, yet he clung to the hope that "genuine residents" would revive the market. He told me, "The need for homes is also increasing. You know prosperity rates have gone up, individual nuclear families, husband-wife working, there is more money to buy. There is genuine residents are also rising. So maybe it might just balance out." The existence of such residents counted as a "market fundamental." One op-ed piece argued, for example, that price appreciation would continue because the industry was backed by "fundamentals" such as "rising income levels, resulting in increased demand for quality constructions and aspirations for better locations in residences. The emergence of nuclear families and double-income households is an associated factor" (S. Mehta 2007).

Investors and developers argued that a certain kind of person—one who, unlike the majority of Indians, earns well, lives in a nuclear family, and has a spouse who works—guaranteed future demand for real estate, and, thus, buoyant prices. The resulting "end user" or "genuine resident" eerily resembles a generic globally elite consumer. The term "genuine resident" suggests that these are real rather than fictional people, actual people who guarantee real estate demand because they buy houses for living in them, not speculating on them. The "genuine resident" is also an exemplary resident, the best kind: a modern, global consumer, a well-paid professional (see chapter 6). To explain the emergence of this type of person over the past decade and to predict their rising numbers, developers and investors told a story about growing prosperity and cultural convergence with the "developed" world.

The marketing director at a Gurgaon-based real estate development company, like many I interviewed, used this dominant narrative to explain the real estate boom. He began:

> The real take off [in the real estate industry] has again been to the end of [the] '90s and beginning of 2000. These corporates coming in, these multinational companies from the US and from all over the world, has led to a lot of changes in the culture.

The narrative begins with the entrance of multinational corporations (MNCs) and the rise of the IT industry, both of which offer young Indians well-paying jobs and "exposure" to the West (thus the "changes in the culture"). This has transformed attitudes toward housing:

> With the younger generation earlier, historically, how it used to be was that a person or a child completes his education, goes to college, then has to struggle to find a job, and then, [when] . . . he is 40–45, he's at a position where he can afford to buy a house.[1] So that was more of a—a house used to be considered as, you know, it's a legacy: your grandfathers' and great grandfathers' properties were inherited as we moved along.

Instead of inheriting houses, according to this narrative, Indians now buy them at a young age. There is also a trend toward new family structures:

> How it's changed . . . was that with the these multinational companies coming in, jobs being created, the younger talent being harnessed, disposal incomes increasing, changed the traditional family where it was more of a joint family living concept. Exposure has led to a lot of nuclearization of families which means like in the West we see couples living independently. They are earning [a] handsome amount of salary . . . and the mortgages coming in cheaper, that has been the real driver for the change.

Remunerative employment with new economy firms has resulted in several related trends that stimulate demand for housing. These are the four main elements of the post-liberalization social change story: first, Indians can now afford homes at a much younger age than in the past; second, women are entering the professional workforce, leading to double-income households; third, young couples have new attitudes to spending and debt and are thus willing to take mortgages; and fourth, they want to live as nuclear families, a choice their new economic status affords.

Real estate developers and investors have not conjured this story about social change and consumer demand out of thin air but from the Indian media. Newspaper articles on real estate routinely refer to the nuclearization of families and the decreasing age of home-buyers (Chatterjee 2007; Kulkarni 2006). A barrage of English-language media celebrates rising corporate salaries; profiles the young, talented software engineers who hop from job to job in search of better pay; and highlights the challenges of being a working mother.[2] Clues about new lifestyles abound in soft features on the accoutrements of Western-style corporate living—power suits, wine, and modern home decor.[3]

In fact, both the media and the real estate industry hype a social reality that only a fraction of the population could possibly experience. In 2008, of a working population of more than 400 million, the IT industry employed just over two million people, a group of the "largely urban, middle class, and high or middle caste" (NASSCOM 2008; Upadhya 2007, 1863). Only 15 percent of urban Indians are college graduates (Bijapurkar 2007, 202). The apparel industry and domestic service—not IT and finance—are the largest employers of urban women, only 16.6 percent of whom engage in paid economic activity at all (Jayashankar 2007; see Bijapurkar 2007, 211–13).

Even white-collar workers in India are not living the fast-paced, high-earning corporate life. A survey of 16,500 workers in "supervisory, non-manual jobs" concludes that,

> contrary to the stereotypes, most of the white-collar employees are over 35, and have put in almost 12 years in the profession . . . Half of white collar workers are plain graduates drawing an average monthly salary of Rs 13,000. Around 70 per cent belong to single-income households and an equally big number of them come from non-metro cities. (Goyal 2007)

Apparently, only "the brightest, smartest, wealthiest and the youngest" Indian executives "hog all the limelight and make it to glossy magazine covers" (Goyal 2007).

Investors, consultants, and developers tell a tale which is only fractionally true about the emergence of a young, high-earning demographic, and they project that story into the future, forecasting the development of a prosperous, internationally familiar, consumerist Indian society. I investigate the stories developers and investors tell about demand and the forms of knowledge that inform those stories. A phalanx of experts—retail strategists, marketing professionals, and international consultants—have elaborated a new model of Indian society that explains the development of "Consumer India" (Bijapurkar 2007) and creates expectations of its growth. I trace this model from its origins in social science surveys to consultancy reports and conversations with developers, who use narratives about future consumers to enhance their own value in the eyes of investors. I show how ideas about consumers shape producers' value projects; consumers—even largely imagined ones—are needed to make markets.

Industry discourses about "Consumer India" link imagined consumers to time (the near-future) and place (particular Indian cities) constituting what linguistic anthropologists would call a *chronotope*, a "representation of time and place peopled by certain social types" (Agha 2007b, 321; Bakhtin 1981). This chronotope—a future of Indian metros populated by global consumers—is a "possible world" (Agha 2007b, 322) that real estate industry members have adapted from social science research and consultancy reports in order to advertise Indian real estate to investors, assuage anxieties about future demand, and strategize about where and for whom to build. The Consumer India chronotope implicitly contrasts with India's past (and in some places, its present)—which, in the stories industry members tell, is dominated by extended families, traditional values, an aversion to credit, low disposable incomes, and the attitude that a house is a legacy that one should pass on to children—all attributes that make India a problematic place for selling real estate.

The "India story," however, transforms these past inadequacies into possible future profit. It connects the now of engaging with industry reports with the future conjured by those reports because it promises that economic growth will automatically produce social change. Elaborating on the hierarchies described in chapter 3 which place India "behind" more "advanced" nations, I show how industry members project those hierarchies onto people, places, and goods in ways that guide their actions. The top of the hierarchy and the end point of change is the possible world of Consumer India projected in industry discourse. While industry members presume that the number of wealthy Indian consumers and global Indian cities will automatically grow over time, they use this chronotope to guide their attempts to build those places and create those consumers now.

A Market Called India

After the 1991 economic reforms, the Indian government and Indian corporations were eager to show potential foreign investors that India was a vast, untapped consumer market, rather than a land wracked by poverty and famines. They did so by promulgating the idea of a large, consuming Indian middle class, an idea which has characterized media and scholarly coverage of India since (Fernandes 2006). In a recent book on Indian consumers, one Indian marketing consultant confirms:

> The Great Indian Middle Class was a seductive idea that was conceived, packaged and sold to the world by India as part of its sales pitch for foreign direct investment in the early to mid-1990s when all it had to offer was a GDP per capita of less than US$20 per month, and a lot of optimistic conjecture about the future. (Bijapurkar 2007, 84)

An array of post-liberalization consumer surveys have attempted to ascertain the size and contours of the Indian middle class. In so doing, they have produced a powerful new image of Indian society, of which "middle class" is just one element. These surveys depict India as a pyramid of social classes, segmented by income and ownership of consumer goods. In contrast to an earlier, colonial, mode of knowledge that catalogued intra-societal *difference* (see Cohn 1990; Dirks 2001; Pinney 1997), this new social knowledge is obsessed with *convergence* on global elite norms of consumerist personhood.[4] Like the models of social organization that guide transnational corporations' marketing strategies, this new model of Indian society "groups people according to spending habits or *lifestyles*, in contradiction to the multiple, collective forms of identity that might for the basis for group affiliation and meaning creation—tribal or ethnic group membership, kinship, class, nationality, religion, and political allegiance" (Applbaum 2000, 260, original emphasis). It flattens the immense social variety that fascinated earlier generations of social scientists, conflating society with market.

This pyramidal image of Indian society originated with an influential set of reports by the National Council of Applied Economic Research (NCAER), an Indian organization, on its Market Information Survey of Households (MISH), an annual 300,000-household consumption survey it has been conducting since 1985–86.[5] Using the MISH data, the NCAER estimates the size of the market for different consumer goods and classifies consumers by income, location, and occupation. Beginning in 1996, the NCAER has used income, consumption, and other "educational and asset owning characteristics of the population" (Rao and Natarajan 1996, 232) to portray the Indian market as a stratified tower of five classes: the Very Rich, the Consuming Class, the Climbers, the Aspirants, and the Destitute.

The 1993–94 MISH survey lumped all households earning more than Rs. 86,000 annually into one consumer-income bracket. However, at the request of multinationals and manufacturers, the Council began estimating the number of the "very rich" in India (Rao and Natarajan 1996, 206). It expanded the classification scheme at the top of the income pyramid, dividing the Indian populace into the groups Deprived, Aspirers, Seekers, Strivers, Near Rich, Clear Rich, and Sheer Rich. The top 6 percent of the population is now elaborated into five categories, while the bottom 70 percent of the population remains in the undifferentiated category "Deprived." Although more than half of Indian households cannot afford to buy a color TV, three out of seven consumer classes are labeled "rich" (Bijapurkar 2007, 93).

To understand just how radical the MISH is as a tool of social knowledge, it is illustrative to compare it with an older consumption survey, the National Sample Survey (NSS).[6] Although both surveys produce a statistical model of Indian society, the NSS quantifies Indian living standards in the service of a development-oriented state, while the MISH quantifies Indian consumer demand in the service of corporations. The NSS measures monthly consumer expenditure by tabulating spending on basic foods, clothing, fuel, education, and medical expenses in order to assess the living conditions and nutritional status of the populace. While the Indian Planning Commission uses these statistics to establish the poverty line, corporations have limited use for them because the NSS does not generate the size of Indian markets for particular goods.

By contrast, the MISH measures the consumption of particular manufactured products like shampoo, packaged biscuits, lipstick, and motorcycles to explain potential markets to industry (Rao and Natarajan 1996, ix). In fact, NCAER presents a social model based on the consumption of such products. Their *India Market Demographics Report 2002* segments Indian society purely on the value of the consumer goods that households in each category own: "The major assumption underlying this categorization is that a household owning a high-priced product is assumed to own most of the goods falling below the price-line indicated by that product" (NCAER 2003, 66). They thus relate a hierarchy of people to a hierarchy of goods, and they presume "that consumers move up the ladder with regard to their product ownership" over time (NCAER 2003, 69). Since the MISH does not measure food consumption, it cannot be used to estimate poverty as defined by the Planning Commission (cf. Lal, Mohan, and Natarajan 2001; Bery and Shukla 2003). While the NSS does not measure income at all, the NCAER partially bases its market structure on income data so that industry readers can estimate consumer spending capacity.

Unlike the NSS results, the MISH data is private (Deaton and Kozel 2005, 18). The NCAER recuperates the estimated two crore cost of conducting the survey by selling "data for many selected manufactured consumer products" directly to industry, or by selling its reports (Rao and Natarajan 1996, 42).[7] The 2004 report *The Great Indian Middle Class*, based on 2001–2002 MISH data, sells for an astounding Rs. 2.5 lakh (or $6,024), making it virtually inaccessible to independent researchers, the general public, and most libraries. The NCAER's own library does not carry a copy.

Although private, MISH data are far from secret. English-language newspapers and magazines publicize the NCAER's findings as colorful, easy-to-read graphics (see fig. 4.1), the World Bank cites them, and business blogs replicate them (*Business Today* 1996; Chakravarti 1995; World Bank 2000). For example, the McKinsey Global Institute, the research arm of the international management consulting firm McKinsey and Company, has published a study entitled *The 'Bird of Gold': The Rise of India's Consumer Market* based on the 2001–2002 MISH findings (Ablett et al. 2007). All of the major Indian business newspapers published summaries of the *Bird of Gold* report, as did the *McKinsey Quarterly* and India's Minister of Commerce and Industry in his latest book.[8] Thus many people have encountered the MISH findings as simplified regurgitations of the McKinsey report's executive summary, their forecasts reported as near certainty or transformed into bullet-pointed statements easily called up on a Blackberry. This is social knowledge for the global business world.

Marketing agencies, banks, MNCs, and consultancies now produce this social knowledge too. The Indian affiliates of the international firm Young and Rubicam, for example, have developed a NCAER-like hierarchy of five consumer attitudes (Bijapurkar 2007, 142). The Indian marketing firm Hansa Research has culled data from its Indian Readership Survey to create a "Household Potential Index" which scores households based on their consumption of premium goods (MRUC—Hansa Research 2006). Like the NCAER, Hansa Research arranges India's social classes (in this case, eight) in a diagram they call "The Great Indian Pyramid."

Time: The Mantra of Growth

The NCAER reports and their spin-offs do not merely produce a static image of society as a hierarchy of consumers; they have popularized a theory of income-driven social change which produces Consumer India over time. According to the NCAER, "over the years, the bottom layer [of the market structure] will narrow further, and the top will expand, so that it will approximate more to a diamond" (Rao and Natarajan 1996, 231) as India's economic growth produces increasing incomes which push consumers into higher consumer

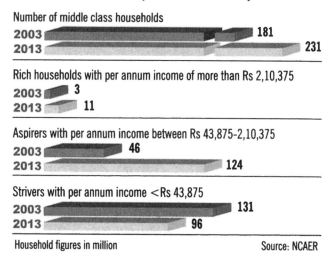

From Pyramid to Diamond

Millions of Indians would have joined the middle class by 2013.

Number of middle class households

2003 — 181
2013 — 231

Rich households with per annum income of more than Rs 2,10,375

2003 — 3
2013 — 11

Aspirers with per annum income between Rs 43,875-2,10,375

2003 — 46
2013 — 124

Strivers with per annum income <Rs 43,875

2003 — 131
2013 — 96

Household figures in million   Source: NCAER

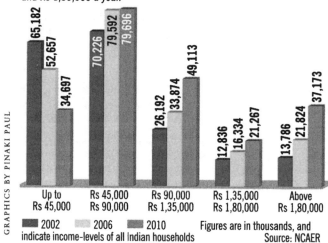

The Rich are Coming

By 2010, there will be 130 million households earning between Rs 45,000 and Rs 1,35,000 a year.

	Up to Rs 45,000	Rs 45,000 Rs 90,000	Rs 90,000 Rs 1,35,000	Rs 1,35,000 Rs 1,80,000	Above Rs 1,80,000
2002	65,182	70,226	26,192	12,836	13,786
2006	52,657	79,592	33,874	16,334	21,824
2010	34,697	79,696	49,113	21,267	37,173

GRAPHICS BY PINAKI PAUL

■ 2002 ■ 2006 ■ 2010   Figures are in thousands, and
indicate income-levels of all Indian households   Source: NCAER

FIGURE 4.1. NCAER statistics are often quoted in popular magazines.
Source: Shukla 2007.

categories. Even the names of the NCAER market classes—Climbers, Aspi-rants, Seekers, and Strivers—convey upward social mobility, a trajectory and thus a narrative about the future. Only the Destitute are doomed by their inert name to remain poor.

The NCAER's offspring, *The 'Bird of Gold': The Rise of India's Consumer Market*, is equally obsessed with income growth and social mobility. It predicts:

> As Indian incomes rise, the shape of the country's income pyramid will also change dramatically. Over 291 million people will move from desperate pov-erty to a more sustainable life, and India's middle class will swell by over ten times from its current size of 50 million to 583 million people. (Ablett et al. 2007, 10)

The constant harping on the *future* of the Indian consumer market serves many purposes. It diverts attention from India's current poverty and rhe-torically converts the poor into future consumers.[9] Reading the quote above, one might miss the admission that members of India's middle class currently number only 50 million (out of a total estimated population 1.13 billion in 2007).[10] Elsewhere in the report, the authors admit that this group, earning between US$4,400 and US$22,000 annually, represents only 5 percent of the population (Ablett et al. 2007, 46). Even if one estimates this group to be 10 percent of the population, as another marketing analyst does (Bijapurkar 2007, 87), the term "middle class" refers to the *topmost* portions of the income pyramid today; these are not middle-income earners but elites (fig. 4.2).

In order to make a plausible argument for the existence of a large con-sumer market in India, the McKinsey Global Institute (MGI) must brush past the fact that 95 percent of the populace earns less than US$4,400 per year, in-sisting, "by 2015, however, a bulge of aspirers and seekers will work its way up the income ladder; by 2025 India will transform itself into a nation of strivers and seekers with 128 million households, or 41 percent of the population, in the middle class" (Ablett et al. 2007, 46). Liberalization is the lynchpin of this predicted social transformation; the MGI warns that their forecasts depend on the Indian government's commitment to the path of economic reform (Ablett et al. 2007, 109).

With such predictions, the MGI projects a vision of India that conforms with commercial hopes. In a condensed version of the report, its authors de-scribe India as a retailer's paradise:

> Opportunities will blossom as millions of first-time buyers step up to cash registers and as the bulk of consumer spending moves from scattered, hard-to-reach rural areas to more concentrated, accessible urban markets. Indian consumer spending will shift substantially from the informal economy, with

THE SHAPE OF INDIA'S INCOME PYRAMID WILL CHANGE
DRAMATICALLY AS INCOMES GROW

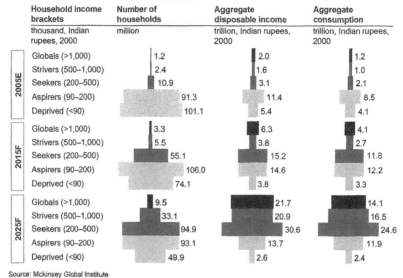

	Household income brackets	Number of households	Aggregate disposable income	Aggregate consumption
	thousand, Indian rupees, 2000	million	trillion, Indian rupees, 2000	trillion, Indian rupees, 2000
2005E	Globals (>1,000)	1.2	2.0	1.2
	Strivers (500–1,000)	2.4	1.6	1.0
	Seekers (200–500)	10.9	3.1	2.1
	Aspirers (90–200)	91.3	11.4	8.5
	Deprived (<90)	101.1	5.4	4.1
2015F	Globals (>1,000)	3.3	6.3	4.1
	Strivers (500–1,000)	5.5	3.8	2.7
	Seekers (200–500)	55.1	15.2	11.8
	Aspirers (90–200)	106.0	14.6	12.2
	Deprived (<90)	74.1	3.8	3.3
2025F	Globals (>1,000)	9.5	21.7	14.1
	Strivers (500–1,000)	33.1	20.9	16.5
	Seekers (200–500)	94.9	30.6	24.6
	Aspirers (90–200)	93.1	13.7	11.9
	Deprived (<90)	49.9	2.6	2.4

Source: Mckinsey Global Institute

FIGURE 4.2. The McKinsey Global Institute focuses on future predictions since present income data is so bleak.

Source: Ablett et al. 2007.

its individual traders, to the more efficient formal economy of organized businesses. (Beinhocker, Farrell, and Zainulbhai 2007, 52)

The MGI uses the future tense to disallow an Indian consumer market characterized by a large informal economy and few consumers, many of them in hard-to-reach rural areas. Similarly, claims about the creation of a "massive middle class centered in the cities" describe an alluring possibility, not a present reality (Beinhocker, Farrell, and Zainulbhai 2007, 51). The term "middle class" indexes the *potential* growth of large consumer markets in India. It also conjures a minimum standard of consumption of international, branded products—an international lifestyle, albeit one unattainable to those with median Indian incomes today.

A belief in social mobility and income growth bridges this gap between future potential and current reality; it also enables businesses to target the richest classes of Indians. Drawing on the MGI findings, they can assume that while the current market for their global products is small, it will grow as the number of consumers does. The same companies talking about a future middle class, their enthusiasm fueled by articles like "The Market Makers: How India's Middle Class of 300 Million Became Not Just One of the Largest

Markets, but a Global Phenomenon" (Shukla 2007) craft marketing strategies aimed at the few Indians who have money today, those in the income strata *above* middle class.

The MGI authors outline two strategies that a multinational company might take as it enters the Indian market. The first is to wait for the rich (here, "the global class") to grow in number. As they point out, "the global class in India is already able to afford internationally priced products," and, according to their predictions, it "will grow at a rate of 8.6 percent to reach almost 2 million households by 2010." The second strategy is to focus on India's many poorer consumers: one could "drive price-points down and face the consequent pressure on margins, but tap into the extraordinary volume that these emerging markets offer" (Ablett et al. 2007, 103; cf. Prahalad 2006). According to Indian marketing expert Rama Bijapurkar, most international companies have chosen the first approach; they are "more comfortable" targeting high income consumers without having to innovate India-specific business models (Bijapurkar 2007, 60, 255).

Targeting India's wealthy requires little innovation or localization from multinationals because they believe that members of the top echelons of Indian society resemble consumers elsewhere in the world. The McKinsey Global Institute makes this assumption obvious by relabeling the topmost class in the NCAER consumption-income pyramid "Global." They thus assume that Indians who make US$22,882 (one million rupees) or more "have spending habits similar to those of their developed-country counterparts—branded apparel, vacations abroad, electronics, and cars will all be high-priority purchases" (Ablett et al. 2007, 72). Global Indians include "senior corporate executives, large business owners, politicians, big agricultural-land owners and top-tier professionals," and also, what *Bird of Gold* authors call "a new breed of the upwardly mobile—mid-level executives of graduates from India's top colleges who are able to command premium salaries from international companies" (Ablett et al. 2007, 44). By lumping rural landlords and urban executives in the same class, the MGI assumes that the allure of an internationally standard package of consumer goods cuts across other social divides.

With increasing incomes and consumption, the MGI and NCAER perpetuate the belief that tastes will automatically change. People will move up a hierarchy of goods, consuming more "branded apparel" and less *paan* over time, eventually becoming middle class, if not Global Indians, with tastes just like consumers elsewhere in the world. This movement toward generic international consumer status cuts across regional, ethnic, religious, caste and other affiliations. By showing everyone climbing an imagined income ladder and harping on growth, these studies portray poor people as potential rich people. They achieve the amazing feat of discursively transforming India into Consumer India.

Social Types: Targeting the Top

Taken up by marketing and consultancy firms, the NCAER-McKinsey model of social organization has informed countless corporate strategies. Indian real estate developers also use this model in their own value projects. They reproduce NCAER diagrams in their market research reports, investor presentations, and stock market prospectuses to demonstrate demand (see fig. 4.3). They also conceive of their target customers as organized in a NCAER-like hierarchy of classes. The consumer at the apex of the NCAER pyramid is the bellwether of real estate demand that we encountered at the beginning of the chapter: the high-earning, professional couple with international tastes and consumerist attitudes, the "genuine resident." Here I elaborate on this social type that is so central to the Consumer India imaginary by examining how real estate developers alongside other foreign and Indian companies that sell housing-related goods—kitchenware, home furnishings, or interior design magazines—imagine their elite target audience.

Marketing professionals for real estate and related firms use the term SEC A, or Socioeconomic Class A, to refer to elite consumers. Developed by the Market Research Society of India in the 1980s, this scheme ranks Indians

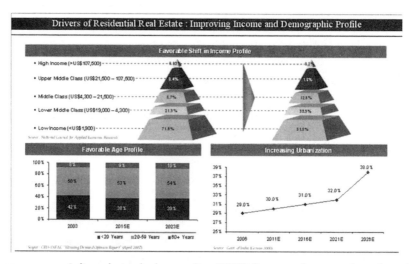

FIGURE 4.3. Indian real estate developers replicate NCAER diagrams to demonstrate future demand in their reports for investors.

Source: Emaar MGF Land Limited 2008.

based on the education and occupation of the "chief wage earner" in each household, from SEC A1, the highest, down to SEC E2, the lowest, with separate rankings for urban and rural dwellers (Bijapurkar 2007, 130). The head of a SEC A household is well-educated, "a graduate or postgraduate who is either self-employed or in a middle or senior level position if employed," and SEC A1, with only two million households, "is the miniscule group that all international lifestyle, luxury brands target" (Bijapurkar 2007, 133). My informants also use euphemisms for SEC A: "professionals who are doing very well," "a certain income class plus," "a very affording class," or "the consuming upper middle class." They refer to the very wealthy as "High Net-Worth Individuals" or HNIs. If pressed, real estate developers put their target consumer's annual income anywhere above seven lakh rupees per year, (with one Indian developer claiming his clients made 60–70 lakh annually). Based on this income range, McKinsey would classify developers' target audience as Strivers and Globals, the top two classes.

The SEC A person is first and foremost a consumer. The marketing director for an Indian home accessories company that sells expensive, modernly styled trays, vases, silverware, and tea sets described her firm's target consumer as having a disposable income of Rs. 40,000 a month and living in a high-rise condominium:[11]

> You come to his lifestyle, he is . . . decently qualified—one benchmark. Second, he would be either golfing or going for a swim or maybe to the gym for sport. The third thing, well-traveled. Maybe one tour abroad. Owns a car, might be having a second car too at home. Usually a double-family income, and preferably a 70 percent skew towards nuclear family. Reads the current magazines, looks out for the current trends, have a fascination for watches. Women, particularly conscious about shoes and bags. OK, ah, doesn't over-dress. That understated dressing statement is more or less what they would follow—[This] *is* the bracket that we think we are in.

This is a description of an undistinguished consumer: someone whose leisure is commodified and whose interests (current magazines, trends, and watches) coincide with marketers' desires. This seeming banality has important implications. This person does not live in the highly segmented consumer universe of the United States, where marketers have adopted anthropological and psychological research methods to elaborate distinct consumer types like "shotguns and pickups" or "Hispanic mix residents" (Cohen 2003, 299; Turow 1997). Rather, he inhabits India, where consumers themselves are novel, and, in this imaginary, relatively homogeneous and undifferentiated.[12]

The SEC A consumer is also "international" in outlook. One informant described his target audience as "wanting to catch up with the rest of the world, of his contemporaries or peers, wherever they may be." Developers believe that through travel, media, and work in the IT sector, Indians are increasingly aware of international trends. One developer, building homes in Gurgaon that cost approximately four crore rupees (or just under $1 million) each, said, "Our customers would be increasingly educated—not in the sense of the literal sense—I'm just mentioning they have traveled, they have understood, they have seen it. They want that kind of a thing from you. So you have to address them." Educated by travel abroad, his consumers demand the same products back home.

Alongside the internationally savvy consumer at the top of the consumer pyramid, homes and home related products are also highly ranked. The editor-in-chief of a home decorating magazine explained, "After the nitty-gritty is out of the way, you're fed and you're clothed, and you have a fridge, AC, car— all the necessities, then the second stage is a home and home decorating." Note how she redefines "home" as luxury, rather than basic necessity; homes are the consumer durable that outranks cars and ACs. Homes and consumers also exist in a hierarchy of refinement. Having evolved beyond basic necessities, consumers of high-end houses search out uniqueness or "aspirational quality," explained the developer who is building apartments in Gurgaon that cost four crore rupees each:

> But as you move forward, as you move up the food chain or the market segments, then the person will look for some special quality. It could be Italian marble. It could be the design of the house. It could be the size of the house. It could be features. But, then if you move forward then, or move up, rather, then people are going to look for what are, how is this place unique when compared to other places?

The developer's repetition of the terms "forward" and "up" provides a powerful image of the arrangement of the consumer segments, and the term "food chain" evokes ecological images of competition and consumption.[13] A kind of natural or even biological evolution, in this narrative, is tied to capital increase, understood as a space-time through which people can move. Those at the top of the capital-consumer hierarchy have the privilege of moving beyond the "brick-mortar" issues of concern to those in the lower-income brackets.

The top of the consumer pyramid is a competitive place to do business. Explaining his company's "top-end luxury retail" strategy to me, a retail consultant for one of the largest real estate developers in the country started talking about the "more mass market" and then paused. He added the qualification—"the more mass market, which isn't the mass market and that is the other thing people get wrong." He proceeded to draw me a quick graph, with income on the Y axis and population on the X axis, which showed a very small spike of population at the high-income end and the rest of the population as a block earning very little. Pointing to the narrow spike, he said, "so inside that may be your luxury but also your regular mall, and it's a very narrow margin before you hit that area there," referring to his representation of the bulk of Indians. "And so Indian retail has to recognize [that] everybody is after almost the *same* marketplace." Although the different malls that have been built in India to date—discount, big-box stores like Big Bazaar or luxury malls like DLF's Galleria—might appear to serve different consumer segments, they really cater to the same small population.

It is a small market indeed. The cost of a new apartment in Gurgaon in 2006–2007 hovered around one crore (10 million) rupees. In other Delhi suburbs, NOIDA or Ghaziabad, one could find new construction for about 30 lakh (3 million) rupees—more than fifty times the Rs. 54,000 that the average Delhiite makes in a year (itself more than twice the national average) (*Times of India* 2006). According to a senior manager at HDFC, an Indian housing finance corporation which handles about 30 percent of housing loans across India, in 2006–2007 the average *monthly* income of a mortgage-taker was Rs. 42,000. Even to claim that "the consuming upper middle class has been the real target of developers," as Delhi-based developer Unitech's Director Sanjay Chandra did at a real estate conference in 2007, is to understate the social position of their target group and exaggerate its size.

Perhaps that is why real estate developers and others fervently believe that, over time, the pyramid will become diamond-shaped and more people will join SEC A and the market for houses and home-related products: their market is, at present, so small. A senior manager at HDFC told me that since developers working in the National Capital Region assume that salaries will increase 15 to 20 percent a year, they expect the market for high-end homes to grow. I asked the CEO of an Indian media conglomerate that publishes an interior design magazine and a home decorating supplement whether he could imagine a home magazine aimed at a SEC B or C audience. He replied, "Well, not immediately, but I would believe that as we progress in time it should be possible. . . . Again, because it's a hierarchy of needs. And as people evolve at the higher level, there are many more people who are getting into the entry level." This CEO conceives of Indian society as an escalator of progress, continually making space for people at the "entry level" as others progress upward. Belief in growth allows companies to target the small group of international consumers at the top of the NCAER pyramid today with the expectation that incomes will soon increase, tastes will trickle down, and the market will expand.

Creating Indian Consumers

The McKinsey Global Institute contends that liberalization-induced income growth drives the development of Consumer India; a process of natural convergence, requiring no specific agency, links income growth to new consumer habits. My informants, on the other hand, used the term "exposure," as did the press: Indians are now "exposed to the best global consumption culture" (Shukla 2007, 146) through television, the Internet, travel, and employment in the IT industry. While "exposure" sounds like a passive process, it is not. The firms I profile here actively "penetrate" markets, win over consumers, and convince them to upgrade their tastes.[14] They do not simply wait for a new consumer society to grow; they build it. Rather than rely on existing "genuine residents," they cultivate them. And they use the NCAER-McKinsey model of Indian society as a resource in doing so.

The CEO of a major Indian media company told me that his firm "map[s] markets to see how they are progressing, and which markets can afford what kind of advertising spend and then particularly we tailor-make our products." His company engages in a recursive process with its market research team, continually testing the size of various emerging submarkets—women, youth, home-owners—to see if they can support targeted advertising from other firms looking to attract SEC A or Global Indian consumers. Those submarkets deemed sufficiently large earn new media formats designed for them: regional versions of the company's news magazine, new niche magazines, or free supplements (called "line extensions"). Reaching out to readers through new media, the CEO believes, cultivates future media consumers. He explained how his firm decided to produce regional language editions of its news magazine:

> English is the mainstay for people who are successful, but there are a lot of people who are not comfortable in English, who probably, the next generation would be comfortable in English, and, you know, to have them go through that transition, give them [magazine title] in the language of their choice and as the next generations come up, they will move towards from their local language to the English language edition.

He sees providing regional language editions as a means of exposing the next generation to the magazine and training Indians toward the English edition over time. Of course, he understands English to be the more prestigious language, that of the "successful" in India today. The line extensions, free supplements about home decor, women in the workplace, or higher education, are similarly "aspirational, not all of it would be relevant and would come and touch people's lives, but you'd like to know how people who have arrived in life in the developed world are spending their money and time." Driven by magazine sales and advertising revenues, this company trains its readership toward new media products and higher-end consumption patterns. "Exposure" is a money-making proposition.

Marketers introduce even those Indians with the incomes to qualify as SEC A or Global consumers to new products and ways of living. This is essential for foreign firms entering the Indian market without changing their business model or product line. One American mall development and management firm looking to build luxury malls in India found that even wealthy Indians do not regularly buy luxury brands. As the firm's Indian consultant Sumit explained, "there are many customers in India who have got money, but they are not aware of why a Valentino or why this brand." The solution: "We need to actually expose this customer to this particular lifestyle."

Sumit plans to expose consumers to luxury lifestyles through careful management of his mall's mix of tenants, which also solves the problem of the relative lack of high-end retailers in India:

> In India, we do not have so many luxury and premium brands that we can fill a shopping center, so we need to do a mix of it, a mix of maybe starting with Mango or starting with a Calvin Klein, or maybe starting with a Levis and going till LV [Louis Vuitton]. So a person who is buying a Levis today, tomorrow can buy a Diesel, or maybe he'll buy a Guess, and slowly he'll go to maybe Versace jeans. But till the time I don't expose him to Versace, he'll never be able to go and buy it.

Like the media CEO who believes in a hierarchy of languages, Sumit believes in a hierarchy of retail brands. By mixing high and low brands in one mall, he plans to train shoppers up the brand hierarchy from Levis to Diesel to Guess to Versace until they habitually buy luxury: the consumer "slowly graduates and he, after maybe three years, four years, he'll regularly go to Versace." In a country where most people do not wear branded or ready-made apparel, buying a foreign brand at a fancy new mall is itself a statement of prestige, means, and modernity. Sumit contends that the cachet of the mall can be pushed further: after training consumers into luxury shopping, he can change the tenant mix of the mall to include more high-end retailers over time. In the end, his American employer should have both malls and consumers that fit its international model.

Sometimes, to sell a particular product, marketers inculcate the idea of consumerism itself. One Delhi-based real estate developer, responding to the nuclear family trend, foresaw a market for retiree housing. His son, Anand, investigated the possibility as a master's student in real estate in the US. While he visited retirement homes in Florida, his father hired a consulting company to research the viability of the concept in North India. Eventually, they built a series of modest, five-story buildings about an hour outside of Delhi and offered one-, two-, and three-bedroom flats to people over fifty-five. They included a central green space, organized activities, and on-call medical service and marketed the project as "India's first retirement resort." They've now replicated the project in other cities.

Initially, however, they had trouble making sales because of the age restriction. Retirees were reluctant to purchase a home in which their children could not live after they were gone. Anand explained the biggest difficulty he had marketing the project:

> [It was] convincing a customer that it's all right if your children cannot stay after you are not there in your house. They are not going to stay anyway because this is [a Delhi suburb]; they are working in Delhi. They are not going to go to [a Delhi suburb] to stay. Just that thought process breaking. That it's all right, you are getting a lifestyle. They'll still get that asset you own, which will be theirs, and we will help them.

In order to reassure potential buyers, the firm offered to help residents' heirs resell the properties or rent them out. As Anand says, residents' children could still inherit the property as an *asset*, just not as a place to live. Resistance to buying the retirement homes indicates a crucial difference in attitude between Anand and his potential customers: the former sees the house as a financial asset that can easily be made liquid, while the latter conceives of it as something to be used, lived in, and passed on to future generations.

Anand saw the difference in attitude in terms of a culture of parental responsibility:

> It's a big, big thing in India. Parents work, work, work, get their children up, and still after they retire, also, still want to give. We want to change that thought process. Here you have a lifestyle, which is against the Indian thought process, . . . we are telling them, first look at yourself—now they [children] are settled, they are doing well for themselves. You don't have to worry about them. If you have brought them up good, they are good. So what we are saying is, forget about them right now. Live your life first and whatever you have left, just give it to them, and we will help you whenever we can as a company.

Anand asks retirees to stop worrying about their children and think of themselves. As he repeats, he is selling a *lifestyle*: not just a house, but a personal consumer choice and a new way of living. The marketing copy for the project reiterates this message: "You've worked hard and fulfilled your responsibilities; now it's time to think about your needs, your comforts and your peace of mind. It's time to enjoy life independently and on your own terms."

Anand's retirement project does not merely fit a "need" arising from the trend toward nuclear families; it also has the potential to transform people's thinking and behavior. The seemingly simple act of purchasing a condominium in fact invites buyers to embrace a new understanding of themselves, their families, and their priorities: to embrace individual self-fulfillment through consumer choices. Anand's difficulty marketing his new retirement homes casts doubt on the stories with which we began this chapter, narratives about how economic liberalization created "genuine residents" for real estate products. If the process of selling condominiums invites potential buyers to reconsider homes as commodities through which they can attain self-fulfillment, is the idealized real estate consumer the cause or the outcome of the real estate boom? I have argued here that in accommodating perceived social trends, developers aim to create consumers. Anand and Sumit are each doing their small part to "educate" Indian consumers, "exposing" them to new products and ideas with the hope of making markets for their products. Like other marketers, developers, and consultants, they are effecting the changes which they see as inevitable, helping to make NCAER knowledge self-fulfilling and bring Consumer India into being.

Place: A New Map of Consumer India

Just as real estate producers conceive of the Indian market as a hierarchy of consumers, they imagine India as a hierarchy of places. As they project the narrative of social progress that produces their ideal elite consumer onto the national geography, they classify certain places as behind others in their progress toward "modern" or "Western" consumer society. Such classifications are "value-making acts [that] do not end with themselves, but go on to make many other things" (Ferry 2013, 20). Developers and investors use this geographical conceptualization of social progress to decide in which cities to build. As they do so, they transform their geographical imaginary into a reality, a new India.

Not surprisingly, the geographical imaginary of Consumer India ignores Rural India—that undifferentiated category that includes both prosperous

Punjab and impoverished Chattisgarh. Despite occasional exhortations to tap the rural "market at the bottom of the pyramid" (e.g., Carvalho and Subramanian 2007), most marketers focus on cities because they offer concentrations of wealth easily accessible through existing transportation and communications systems (Ablett et al. 2007, 91). Moreover, many marketers consider cities the future of consumer behavior and rural areas the past; they are "two different worlds, about ten years apart in terms of consumption behavior" (Bijapurkar 2007, 93).

Various ranking devices help companies decide which cities have the most promising consumer markets. The McKinsey *Bird of Gold* report ranks Indian cities by population using a familiar pyramid diagram. International companies need look no further than the eight top tier cities for their market, as they account for 39 percent of the country's disposable income, and 60 percent of the urban Global households (Ablett et al. 2007, 73–75). The *RK Swamy BBDO Guide to Urban Markets*, developed by I. Natarajan (formerly of the NCAER), attempts to measure cities' "consumer potential" based on the number of consumers in a city, their incomes, consumption behavior, and "awareness levels" (media exposure and literacy rates) (Challapalli 2004).

The real estate industry has its own, related, city rankings. Real estate developers and investors want to know where international companies will locate their new headquarters and outsourcing units in India. International companies, Business Process Outsourcing units, and IT firms not only require new office space; they also employ the high-earning, internationally exposed "genuine resident." International consultancies like Ernst & Young and Jones Lang LaSalle, magazines such as *Business Today* and *Realty Plus*, securities firms, and investment banks provide guidance to firms, investors, and developers by ranking Indian cities in terms of labor costs and availability, the ease of doing business, livability, and other measures.[15]

The most prevalent ranking system for Indian cities, now firmly embedded in the Indian real estate lingo, is the international Tier I/II/III classification (fig. 4.4).[16] This ranking is not based entirely on population, but on the size of the real estate market and the presence of the IT industry in a particular city. For example, Kolkata is India's second largest city by population, but it is usually considered a Tier II or Tier III city along with smaller cities judged able to "provide the basic requirements to attract IT offshoring activities and become the next tier of successful cities" (Jones Lang LaSalle 2006a, 7). The rankings represent the penetration of multinationals, hand-in-hand with the real estate industry, into Indian cities; changing classifications over time indicate the movement of such firms beyond Delhi, Bangalore, and Mumbai.[17]

Just as the label "middle class" renders Indian society legible to foreign

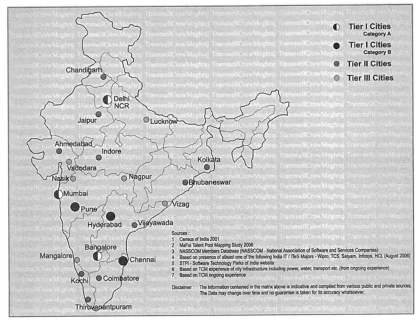

FIGURE 4.4. International property consultancy classification of Indian cities.
Source: TrammellCrowMeghraj 2006.

corporations, these classifications are intended to render Indian cities legible to foreign investors as members of global categories. They also enable international comparison: should firm X outsource to Manila or Delhi, Sao Paolo or Pune? Jones Lang LaSalle reminds readers that "low cost destinations elsewhere in Asia (e.g., Manila, Dalian, and Tianjin) along with those in Central Europe (such as Prague, Budapest, Warsaw and Krakow) and Latin America (e.g., Sao Paulo and Buenos Aires) are all competing for the same market as Tier III cities in India" (Jones Lang LaSalle 2006a, 8). Providing standardized, comparable data, these rankings are vital instruments in the international competition between cities that liberalization has unleashed.

As with the forms of ranking discussed in chapter 3, here evidence of deficiency is seen as a sign of future growth. City rankings reinforce the idea that some cities are trailing behind others in the race for development. However, lagging Tier II and III cities also present an opportunity for investment, growth, and profit. Writes one consultant, "In the next two to three years, Tier II cities will witness growth at breakneck speed compared with Tier I cities. In terms of quantum and depth of real estate development, Tier II cities are about 18–24 months behind their Tier I counterparts" (Gupta 2007, 10). Tier II cities are the new frontier for corporate and real estate industry expansion.

In order to guide expansion, city ranking reports present predictions, transforming data about the present into a measure of future potential. A 2006 Jones Lang LaSalle report on Tier III IT destinations "presents our *expectations* of successful (winning) Tier III cities *in the future*, to assist both occupiers and real estate investors make more informed location decisions" (Jones Lang LaSalle 2006a, 3, emphasis added). Similarly reports on "hot emerging destinations" predict "focus areas" of real estate and MNC investment for a particular year and highlight overlooked Tier III candidates (*Realty Plus* 2007, 2008).

Much as the McKinsey Global Institute and NCAER forecasted the growth of India's consumer markets in order to stimulate international firms' interest in India, and thus the development of the market, these reports predict growth in order to make it happen. Moreover, the idea that "Tier II cities are about 18–24 months behind their Tier I counterparts" rests on the assumption that Tier II cities are Tier I cities in the making. Like models of social change that assume that most Indians will eventually achieve an internationally recognizable middle-class consumer status, these reports assume that all Indian cities will eventually replicate Mumbai, Delhi, or Bangalore.

Members of the Indian real estate industry share this expectation of metropolitan convergence. After more than twenty years developing Gurgaon, India's largest real estate developer Delhi Land and Finance (DLF) has expanded its construction activities to include cities all over India. A DLF employee assured me that

> there is a marketplace in India where what happened in Gurgaon in the last
> five years, even from malls to offices and even to homes, can be replicated down
> the food chain all over India, in lesser markets that are looking to develop,
> where they don't want more sophisticated product because they are just starting.

Through a process of product replication, the "lesser markets" can be made like Delhi's suburb Gurgaon, a successful offshoring hub and the location of many MNC offices. Note his evocation of the "food chain" metaphor, which recasts hierarchies as natural. The mall, office, and home designs developed in Gurgaon can be exported down this evolutionary hierarchy of urban places to less developed places in India—albeit with some small alterations, like less sophisticated products for cities "just starting" out.

Tier II and III cities do not merely trail Tier I cities in the provision of corporate infrastructure: my informants believe that the levels of the urban hierarchy represent a cultural lag in the progress toward modern/Western consumer society. As an analyst at a real estate fund commented, "It takes a generation for a city to graduate from Tier II to Tier I. And there are cultural issues, as well, which take time to change." In a telling moment, a brochure designer who has worked on several real estate projects confused the urban classifications Tier I, II, III with the socioeconomic categories A, B, C, D: "See what happens is there are segments. India is divided into three tiers—A category, B and C is a category, and D is another category. So B and C would be smaller towns." His use of the word "tiers" but the labels A, B, C, and D for classifying cities suggests a powerful equivalence between the hierarchy of consumer segments and the hierarchy of cities, especially as he went on to talk about the unsophisticated nature of B and C city media consumers. Similarly, marketing expert Rama Bijapurkar has correlated "acceptance of modern retailing and entertainment venues" with an urban hierarchy in which each city has the name of a consumer mindset, either escapist, striving, or arrived (Bijapurkar 2007, 143).

The overlap of language describing the processes of consumer evolution and urban development suggests that my informants conceive of the pyramid of consumer classes as geographically distributed. For the most part, they think of small towns as B and C consumer markets. Analogous to the Aspirer class of consumers rather than the Globals, they are trickier to serve and further from the ideal of international consumer taste. With economic growth, "India's middle class will begin to move beyond Tier 1 cities and spread into Tier 2, 3, and 4 cities," predicts the McKinsey Global Institute, conflating growth and movement (Ablett et al. 2007, 76). By this logic, economic growth will transform Indian people into middle-class consumers and Indian cities into Mumbai-Delhi-Bangalore clones, creating diamonds out of both urban and consumer pyramids.[18]

This emerging geography of demand for real estate maps progress toward international consumerism. The DLF employee continued:

> Where we might have trouble is in Tier II or Tier III cities in states that are not so forward, beyond the major cities. So Indore in MP [Madhya Pradesh], not too much of issues. But the minute you go down to some other city—the deeper you go the deeper the problem for the product configurations. We'll have to track this.

His understanding of different real estate markets takes on a three dimensional quality as spatial axes of progress intersect. The company's replicable design, construction, and marketing models will only take them so far, the "deeper" it goes "down" the urban hierarchy. In those far reaches of the "states that are not so forward" the markets are raw, consumers are unexposed, and existing product configurations become problematic. This is the frontier. It is not an external border, coincident with the national boundaries, but an internal one whose dimensions—measured in terms of consumer habits and attitudes—must be tracked.

Like other frontier stories, this one fuels market expansion (see Tsing 2005). While international property consultants straightforwardly describe the growth of Tier II and III cities as the result of the growth of the IT industry, IT companies rely on real estate developers' *prior* construction of office space as they move to new cities.[19] Developers read about the possibility of IT expansion and then construct the buildings that enable it. Real estate development is the vanguard of capitalist activity—a speculative forerunner that makes other types of capitalist activity possible—and that development is predicated on consultancy reports that fuel the trends they describe by helping to guide firms to provide the infrastructure for future expansion. Especially since it organizes the world hierarchically, this speculative knowledge provides developers with paths of action: an ever-diminishing set of frontiers "down" a hierarchy of places that promises years of profitable transformation.

Many Delhi-based real estate developers are already moving down those paths by expanding into the neighboring states, with projects in Jaipur, Lucknow, and Chandigarh.[20] One developer, TechBuilder, is planning a 500-acre township in Jaipur, with housing for 40,000 residents and an IT park with 6.5 million square feet of offices for "65,000 IT professionals and support staff," according to the project brochure. A complete environment, it will include an "exclusive" five-star hotel, parks, schools, and shopping malls. The firm's marketing director, Gurdeep, described his company's decision to build its Jaipur project as a mix of creating demand and anticipating it:

> So far it's a very traditional sleepy town where activities have now started happening. These MNCs are occupying. GE [General Electric], for example, is present in a large setup out there. And again we are following. We are following the rule that we are going to create the demand whether in terms of infrastructure, in terms of millions and millions of square feet of office space, millions and millions of square feet of residential.

Because GE already has a facility there, TechBuilder is willing to take a risk that a "sleepy town" can attract the multinational corporations necessary to support its proposed development. TechBuilder is both following GE and planning to "create the demand" for its ambitious project on the frontier.

Like the DLF employee, Gurdeep believes the Gurgaon model can be replicated:

> Basically Jaipur is currently ten years behind what Gurgaon was. So it has the potential to be the next Gurgaon. What does an MNC or a BPO [Business Process Outsourcing firm] look for? They look for good infrastructure. They

look for educated—skilled, rather, I would say skilled—manpower, and Jaipur has the right ingredients to be the next alternative to Gurgaon with the man-power. Gurgaon, if you see, it has a population of ten lakhs, and Jaipur is close to about 3.8 million, so the opportunities are huge.

Jaipur is not just different from Gurgaon, but *behind* it—a lag which provides an opportunity for his firm to develop Jaipur into "the next Gurgaon." Pars-ing multinational corporate logic, Gurdeep believes that cheap labor in Jaipur provides an incentive for companies to move from nearby Delhi.[21]

TechBuilder will construct the missing infrastructure such firms require: "That's where the bet comes in that we have to create the infrastructure to provide these companies an alternative," Gurdeep said. His use of the term "bet" indicates risk, and, indeed, when he spoke to BPO firms, they told him, "You guys are crazy doing something in Jaipur." But then, "several other com-panies like SAP and Oracle [multinational software firms] and those sort of companies that we have met, they said that we are open to shifting to Jaipur, but where is the infrastructure? So our risk is limited to constructing." On the one hand, his firm is taking a risk, producing space in advance of demon-strated demand from multinational corporations. On the other hand, it is acting in accordance with received wisdom, consultancies' premonitions, and a few potential tenants' expressions of interest. The ideas about people, places, and time popularized in consultancy reports and other industry media in-form the construction of the built environment, guiding firms like Gurdeep's to create landscapes for imagined consumers and to help bring Consumer India into being.

Conclusion: Rescaling Global Living

In 2008, Kamal Nath, the Minister of Commerce and Industry, described In-dia's transformation since the 1970s using familiar language. By 2004, when he began his term,

> a distributional society had given way to an aspirational society. Across the na-tion, in both rural and urban areas, the climbers were aspiring and the aspirers were consuming. The horizon of expectations was expanding at all levels. The prevailing conviction was no longer that "life should be better for my chil-dren." Instead, it was that "life should get better for me," and in the next few years, if not right now. (Nath 2008, 75)

Not only does Mr. Nath employ the language of the NCAER, he also gen-eralizes, describing the "prevailing conviction" common to "both rural and urban areas" as though this impatient attitude is a society-wide phenomenon.

Like those in the real estate industry who speak about the post-liberalization income growth of the well-educated, upper-caste, and upper-class youth employed in the IT industry as though their experience is broadly representative, Kamal Nath tells a partial story. He also describes an ongoing process in the past tense, transforming the predictions of the international consultancies into a description of fact. According to Mr. Nath, India is not developing into an aspirational society; it already is one. His generalization hides his partiality, and his use of tense hides the ongoing work of *creating* the aspirers, climbers, consumers, and convictions of an aspirational society—work, that, as we have seen, real estate developers, investors, marketers, editors, graphic designers, and others undertake every day.

New buildings themselves have come to symbolize the social changes that liberalization is thought to have wrought—namely, the rise of a consumerist Indian middle class. However, as I have shown, buildings themselves are predicated on this story of liberalization-induced social change. It may not be surprising to learn that real estate developers (like those in other industries) make decisions based on predictions of demand. However, these predictions require closer scrutiny because they hinge on a story about the Indian middle class which is told so often by journalists, government officials, and academics that it has become common sense. I mean to remind us that Indian government and corporations have promulgated this story about the Indian middle class in a bid to sell India to foreign corporations. Investors, corporate managers, and developers have used this story to plan corporate strategies, including inculcating the very consumerist desires that stories about social change suggest will naturally evolve and building the infrastructure for urban growth that consultancy reports suggest is inevitable.

Both constructing buildings and forging a new consumer society depend on the semiotic work of sorting, labeling, grading, and rating—that is, attempts to make value. The NCAER, the McKinsey Global Institute, Hansa Research, and others have sifted through the complexities of India's social order, using the lens of consumer activity to create new classifications. Similarly, Jones Lang LaSalle and other international property consultants have ranked localities in order to shoehorn them into international categories. These are value projects aimed at rendering India legible to foreign investors and companies by establishing transnational equivalencies. These various consultants create analogies between hierarchies of people, goods, buildings, and places and reinforce the idea that class is a measure of global outlook. The slippage between Indian and international categories—between multinationals' mass market products and the elite Indians who can afford them—fosters a productive misrepresentation: "Middle class" refers to the rich but conjures the common man.

Rating produces hierarchies, and these organize activity by orienting it along a trajectory of progress. Hierarchical models of Indian society are similar to the gap-prediction logics used to attract investors (chapter 3) in that they discursively transform problems (in this case an impoverished population) into opportunities (*future* consumers)—and in that they draw on development discourses. By identifying deficiencies, hierarchies create the frontiers of capitalist activity and orient that activity toward particular end points. Hierarchies establish a means for moving from the past to the future, from the traditional to the modern, and from the Indian to the international. These hierarchies create a fractal geography of nested dichotomies—West/India; Tier I cities / Tier II cities; urban/rural—which, recursively applied, could extend the frontier of capitalist improvement indefinitely.

Because it orients actors toward the future, the new social knowledge promulgated by the NCAER and other consultants provides an alibi for treating the social relations of the present as simply a passing phase in the inexorable movement toward a different social future, enabling developers and others to target the wealthiest Indians today and assume that they are the leading edge of future demand. The result is discourse about the middle class and construction for the wealthy; a proliferation of luxury malls, swanky apartments, and golf courses in a nation with an estimated housing shortage of more than 24 million units (National Building Organisation 2008). Of course the wealthy are a lucrative market, but it is the assumption that they are the *future* of the market and that their tastes are (or are soon to be) just like those of consumers elsewhere in the world that draws real estate developers and multinationals to wooing them.

As they do so, they construct buildings, design advertisements for them, and publish home decor magazines. These various media translate the business discourse of hierarchies and ratings into structures of aspiration for wide audiences, exposing those Indians able to participate in consumption today to new products and preparing the groundwork for those who cannot. Just as media moguls plot to train readers to appreciate lifestyles beyond their means, buildings provide a spectacle of modernity or a "simulacrum of inclusion" for nonelites (Guano 2002). Even before new buildings are constructed, large hoardings along construction sites' boundary walls proclaim the virtues of global living. From Kolkata to Kochi, the visual space of Indian cities is saturated with images of light-skinned people playing tennis, using their laptops, drinking wine, swimming in pools, shopping, and dining out. Thus the products of the new hierarchical social knowledge broadcast images of how a very small percentage of the population lives. They scale up expectations about global living while concentrating resources—land, infrastructure, amenities—on wealthy consumers and locales. While promoting a prosperous future, they exacerbate the uneven geography of the present.

PART II

Conflict and Commensuration

Transparency and Control

Introduction

In June 2005, I accompanied Vinay, a young developer who worked with his father, to the municipal corporation building in one of India's metros. Inside, its halls were teeming with men in bureaucratic uniform: drab button-down shirts and brown pants. Vinay stood out in his deep blue shirt and snappy black trousers. The mint green hallways of the planning wing were crowded and hot, with no fans. Boys ran in and out with glasses of chai in wire baskets. Vinay was sweating, and he seemed a bit nervous. "I hate doing this, man, I just hate doing this," he complained. We had come to do a little bribing.

Vinay wanted to remove a staircase from the plan for one of his buildings. For the signature of the deputy chief planning engineer bestowing final approval on the drawing, Vinay had counted out Rs. 5,000 and carefully placed it in his right front pocket before coming into the building. He had other bills in his left front and right back pockets. He told me, "What'll happen is I'll go in and ask how is he doing, ask after his health, some niceties. Then we'll shake hands, he'll open his drawer, and I'll just put the money in. Done." We were waiting in the hallway for the "liaison architect," an intermediary who arranges these meetings, usually between the developer's "design architect" and the appropriate clerk or official. Vinay wanted to come himself to make sure he's not asked for too much money. For this signature, he will pay the clerk Rs. 2,500 and his boss Rs. 5,000, as arranged by the liaison architect and the clerk in advance.

I asked Vinay how many times in the life of a project he has to come here. He replied,

If you don't make any revisions, then once at the beginning for approval of the plans. Then for the NOCs [No Objection Certificates]—fire, lift, drainage, etc., then again for the completion certificate. So that's three, if you don't revise. And when you've poured the first [concrete] slab, then you send your car and you bring the chiefs down to the site and they just see that everything's going as per the plan.

The liaison architect arrived and told us our appointment was not for half an hour, so we went upstairs to two other offices to deal with other matters. Vinay ducked into one office and came out ten minutes later, disgruntled. The official had signed all but one of the forms he needed and then had been transferred. For the one remaining signature, the official's replacement was asking for as much as Vinay had already paid. Nevertheless, Vinay paid him.

Part 1 of this book introduced the foreign developers, private equity funds, and investment banks that have invested in Indian real estate since foreign direct investment was further liberalized in 2005. For them, Vinay's routine visit to the planning office would be a nightmare. Regulations in these firms' home countries prevent them from bribing foreign officials, a requisite step in the construction and approval process.[1] More importantly, navigating local planning bureaucracies requires local knowledge and connections. Even Vinay, involved in his father's business for five or six years, relies on the liaison architect as an intermediary; still, he found he had to pay twice for the same job. Most developers operate through several layers of contacts: design architect, liaison architect, clerk, official. Even then, as Akhil Gupta points out, bribing is "not . . . simply an economic transaction but a cultural practice that require[s] a great deal of performative competence" (Gupta 1995, 381). The Indian-born, US-trained representatives that many foreign investors send to India to find investment opportunities (never mind their European and American counterparts) often lack the social capital and district-level contacts needed to buy land, change land use, and obtain permits—in short, to construct buildings in India.[2]

Navigating local bureaucracies to bribe planning officials is just one of a number of hurdles that foreign investors encounter as they try to invest in India real estate. First, foreign companies face legal hurdles in buying agricultural land. Second, land holdings are extremely fragmented, making assembling large tracts of land for construction projects difficult and time consuming.[3] Third, from the point of view of a foreign investor, the land titling system in India is extremely complex, a Pandora's box of village-level records, many in dispute between various parties. There is no title insurance to cushion the blow if someone should appear months or years into a project to dispute the land title, and the Indian courts are a notoriously Dickensian place to settle such disputes.[4] Since investors plan to sell their assets in the future, land title complications jeopardize their ability to "exit" a project profitably. The analyst for an international real estate fund asserted, "We will not invest until all the land has been aggregated, has been put into the investing company, is clean, is usable, is transferable, is zoned for the right purpose. [It] has to be. If it's not happening, we are not investing."

Given this impasse, foreign funds turn to Indian real estate developers, who now find themselves in a lucrative position as intermediaries. Many Indian developers have already assembled large parcels of land (a practice locally called "land-banking"), and they are adept at negotiating the legal and political hurdles of land development. As a result, they assemble and clean land for international investors and developers: they bring parcels with clear titles, land use change approvals, and other permits into a joint venture where the foreign partner provides funding, serves as the developer, or brings other expertise to the project. By taking on the initial risks in the development process, navigating local politics, and assembling land parcels (often using intimidation, extortion, and violence), Indian developers transform Indian land into an internationally legible asset, a profitable route for foreign investment.

Indian developers, for their part, are interested in working with foreign investors in order to fund ambitious plans to "scale up" their businesses. Most had previously worked in only one market in India and now plan to expand into new cities. For example, Delhi Land and Finance, which focused on developing Gurgaon throughout the 1990s, was constructing projects in fifteen cities throughout India by 2006. According to a senior staff member, the firm had grown from roughly 300 employees in 2005 to 1,300 in late 2006, with plans to triple in size by 2010. Parsvnath Developers developed 3.46 million square feet in its first sixteen years of existence, primarily residences in the National Capital Region. By November 2006, when Parsvnath went public, the company was planning to build 108 million square feet of townships, IT parks, hotels, and malls across North India—all in five years (Batlivala and Karani Securities 2006). Another firm, Aerens Gold Souk International Ltd., opened its first gold and jewelry mall, Gold Souk, in Gurgaon in 2004. In the spring of 2006, the company announced that it would build one hundred such malls in one hundred cities in one hundred months (*Hindu Business Line* 2006). Many other companies also announced extensive construction plans: grand townships (some upwards of 1,000 acres), multiple shopping plazas, housing developments, and IT parks in numerous cities across India. Given the difficulties of agglomerating land, these were ambitious plans indeed.

To realize these ambitions, developers needed money "at a very fast velocity and in great quantities," as one developer put it. As the real estate boom was cresting in 2006–2007, real estate developers were searching for capital.

Domestic institutional finance for the real estate industry had improved significantly since the late 1990s through a series of government initiatives and the rise of mortgage lending. However, the Reserve Bank of India (RBI), concerned about rising property prices, made it progressively harder for developers to obtain capital in India in 2006–2007. Pre-sales of housing units, a traditional source of funds, were also down, as consumers increasingly demanded to see finished construction before buying and interest rate hikes slowed the residential market.

Whether they had tied up all their money in land and now needed money for construction, or they were trying to buy land in order to expand their operations, developers sought international financing through two main routes.[5] First, they could elicit investment from a foreign fund, forming a joint partnership company (JV), or a special purpose vehicle (SPV) for the purpose of carrying out a particular project.[6] Second, a developer could go public, listing either on the Bombay Stock Exchange (BSE), where foreign institutional investors are significant shareholders, or on foreign stock exchanges such as the London Stock Exchange Alternative Investment Market (AIM).[7] Either way, Indian developers found themselves appealing to foreign investors for funding.

However, investor-developer partnerships were not without their frictions. Part 2 of this book examines conflicts between investors and developers, which reveal their divergent value projects and ways of working. As they attempted to bridge these differences to create an international market in Indian land and buildings, investors challenged their potential partners' expertise and strove to change the way they worked; they did so, in part, by describing Indian real estate markets, practices, companies, and people as "nontransparent." Transparency talk, I argue, served as a resource in their value project of gaining control of partnerships and changing business practices.

Here I depict foreign direct investment as a disciplinary project, not as an automatic flow of money. Foreign investors' calls for transparency are attempts to govern: attempts to devalue Indian developers' expertise, to obtain favorable investment terms, and to urge Indian developers to transform themselves into legible intermediaries (and less risky partners). Indian real estate developers have responded with their own transparency claims, weaving a narrative of the industry's transformation and reinventing themselves to fit foreign expectations, but their value projects are shaped by their contradictory position as intermediaries; I take this up in the next chapter. But, first, let us turn to foreign investors.

Transparency Problems

Foreign fund managers evoked "transparency" to describe interactional failures with Indian real estate developers and to express their own lack of power navigating a place they do not understand or control. Simon, the head of the Indian office of a London-based real estate private equity fund, told me the following story with vehemence and animation. He was frustrated with an Indian developer in Cochin about a construction project in which he hoped to invest. Before meeting the chairman of his potential partner firm, Simon and his colleagues visited the project site, spoke to brokers and other real estate companies in the area, and met with the company directors: "We met with the directors of the company in one city, who gave us all the information, who gave us what we thought to be a certain amount of comfort on the clarity of the transaction." However, when they met with the chairman, the deal unraveled:

> Day two, we sit down to meet with the chairman, who doesn't even bother getting out of his seat, with his arms crossed, to say, what can we do for you? Knowing exactly why we're here. . . . So we play the game. "Thank you for offering this opportunity to us. We are very interested in it. We believe this is the deal." We tell him the five crores per acre and the one million square feet that we've been by told, by *his* company, by *his* directors. He says, (exaggerated Indian accent for first three words), "*No, my land* is worth eight crores and we're creating one-point-five million square feet." See you later, mate.

Simon voiced his exasperation by walking away from the deal: "See you later, mate" is addressed to the Indian chairman. It was not the price of the land per se that bothered Simon, but the sudden increase in value:

> When somebody tries to increase his value by 50 or 60 percent within a period of a week and then increases FSI [Floor Space Index] by another 50 or 60 percent within a period of a week, after getting the information *from* that company, *within* that company, *from* his directors, (pause) doesn't give you a huge amount of comfort.

Strikingly, what bothered Simon most about the entire episode was the *inconsistency* of the Indian developer—the capriciousness of the changing deal terms suggested that the chairman might be greedy or that the chairman might not know or control what his employees say. Simon emphasizes that all of his information came directly from the company whose chairman changed the terms of the deal. The chairman's inconsistency about the deal did not give him "comfort," while his earlier investigations and meetings had provided "some comfort on the clarity of the transaction." When Simon found "comfort," "clarity," and consistency lacking, he walked away from the deal. He told me this story as an example of a problem with an Indian firm's "transparency." The term here means a kind of interactive consistency that Simon felt is necessary in a business partner, and the chairman's inconsistency was a "deal breaker" for Simon.

Clearly, Simon is talking about power—his own lack of it. The Indian developer held power in this failed transaction: the power to dispense information, to delineate the scope of the project, and to determine the price of land. Ultimately, he had the power to exclude Simon from a potentially profitable deal. Simon articulates his own lack of power by labeling the Indian developer as "inconsistent" and "nontransparent."

Simon complained later in our interview about a range of "partnership issues":

> When you think you've got a certain partner and they want to bring in their partners and make friends and they want to be on the board and at the end of the day, the lack of transparency because there's too many people sitting on the board. Ego becomes a problem, everyone wants to have a say in the matter. Timelines get, you know, get uhm, get muddied. You know, your lawyers and your accountants making a shitload of money trying to finalize the shareholders' agreement, whereas it keeps being changed every five minutes. It's not a way to do business.

Again, he related the issue of transparency to a question of consistency. He thought it was no way to do business if your partner tries to "bring in their partners" without warning, if the board gets too large and unwieldy, and if agreements keep changing "every five minutes." When Simon discussed inconsistency and lack of transparency, he meant his own lack of control over his Indian partners, whose behavior hints at agendas and social connections that Simon did not understand and could not foresee. He expressed these anxieties as concerns about time, which was a constant refrain among investors because funds have deadlines for deploying their money in India and, as we will see in chapter 8, earning returns requires careful time management.[8]

EuroFund, a European real estate fund with which I did participant observation, also had difficulty interacting with partners and finalizing deals. They had negotiated with one potential partner (Mr. M) for five months before they realized he had been simultaneously talking with another investor who he wanted to bring in on the deal. EuroFund's managers liked neither the third party nor the fact that Mr. M had been negotiating with him in secret. They also did not like the fact that Mr. M refused to show them the two plots of land they were considering; they later discovered that one of them would have been difficult to develop because it had very little road frontage.

EuroFund finally formed a joint venture with a large Indian development firm (I will call it BuildIndia) to construct an office complex. EuroFund's managing director, Jeremy, expressed dismay at how long the negotiations took: "We first met with [BuildIndia] in August 2006. It's now February 2008 and we haven't signed the agreement document yet. That's just one transaction. And we're still wondering, do these guys really trust us enough to be responsible for the day-to-day construction of the building?" Such protracted negotiations and uncertain timing are difficult for EuroFund to weather because they have promised returns to investors in a set time frame. Moreover, for Jeremy, the length of negotiations indicated mistrust. For contrast, he told me about a fifty million dollar contract that EuroFund had signed with an American firm, several years ago. While that deal had taken four months to negotiate, an immense amount of time by Western real estate industry standards, it paled compared to the fund's troubles finalizing deals in India.

The terms of the agreement also indicated mistrust to Jeremy. While EuroFund routinely acts as the majority partner in its overseas ventures, BuildIndia insisted on a 50:50 partnership. Jeremy explained, "Usually, when we get partners, they are quite happy to be in a minority and to have a smaller voice. . . . They want to be in business with us because they know we know what we are doing." EuroFund also usually does "all the accounting and bookkeeping and we'll manage the bank account and we'll organize with the accountants to prepare tax returns." However, BuildIndia wanted to hire a third party (an employee of the joint venture) to do this work. Jeremy told me, "I was genuinely affronted. The implication of this is they think we're going to try to steal from them." Jeremy interpreted his lack of control over the project as his Indian partner not trusting him. But then, Jeremy also admitted that he did not trust the third party: "I think this is the only time we'll ever have not basically been taking responsibility for the accounting. And it worries me. I mean it just worries me about whether it's going to be done right."

By the time I left India, Jeremy was quite frustrated. He complained, "We [EuroFund] have a tremendous reputation for integrity and honesty. But in India, they think we'll act like Indians: 'they'll rip us off.'" He felt that Indian businessmen generally operated with a de facto assumption of mistrust and a competitive, rather than cooperative stance. He continued, "There are ruthless, bloody-minded businessmen in [Europe] and everywhere else too, don't get me wrong. But we are almost completely transparent in [Europe]. You know who those people are, and if you choose to do business with them, you do so with your eyes open."

Jeremy was frustrated by a different mode of working and by his lack of knowledge of Indian players. He found it impossible to operate "with his eyes open," using the metaphor of "seeing" to express his difficulty navigating an unfamiliar business culture. Through the discourse of transparency, foreign investors expressed their own ignorance of the Indian real estate market, its culture, and its participants. Simon admitted his own lack of local knowledge: "The local guy has the mindset, has the language, has the knowledge, has the way the deal is done in India, whereas a foreign company is learning that on a daily basis."

Not only foreigners used the term "transparency"; it has become a widespread idiom in India. For example, Rajesh, the vice president of an Indian real estate development firm that operates in the National Capital Region, characterized his own working methods by their lack of transparency. He was talking about "Indian work habits," and I asked him for an example. He said,

> Transparency. Transparency. When I come to the table, and I'm talking to a foreigner, I'm a little vague and I don't want to reveal all my cards. I don't know what I'm fearful of—maybe the information that I reveal may be used to, you know, either take away my money from me or my control of equity from me. Or something. Somehow, this foreigner will harm me. There's a fear at the back of my mind.

If Jeremy and Simon are concerned about control, so is Rajesh. His concerns stem from a way of working that privileges social connections. Rajesh continued,

> It's a way of thinking that up till now, what I have been doing is I know so-and-so minister, I can get this work done, but I don't want to share it. Otherwise all sorts of jokers will come to me. So I've got into a habit of thinking that whatever my connections or networks are, or my ways of getting things done are, is exclusive to me and I need to guard it. So that is who I have become, you know, in all my dealings, in all sectors of life that I go to.

Unlike large, multinational firms, managed through formalized, impersonal, and institutionalized processes (Chandler 1977; Yates 1989), Indian real estate firms are generally run by a single proprietor and his family. If the former operates through the mechanical objectivity of depersonalized business systems (Porter 1995), the later operates through networks of personal trust and discretion.[9] Rajesh accomplishes work using his personal connections to government officials, ministers, and others. In a system based on such personal networks and individualized interactions, he feels he needs to guard his contacts closely, lest "all sorts of jokers" attempt to exploit them (and him). He

feels his efficacy is based on the "exclusivity" of his contacts, and so guarded-
ness becomes part of his "work habit."

He went on to say that even when a potential partner shows interest—he
"comes along and says, 'I'm here, you guys are making money legitimately,
and I want to participate in it. Why don't you tell me all that there is to be said
and I'll take a call on that?'"—an Indian businessman will "not [be] revealing
all his cards at one go." He explained,

> Every time you come back to him, one little piece, which is then impact[ing]
> on the financial flow or the amount of equity that you need to bring in, or
> the timescale that you are required for you to bring in, somewhere, you are
> affected. "So why don't you tell me in the beginning?" So that's a work habit
> that was there.

In Rajesh's depiction, the Indian businessman metes out important details of
the deal as he sees fit, much to the frustration of his potential partner, who
asks, "So why don't you tell me in the beginning?" Information is power, and
the Indian developer, in this portrayal, controls the situation by controlling
the information he imparts.

The inconsistency that frustrated Simon and the mistrust that bothered
Jeremy are, according to Rajesh, elements of a commonplace interactive mode,
a "work habit" enabling Indian businessmen to guard contacts, maintain control, and test potential partners. Foreign investors' frustrations highlight divergent modes of doing business—or even just lack of social knowledge—
which investors saw as threats to the viability of partnerships and risks to
the productivity of capital. Foreign financiers' complaints about transparency
signal their own ignorance in such a market and the control Indian real estate
developers have maintained over real estate projects in which financiers are
anxious to invest.

Transparency as a Disciplinary Project

When foreign investors use the term "transparency"—or any number of related tropes of visibility, legibility, opacity, clarity, or cleanliness—they draw
on a prevalent discourse about "disclosure." For example, the *Economist* explains that transparency is "a buzz word for the idea that the more information
is disclosed about an economic activity the better" (*Economist*). Economists,
politicians, and powerful international organizations such as the World Bank,
among others, have propounded the idea that more information makes better
governments and markets, leading to economic development (see Hetherington 2011, 4, 156–8). As a result, the idea of transparency as disclosure has ani-

mated numerous political and business reforms: from the World Bank's "good governance" campaigns (Abrahamsen 2000), to the Right-to-Information Act in India (Webb 2013), to civil service reforms in the United Kingdom (John 2011; Miller 2003) and various measures of "corporate governance."[10]

Anthropologists have argued that the idea that "transparency" is merely a matter of "disclosure" hides the powerful disciplinary work that transparency projects perform. Building on James Scott's work on "legibility" (1998), anthropologists have shown that transparency projects do not merely seek to reveal information; they are themselves tools of power in that they simplify, standardize, and transform practices and people (Mahmud 2014, 155–186; Strathern 2000). Matthew Hull argues that "as political projects of civil society, transparency initiatives are attempts to turn the modernist regime of surveillance on government itself, not only to see the state but also to see like a state" (Hull 2008, 515).

Anthropologists have theorized transparency as a matter of state disciplinary projects and civil society resistance, but the investor complaints that I discuss above also point to transparency as a *corporate* disciplinary project. Similar to state projects, achieving corporate "transparency" does not entail merely "maximizing disclosure" but enacting far-reaching corporate change. As international political economist Jacqueline Best has written, "The call for a spirit of transparency is not so much an attempt to bare the economy's true face to the world as it is an attempt to remake that face the world over by *imposing new financial norms and practices*" (Best 2005, 144, my emphasis).

These new corporate procedures can be "agents for the creation of new kinds of subjectivity: self-managing individuals who render themselves auditable" (Shore and Wright 2000, 57). In her ethnography of the privatization of a baby-food factory in post-socialist Poland, for example, Elizabeth Dunn documents how corporate reforms implemented in the name of accountability and transparency reconfigure employee social relations, control workers, and transform them into "individual, partible, and 'privatized' persons" (2004, 127).

This understanding of transparency as a disciplinary project informs my argument that foreign investors, anxious to profit from Indian real estate projects, aim to impose financial practices on their Indian partner firms in order to better control them and transform them into legible intermediaries.[11] Calls for transparency may seem like neutral calls for information, but with corruption as the implied antonym to transparent, they carry a potent moral imperative (see Fourcade and Healy 2007; Garsten and Montoya 2008). By invoking "transparency," investors devalue their partners' practices and make their own business practices seem like universal standards, opening the way for corporate reform. As we shall see, the quest for transparency involves transforming how Indian developers organize and conduct their business as well as transforming their *person*—their practices, behavior, dress, and speech—in order to make them credible partners, solid links in an emerging chain of capital accumulation.[12]

Risky Investments

Complaints about "nontransparent" partners signal investors' lack of control in an unfamiliar context. "Risk" is a related term for capturing this unfamiliarity—but it also suggests the possibility of profit. Talking about transparency and risk, investors discredit Indian practices and people, even as they discursively create economic opportunities.

Suraj, the head of real estate in India for an American investment bank, explained to me that he thought his bank would soon set up a fund devoted exclusively to Indian investments because India was a "riskier" market than others.[13] According to Suraj, investing in Indian real estate amounts to "buying risk" because in India, "the market isn't transparent, it's not institutional, you're dealing with owner-driven development businesses." Note that here, Suraj, like other investors with whom I spoke, uses the term "transparent" to identify differences between international and Indian real estate practices; Indian firms are "owner-driven," not institutional, and he understands these differences as risks.

Suraj characterized the lack of transparency in Indian real estate as a "market failure":

> The market failures . . . are so dramatic that there's a huge opportunity for people in my business here. . . . Because there's just—there's a big market failure in terms of information. . . . It's the lack of transparency with land and the lack of transparency with everything else is—is, is, huge. . . . So if we can solve [that], [then] there's money to be made. That's the reason we're here. I think that's the reason *anyone* is here. Although they may or may not be able to articulate it, I'm sure . . . they [investors] instinctively recognize there's a big opportunity here.[14]

I interpret this passage to mean that Suraj sees opportunities to profit from the "market failures" and "lack of transparency" in the Indian market. When he says, "So if we can solve . . . ," I don't think he wants to eradicate such market failures ("solve" them in one sense) so much learn how to exploit them as an advantage ("solve" in another sense). In glossing problems with land and information in terms of transparency and "market failures," Suraj uses the language of transparency to negatively characterize Indian real estate markets as inefficient and imperfect.

However, "market failures" also provide a "big opportunity" for profit. An international property consultancy report summarizes the inverse relationship between risk/profit and transparency:

> To an investor, high transparency eases the free flow of information and capital, but also makes it harder to find undiscovered bargains or to earn a "risk premium." Efficient markets tend to display "convergence to the mean." Less transparent, inefficient markets tend to have a wider dispersion of results, which favor or penalize participants in the market, depending on which side of the trade they sit. (Jones Lang LaSalle 2006b, 3)

Like arbitrageurs who capitalize on price discrepancies, investors in Indian real estate hoped to capitalize on the "failures" of transparency in the Indian market. That is, they hope to turn risk into profit (cf. Zaloom 2006, 93). As EuroFund managing director Jeremy explained to me, "for the complexity and the difficulty of getting something done here [in India], you should be entitled to a somewhat greater return." Jeremy feels that a 20 percent after-tax return was "about the minimum I think is a reasonable level given the risks and complexities of investing in India today."

Similarly Suraj estimated that his fund could provide investors with returns 5 to 10 percent higher than they might earn elsewhere:[15]

> I think, in general, expect to deliver more than we would elsewhere. That's pretty much all we can say at this point. I think it would *have* to be somewhere in the region of 500 to 1,000 basis points, 5 to 10 percent higher in terms of overall return. Investors elsewhere expect—although I'm not necessarily sure it can be delivered—expect the 5 percent higher for India risk . . . They are significantly higher than risks that you would take in other countries because of the lack of market transparency and the fact that it *is* development, you know, the fact that there is construction capacity constraints, and all of that other stuff.

Financiers like Jeremy and Suraj (and apparently the investors whose money they manage) felt that they must "deliver" returns that *ought* to be higher in India, because of the way real estate markets in India operate (the "lack of market transparency") and because the buildings in which they are investing are not yet (and might never be) built. Suraj doesn't know if he can meet ("deliver" on) investors' expectations, as he went on to explain to me, because he is not sure if these expectations of higher return are warranted. Nevertheless, discourses about risk created possibilities for profit. Investors' expectations about "India risk" informed fund managers' negotiations with Indian developers over the value of land and the cost of capital; they helped fund managers justify charging a "risk premium."

Investors assumed that India real estate markets "lacked transparency" and were thus "risky" because they read the numerous international property consultancy reports that quantified and ranked that risk, using the mantle of economic expertise to authorize their pronouncements. For example, the Jones Lang LaSalle Global Real Estate Transparency Index rates countries on a scale of one to five, "opaque" to "highly transparent," in order "to help real estate market participants identify opportunities around the globe" and to "evaluate market risks" (Jones Lang LaSalle 2006b, 4).[16] Jones Lang LaSalle defines transparency explicitly in terms of what "the new generation of cross-border investors and occupiers typically seeks," including

- Accurate market and financial information
- Reliable performance benchmarks
- Enforceable contracts and property rights
- Clarity regarding the taxation and regulation of real estate
- Fair treatment in the transaction process
- Ethical standards among professionals hired to transact business (Jones Lang LaSalle 2006b, 3)

The index measures progress toward these investor demands through five "sub-index" measures that correlate well with the concerns of the investors I spoke with in India.

The Jones Lang LaSalle transparency rating identifies familiar and enforceable environments for international capital. The index identifies practices as well as information as necessary for creating a hospitable environment for investment, and implies that practices that don't meet international investors' standards are unfair, unethical, and unreliable. Not surprisingly, the "high transparency" markets include those in Europe, North America, and Australia, while the most "opaque" occupy Eastern Europe, Russia, and much of Latin America and Asia. "Transparency" labels markets that meet investor criteria; a low score discredits countries that vary from this norm.

Like the Jones Lang LaSalle report, investors used "transparency" to gloss a wide range of problems they saw in India: lack of information, bureaucratic uncertainty, and unacceptable business practices. First, they complained that statistical information about real estate projects was lacking. Second, foreign investors worried about uncertainties with land title; they did not want to find themselves with a property they did not own and thus could not sell. Third, investors saw the cash transactions and bribes routine to the Indian real estate business as risks because of international anti-bribery laws and investment regulations in their home countries. This was a matter of reputation as well as legality. EuroFund's controller explained to me that what he called the "culture of corruption" in India was a problem: "Our reputation means everything to us. We don't want one mistake in one far-flung office splashed across the front page of the *Wall Street Journal*. That would ruin us."

Finding information, getting permits, and checking land titles are all bureaucratically complex processes that require a great deal of local knowledge and social connections and which, even with such knowledge and connections, is fraught with uncertainty. Rather than rely on statistical indicators, Indian developers cultivate networks of people and accumulate experience in order to gauge prospective projects based on "gut feel." Similarly, dispelling land title risk involves a lot of legwork with village *patwaris*, local courts, police offices, and sub-registry offices of the Stamps and Registration Department.[17] Thus, investors' complaints signal their desire to divorce real estate development from local knowledge and social relations, to make an uneven terrain legible to outsiders like themselves (Scott 1998). They want to dissolve the economy of knowledge which they find themselves having to navigate—knowing full well that doing so would diminish the possibility of profits.[18]

Suraj's comments about "market failures," the Jones Lang LaSalle Global Real Estate Transparency Index, and complaints about land titles, bribes, and developers are all forms of "boundary work." As Thomas Gieryn argues in the context of scientific rhetoric, "when the goal is *monopolization* of professional authority and resources, boundary-work excludes rivals from within by defining them as outsiders with labels such as 'pseudo,' 'deviant,' or 'amateur'" (Gieryn 1983, 792, original emphasis). In this case, the labels "opaque," "non-transparent," or "unprofessional" do the work of identifying "outsiders." As "value-making acts" (Ferry 2013) or "value projects" (see Nakassis and Searle 2013), such labels devalue real estate practices in India while bolstering the value of investor expertise—but they also simultaneously increase the value of investing in India by highlighting (and perhaps even discursively creating) the kinds of risk that produce profit.

Financiers want to disentangle Indian land from the local bureaucratic procedures, networks of power, and knowledge that make it such a complex thing to trade. But while the idea of transparency suggests a simple freeing, the commoditizing project is really one of re-entangling land with new processes and social relations: investors' own. Thus, far from simply disclosing, transparency discourses enable foreign investors to transform their own lack of knowledge and local contacts into a sense that *Indian real estate markets are deficient but profitable*. Like the development hierarchies that investors invoked in the previous two chapters, investor complaints about a lack of transparency in India establish their own practices as superior and naturalize them as universals; they thus legitimize interference as "improvement."

Rendering Indian Developers Transparent: The Investment Process

Investors often projected their frustrations with Indian real estate markets onto Indian real estate *developers*, displacing ideas about things onto people. If investors need partners with the connections and knowledge to navigate the market—as Jones Lang LaSalle recommends, "knowledgeable, trustworthy advisors or local partners are especially important to help cross-border market participants navigate markets with lower transparency" (Jones Lang LaSalle 2006b, 3)—those same connections and knowledge mark their partners as possibly suspect and unruly.

Industry members use terms like "clean" and "transparent" in their analysis of developers' business procedures. An independent consultant explained that "clean" partners are hard to find:

> Indian developers are financially unsophisticated in terms of formal accounting systems. So you do the due diligence and all these gray areas crop up, that in the Indian context are not significant. But to the foreign investor, they're huge red flags. So transactions fail because of that. They [foreign investors] expect everything to be squeaky clean. But it's never squeaky clean. The transparency is not there.

By "formal accounting systems," the consultant means those of potential foreign investors: Indian developers do not engage in the same procedures as foreign investors.[19] Foreign funds remain accountable to investment committees in New York, London, and Hong Kong that vet potential investments. Even if a fund manager in India has become comfortable with the informalities of Indian business, investment committees need formal documentation and accounting that meets their requirements in order to approve projects.

Two consultants with one of the international real estate consultancies explained why deals often fall through:

CONSULTANT A: Somewhere down the line there is title clearance slip. Developer assures, "Everything is fine, everything is cleared." Legal division pulls out twenty question marks, developer cannot answer them. "No, no we will take care of it. We have people in the government offices."
CONSULTANT B: And you know they might actually take care of it.
CONSULTANT A: They will, but the investment committee cannot take it. They can't rest it [a deal] on a handshake.

The developers' way of working—"we have people in government offices"—
often does not meet the formal requirements of investment committees or
legal divisions, especially with major issues such as land title. Foreign firms
like written assurances, not verbal ones. As the representative of a pension
fund looking to invest in Indian real estate explained, his fund is looking for
Indian partners with both "a good reputation" and "proper internal structures." He concluded, "The partner needs to be institutionally friendly." In
short, foreign investors are concerned with a developer's ability to become
"institutionally friendly"—that is, to operate in a way that conforms to the
conventions and regulations of foreign investment committees.

When foreign investors discuss their partnership strategies, it is clear that
ensuring that conformity and gaining control are their main goals: they attempt to guarantee the return of their capital by changing the way their Indian
partners structure their companies and do business, rendering them legible,
acceptable partners whom they can control and from whom they can profit.
For example, one fund manager provided a tidy classification that mapped
length of operation to tractability:

> The established player doesn't want the value added. "I'll just take the money,
> thanks." The emerging player is getting lots of opportunities, so you need to
> help him stay focused on what you're doing. The new developers—you need
> to help them set up an organization.

By "value added," he means the advice and organizational interference that a
new developer might be more willing to accept. Keeping an "emerging player
focused" means controlling the projects he works on. Another fund manager
told me that his fund specifically sought out "new developers," precisely because they are more easily molded:

> We are trying to pick up new developers, because, you know, certain people
> have done certain things and their mindsets are now fixated. But there are a
> lot of new young guys who want to do certain things, who have more fire in
> their belly. So you're trying to incubate those kind of development compa-
> nies, and saying, we will provide you capital, we will provide you our global
> perspective.

Again, by "global perspective," he means advice. He felt that a new company,
working on its first or second project, "will have a huge desire to execute it
well" but will not yet be "fixated" on a particular way of doing business. This
bodes well for the investor's chances of controlling how the project is done
and achieving a return on his investment.

Suraj has also had luck working with "start-up" firms.[20] He told me his first deal was with a young firm, enabling him to have "a significant hand in the development of the organization." Suraj told the firm's owner that he wanted him to focus on acquiring land and building relationships, and to hire a CEO to run the company. He told him, "You've got to hire a CEO that will to do X, Y, and Z, and you're never going to be that CEO." Although this was "a difficult thing for anyone to hear," the partner complied, transforming the organizational structure of his firm into a corporation run by a CEO and Board of Directors, something familiar to Suraj's fund's investment committee.

Suraj has been surprised to find Indian developers "open" to such demands. He concluded,

> They're [Indian developers] all focused on the idea of creating value for themselves. They're very entrepreneurial and capitalist in that sense, and to the extent that you are ah—and even if it means an ostensible lack of control, I think they're, they're—the surprising answer is that they're really willing to give it up in the face of potential value creation for themselves.

The "value created" through tie-ups and public offers includes both prestige and profit. Investors believe developers are interested enough in such value to give up control of their own firms.

When Indian real estate developers refuse to adopt foreign investors' working methods, they can lose out. The senior vice president of an American private equity firm, an Indian man, told me about a deal that fell through. The project looked promising—approvals in place, land with a single owner, good location—when, "suddenly we realized the partner doesn't have the mindset in which we want to operate. He was a local guy." Note how he uses local-ness to cast doubt on his potential partner. Explaining the differences in "mindset" between his international investment firm and the "local guy," he said,

> We want to bring in certain systems and processes. We want to have certain disclosure norms. We want to have how we'll monitor the certain project. Maybe we want a project manager team, we want a certain level of, you know, people with certain credentials to manage each of the projects.

The Indian developer questioned the cost of hiring professional managers and tracking systems, so the US investors, concerned that they would not be able to achieve a level of control over the design and construction process that made them comfortable about investing their money, backed out.

Some Indian developers choose not to subject themselves to investor controls. For example, Govind, a developer in the National Capital Region, had been approached by various foreign investors (Morgan Stanley, Merrill Lynch, Trikona Capital, and others) but was ambivalent about foreign direct investment. He found potential investors' reservations to his way of working unrealistic, commenting "It's a very *homegrown* industry, the real estate industry. There's no *set* norms, there's no set rules—you can't go by, there is no *by the book* over here. You can't do it by the book." He doesn't believe real estate can be done in India in a formal, "by the book" manner. He told me he would rather hire an international consultant than work with a partner who would insist on change:

> Why do you need a strategic partner, you know, who will tell you how to do things and say "OK, now"—there is too much interference. See this is a very delicate issue. You are used to a particular way of functioning, you have professionalized your set up, but still you want independent decision making because that is what sees you through real fast. So right from day one, getting so much of interference is not going to be very easy because you are, you know, you have be conditioned to a particular way of functioning. So changing yourself overnight is not possible.

He had yet to agree to a joint venture with a foreign firm because he was wary of such "interference." He did not want to give up his "independent decision making," his ability to move quickly to take advantage of opportunities, and his usual ways of working. In short, he did not want to give up control over his firm.[21]

Going Public

Many developers, however, *have* formed a joint venture with a foreign investment company, or they have taken their company public, attracting foreign investors to buy shares through a listing on the Bombay Stock Exchange. Both avenues to investment require some change on the part of the developer. Just as a joint venture often necessitates loss of control, listing on the stock exchange ("going for an IPO") requires meeting the stringent disclosure requirements of the Securities and Exchange Board of India. A large number of Indian realty and construction firms listed on the Bombay Stock Exchange in 2006 and 2007 (table 5.1). In addition, the London Stock Exchange Alternative Investment Market (AIM) attracted public offers from the Indian firms K Raheja (Ishaan Real Estate), Hiranandani Constructions (Hirco), Unitech (Unitech Corporate Parks), India Bulls (Dev Property), and West Pioneer Properties. In 2007, the press reported many other firms planning initial public offers (e.g., Hussain 2007a, 2008a; Sukumar 2007).

Prior to the initial public offer, these firms often attract private equity (PE) investment from firms such as Citibank, Morgan Stanley, Lehman Brothers,

TABLE 5.1. Selected real estate and construction firms on the Bombay Stock Exchange.

	Issue	Issue Amount
Company	Opening Date (day/month/year)	(Rs. millions)
Sadbhav Engineering Ltd.	03.02.2006	536.5
Pratibha Industries Ltd.	16.02.2006	514.2
B. I. Kashyap & Sons Ltd.	20.02.2006	2,000.2
Tantia Constructions Ltd.	27.03.2006	217.5
D. S. Kulkarni Developers Ltd.	25.04.2006	1,336.5
Patel Engineering Ltd.	03.05.2006	4,250.0
Unity Infraprojects Ltd.	19.05.2006	2,324.0
GMR Infrastructure Ltd.	31.07.2006	7,885.0
Gayatri Projects Ltd.	26.09.2006	855.5
Lanco Infratech Ltd.	06.11.2006	10,673.4
Parsvnath Developers Ltd.	06.11.2006	10,897.7
Sobha Developers Ltd.	23.11.2006	5,691.7
Akruti Nirman Ltd.	15.01.2007	3,618.0
C&C Constructions Ltd.	05.02.2007	1,242.4
Abhishek Mills Ltd.	20.02.2007	410.0
Orbit Corp. Ltd.	20.03.2007	1,001.0
DLF Ltd.	11.06.2007	91,875.0
Roman Tarmat Ltd.	12.06.2007	507.5

Source: Adapted from Builders' Association of India photocopy, "Real Estate Industry," n.d.

Old Lane, Trinity Capital, Quantum, etc. Chetan, a public relations agent who has worked with many real estate firms during the listing process explained,

> In the last one year, PE [private equity] interest has changed the whole thing. They're advising. They bring X money and say, "Listen to us." And developers listen because they know that if their value goes up, they'll make money. So those guys are forced to listen to them. It's mutually beneficial. We also come in there. A lot of PEs know what a PR [public relations] agency can do in terms of producing the right profile.

Private equity investors promise to transform Indian real estate companies, enlisting public relations firms to give them the "right" profile to attract foreign investors. In short, private equity firms promise to make Indian developers both credible and profitable by making them legible to international investors. After the private equity firm, in conjunction with its international investment banking partners and public relations firms, works with the Indian real estate developer to change his company's internal structure (adopting a board of directors, hiring professional financial officers, putting in place construction monitoring or other business systems) and its accounting practices, the private equity firm will take the development company public and sell their shares at a profit. For example, Citigroup Global Markets had stakes in real estate developer DS Kulkarni, which went public in May 2006. Delhi Land and Finance attracted $600 million investments from DE Shaw and Company and Lehman Brothers Holdings, Inc. before its initial public offer in June 2007 (Raja D. 2008b). Similarly, Emaar MGF had garnered investments from Citibank, New York Life, and JP Morgan.

While Chetan's firm works on the public relations aspect of the listing, building up the real estate firm's reputation in the business papers with rosy feature stories, profiles, and advertisements, the private equity firm's other consultants go to work on the developer's books. Chetan recounted one developer who had yet to tie up with a private equity fund:

> We had one small guy [developer], he wanted to raise money, so he called us. He said, How do we go about it? I asked him, [developer's name], have you done any valuation of your company? He asked me, what is it? (Laughter.) So I said, look, what we can do is, you put some of these PE [private equity] funds or merchant bankers on to you. They will advise you how to go about it.[22]

This developer's firm is an unknown quantity, an entirely unvalued asset vis-à-vis global capital; in fact, the developer does not even know what a valuation is.[23] Chetan suggests that private equity funds and merchant bankers will teach him how to do a valuation, thus beginning the process of making his firm a globally recognizable entity so that he can raise more capital.

Many Indian real estate companies keep such a large percentage of their income in black money that outside auditors, examining their "official" accounts, would severely undervalue them—a problem since the private equity fund wants a high valuation at the time of the initial public offer so that the developer's shares will fetch a high initial price. Exactly how international consultants and auditors clean up developers' books was a process that few of my informants admitted to understanding. A young consultant with an international consultancy commented that it was a process of "financial engineering by the good old people of the top five consulting firms, audit firms." Another informant commented that Indian real estate firms have been declaring their black assets over a period of a few years, resulting in what look like sudden and extraordinary profits.[24]

The private equity firms, bankers, lawyers, and public relations firms involved in the initial public offer not only launder the company's books; they also clean up the director himself. "Going public" requires an entirely new communicative orientation for the developer, who must now address new audiences—representatives of investment banks, institutional investors like pension funds, and Indian brokerage houses—in new forums.[25] Consultants train developers how to operate under Security and Exchange Board of India regulations and how to act in front of these new audiences. For example, developers are prohibited by law from speaking about projects that are not listed in their initial public offer prospectuses. Chetan described developers' typical pre-listing attitude: "In India, the CEOs and proprietors and directors, chairman, they take their liberty: it's my company, I can speak whatever I want." However, "once you are planning to raise money from the public, you have to be careful. You have to be—you cannot say anything which you cannot substantiate in the offer document." Reiterating this lesson to developers, practicing question-and-answer sessions with them before press conferences and investor presentations, and monitoring their public statements, Chetan and his associates are imparting a new form of discipline, teaching them the interactional style required of the chairman of a listed company and preparing them for a new mode of publicity.

Coached by merchant bankers, private equity firms, and public relations agents, Indian real estate developers have thus begun conforming to international accounting, interactional, and business systems' norms. Conformity—and the international credibility it engenders—is extremely profitable. Omaxe grossed Rs. 550 crore, Delhi Land and Finance more than Rs. 9,000 crore, Purvankara more than Rs. 1,250 crore, and Parsvnath about Rs. 1,000 crore from their respective public offers (Jha and Guha 2007b).[26]

The process of making an Indian developer legible considerably raises the value of the firm—and of the investments a private equity firm has previously made. For example, the venture capital branch of Citigroup, Citi Venture Capital International, sold 40 percent of its stake in Emaar MGF to the investment firm DE Shaw before Emaar MGF's public listing at a price based on the valuation of Emaar MGF shares for the listing. At this price, Citi Venture had increased the value of its investment by 3.5 times between November 2006 and January 2008, that is, in just over a year (Raja D. 2008a).[27] Three other firms also invested in Emaar MGF just before the public offer to cash in on the expected post-public offer rise in the share price.[28]

Incorporated as a joint venture in 2005, Emaar MGF had not completed any construction by February 2008, when the public offer was scheduled. It had built no properties. The buying and selling of its shares prior to the public offer constitutes speculation on the worth of the company (based on its land) and the future rents it planned to accrue through buildings it had yet to build, or, perhaps merely on the continued buoyancy of the Indian stock market and the glamour of Indian real estate.[29] Chetan corroborated the idea that the value of the company raised through the initial public offer process has little to do with a developer's productive activities (construction or land conversion), but with his firm's image, which public relations firms like Chetan's help to establish. Chetan's work—like that of the bankers, accountants, and private equity analysts who make Indian real estate companies legible, and thus investable—may not be the labor of constructing buildings, but it is the work that makes spectacular accumulation possible.

Conclusion

Foreign investment is in not just a matter of moving money, but of transforming the object of investment—in this case, Indian firms (and as we'll see in future chapters, Indian buildings)—so that, in fact, they can be invested in. Financiers do so in order to produce legible, investable, tractable partners who can help them navigate what they see as an unfamiliar—and thus profitable—market. Fund managers attempt to control their partners through engendering conformity to international business practices. Fund managers like Suraj attempt to standardize their potential partners' operations by dictating the terms of their joint ventures and using intermediaries such as investment bankers and PR firms like Chetan's to provide them with the tools for projecting a new image. Thus "transparency" is not merely a state in which more information is available, nor is it something that only states and citizen-activists are interested in imposing. Transparency is a persuasive model of business organization, personal appearance, and interaction. Investors struggle to impose this model on their Indian partners in order to transform them into acceptable intermediaries who can help them turn "India risks" into profits.

Yet transparency is the language that investors use to maintain differences between international and Indian practices, land, markets, and people, even as they try to standardize them. Investors use transparency discourses to describe the risks of working in India and the frustrations they feel in forging partnerships over difference, thus signaling both financiers' disciplinary project and their struggles in implementing it. The moral tones of the discourse, its connections with institutions of global governance, and its resonance with colonial stereotypes about the untrustworthiness of subaltern others make it a useful tool in the boundary work that investors do to convince potential partners to change. The discourse serves to naturalize those changes, making them seem universal, unproblematic, even morally upright.

The fact that Rajesh, the vice president of a development firm in the National Capital Region, used the term "transparency" to describe his own activities with no prompting from me suggests that this discourse has been taken up by Indian developers themselves. However, not all Indian developers want the "transparency" that comes with an international partnership; many, like Govind, see it as a loss of control and as a threat to their ability to generate profits. As I show in the next chapter, Indian developers do not merely blindly comply with investor demands—for as we have seen, investors' complaints register their frustrations; rather, they use international investment to advance their own value projects, which combine attracting international capital with constructing local prestige.

Developers' Quest for Credibility and Capital

Developer's Credibility Problems

In the 2006 Bollywood comedy *Khosla ka Ghosla*, the realtor Khuranna steals the plot of land in which the middle-class hero, K. K. Khosla, has invested his life savings.[1] The two couldn't be more different. Khosla is soft-spoken, polite, and anxious, while Khuranna blusters and yells. The former lives in a modest house in Delhi; the latter in a palatial suburban home with a skylit dome, columns, and interior fountains. The former has painstakingly saved a lifetime of earnings from his salaried job; the latter has grown rich swindling people of their property.

The film pits Khuranna against another character: an actor playing a Dubai-based Non-Resident Indian (NRI) named Sethi, who Khosla's children are hoping will lure Khuranna into a fraudulent land sale, producing the money they need to get their father's plot back from Khuranna. Khosla's children provide the actor with all of the props of a successful NRI: a Mercedes with a driver, an obsequious secretary, two mobile phones, and a suite at a five-star hotel. When they meet for the first time, Sethi is aloof and cool, dressed in a dark suit with a silk cravat. Khuranna slouches in his chair, his shirt unbuttoned to reveal his gold chain. A driving cap is angled sportily on his head. He fingers his sunglasses and his oversized Nokia 9500 phone.

It is clear that Khuranna admires Sethi, taking his stiff formality (a byproduct of the actor's discomfort with the deception) as a sign of superiority. In one of the last scenes of the movie, Khuranna has invited Sethi back to his house for a drink. Sethi sits upright in his seat while Khuranna leans forward and drunkenly admits, "*Mera problem kya hai, sir, abhi bhi mai piche ho jata hai*." (My problem is, sir, that even now I am behind / I haven't progressed). He makes a face and looks at his associate, hovering in the background, "*Choti log ki company hai na sir*" ([It's because] I keep company with inferior types).

He follows Sethi out to the car, urging him to become his real estate partner. When Sethi drives away without responding, Khuranna wanders into the lawn to take a leak.

Khuranna presents an unflattering stereotype of the developer. He is crude and dishonest, with unfortunately low-class habits: he hikes his trousers, scratches his crotch, and laughs with a splutter. He embodies the popular perception of real estate developers that many developers themselves would like to overcome. Indian real estate developers have never enjoyed a good reputation, but today they face a new problem: living up to the expectations, demands, and operating protocols of potential foreign partners used to interacting with "transparent" corporations run by CEOs and boards of directors.

While these new partnerships present problems, Indian developers have also embraced investors' calls for increased transparency because they coincide with their own project for self-improvement and their desire to be seen as world-class professionals, not real-life Khurannas. That desire is also stoked by other concerns. The entrance of Indian corporations into real estate highlights the noncorporate status of most developers. In addition, because of changing middle-class aspirations, they find themselves on the wrong side of the divide between the persona of businessman and that of professional. Their reputation as shady businessmen has also hurt their ability to gain Indian consumers' trust (see chapter 8 for a more complete discussion of this problem). Thus, Indian real estate developers' quest for international finance is also a quest for local respect.

Similar to Bollywood filmmakers' attempts to "gentrify" film production (Ganti 2012a), Indian developers seek to upgrade their image and rationalize their businesses. This value project entails telling a narrative about industry transformation and displaying a range of emblems of professionalism, world-class status, and transparency. This image work is central to their attempts to attract both investors *and* consumers, and thus to accumulate capital and create domestic and international markets. More than just a cynical attempt to garner foreign investment, moreover, I argue that the Indian developers with whom I worked used foreign investment itself as a sign of credibility to do their own interactional work in domains beyond capital accumulation.

While striving for respectability, however, many developers also defended practices that foreign investors, local activists, and others within the industry discredited, betraying an ambivalence wrought by their own structural position as liminal intermediaries about their projects of self-fashioning. They simultaneously summoned the figure of the transparent, global professional *and* the corrupt local fixer in interactions with me and with others in the industry. Here, I explain this paradoxical self-presentation as a function of

Indian developers' position in the market. As intermediaries to global capital, real estate developers find themselves caught in a double bind: in order to participate in the international market in Indian real estate, they need to appear "clean" and "transparent," yet their position as intermediaries requires that they do the "dirty" work of land agglomeration that, at the same time, continually marks them as not-quite-global players.

A Murky Business

Almost everyone I met described real estate as a "murky business" populated by untrustworthy scam artists. For example, a journalist on the real estate beat for a major business daily provided this unprompted description as she gave me advice for contacting and interviewing Indian developers:

> Real estate is an unorganized sector so the rules applied to interviewing people are not the same. A lot of these people don't even understand English. They are not transparent. They don't keep proper audited balance sheets. So you have to pressurize them to get the real figures.

For this journalist, being "not transparent" involves more than just shady accounting practices; indeed, the journalist disparages a style of interaction she sees as secretive and downright ignorant. Moreover, the journalist casts aspersions on developers' class backgrounds; she writes for an English-language publication but she thinks developers "don't even understand English." Hence different "rules" apply to interviewing them: talking with a real estate developer is not a conversation but an interrogation requiring that one "pressurize," that is, apply pressure, to get "real" information. She advised me, "You can't just take what they give you. You have to ask hard and tough questions." Linking "transparency" to class, language, interactional practices, and intelligence, she suggests that developers are crass, ignorant, devious, unprofessional, and nontransparent people.

This multivalent use of "transparency" to suggest a range of characterological features seems to exceed the ways in which scholars have conceptualized "transparency." Indeed, in what follows, I argue that "transparency" is more than a state where more is visible, as business discourses suggest, or a disciplinary project of transforming procedures and thus controlling people, as I suggested in the last chapter (see John 2011; Mahmud 2014; Strathern 2000): it is also a figure of personhood, a stereotypic type of person that one can perform semiotically.[2] In order to understand developers' attempts to perform "transparency," we must first trace how real estate came to be associated with negative figures of personhood by looking at the history and structure of the industry. Characteristics of real estate firms—practitioners' varied backgrounds, their association with the black economy, and their organization as family-run enterprises—marked them as nontransparent and nonprofessional in 2006.

Established firms in the National Capital Region today started as construction (e.g., Ansals, 1967) or engineering firms (e.g., Unitech, 1972) in the 1960s or 1970s, executing contracts for the government, the largest building client before economic liberalization (Namburu 2007; Surendar and Sinha 2008). In the late 1940s, Delhi Land and Finance (DLF), arguably the first property development company in Delhi, began selling plots of land to individuals in the wake of the influx of partition refugees. The firm developed approximately eighteen residential colonies (or neighborhoods) in South and West Delhi before the 1957 Delhi Development Act prohibited private real estate development in the capital (Damodaran 2008, 284–87; Kacker 2005).

A number of Indian construction, engineering, and architectural firms first worked in the Middle East and North Africa in the 1970s and 1980s. For example, Delhi-based Unitech and Bombay-based Kalpataru both began as engineering and construction firms; the former had significant contracts in Libya and the latter was based in the United Arab Emirates between 1974–1982 (Damodaran 2008, 37; Kalpataru Group) Charting an illustrative trajectory, PNC Menon, from Kerala, moved to Oman to do interior decorating in late 1970s and then started construction firms in Oman, United Arab Emirates, and Qatar. He moved to Bangalore in 1995 at the height of the last real estate bubble and established Sobha Developers. With his earnings from taking the company public on the Bombay Stock Exchange in 2006, he made the *Forbes* billionaire list in 2007. The firm now constructs projects all over India, including in the National Capital Region (*Forbes* 2007; Sobha Developers).

With the exception of Delhi Land and Finance, whose proprietors are Hindu-Jats (agriculturalists), real estate has traditionally attracted entrepreneurs from upper-caste Hindu mercantile communities.[3] There are few Muslims in the industry; two prominent exceptions are Irfan Razack's Prestige Group in Bangalore and Siraj Lokhandwala's Lokhandwala Construction in Mumbai. Both men come from trading communities, the Memons and Bohras, respectively (Namburu 2007, 218).

Like other Indian businesses, real estate firms have been run as family concerns, with sons joining their fathers in business after their education. Often sons will informally divide responsibilities within the company, for example, one looking after sales and the other construction. These divisions sometimes become part of the corporate structure, with brothers each heading an arm of the company, and, occasionally, separate companies.

Indian real estate firms are usually managed centrally, by the proprietor and/or his sons. Rather than formalized systems of control which diffuse decision-making capability through the company to people in defined roles, these promoter-owners make even minor decisions at all levels of the corporate structure. As a result, the identity of the owner is intertwined with the identity of the firm; brand names rely on the highly publicized celebrity status of a firm's owners.[4] The media perpetuates this cult of the owner, profiling K.P. Singh (DLF), R. Chandra (Unitech), D. S. Kulkarni (DSK Group), among others.[5]

Especially before the late 1990s, Indian developers financed their projects through personal connections (see chapter 1). In order to buy land, they asked acquaintances to co-invest. It was also common to partner with landowners, and a few appealed to large Indian corporate houses for funding.[6] The son of one developer described how his father, when he moved to Delhi in the 1990s, had difficulty finding financing because "he didn't know anyone. Delhi is a close-knit, cliquey society. . . . He only had a few friends." He eventually convinced one friend, a jeweler, to bankroll his farmhouse development, and he also used the jeweler's personal contacts to sell the houses. The architect Bimal Patel describes a typical transaction in Ahmedabad, in which the developer's acquaintance, a textile trader, lent 80 percent of the money needed upfront for land at 18 percent interest; in addition, he received 40 percent of the final profits from the project. The developer and his financier agreed on these terms without drawing up written documents (Patel 1995, 31–38).

Real estate developers also depended on brokers to bankroll construction by buying blocks of property in advance (Kumar 1982, 2002), or they financed building construction (and sometimes land purchase) through pre-sales. Today, condominium buyers often pay for their apartments in installments, with payments due as the concrete slab is poured for each floor of the building. As the building goes up, the money to build it rolls in. Often pre-sales were conducted by word-of-mouth. In Patel's example, the developer only presold apartments to buyers who knew at least one other person the developer trusted (Patel 1995, 36).

Alongside gold and movies, property has long occupied a key position in the circulation of "black" or untaxed cash assets. Although the "black" or untaxed economy in India is vast—Kumar estimates that it accounted for 40 percent of GDP in 1995 and that it still extends into almost all aspects of life (Kumar 2002, 72)[7]—the real estate sector's dependence on black money and undeclared interests has contributed to popular perception of it as a "murky business." As Patel suggests, "for most lay people it is not entirely clear what it is that developers do, how they profit from development, and how they are able to amass large fortunes in relatively short periods of time" (Patel 1995, 42). One real estate lobbyist estimated that, even today, "eighty to eighty-five percent of this sector is unrecorded, black money. Even government doesn't have an idea what is the total worth of the sector." The lobbyist conflates a lack of statistical knowledge with tax evasion and suggests further impropriety. Like other negative terms carrying a heavy moral charge, the term "black money" suggests criminality, even though "black" profits can be made through legal transactions.[8]

Even industry members described developers' reputations derisively. I spoke to a Bombay-based developer at a conference who evoked America's "Wild West" to explain the lawlessness of Indian real estate. He acted out the iconic shady deal—all whispers and nods—and claimed that developers used to get money "from a guy in a white shirt and white pants, sitting at a table with a stack of cash and a gun." This association with politics (as indexed by the man in white) both stemmed from a lack of formal funding and perpetuated it. As a veteran real estate consultant explained,

> There was no funding which was available to the developers: no bank or a financial institution would touch a real estate project with a barge pole. Real estate was a dirty word. A developer is bound to be a crook, and you could use some other word. . . . But I'm just saying, you know—unreliable, and real estate market was operated by local brokers and everything. So there was no funding.

Thought to be a "crook" or an "unreliable" local broker, a real estate developer could not access institutional funding. Conversely, his lack of formal, "white" financial backing contributed to his association with illegal practices.

Real estate developers do sometimes earn their unsavory reputations. As they agglomerate land, real estate developers accrue not only unrecorded capital gains ("black money" in one sense) but also the proceeds of violence, intimidation, and fraud ("black money" in the more inclusive sense).[9] Developers are notorious for using brute force, intimidation, and deceit to obtain land (see Carney 2008; Reddy and Reddy 2007). Developers routinely operate through subsidiary companies and agents to hide their interest, subvert land ownership regulations, and obtain better prices from farmers. They "flex their muscles" with reluctant landowners—either by sending in thugs or by exploiting government connections.

One informant told me that Delhi Land and Finance coerced his uncle into selling land in Gurgaon by sending him letters, purportedly from the Haryana authorities, informing him that his land was to be taken by eminent domain at a low price. This story is consistent with evidence that has since surfaced that Haryana Chief Minister Bhupinder Hooda's administration threatened to acquire 1,350 acres land for "public purpose" from farmers at low rates between 2006 and 2008; the land was never used for public purposes but instead licensed to builders who used the threat of state capture to convince landowners to sell cheaply. The administration then allowed builders to violate density and minimum project size requirements, to build on environmentally restricted sites, and to acquire permits without proper documentation (Singh 2013). Politicians like Hooda often profit from speculation themselves, blocking or speeding up the approval process for their own gain.[10]

Land acquisition politics have intensified with the skyrocketing prices in land. Simultaneously, rising land values have transformed real estate into a highly visible and lucrative business since 2000, luring entrepreneurs from other fields to join the construction rush.[11] Relatively new firms in the National Capital Region include those whose promoters were contractors (Unity Group, Som Dutt Builders); engineers (Ashiana Housing and Finance, ATS Infrastructure); returned NRIs (Silverglades, Malibu Towne); brokers (Parsvnath); or employees of more established real estate companies (Vipul). One developer, who had worked in the US and Saudi Arabia, returned to India to be closer to his family but was dissatisfied helping with his father's jewelry manufacturing business. He remembered, "I went to buy a house and saw the price rise three times in three months. I thought to myself, I'm in the wrong business!" So he bought land and eventually began building high-rises and villas. Some developers started their firms to exploit land they had inherited or acquired for investment (Vatika, Suncity, MGF, and Raheja). They began selling one- or two-acre plots to individuals for building "farmhouses,"[12] and later constructed multistory buildings and commercial complexes.

Other non-real estate related businesses and industrial houses have diversified into real estate, continuing a trend that began in the early 1990s (Sheth 1993): the consumer electronics company Videocon now runs Videocon Realty and Infrastructure; the Essel Group, which also includes Zee Entertainment and DishTV, controls a stake in Suncity Developers; the Jaypee Group, an engineering, cement, and hydropower company, has been developing hotels and townships in the National Capital Region; and the Luxor Group diversified into real estate in 2003 from manufacturing and importing pens by investing heavily in commercial real estate projects in the National Capital Region with the Uppal Group. Other large companies have turned extensive landholdings into new assets by developing them. For example, the industrial conglomerate Tata Group developed a full-fledged real estate and infrastructure business in 2007, beginning by developing excess land owned by its group companies (Unnikrishnan and Pandey 2007).

Such large corporations with established brand names cast a shadow of doubt on smaller developers whose operations are not corporatized and highlight the historical legacies which cloud the industry's reputation. Overall, the heterogeneous backgrounds of industry members and their involvement with the black economy have led to a situation in which developers have historically been stereotyped as untrustworthy and even criminal.

Boundary Work

On the one hand, the entrance of large, trusted Indian corporations such as Tata, Godrej, and Reliance and of "professionals" from other businesses—and of course the industry's sudden profitability—has given the industry a certain legitimacy, or even "glamour," as one consultant described it. On the other hand, the entrance of "corporates" has made industry members sensitive to the industry's lack of professional status, which they often gloss with the term "disorganized." This is a negatively loaded catch-all that refers to lack of regulation, lack of barriers to entry, numerous small firms, and black-market connections. Chetan, who has done public relations for several real estate firms, summed up the situation: the "reality sector in India has a bad name. Mostly localized people and a lot of black-money-handling people and [there] is, like, nobody to regulate: it is disorganized."

Avinash, a consultant, discredited one Delhi-area developer as "a scamster. He's a petty contractor. They've never delivered. And the staff—it's all his family, friends, and relatives. They're making tons of money, but the major portion of their sales proceeds come in black." Note that Avinash's comments conflate person and company. He substantiates "scamster" with the developer's background as a contractor, his recent entry into the business ("they've never delivered"), his hiring of family members, and his reliance on black profits. Indeed, many developers are new to the business and rely on kin networks and informal sources of finance. These common characteristics are now perceived as liabilities. Inversely, Avinash's negative descriptors point to new markers of credibility: professionalism defined by white/check dealings, hiring educated nonrelative employees, and a construction track record.

Avinash's disparaging remarks are a form of "boundary work," an attempt to construct authority by drawing rhetorical boundaries between oneself and others (Gieryn 1983; Ganti 2012b). As Indian developers distinguish themselves by disparaging their competition, they often tarnish the image of the industry as a whole. For example, the corporate communications manager for the Indian firm Taneja Developers and Infrastructure publicly called for more regulation of the industry in an editorial in the *Hindustan Times*, complaining, "While reputed developers have zipped through the learning curve to become professionally competent, many fly-by-night operators draw attention through their lack of transparency and inflated land bank claims" (Michael 2007). Using the same language as many foreign investors, he attempts to distance himself from "fly-by-night" or "nontransparent" developers and distinguish himself as among the "professionally competent." In so doing, he contributes to the general image of the industry as unprofessional, inexperienced, and shady.

Similarly, the rash of inexperienced entrants to the industry bothered Gurdeep, the marketing director for a Gurgaon-based real estate developer:

> I just hope that people are realizing that it's not as easy, just building. I mean, you know, these days in building construction specifically, there are agents, there are brokers who have become developers. It's our core business. I mean, we can't tomorrow be going into mining or setting up a telecom company just like that, but people who used to sell property for us, three years back or four years back, are making buildings, and talking about high technology and all that, but this is all crap from my point of view.

He emphasizes that real estate development is a specialized industry: "It's not as easy (as they think), (it's not) just building" and that development is his "core business" and expertise (by contrast to a broker who has recently ventured into construction). Here he exploits the other key marker of developer credibility: the ability to construct buildings, in local parlance, to "deliver." The labels "broker" and "landowner" pin a competitor as merely a dealer, not a constructor. By using these labels, the marketing director questions his competitors' construction ability and thus their capacity for making good on their promises; he questions their integrity as people, not just as companies.

Ironically, this informant later told me that his firm had started as a landholding company. Before 1999, "we used to sell farm lands to people, one acre each, two acres, and people used to build their farmhouses." While he derides brokers-cum-developers, his firm began as "just a business house which was selling land." What is the difference between "just a business house" and a broker? *Claims* to expertise matter, especially when they can be backed up. From a swivel chair at a blonde wood conference table in a modern office with polished black floors, Gurdeep could point (in English) to his firm's private equity deals with major foreign banks and its completed projects as evidence of credibility. He compared his company with others, estimating that in terms of millions of square feet completed, they were well ahead of Omaxe and Parsvnath, and "third in India behind DLF and Unitech." In addition to delivery, Gurdeep himself commanded the proper registers of speech and dress to embody the kind of transparency and capability that he accused other developers of lacking.

As Indian developers compete for investors and consumers, they delineate boundaries between real estate development and "just building," between brokerage and construction expertise, between themselves and their "fly-by-night" competition in a "disorganized" industry. Where the boundary falls could determine who signs up with a prestigious, foreign fund for a multimillion dollar project and who does not.

Aspiring Professionals

Reputation is a matter of attracting business, but it is also deeply personal, a matter of status and pride. Industry members narrated to me the personal difficulties they faced countering the perception that real estate was not "professional." For example, Ashish, a veteran real estate consultant who entered the industry in the 1990s, told me that his family had been appalled by his decision, especially as he had been educated abroad. He described his early experiences,

> Wherever I went it was a bit embarrassing because you went to parties and they would say, "Oh, you are a broker?" "No, no, no, but we are professionals and everything." I think first two years, specially first two to three years, were very very tough, personally . . . starting the business from scratch, nobody knows the brand in the market. They didn't understand that real estate could be done professionally.

Note his embarrassment at being called a broker in social settings, and how difficult he found it to repair this reputational damage when popular perception pitted "real estate" against "professional." For him, the challenges of starting a business coincided with the personal challenge of forging a professional identity in real estate.

Being a professional is all the more important in India today. With the rise of white-collar employment in the service sector since liberalization, the Indian middle class has reoriented its aspirations from government employment to banking and multinational corporate jobs (Fernandes 2006). This shift has expanded the definition of "professional" from the professions (doctors, lawyers, engineers, civil servants, teachers)—many of which traditionally included the self- or government-employed—creating a desirable new persona: the figure of the high-earning, educated professional associated with international corporations, the new economy, and white money (similar to the imagined consumers discussed in chapter 4).

The "professional" is a transparent kind of person: educated, corporate, paid in "white" money. As a social type, the figure of the "professional" was defined in contrast with the "businessman"—since liberalization recast as a shady, uncouth trader, a small-time operator associated with pre-liberalization business practices and the black market (see Bijapurkar 2007, 213). While real estate developers have long been stigmatized, they have come to stand in as the exemplar of the category of businessman and thus as the opposite of "professional." Real estate developers, then, find themselves on the wrong side of a widening chasm of respectability.[13]

Information technology workers embodied the "professional" for the Indian developers with whom I spoke.[14] Indeed, Indian real estate developers often compared real estate with the information technology industry and found themselves lacking. For example, one developer explained to me that the information technology industry "is all professionals. It's all the IT and the engineers and managers. Totally. See, nobody can enter there. No free player can enter there." By contrast, with real estate development, "it's like anybody and everybody can—anybody with a huge stretch of land can build a township, you know." For the developer, an industry with "professionals" is one that is closed to most people; real estate's openness to "anybody with a huge stretch of land" is a mark of inferiority.

Developers fulfill their aspirations for professional status, in part, by building for "professionals." In marketing materials targeted at Indian consumers, developers insert their properties into "professional" lifeworlds, picturing light-skinned inhabitants with briefcases and laptops and addressing professionals in their ad copy. They often boasted that only professionals lived in their communities—particularly information technology and multinational corporate employees. Developers make these linkages between their constructions and this prestigious persona to attract Indian consumers and foreign investors (see Searle 2013). But they also market their buildings to professionals, I suggest, because it is prestigious to be the kind of developer who builds for this kind of person; it marks the developer of such buildings as also transparent, professional, and credible. Developers seek both economic and cultural capital, and the two are entangled. Building for information technology and multinational companies (and their employees), real estate developers respond to economic trends (like the predicted growth in information technology firms described in chapter 3), but, especially in housing markets, these are not the only nor the wealthiest consumers: they are particularly prestigious ones.

I interviewed an Indian man who had grown up and trained as an engineer in Delhi; after starting several non-real estate businesses of his own, he had become the managing director of a foreign fund. He lived in an apartment in a sought-after building in Gurgaon, one he characterized as the "best" because of "the quality of people who live there. . . . Professionals, largely. Very few businessmen." He was so adamant about differentiating businessmen from professionals and about the prestige of his address that it struck me that his choice of residence was an emblem of professional status *for him*: it was integral to his personal negotiation of stigmas of being a "nonprofessional," in effect a "businessman," working in real estate.

Professionalization Project

To redeem real estate's reputation as a field of "businessmen" and gain respectability, real estate industry lobbying groups, international property consultants (CB Richard Ellis, Jones Lang LaSalle Meghraj, Knight Frank, etc.), the press, and individual developers have used the language of professionalism and transparency to describe the industry. They collectively narrate real estate's transformation, beginning with a description of a corrupt and troubled past. For example, Bombay developer Niranjan Hiranandani reminisced about the old days to the *Economic Times*, "I still remember those days. Ministers used to instruct their personal assistants not to write our names in appointment diaries. We were considered on par with underworld dons like Haji Masaan and Yusuf Patel," but continued with the industry's metamorphosis: "We are witnessing the transformation now. There is a sea change in the mindset of administrators and financiers" (*Economic Times* 2007d).

Lobbying groups have been working to "bring this nascent, unorganized business to industry status," according to Sumit Jha, deputy director of The National Real Estate Development Council (NAREDCO). Groups such as NAREDCO and the Confederation of Real Estate Developers' Associations of India (CREDAI) have begun organizing conferences and publishing glossy newsletters in their bid to deflect negative attention without bringing in government regulation. For example, NAREDCO has initiated a code of ethical practice for its members, a certificate program for real estate salespeople, a rating scheme for developers,[15] and a quarterly magazine.

Developers, their marketing staff, and the press have worked to build real estate's credibility and status among Indian consumers, Indian investors, NRIs, and foreign investors. Developers issue "brand-building" advertisements to familiarize the public with their firms' merits. Viewing company growth as a marker of success, they advertise their quarterly earnings in full-page spreads in the business papers. Size matters: developers tout their "pan-Indian presence," the millions of square feet they have under construction, and the number of different kinds of buildings they will construct. New magazines devoted entirely to coverage of the real estate industry (including *Realty Plus*, *Real Property Times, The Realtor, Real Estate Observer,* and *Real Estate Watch*) heighten the industry's image with gushing developer profiles (fig. 6.1). Developers' webpages narrate company histories full of glowing pronouncements about future projects and company growth. Many tout their "professional" staff, for example, the "highly qualified, young, dynamic, creative professionals with extraordinary business acumen and insatiable thirst to work with passion" at SG Estates or the "dedicated team of professionals practically from all the fields" at Taneja Development and Infrastructure (SG Estates; TDI).

Just as developers deploy emblems of "professionalism" and evidence of corporate growth to distance themselves from the figure of the unsavory businessman, they also mobilize emblems of "world-class" status. Many developers hold meetings in five-star hotels.[16] They drive imported cars and insist on speaking English. Many have renovated their offices or moved into buildings they have constructed. Their offices' divergent styles signal variety in the quest for a new image—from Unitech's ultra-mod main office in chartreuse and white, to Delhi Land and Finance's marble-clad stairwells, to Taneja's reappropriation of a colonial bungalow in central Delhi, complete with an ornate wood-paneled waiting room and neatly clipped front lawn. Most common was an international corporate modern look: sleek black leather couches, glass partitions with oversized chrome hardware, and large flat-screen TVs showing company videos.

One prestigious marker of international success is entrance into the *Forbes* list of billionaires. Developers who had "achieved global recognition" on the Forbes list in 2007 include K. P. Singh (DLF), Ramesh Chandra (Unitech), Pallonji Mistry (Shapoorji Pallonji Group), Vikas Oberoi (Oberoi Constructions), and Pradeep Jain (Parsvnath Developers) (Bisht 2007; *Forbes* 2007; A. Kumar 2007). An article in the *Real Estate Observer* compares real estate favorably to information technology: "A boom in the real estate sector has visibly led to a mushrooming of Indian billionaires on the Forbes list, a trend, reminiscent of that seen in the IT sector once" (Bisht 2007). Books like *India's Global Wealth Club: The Stunning Rise of Its Billionaires and the Secrets of Their Success* (Hiscock 2008) place real estate developers alongside other Indian entrepreneurs in an international race for profit.

International property consultants' reports celebrate the industry's transformation, adding to developers' own attempts to burnish their image. For example, an Ernst & Young report includes an entire section titled "Metamorphosis of Indian Real Estate Industry," and Jones Lang LaSalle Meghraj presents a "before" and "after" picture of industry transformation in a chart

Siachen of New York. We have also won a Rs 300-crore deal to build a five-star hotel and are in the process of closing one of the largest deals with a hotel operator. So things are going the right way. We have extended our operations to Kolkata, Chennai and Delhi.

Q *Analysts are warning of a possible price correction. Do you think the property market is overheated? Will the current prices, in your opinion, be sustainable in the long run?*
A In my personal view, without upsetting anyone, a 10%-20 % correction in property prices is very good for the industry because there are various unorganized developers who are creating unrealistic price mechanism, making it unaffordable for genuine home buyers. But if the correction is made, then the absorption level also goes up because we will be able to give the people the right product with the right kind of pricing. So I think a correction will be good. Already there is a certain amount of correction taking place all across but only in the peripheral areas of the cities and not in the CBDs. Like in Bangalore, it is in the Whitefield areas.

Q *What role do you think REIT and real estate mutual funds will play in shaping the future of this industry?*
A First, the return in the real estate sector is far more healthy and impressive than the other sectors in the country. I think real estate mutual funds are just going to help developers come in, support them and hold hands for large acquisitions where banks don't really help much. As for REIT, it involves purely strategic finance investors looking at instruments like insurance.

Q *You recently had a deal with Mor-*

gan Stanley. How did you come about it?
A They were pitching in and felt that entrepreneurs aged between 25 and 35 would be good to work with. They found that advantage with us. In the last five years, we have done reasonably well for ourselves and are quite transparent in our operations. That perhaps worked in our favour. Further, there are credible projects to be seen on the ground.

Q *A lot of joint ventures and tie-ups are taking place across the country with various foreign companies. You also received $100 million funding from Siachen of New York. How do you think these JVs and tie-ups lead to the growth of the real estate industry in the country and what advantages do these have in the long run?*
A The government of India has stringent laws (especially in land) where you can't really repatriate profits for three years, need to bring in an 'X' amount of money and can't invest in property below a certain size. So it's not like it is going to be out of the reach of a lot of people. On the contrary, with foreign partners coming in, there will be good opportunities for developers like us. These will also bring in more transparency in the projects making the future homebuyers understand that regulations and global quality standards can be met. These are the advantages these tie-ups will have.
Further, a lot of unorganized players using dubious means will get cut off and the quality players who want to do good job will exist. Various players who want to come

> **FARMERS NEED TO BE COMPENSATED FOR THE LAND TAKEN AWAY FROM THEM FOR DEVELOPING THE SEZs. FOR THIS, THE GOVERNMENT NEEDS TO PLAY LARGER ROLE.**

FIGURE 6.1. New real estate magazines heighten the industry's image with gushing developer profiles. Here, Nitesh Shetty, managing director of Nitesh Estates in Bangalore, performs professionalism with his attire; the foreign investment he has garnered ($100 million from New York private equity firm Siachen Capital); and the stance he takes in the text, distancing himself from "various unorganized developers" and pledging to "bring in construction on a global benchmark and achieve international standards in the quality of our products. We aim to get the entire management of projects handled by a professional team."
Source: *Realty Plus* 2006c.

that compares 1996/7 and 2006/7 (Ernst & Young 2006, 4; Jones Lang LaSalle Meghraj 2007, 4). Bolstering the industry's narrative of transformation, India's rating improved in the 2006 Jones Lang LaSalle's Real Estate Transparency Index (*Realty Plus* 2006b; Chittum 2006); and the 2008 Transparency Index projected this trajectory of industry transformation into the future, predicting an improved score in 2010 (Jones Lang LaSalle 2008).

All together, these varied efforts constitute a collective value project: an attempt at transforming the social persona that the Indian consuming public and potential foreign investors associate with real estate developers by linking them with signs of professionalism, world-class status, and transparency. Developers themselves *perform* these qualities by becoming members of professional groups, speaking English, and associating themselves with particular locales. Other signs like media descriptions and consultancy ratings also now portray them in a similar light.

Developers' value projects demonstrate the imbrication of economic and cultural capital (cf. Bourdieu 1986). While money buys items of conspicuous consumption (imported cars, penthouses, etc.), developers have also re-deployed signs of wealth as signs of cultural and social capital. Thus, they tout quarterly earnings, entrance to the Forbes list of billionaires, or driving a Porsche, alongside other signs that they can be trusted to "deliver" (boasts about millions of square feet constructed, land assembled, houses sold). Economic capital thus advertises having the social connections to "deliver" and the cultural capital to create global partnerships.

Investment as Credibility

The story of industry uplift that developers, consultants, and journalists narrate treats foreign investment itself as an index of credibility. Using almost the same language as the Ernst & Young report cited above, *The Economic Times* writes,

> Today things have changed. More than six US-based private equity firms like Goldman Sachs, DSP Merrill Lynch, Morgan Stanley and JP Morgan have started investing in Indian real estate market. . . . Opening up of the market to foreign investors by relaxing the FDI [foreign direct investment] norms in 2005, growth of private equity and rising demand for high quality real estate are gradually transforming Indian real estate business into a more transparent and accessible market. (*Economic Times* 2007d)

Involvement of these large, internationally known investment banks acts as a stamp of approval for the industry as a whole. By citing Indian developers' access to international capital as evidence of the industry's transformation, such reports encourage the very activity they describe.

Moreover, because international investment is generally associated with transparency and professionalism—as well as carrying the cachet of the foreign—Indian developers use investment in their own image work. Joint ventures with foreign firms, private equity investments, public offers (which attract foreign institutional investors), and hiring international consultants exceed the accumulation of capital and expertise: they are emblems of credibility that Indian developers use in their own efforts to change their reputation in India. Alongside the economic capital that investment brings, credibility has its own value as a measure of self-worth and status.

In order to build reputations as credible firms, developers boast of hiring international consultants. For example, Delhi Land and Finance chairman K. P. Singh told the *Business Standard*, "Two years ago, Rajiv [his son] got McKinsey to restructure the company. They did a great job and we paid them a lot of money! Then Rajiv gave a $13 million order to IBM for our systems." (Rai and Zarabi 2007). Note that the value of hiring these international business consultants lies in the work they do creating "world-class" business systems *and* in the bragging rights it provides. Like imported goods which are costly and thus prestigious, McKinsey's expertise and IBM's business systems came at a cost that Singh is happy to report was high. This corporate conspicuous consumption is a bid to reinforce DLF's credibility and Singh's prestige.

Many developers approach public offers as a means of publicly demonstrating compliance with international norms of transparency; doing so conveys credibility and thus contributes to their professionalizing project. For example, a little over a year before Emaar MGF's attempt to list on the Bombay Stock Exchange, the chairman of the firm's Dubai-based partner (Emaar Properties PJSC), Mohamed Ali Alabbar, told *Realty Plus* magazine,

> Our intent of going public is not just to raise capital. It is mainly because I like the transparency that comes with the publicly listed companies. As a listed company, we will be keenly watched by the public and the authorities. And as such there will be pressures on us to perform and meet targets in an aggressive manner. (*Realty Plus* 2006d)

Ali Alabbar discussed going public as though it were a transparency challenge. He hopes to prove to the world that his firm can comply with Security and Exchange Board of India regulations and, once "keenly watched" by the public and the regulators, reveal that his firm can meet high standards of performance.[17]

In communicating profitability to potential Indian investors at an investor presentation in advance of the public offer, Emaar MGF's managing director, Shravan Gupta, appealed to international investment and partnerships as evidence of "world-class" credibility and potential profits. He insisted, "We have a number of marquee investors: Citigroup, New York Life, JP Morgan. This shows the confidence the global community has shown in the integrity of our business." He added later, "This is a stamp of approval from the best." He also proudly listed his firm's other international partners (two Australian construction firms, an American project management firm, and a Singaporean school) and reminded the audience that the firm is itself a joint venture, "the largest FDI [foreign direct investment] in the sector," between Delhi-based MGF and Dubai-based Emaar Properties PJSC, "the world's largest private development company," according to Gupta (fig. 6.2). Like an advertising testimonial, Gupta implied that if these established international companies have invested in or partnered with his firm, Indian investors should feel comfortable buying shares.

Just as working with foreign partners confers prestige, "there is an ego element involved" for the firm going public, explained Chetan, a public relations agent who has worked with many real estate firms during the listing process. When Delhi Land and Finance (DLF) announced plans to go public in the spring of 2006, the Indian business press interpreted the decision as a personal accomplishment for the company's chairman K. P. Singh. A month before the offer, one journalist predicted,

> With a forthcoming public issue of nearly Rs 10,500 crore for a 10 per cent stake in DLF, Singh, with a holding of 90 per cent, will be catapulted to the global stage as the fifth richest man in the world and the richest resident Indian (worth Rs 90,000 crore or around $20 billion), pushing Azim Premji to the second Indian slot. (Menon 2006)

The journalist (and others in the press) understands the public offering as a route to personal glory. Providing wealth legitimized by both the Security and Exchange Board of India and foreign institutional investors, the public offer would enable Singh to compete on "the global stage" of capitalist entrepreneurs. It could transform him from Indian real estate developer to world-class professional.[18]

However, after running into minority shareholder opposition, Delhi Land and Finance had to withdraw its prospectus and cancel the listing.[19] Chetan, the public relations agent, commented,

> You know, DLF was so upset about the IPO [initial public offer] process being derailed, they did all these things to get back. Because for them it's a reputation. "They couldn't do that, you know, they may be big, but they couldn't go

FIGURE 6.2. Emaar MGF full-page advertisement. This advertisement on the front page of a major business newspaper was part of the company's brand-building campaign in advance of its attempted initial public offer in February 2008.

Source: *Economic Times*, February 5, 2008.

for it. Their books are all bad, that's why." You know, so then the reputation
factor comes in. Once you go through it, they feel that OK, we are listed company, we are answerable to SEBI [Securities and Exchange Board of India],
government, our investors. So it's like, whatever they do, it's fine.

Chetan feels that the failure to list cast a poor light on DLF's operations; he
even suggests that the public might have suspected improper accounting
and dubious dealing: "Their books are all bad." The firm's subsequent listing
in June 2007, then, provided its promoters an opportunity to reverse public
opinion.

These examples cast attracting foreign capital as a matter of reputation *and*
profit. Successfully engaging the new modes of publicity involved in a public
offer, developers can demonstrate transparency and respectability. Developers advertise their foreign partnerships and successful initial public offers as a
way to fight the stigma of real estate and appeal to potential Indian investors
and consumers. Shravan Gupta, K. P. Singh, and other developers use foreign tie-ups to present themselves as global professionals comfortable working with other global professionals, their firms on par with others the world
over. To garner foreign capital and local trust, they must appear wealthy—
but a certain kind of wealthy: they need to mark their wealth as "white" by
deploying it in particular ways (paying for McKinsey and IBM expertise, for
example) and by themselves appropriating the symbols of professional success (speaking English, imported cars, NAREDCO membership, upscale residences, etc.). Foreign investment is both the outcome of such displays and
part of the display itself.

Double Bind

We might read the self-presentation of Indian developers like Shravan Gupta
and K. P. Singh as examples of the reproduction of a "transnational capitalist
class" (see Robinson and Harris 2000; Sklair 2001). However, Indian developers have become vital to the internationalization of Indian real estate precisely because they are intermediaries who can *both* conform to international
expectations *and* engage in the local practices discredited by international
financiers. Their ability to "deliver" land and buildings requires that they navigate a system of land procurement and a government regulatory process that
does not meet international standards of "transparency." Indeed, there is evidence that not only politicians but organized crime has played an increasing role in land dealing *since* liberalization (Carney 2008; Weinstein 2008).
Indian developers find themselves in a double bind: they must be "transpar-

ent" to garner investment but at the same time must continue bribing local officials and "cleaning" land to remain valuable intermediaries. Thus, even while attempting to distinguish themselves as transparent global professionals, the persona of businessman still has its attractions and necessities.

Govind, a developer in the National Capital Region, represented himself as a "new" real estate developer. Educated as an engineer, he spoke English, drove an Audi, and dressed with restrained elegance. He described his business partners as "all professionals, really." When they started their company in the late 1990s,

> there is no greed really to make a quick buck, but the greed was there to actually do something different and to be known in the market as somebody very clean and as a group who's clean and, you know, they can be trusted, and they're very transparent and stuff like that.

He differentiated his business from those of other developers just looking for "quick money" and sought customer trust through being "clean" and "transparent."

Despite this seeming alignment with investors' calls for transparency, Govind was ambivalent about foreign investors, who, he claimed, lacked the local knowledge to do business in India, to deal with "the politician who wants his cut, . . . [with] the criminal who wants his cut." He continued: "And it's not easy. You have to get around everybody, you have to keep them happy. So these guys [investors] get scared." He concluded,

> See, they are *bankers*, they are not real estate people. We are real estate people. So in a JV [joint venture], it's like a marriage between a—what do you say?— an Aries and a Taurian or whatever. (Laughter.) So they don't know the dynamics of the trade, and we say why can't they just put the money on the table and let us do the work? Because we are confident we'll deliver. And they say, "No, but it shouldn't be for so much." Then they run their numbers, through statistics on this page and that page and this survey and that—that's also not going to happen in a hurry. (Laughter.)

He scoffs at foreign investors' reliance on number crunching and their inability to handle politicians and criminals, as he can. In the end, they are "just bankers," while he is a real estate developer, equipped to deal with the fast pace and dirty politics of Indian real estate. Conjuring the gangster and distancing himself from cautious, fearful bankers is critical to Govind's ability to convey his effectiveness in "delivering" buildings: being a good real estate developer requires the ability to act quickly, ruthlessly, and fearlessly with unsavory characters. He might even be one of those unsavory characters himself, he hints. Govind's double-voicing (see Bakhtin 1981) of both the global professional and the local gangster are what define his identity as a real estate developer.

Similarly, Avinash, an independent consultant who brokered deals between developers and foreign funds, both distanced himself from and embraced "unsavory" activities. In one interview, he mentioned that he had left his previous consulting partner just two weeks previously because he learned that he was involved in "repugnant" business activities, about which he refused to elaborate. However, one day in 2014, after regaling me with stories about crooked Indian developers stealing from credulous foreign investors, Avinash gave me an impassioned defense of corruption. Ironically, we were driving through central New Delhi streets congested because of an Aam Aadmi Party sit-in.[20] As anticorruption activists blocked nearby Rajpath, Avinash boasted of his own ability to get a building approval from the municipal authorities in Bhiwadi in record speed at minimum cost (Rs. 20,000).[21] Not only were such activities indispensible to real estate production, he argued, but he was quite good at them.

If real estate developers like Govind and Avinash continue to cite the local fixer in their self-presentations as they celebrate their local expertise, this ambivalence does not reflect an "incomplete" or "failed" transformation. Just as Frank Fanselow argues that bazaar traders' "unscrupulous" practices are "not a function of the actor's ethic but of the rationality of the market" (Fanselow 1990, 262), Indian developers' mixed messages are a function of the structure of the globalizing market in which they operate. They occupy contradictory, liminal subject positions. Indian developers, I would argue, are "reflexive[ly] orient[ed] to an experience of being beholden to multiple mandates at the same time" (Nakassis 2016, 16). Their liminality is structural, not temporal: they are not "on the way" to new social status so much as caught in between, such that their position as intermediaries both enables and threatens their professionalizing project.

Indian developers' liminality stems from their position between two different systems of value signaled by two different types of money. "White" money indexes transparency, professionalism, efficiency, and global aspirations. Developers today claim to operate more and more "in white," just as they build houses for professionals and claim to be professionals themselves. But "black" money also has its attractions: black money, as the "sedimented embodiment of accomplished power" (Parmentier in Björkman 2014, 629), is a "talisman of networks of access to the worlds of opportunity and promise inhering the city's enigmatic economies" (Björkman 2014, 628). It indexes local efficacy: wielding sociopolitical networks, navigating bureaucratic claims, and negotiating with local power brokers. To be successful—to garner capital, construct buildings, and accumulate profits—Indian developers need both "white" and "black" prestige, both "white" and "black" efficacy.

The aura of "black" efficacy was often palpable, even in the most "professional" of displays. The Emaar MGF investor presentation in early 2008, for example, was an impressive performance of professionalism: a phalanx of somber-suited men spoke about the company's promise from a dais in the ballroom of a five-star hotel decorated with seven-foot-high posters of future projects. The presentation included slickly produced videos and investor kits in logo-ed binders. And yet, probably everyone in the room knew about the connection between the Guptas and a court battle that had been in the papers intermittently over the previous nine years.[22] Shravan Gupta's brother, Siddharth, an executive director at Emaar MGF, was a passenger in a drunken hit-and-run car accident in 1999, in which six bystanders were killed. The driver, Siddharth's friend, was the son of a wealthy arms dealer and the grandson of a former Navy Chief. After driving away from the accident scene, they went to Siddharth's house, where his father ("businessman Rajeev Gupta" in the press) helped wipe bloodstains off the BMW (the press always mentions the make of the car). Rajeev Gupta was later convicted of destroying evidence; Siddharth was exonerated (Kumar 2008).

We might interpret Shravan Gupta's show of global professionalism as an attempt to dispel this black mark on his reputation. Rather, his clout came from both his international partnerships *and* his local power. The court case connected Emaar MGF to a very powerful network of people who could drag a court case out for nine years, buy off witnesses, and expect to kill people without going to jail. At the end of the investor presentation, Emaar MGF's CFO summarized the company's selling points: "Our land banks, our scale of operations, our construction execution capability with joint ventures, our board and management—who are using their experience to benefit investors. We are a very compelling story." Both local networks and international ones make a "compelling story."

The Value of Expertise

As foreign funds and Indian developers make deals, perceptions of credibility, reputation, and expertise translate into profit and loss, and the contradictions of developers' value projects come to the fore. Developers' liminal position as intermediaries enables them to take on the persona of the businessman or the professional strategically, to differentiate themselves from or align themselves with others in interactions as they vie for capital and prestige. Yet this double-voicing creates ambivalence about a developer's financial and moral worth. Investors might ask, if a developer has the social networks to deliver land, permits, and buildings, might he also abscond with our money? This ambivalence is a problem when developers and investors attempt to quantify the value of a developer's expertise and his contributions to a joint venture project.

Indian developers and their foreign partners indirectly determine the value of expertise as they negotiate profit sharing agreements and haggle over the price of land.[23] If the Indian real estate developer is "just" a landowner, how much profit can he claim? What is the value of his local expertise and the risk he assumes in the land development process? Paradoxically, when developers are successful at appearing like global professionals, they erase evidence of their own labor and undermine their own value. Thus, they often defend their own expertise as local knowledge and political connections—diminishing their attempts to bill themselves as transparent, international players and resist the labels "landowner" and "broker."

In general, Indian developers believe that land prices should be high to remunerate their work in assembling and "cleaning" it, while foreign investors predictably complain that such high land valuations cut into their returns. Ashok, the head of land services for an international property consultancy in India explained that "a lot of mid- and large developers actually bought land four years ago and now the price is three times what they paid. So they quote today's price to the fund." Foreign funds, of course, think they should be charged the lower "historical" price.

In the absence of reliable land valuation data (see chapter 3), Ashok explained, "Many landlords see what their neighbor's land went for X and say, so mine should sell for X+1." Sumit, the mall developer, questioned this valuation approach: "Now we turn around and say, see, that particular deal was done—I don't know for what reason. What was the compelling reason for that company to actually put in that kind of money?" He feels that valuations based on other deals are often unjustified.

Indian developers also commonly work backward from their profits to determine the land price, but when maximizing their profits, they assume only "an IRR [internal rate of return] of 10–15 percent" for the foreign firm, according to Ashok. This is far short of the 25–30 percent that most funds would like to make. Alternately, for very profitable projects, they promise the fund a 20–25 percent return, but through an unevenly weighted promote structure; by putting up 50 percent of the equity, the fund will get back only 20 percent of the projects' profits, with the Indian developer keeping the other 80 percent.

Potential investors see these various tactics as greed, pure and simple. Simon complained about

> landlords and developers making a hundred and a hundred and fifty percent on their land. Offering you land at five crores an acre, whereas you know they bought it three years ago at fifty lakhs. Then trying to justify the price. And then putting the price up because their cousin around the corner just sold it for seven crores. That doesn't work. And then wanting a management fee. And then wanting a promote. And then trying to cap the IRR [internal rate of return].

He clicked his teeth disapprovingly and added, "It doesn't work. It just doesn't work." As Avinash admitted, such tactics do amount to overvaluation: "Which isn't to say that the Indian developer doesn't say, 'I've got a bunch of idiots [foreign investors] coming in today, let's milk them for all I can.' So they overvalue everything and leave nothing on the table for the investor." As a result, a lot of investors "come in expecting a 35–40 percent return, and they can't find a project for more than 20. The developer says, if I put in all the hard work to get it to this stage, why should I give up my profit?"

Indian real estate developers, by contrast, justify high land valuations by reminding foreign investors of the work they do. As one developer explained to investors at a real estate conference,

> the land that the developer buys—it's a semi-cooked product. The investor isn't coming in when the land is in agriculture. To change the use, you need to show construction permits. What we bought and what we are passing on to you is totally different.

This developer argues that he has "added value," to use a phrase my informants commonly used; he is selling on to the investor a "totally different" product, one with a higher value than mere land. Another said bluntly, "if you come on board at the land level, then that return is there for the asking. Come, join us. If you expect that we should get land, approvals, and then [you] get 20 percent, that's unreasonable." In his opinion, if a foreign investor wants to buy into a project early, pay for the land, and assume the risk of getting permits, then he is happy to share the profits with the investor. It is "unreasonable" however, to expect the developer to research titles, aggregate land from different owners, and negotiate with politicians and bureaucrats— all the while assuming the risk should these processes go awry and the land prove undevelopable—and still provide an investor with a 20 percent return on his equity. Where foreign funds see inflated prices, Indian developers see remuneration for their risk-taking and local expertise. Indian developers find themselves fighting both for the value of such local knowledge *and* promoting themselves as international professionals.

Schooled in different real estate practices and assumptions, investors see land as an input into a longer development process, not a product of labor (see chapter 8). Moreover, the moral discourse of transparency through which they understand and judge Indian real estate obscures the work of land agglomeration. What Indian developers see as labor and expertise, foreign investors see as "corruption" or "risk"; these are the activities about which they legally cannot know. I once overheard Ravi on the phone at EuroFund telling someone that, according to the Foreign Corrupt Practices Act, he could not hear any more of what the person was about to say to him. Developers' and investors' conflicts over profits are not just a question of haggling over value, then, but of the structural contradictions created by a form of capital accumulation that requires chains of intermediaries. The imperative for developers to be "dirty" *and* "clean" implies that the work necessary for capital accumulation, the transformation of Indian land into an internationally legible asset, is not visible—cannot be visible—to certain members of the chain, even as they call for "transparency."

Conclusion

Anthropologists have argued that "transparency" is a seductive ideal that cannot be achieved in practice, a "fantasy of immediation" in a world dependent on the "the imperfections and impurities that mediation necessarily involves" (Mazzarella 2006, 499).[24] And indeed, the international discourse of transparency that investors used (chapter 5)—the transparency of corporate governance through disclosure—is exactly this kind of "fantasy of immediation." It is a fantasy because markets are not "perfect" and cannot be divorced from mediation—and indeed, if they were, they would not be profitable, as investors and consultants themselves realize.

The very possibility of profit in Indian real estate depends on the transformational work that fantasies of immediation obscure. Foreign investors and their Indian partners hope to profit from transforming Indian land into something that can be invested in from abroad. In order to make money, investors need others to transform agricultural land into buildable parcels, and thus to engage with local politics. The continued non-transparency—from a foreigner's perspective—of the real estate business necessitates developers' work and creates new value for their social connections and local knowledge, creating a profitable niche as intermediaries. Yet it is that very liminal position at the intersection of different regimes of value that undermines developers' attempts at performing "transparency" and perpetuates the utility of being a local businessman.

And yet, in this case, "transparency" is not just an unattainable ideal unrealized because of its own internal contradictions. Investors and developers both use this discourse to do work. While investors clamor for the market information and bureaucratic reforms that would make Indian real estate more "transparent"—more accessible from afar, less dependent on local social knowledge—they also use claims about the "nontransparency" of the market (its many uncertainties and "failures") to value international practices over Indian ones as they assemble global chains of accumulation; to negotiate lower prices on land and real estate development services; to attract Indian partners who believe they need international cachet to get ahead; and to insist on organizational changes that serve their ability to control Indian companies. The same discourses that make India look profitable also devalue Indian knowledge, social networks, and work. Marked as inferior, Indian firms are always already suspect of harboring incommensurable differences. Indeed, they are valued because they are assumed to do so.

"Transparency" is also a stereotypic kind of personhood that one can perform by enacting particular signs; it is not unattainable but frequently achieved in particular interactions for a variety of effects. Deploying "transparency" as a major tenet of their collective professionalizing project, Indian real estate developers have refashioned themselves as "clean," trustworthy professionals in order to seek international capital, respect, and local sales. In doing so, developers have elaborated associations between transparency and other locally desirable qualities—being "world class" and "professional," for example. Thus, transparency in an Indian context is inflected by Indian concerns: it is tied up with, subsumed under, and achieved as a tool in developers' broader aim of appearing as global professionals. Ideas about transparency circulate through international projects of economic governance, but to the extent that they are successful, they resonate as personal aspirations, not just bureaucratic ideals. As a set of qualities associated with social types and performed in interactions, "transparency" can be adopted, transformed, and put to use in value projects that diverge from and perhaps compete with those of international financiers, as we shall see in the next chapters.

Quality Projects I: Constructing Authority

Visiting Gurgaon

On a hot September day, I accompanied five American architects on a tour of Gurgaon. The joint venture between a European real estate investment fund (EuroFund) and an Indian real estate development company (BuildIndia) had hired an internationally famous New York architectural firm to design its project, and this was the architectural team's first visit to India. After more than an hour in grinding traffic, we arrived at one of BuildIndia's office buildings to meet their chief architect, our guide that morning. We reached his office through a winding series of open-air staircases and narrow corridors. As we ascended, EuroFund's managing director Jeremy asked us to keep in mind that this is the office of one of the largest developers in India. We came to a halt in a foyer directly beneath a hole in the drop ceiling that caught the architects' attention. Pointing up at the exposed pipes and wires, the head of the New York firm remarked, "I wish I knew that this was just for our benefit, but I have a feeling it's not!" Everyone snickered. Informed that the man we were meeting was already outside, Jeremy led us back downstairs. As we were walking out, one of the architects commented that he had trouble believing that this was the office of a developer worth billions of dollars. He pointed to mortar oozing from behind the stone on the facade and repeated his boss's comment: "I like that corner detail!"

That morning, we visited some of North India's most contemporary buildings: blue-glass and stone encased office blocks, balcony-laden high-rises, and lush, manicured hotels. Throughout, the architects derided the quality of the materials they saw and criticized a lack of "good detailing." They discussed inconsistent metal work, discolored wall paneling, dirty glass overhangs, water damage, and leaky glass curtain walls. Their commentary extended beyond construction quality narrowly considered to the layout of rooms and the efficiency of office spaces. Nick, an experienced project manager and a member of the EuroFund team, declared that not one of the buildings they saw had "good architecture with efficient floorplates" and all the HVAC (heating, ventilating, and air-conditioning) units were "primitive, very simple systems." Taking stock of the bathrooms in an office building—assessed in terms of "cheap granite [countertops], wood partitions six inches from the floor, almost full height toilets"—one architect said she was reminded of Brazil, where she had done a project several years before.

Their critique also extended to aesthetics. The architects responded to Gurgaon's postmodern pastiche of architectural styles with raised eyebrows, smirks, and sarcastic asides. An architect pointed to a row of classically inspired pediments which, with a chuckle, she likened to the work of Michelangelo. Someone else joked that maybe they could develop "curtain wall wallpaper" to screen out views of offending buildings from their own. The head of the New York firm mocked, "Every time you say attractive, [Jeremy], I don't know if you mean 'attractive' in quotes!"

These various complaints and evaluations—all glossed with the term "quality"—included commentary on materials, construction, labor practices, layout, amenities, and aesthetics. After a morning touring buildings, Nick commented on the group's detail-obsessed behavior to me: we're "looking at how can we do it better," he said. "Most of the time, it's pretty obvious." I examine EuroFund's strategy for producing profit in India, a value project which hinges on the category of quality and the goal of "doing it better" than Indian developers. In what follows, I refer to this value project as EuroFund's "quality project."

Like other corporate quality projects (e.g., Dunn 2004), this is also standardizing project: EuroFund aims to build in India as it would in Europe, the United States, Brazil, or China, and so attract the same multinational corporate tenants. "Quality" means more than craftsmanship or structural integrity in this context: it is shorthand for a built environment conforming to the tastes of an international business elite. EuroFund strives to construct buildings appropriate to a particular semiotic style, to fit them into an international register of the built environment and thus associate them with particular social practices and those who engage in them. Constructing a "quality" building for a global elite, fund employees hope to charge higher rents than their competitors in India. Paradoxically, EuroFund's standardization project (to make buildings in India similar to those for the same audience elsewhere in the world) requires differentiation: the fund hopes to profit from the difference between Indian and international fields of real estate practice and to gain a premium in rents over its Indian competition.

I pay close attention to the work of standardizing and differentiating. I use EuroFund's struggles to carry out its quality project to throw light on the differences between Indian and international real estate development. Moreover, I explore how EuroFund employees identify these differences and how they distinguish their idea of quality from Indian real estate developers' ideas of quality. As the architects' tour of Gurgaon demonstrates, determining a building's quality requires expert judgment: visual acuity, knowledge, and fluency in specific aesthetic registers.[1] These architects are engaged in a process of commensuration, rendering different qualities comparable by a common metric (Espeland and Stevens 1998; Kockelman 2006); however, they are commensurating without recourse to a quantitative measure. The architects' expertise, born of participation in a design community with its own arenas of certification and prestige (see Larson 1993; Olds 2001, 141–157), enables comparison.

However, EuroFund's employees and consultants make claims to expertise in an environment in which they do not necessarily wield much authority, for both the economics and the culture of real estate development in India militate against recognition of foreign construction expertise.[2] Whereas elsewhere in the world EuroFund's consultants' architectural taste may be dominant, one of the institutionally sanctioned "baseline norms relative to which other registers appear deviant or defective" (Agha 2007a, 147), in India, a profusion of similar projects dilute their dominance. Thus, in order to construct buildings for a global elite, EuroFund and its consultants must not only commensurate—measure and compare—they must also construct authority. EuroFund's problem is twofold: it must enroll allies (partners, contractors, consultants, buyers) and control their behavior (Latour 1987).

Here, and in the following chapter, I explore EuroFund's attempts to construct authority, find partners, and transform real estate and construction work processes. Practices and money do not flow seamlessly from one place to another; the globalization of Indian real estate requires work. Nor are the differences that impede (and enable) globalization mere frictions, "the awkward, unequal, unstable, and creative qualities of interconnection across difference" (Tsing 2005, 4), for the actors in this story actively identify, exploit, and bridge cultural difference as they carry out their own value projects and mobilize others to join them.

EuroFund's Strategy

Like other international firms entering the Indian market, EuroFund plans to "focus on the top-end," to offer "'global standard' benefits at 'global equivalent' prices" (Ablett et al. 2007, 103; Bijapurkar 2007, 6). Jeremy articulates this strategy clearly in terms of "quality": he aims to produce "very high quality, high profile buildings in the major markets" in India. The fund intends to replicate in India the construction and investment model it has used in other markets: "The central premise of our company is . . . use better architects, try to do things that are more architecturally distinctive, use better quality products, and over all, build a higher quality building." This "higher quality building" is a *global* building, like those the firm might build elsewhere in the world. One of the fund's directors, Ravi, explained at a PR meeting, "We're doing only those projects that are of global quality . . . [it] will be the best building in whatever city to produce a new standard."

EuroFund's managers hope that constructing "global quality" buildings in India will make them money. Jeremy believes that "if you build a better quality building and better architecture and spend a bit more on materials . . . it will create a higher value in the near term, and it will hold its value better and stand up better over time than its competition." By attending to all aspects of quality—design, materials, efficiency, etc.—EuroFund aims to "elevate the standards of the local industry" as it claims to have done in other emerging markets—that is, to construct a better building than the local competition has and thus achieve rents above market norms.[3] Discussing a potential residential project, Ravi explained, "We want to redefine the price point, actually. If they [other developers] are selling at ten thousand [rupees per square foot] now, I want to push it to fifteen [thousand]." EuroFund has drafted a confidential internal memo with the title "Why [EuroFund] Buildings Cost More . . . and Are Worth It" to help staff communicate the value of EuroFund projects to potential partners and tenants.

EuroFund employees believe that "quality" gives buildings endurance. They assume that their buildings will retain value better than others and that they will achieve a "certain degree of price insensitivity" compared to competitors' buildings. As Jeremy explained, "we'd like to think we've got some degree of protection" in the face of a market downturn. Similarly, Nick predicted that EuroFund buildings would succeed in the future in India: "In the next five or ten years, those that have really started to build the true quality, the true international best standards kind of buildings, are going to be the ones that are successful."

EuroFund employees plan to replicate global quality in India because— reiterating the logics described in chapter 4—they believe they are serving consumers with globally familiar tastes (wealthy Indians, NRIs, or foreigners) who are willing to pay high rents. Jeremy has described his ideal target audience to me as "the wealthy strata of Indians and a mixture of expatriates."

At other times, staff members described potential tenants as either NRIs or "the highest and wealthiest demographic" in India. In a discussion about appropriate residential building design in India, Jeremy, who was quite keen on understanding local housing preferences, commented nevertheless that "I have a feeling that if it's designed and built with the expat in mind, in many aspects, it [a residential project] will also appeal to Indians." Similarly, EuroFund intends its commercial projects for multinational corporations and international investors, many of which already have relations with EuroFund through its projects elsewhere in the world.

EuroFund employees think quality is a language that they share with this audience. Nick (the project manager) told me that for its first Indian office building, EuroFund is "going to hit most of the big multinational corporations who know on a corporate level what [a EuroFund] building is, what a quality building is." Appealing to international consumers already familiar with EuroFund products, the fund has every incentive *not* to innovate for Indian audiences or deviate from its construction and design norms. One of the firm's controllers on a visit from the home office commented that the fund has been very cautious about investing in India: "Despite investor pressure, we are very particular. If we built something like this [EuroFund's rented Delhi office], we'd be run out of town. I know we can do better." He uses the phrase "run out of town" to conjure the disgrace that would befall EuroFund's name should the firm construct anything like current constructions in Delhi—disgrace in the eyes of their multinational tenants: "Our tenants have seen what we can do," he explained. "They know what quality they're getting into."

The imperative for building "quality," then, stems from meeting the expectations of EuroFund's target audience in order to achieve high rents. As one staff member commented, "we're targeting the crème de la crème, so we have to keep the specs [specifications] high." Other international funds and developers share this perspective. For example, Donald Trump Jr. explained to an Indian business daily, "The Trump Organization has always been focused on the high-end of the market. We've turned down deals involving middle-range projects because it wouldn't go with our brand. We have a very wealthy, business-oriented clientele, and quite a few of them are Indians" (*Economic Times* 2007h). EuroFund's reputation, like that of the Trump Organization, relies on catering to a particular consumer base; deviating from it would compromise the brand.

Lowering quality—that is, serving a different audience—moves companies down a hierarchy of prestige. Several Indian developers I spoke with shared this view. One described why he would not construct projects for IT workers (rather than his typical high-net worth and NRI clientele): "their price tag is too low for us to build. They don't want high specs, just a shell. But we can't do a shorty job. We can't do lower specs. You know, they say, 'a Mercedes can never build a Buick'—even if they know it would sell more." He feels that to move down the consumer hierarchy would involve not just "lower specs" (lower material specifications) but a "shorty job" (substandard work). It would violate the intrinsic worth of his company, its identity as a "Mercedes." According to this mindset—shared by EuroFund and the Trumps—high-quality yet affordable construction is a contradiction in terms.

In summary, through their quality project, EuroFund employees hope to attract multinational tenants, reap high rents, differentiate their buildings from competitors', avoid risk of a market downturn, and support their fund's reputation. Thus, EuroFund's value project—their strategy for profit making—hinges on the semiotics of positioning their buildings as "international" and themselves as "experts." Constructing a quality building in India involves EuroFund in attempts to wield symbolic power in an unsympathetic environment. Before we turn to that environment, let us first explore "quality" in more detail.

Quality as a Register

EuroFund employees define "quality" in terms of people; when they speak of "quality," they mean building for a particular clientele. EuroFund employees pointed to the residential complex "The Laburnum" as a model for the best quality currently available in India. A marketing agent for Laburnum's developer, Silverglades, described Laburnum tenants as about forty or forty-five years old,

> They're young but they've reached that height. They're heads of multinationals and expats posted from abroad. Heads of good industries—IT, entertainment, FMCG [Fast Moving Consumer Goods], PR [Public Relations]. Name a big company, like GE, and their top guys are living there: IBM, Coke, Dell, they are all there.

In 2006, Laburnum continued to outsell new construction by several thousand rupees a square foot though it dated from the 1990s, validating EuroFund's strategy: quality attracts international tenants and produces profit. A "quality" building like Laburnum has the marks of refinement and good manufacture that make it attractive to a particular class of people—here, those with international tastes and wealth, like the high-level employees of multinational corporations.[4]

"Quality," as a repertoire of materials and design understood to befit a certain class, is a semiotic register, "a reflexive model of behavior that evaluates a semiotic repertoire (or set of repertoires) as appropriate to specific types of conduct (such as the conduct of a given social practice), to classifications of persons whose conduct it is, and, hence, to performable roles (personae, identities) and relationships among them" (Agha 2007a, 147). Here I argue that "global buildings" are elements of a larger register formation that includes other signs (speech, dress, comportment, etc.). As such, they are associated with models of personhood and behavior and are valorized vis-à-vis other registers.

Conceptualizing "quality" as a register explains the surprise and dismay of the New York architects touring Gurgaon. Not only were they shocked to see "poor quality detailing"; they were shocked that such a famous, well-capitalized Indian developer would occupy offices with open stairwells, dingy corridors, and bad corner details. The developer's office challenged the architects' model of how personhood and place should align (wealthy developer : quality building). Similarly, Paul, one of the architectural firm's partners, was "amazed by the lack of central air-conditioning, even in the most top of the line buildings." He was surprised that even expensive properties lacked the amenities he assumed were appropriate for the class of people buying them.

Quality, then, is a matter of taste, understood as "the practical operator of the transmutation of things into distinct and distinctive signs" (Bourdieu 1984, 174–75). Dismayed at the violation of their expectations of the proper transmutation of things into social signs—their models for linking the semiotic and the social—the architects critiqued what they saw. Bourdieu writes, "tastes are perhaps first and foremost distastes, disgust provoked by horror or visceral intolerance ('sick-making') of the tastes of others. . . . Aesthetic intolerance can be terribly violent" (1984, 56). Distaste is a violent reaction to the violation of often unarticulated but deeply felt models of appropriateness.

When, after looking for an office for EuroFund and a home for his family in Delhi, Jeremy remarked that "this city needs a lot more high quality residential and a lot more high quality office space," he was not criticizing Indian construction on structural or safety grounds, but on aesthetic grounds. When I asked him to explain what was wrong with the buildings he saw, he answered that they were not to his taste. He told me about visiting one office building, "considered one of the good addresses in Connaught Place, where rents are very expensive." Despite the cost, Jeremy found the building "hideous":

> It's a very tall building that actually has an atrium that is open all the way to the sky inside. . . . It's open enough that actually inside the atrium you've got pigeons flying around, living there. And we went up to a high floor, maybe

> the 30th floor or 35th floor, and we got off the elevator and again, you've got
> this open atrium and the sense that you're sort of open to the sky, and ah,
> you know, pigeons flying around, pigeon droppings on things. I mean, it truly
> looked like a set for a science fiction movie about the future after a nuclear
> holocaust or something. I mean, it was just grim, I mean really grim.

While Jeremy noted that this was his own perspective, nevertheless he could
not overcome his incredulity that a tall, concrete office building in central
Delhi has an open atrium with pigeons in it. In fact, his revulsion is so strong
that he likens it to "a set for a science fiction movie about the future after a
nuclear holocaust"—expressing the violation of his expectations about building form and appearance, and about the correlation between rent, design,
and the status of the occupier. Note that he does not describe the building in
terms of facilities or structural integrity. He concluded, "You couldn't imagine, having (a) to go through that environment yourself every day to get to
your own office space, or (b) having people come to see you and come into
this building and experience this." When he says that there is insufficient
"quality" space in Delhi, he means the city lacks space with which he would
want to be associated. There is nothing *appropriate* for him, his associates, or
his clients.

EuroFund's quality strategy entails reproducing in India a register of the
built environment associated with foreign elites and thus with the global
economy. Critiques of the quality of the Indian built environment—claims
that it is currently unsuitable for foreigners—thus evoke repercussions of
stalled economic advancement. Jeremy confided that after a year and a half
in India,

> the universal conversation I have with foreigners is—"How can you live here?"
> The housing is terrible, the offices are terrible. India wants to be part of the
> global economy. But foreign companies are not really fired up about sending
> their people back and forth and having them working where the conditions
> are abysmal.

For Jeremy, economic success requires an environment fit for foreigners. He
commented, "The more sophisticated people [in India] recognize, you know,
sooner or later we're going to have to build something that's a lot closer to
an international standard if we're ever going to be taken seriously as a true
economic superpower."

Some in India share Jeremy's opinion and his understanding of "quality." For example, the well-publicized 2007 Indian Ministry of Finance report, *Mumbai: An International Financial Centre* has imbibed a similar logic,
arguing that a substandard urban environment is a major hurdle in the city's

quest to become a successful International Financial Center (IFC) like London, New York, or Singapore. In addition to the financial reforms necessary to make Mumbai competitive, it argues that "the most critical task in a strategy for making Mumbai an IFC is the challenge of upgrading the city to world standards in terms of the quality of its infrastructure" in order to attract "a globally mobile population of high-level IFS [International Financial Service] providers" (Ministry of Finance 2007, 181). Here, "quality infrastructure" includes not only the provision of basic services like electricity and water but also schools, cultural amenities, and "lifestyle facilities," all of which should be "catering to global tastes" (xxx). Clearly, by "quality" its authors mean befitting the "high-level expatriate staff" of financial service corporations (xxviii). Moreover, the force of the report's argument comes from the consequences of inaction: should facilities remain at "not yet world class" levels (xxviii), Mumbai—and India—will be relegated to a low-skill, low-value position in the global financial economy.

The report presents a geographical analysis of work in the financial sector, arguing that the lifestyle of a skilled IFS worker—indeed IFS production itself—*requires* a certain kind of urban landscape:

> A day in the life of a skilled worker in IFS production may involve an early morning breakfast meeting at a club or hotel, a long commute to work, moving around several different meeting venues within the city throughout the day to meet clients, colleagues in other firms, accountants, lawyers, consultants, along with lunch and dinner meetings before returning home after a 12–16 hour day. (179)

The face-to-face interactions which characterize IFS production entail a series of locales—clubs, hotels, restaurants, and offices—with unfettered transport between them and among similar international sites via the airport (180).

The *Mumbai: An International Financial Centre* authors recast such locales of global financial production as necessities grounded in the monetary value of IFS workers' time: "The more skilled a person, and the higher the opportunity cost of time, the less inclined that person will be to spend time in Mumbai's traffic, or in solving mundane problems of power, water or electricity, or law and order" (180). The authors thus redefine rights over urban space—indeed, the right to the determination of urban space—from public good to private value. The built environment should be a tool for international capital accumulation, they argue, and the value of skilled labor to the international financial system itself serves as the measure of the landscape's efficiency qua tool. "Quality" is a euphemism for a city suited to the conventions of the international financial services industry: the tastes, habits, and pleasures of a particular group of people rendered natural and desirable through appeals to the market value of their time and the threat of economic stagnation.

Indian Developers' Quality Project

EuroFund and the *Mumbai* report share a sense of "quality" as a semiotic register appropriate to an elite foreign audience, suggesting that EuroFund's quality project taps into discourses already circulating in India. In fact, numerous Indian real estate developers attempt to position their buildings as elements of this semiotic register. In doing so, they do not merely replicate international designs in order to appeal to potential multinational corporate clients; they capitalize on the appeal of foreign goods as longstanding markers of prestige in India, mobilizing international emblems to attract Indian audiences. As they enlarge the social spread of the register (from foreign to Indian elites), they transform it, simultaneously disseminating and reshaping "quality" (see Agha 2007a, 190–232). Indian developers thus make claims to quality that compete with—and thus threaten—EuroFund's quality project.

Some Indian developers discursively insert their projects into the life-worlds of foreign financial elites in order to position them as part of the quality register. For example, the Indian real estate developers Suncity Projects and Dhoot Developers closely follow the *Mumbai* report's argument about efficiency in advertising their jointly developed office complex, Time Tower. The Time Tower promotional video begins with an alarm bell's ring and a barrage of businessmen in black suits holding oversized round clocks. A voice-over in British accented English announces that time is in short supply as a black Mercedes with a stressed-looking businessman at the wheel, mobile phone at his ear, fills the screen. Shot with a blank background in a sound studio, the film is eerily nondescript and abstract, suggesting a world apart. It only provides one image of Time Tower's context, reducing bustling hodge-podge Gurgaon to a generic shot of shopping mall signs at night.

The brochure for Time Tower integrates this world apart into the space of international business by recounting an imagined visit from "the New York based CEO of the multinational corporation," able to reach Time Tower from the airport in "ten minutes flat." Time Tower "reminds the CEO of his Manhattan office" and he is "pleasantly surprised to notice the offices of other large international companies" in the complex. By fictionally inserting the Time Tower into the work and travel schedules of a global elite, its promoters signal to potential tenants that this will be a global quality building.

Other developers position their projects as part of the quality register by replicating the style or tone of international advertising material. For example, a pair of Delhi-based designers created the feel of a fashion magazine for a Punjabi mall brochure. They wanted to create "a communication which when it lands on somebody's table like a Esprit CEO who's heading operations here, or like a Next or a Debenhams, then they would get really excited about it." They didn't feel it was as important to communicate to these foreign retail firms the specifics of the project—"you now, how high is the ceiling or what it is"—as it was to talk "the same language as . . . their peers, like in magazines and all, the lifestyle communications." To give the brochure an "international feel," they employed an Indian fashion photographer to shoot South African models in mod outfits, shiny eye makeup, and edgy fashion poses. The designers thought that their glossy, red-and-black brochure successfully reached a multinational retailer audience; the project was a "sell-out."

Advertisers and their real estate developer clients believe they can accrue prestige among resident Indian consumers when they target foreign or NRI audiences; they feel that designing for an international audience will attract Indians too. The two designers above coached the developer to appeal to "multinational retailers, a certain tier of luxury brands," and not merely Indian or Punjabi stores. As one of them explained, "See if you get A-level retailers, then, naturally, the rest will come." Accordingly, they told the developer, "Let's prepare a communication which will get to the A level, don't worry about the B and the C." Their strategy reflects their belief that multinational companies and global consumers top a hierarchy of consumers (the "A level"); that wealthy Indians and NRIs approximate that global consumer; and that those lower on the hierarchy aspire to move up it and so will respond to images designed for the top ("naturally, the rest will come").

Some Indian marketers have expanded the register by crafting messages aimed at Global Indians, NRI or resident Indians with global consumer tastes. For example, in an advertisement, the Taj President Hotel in Mumbai presents itself as part of the international quality register—in fact, as exactly the kind of international business locale that the *Mumbai* report describes (fig. 7.1).[5] Strikingly, it does so using the figure of a cosmopolitan Indian business person. The advertisement depicts a mixed-gendered group of young Indians, dressed in sleek jackets and sleeveless dresses, enjoying sushi and wine in a trendy bar. The caption, "Because business can be demanding," introduces the theme of mixed work and pleasure, suggesting that successful business interactions and glamorous recreation are in fact one zone of social life. The ad copy presents activities the hotel makes possible, many of them requiring a mastery of non-Indian practices and cultural icons, from Swedish massage to risotto, sushi, and Cary Grant. The ad employs Indian emblems too, in part through Indian-international hybrid activities like "dissect[ing] a contract

FIGURE 7.1. Taj President Hotel advertisement. The ad copy positions readers as cosmopolitan hotel visitors presented with a menu of different activities that the hotel makes possible: "Hi. I'm here to (a) Play hardball with clients at your business center (b) Inveigle a crusty banker into investing in a casino after sundowners at the Wink (c) Massage a few egos while I opt for the Swedish version myself. Tonight, I'd like (a) Cary Grant and a hot pepperoni pizza (b) To dissect a contract and a hot appam at the Konkan Café (c) To undress a sushi roll. And perhaps wake up to (a) A smoothie at my doorstep (b) A risotto that tastes great even when it's not an expense write-off (c) The best Penang curry this side of the continent. And don't forget (a) I like my Martinis just the way Daniel Craig doesn't (b) I would rather go to bed armed with goose-down pillow (c) I crave Naushad Ali's Nawabi Kali Dal."
Source: *India Today*, February 18, 2008.

and a hot appam at the Konkan café," thus evoking the persona of a successful, world-wise, yet Indian business person. Bundling place, decor, persona, and activity, Taj Hotels aims to reinforce the association between its hotels and this persona. As such, it elaborates the quality register in India. It is a small contribution to the development of "world-class Indianness" (see Mazzarella 2003).

Other Indian real estate developers seem less concerned with the creation of hybridity than with linking their properties to overt international markers in order to position them as part of the quality register for Indian residents. Developers prominently display the names of foreign architectural consultants in advertisements, and they routinely list foreign clients, tenants, partners, and consultants in their corporate brochures. Certifying their ability to *construct* buildings in the quality register, some boast of having completed build-to-suit projects for multinational clients. For example, the developer Alpha G:Corp advertises,

> Long before the real estate boom took root, our engineers, planners, and architects masterminded landmark projects that have served India's most demanding residents: Motorola, Eriksson, British Aerospace, British Telecom, Cisco, Intel, and Microsoft.

By claiming to have met the "demanding" requirements of non-Indian corporations, Alpha G:Corp implies that they are well-qualified to construct "international quality" buildings for Indian consumers.

The marketing teams for Indian developers craft advertising campaigns to sell an "international lifestyle" to Indian audiences: as the Omaxe Heights brochure promises, "The lifestyle of London, Paris, New York. Right here in India" (fig. 7.2). Unlike the Taj Hotel advertisement, many of these brochures and advertisements eschew mention of characteristically Indian emblems, instead signaling international pretensions through the use of English names such as NRI City or Malibu Town (see Dupont 2005; King 2002),[6] or foreign building features such as swimming pools, Italian marble floors, grand pianos, German modular kitchens, golf courses, and pool tables. Like the "export only" labels proudly displayed on some Indian manufactures, these international emblems bespeak "quality."

The promoters of Central Park II—Belgravia employ this tactic for positioning their project within the international quality register. As I was informed by the marketing agent who gave me a tour, the sample apartment (designed by American interior designer Hirsch Bedner and Associates) combines Malaysian wood cabinets; Thai furniture; a German kitchen with granite countertops and imported washing machine and dishwasher; Kohler bathroom fittings; and imported dinnerware. Black-and-white photographs

FIGURE 7.2. Omaxe Heights brochure. Developers insert their projects into the international quality register by using borrowed images and copy which suggests the international life can be lived in India. This brochure paradoxically (but characteristically) pairs a tagline about cities with an image of country living.

of Venice, beige upholstery, and tasseled pillows simulate the bland elegance of a fancy hotel. Nothing in the Rs. 2.5-crore apartment references Indian manufacture or living traditions.

Developers also convey international quality living through architectural sampling. Developers have built Spanish-style haciendas with tiled roofs and stucco walls; California-esque bungalows; futuristic glass and metal bubbles; Gothic towers with quatrefoils and pointed arches; and modernist concrete boxes with 1980s-style geometric color fields. There is no *one* stylistic indicator of the quality register. For example, at ATS Greens Village in Noida, twenty-five residential towers with the little green roofs of a Spanish hacienda encircle a decidedly neoclassic rotunda-cum-pool house. Similarly, the brochure for Delhi-based Uppal Group's Marble Arch complex in Chandigarh uses British royal insignia (a sketch of Marble Arch in London, a crest with a lion) to advertise strikingly modern architecture (straight lines, glass and metal). Anything "international"—or even several different international genres together—conveys global quality.

While Indian real estate developers disregard the genre distinctions of the West, they are creating one of their own: a flamboyant global pastiche style that is an elaboration and partial transformation of EuroFund's quality register. In a sense, this style predates the current building boom. Patel complained in 1995 that the fast pace of the development process forces architects "to dip into the vast archive of existing architectural images, styles and elements" to quickly come up with designs, resulting in "inchoate collages" of international architectural motifs (1995, 267). The Indian architect Gautam Bhatia sees pastiche as the result of client demands: he coined the terms "Punjabi Baroque," "Bania Gothic," and "Marwari Mannerism" in the mid-1990s to caricature his Delhi clients' chronic sampling of international and historical architectural styles. "The client, unsure of his heritage, uses his new wealth to project a desired image"—that of a cultured traveler of the world—by combining the "pillared porches from an American home, window moldings from an Italian church, Mansard roofs from a French chateau" (Bhatia 1994, 150). We need not adopt the criteria of cultural and historic authenticity that motivates Bhatia's critique to see that Indian developers today continue this practice of architectural eclecticism in order to index prestige and new wealth.

For example, Mumbai-based Hiranandani Developers announces in its brochure for the Hiranandani Upscale township outside of Chennai, "Begone cramped spaces. Goodbye mediocrity. Hiranandanis have triggered a resurgence of good taste." They signal this good taste, "style, grandeur, and elegance," through architectural pastiche:

> The buildings have spacious patios and stylish driveways. The arches are grand and wisely positioned. Dorics and cornices adorn the rugged warmth of greystone. Regal gargoyles and water-spouting lions also impart a sense of majesty. Dramatic atriums, cobbled pathways, theatrical stairways, striking pediments, magnificent rotundas and luxurious pillars—our creations are evidence of both, our keen eye for detail and a perceptive aesthetic that blends form and function.

This list of architectural elements accompanies photographs of Hiranandani's existing development at Powai (a northern suburb of Mumbai), a riot of oversized European architectural elements designed by architect Hafeez Contractor. With domes, colonnades, Mansard roofs, and Medieval gargoyles the Hiranandanis signal quality—not "mediocrity"—and distance their constructions from the "cramped spaces" of government built Nehru-era living. By assembling and recombining architectural elements from abroad, developers build prestige and advertise their own taste. They align themselves with foreign travel, global business, and the liberalized economy while distancing themselves from the drab functional architecture of the state. They are engaged in their own value projects, incrementally building their own quality register even while they forge similarities between Indian and international building.

A Surfeit of Quality

The dissemination of the quality register in India complicates EuroFund's task of enrolling partners, contractors, consultants, and tenants. Indian developers are forging cultural similarity: borrowing, replicating, and recombining foreign markers of prestige in the creation of Indian "international quality" architecture. EuroFund, however, plans to earn a premium over its Indian competitors by distinguishing itself from Indian builders, attracting multinational tenants, and charging high rents. The ubiquity of quality-related terms and of images of Western-style buildings pose challenges to the exclusivity and distinction of EuroFund's buildings and thus to the salability and authority of its expertise. It is to this surfeit of quality words and images that we now turn.

LANGUAGE

Relative language makes EuroFund's task of distinguishing itself challenging. At an internal public relations meeting, Ravi asked, "When we're talking with prospects [prospective partners]—and they say, yes, we're also talking with Emaar, even with DLF or Unitech [large development firms]—how do I say, 'I'm the best'? How do I prove it to them?" EuroFund employees had difficulty finding powerful words to express "I'm the best" for their Indian tagline at the public relations meeting. They discussed the merits of numerous adjectives—best, premier, best quality, leading, global, reputed, respected, celebrated, foremost, unparalleled, unmatched—concluding that most were insipid, overused, or indistinct. At one point, Jeremy complained, "everyone uses the term 'leading.' It's a word you don't even hear."

In the hyperinflated language of Indian real estate advertising copy, every developer is "leading" and "celebrated," every project is "premium," "truly world-class," "luxurious," and "ultramodern." Developers have completed a "staggering" number of "elite" projects, each an example of their "commitment to excellence" or "high quality standards." Terms referencing the international quality register pepper advertisements and brochures, indiscriminately labeling both nine-hundred square foot apartments in the outer reaches of the National Capital Region and several thousand square foot penthouses in central Gurgaon. Their ubiquity makes them suspect: to what do they refer? Bandied about and overused, terms like "high quality" and "world class" have been reduced to mere superlatives, synonymous with "super-luxurious," "prestigious," or "expensive."

One Indian advertising executive whose firm has designed advertisements for several National Capital Region developers told me that he uses the term "world class" in advertisements because it "suggests it's [the property's] got to be premium, it'll be expensive." He told me about a mall coming up in Dwarka, an unglamorous government development on the outskirts of Delhi. The developer, a client of his, bought the land at auction at a very high price and thus plans to charge investors and shop owners the exorbitant rate of Rs. 40,000 per square foot to buy into the project. The advertising executive told me, "Now if I don't use the word 'world class' there, I can't sell it. . . . I can't find another word. We [racked our brains] to see can we use any other word than 'world class'? It didn't have—nothing had similar impact."[7] The property is so expensive that he feels only the phrase "world-class shopping center" conveys the right image.

What does "world class" mean besides "premium" or "expensive"? "Means nothing," the advertising executive concluded. The problem, he determined, is that words like "premium" and "world class" are relative. They mean something different to everyone:

> Premium is relative, *na*? To a guy who is in this office of mine, a person who is only a guy drawing low salary, to him his benchmark of premium will be what? To a person like me the benchmark to the word premium is going to be different. So premium has no standardization. . . . His aspiration is also to buy premium, as much as my aspirations are to buy premium. For me premium would be a golf course house, but for him premium may be just buying a flat would be premium for him.

Suggesting something different—but equally desirable—to different audiences, these descriptive terms fail to refer consistently to the same set of emblems. Is "premium" a golf course home or an ordinary apartment?

The relativity of these terms is appealing to advertisers but threatening to EuroFund, whose India strategy rests on the rent-generating possibilities of an exclusive definition of quality. Others need to see EuroFund constructions as authoritative, authentic tokens of the international quality register in order for the company to gain the high rents it seeks. If premium means something different for everyone and if quality is in the eye of the beholder, then why partner with EuroFund or rent one of its buildings?

Surprisingly, the ranking system that the international real estate community uses—Grade/Class A, B, C—is also a relative terminology, referring to one thing in India and another abroad. In the 1990s, when multinationals began searching for office space in India, a Grade A office building met only their minimum functional requirements. Anshuman Magazine, the chairman and managing director of CB Richard Ellis, the first international property consultancy to establish an office in India, recounted,

> So any building which had sufficient power, 100 percent power back up, and central air-conditioning was an A Grade building. It may just look like a dust-bin, but if it offered all these three things, you know. Fourth, of course, also important, . . . was contiguous large space. So there were hardly any buildings where . . . you could take 10,000 square feet on a floor. So these four things will define an A Grade building.

Multinationals were looking for "A Grade like you would see in the US, anywhere: there's a nice lobby, there's proper good construction, the building looks nice," but in the mid-1990s, Mr. Magazine had to struggle to find buildings that met the minimal criteria of electricity, air-conditioning, and sufficient space:

> I think we could only define one building in the city [Delhi] which was A Grade, and it wasn't really A Grade to international standard, but close to it, and the next building again we categorized as A Grade, but then we defined A Grade because we didn't want to mislead or raise expectations . . . of someone coming and saying it is A Grade so they suddenly think it's A Grade.

Note his difficulty: he did not want to mislead his international clients by using the label "Grade A" for buildings which he felt were not "really A Grade to international standard," so he specified exactly what he meant by Grade A. If there is an "international Grade A" and an "Indian Grade A," the term "Grade A"—which sounds very much like a standard—must not be one. Like "premium" or "world class," Grade A is a relative measure.

In fact, the Building Owners and Managers Association International (BOMA), a standard-setting lobby for the commercial real estate industry, describes its building class system as "a *subjective* quality rating of buildings which indicates the competitive ability of each building to attract similar types of tenants" (BOMA, emphasis added). BOMA provides only a general definition of a "Class A" commercial building since it is a relative measure:

> Class A: Most prestigious buildings competing for premier office users with rents above average for the area. Buildings have high quality standard finishes, state of the art systems, exceptional accessibility and a definite market presence. (BOMA)

This definition provides only one quantitative measure—rent—and a number of qualitative descriptors.[8] What counts as "market presence" or "high quality standard finishes" or "state of the art systems"? Who are "premier office users"? What constitutes a "prestigious" building? According to BOMA, Grade A is a context-dependent categorization; it means "the best in a particular market." But what—or who—constitutes the best?

While real estate consultants consistently refer to the Grade A office market in India, EuroFund employees questioned this categorization. Jeremy commented to one of the visiting architects that one building, "widely regarded as the best in Delhi," would actually be "Class B space in a secondary market in [Europe]." The relativity of such terms provided both a space for Indian developers' claims of producing international quality buildings and EuroFund's critiques. Before we turn to how EuroFund distinguishes itself through critique in this context, let us consider another aspect of it: images.

IMAGES

Images offer EuroFund no more definitive terrain for proving its expertise than does advertising language; images are now easily replicated, circulated, and manipulated. As we have seen, Indian developers and their architectural consultants borrow architectural elements from around the world. The architects I interviewed in India referred to books of American, European, and Chinese architecture for design inspiration, as well as to digital photographs they had taken while traveling. Many worked as associate architects for foreign architectural firms.[9] Graphic designers were equally connected to international trends. They subscribe to international design and fashion magazines, collect books, and browse the Internet. As one graphic designer explained,

> So our entire team, we have a twenty-member team—all of them are surfing, seeing blogs, seeing lifestyle trends. So, a lot of time is going into researching, reading up, seeing in terms of what's happening abroad. To a certain extent, what's happening now in India is actually what is happening abroad also. It's quite related.

Many architects, graphic designers, and computer modelers do projects for international clients; they believe their own work is on par with designs produced elsewhere in the world.

These designers have produced a deluge of images for real estate marketing which help to position developers' projects as part of the quality register. Billboards for proposed real estate projects clutter the streets of Indian cities, and large, colored advertisements for housing and malls fill the newspapers. At real estate exhibitions and developers' sales offices and websites, animated computer renderings lead potential buyers on virtual tours of residential complexes that have yet to be constructed. Many of these still images and "walk-throughs" are convincing simulacra (fig. 7.3). Created entirely on the computer, they mimic the textures, lighting, and depth of actual architecture.[10] These signs for nonexistent objects require little capital or effort to manipulate, and like verbal advertising promises, they lend themselves to hyperbole.[11] Advertising images represent buildings before they are constructed, showing finished skyscrapers where only a muddy field or partially excavated hole currently exists. Making aspirations concrete, they are critical to developers' attempts to draw investment (large investments, life savings) from potential buyers *in advance* of building construction.[12]

Developers also use stock photography purchased from international image banks such as Getty or Corbis to position their projects as international quality constructions. These "build the lifestyle," as one designer put it, by depicting scenes of light-skinned people engaged in luxury pursuits in patently foreign locales. Advertisements and brochures often picture shingled pitched-roof houses, New England fall foliage, or recognizable places such as New York City's Central Park.

Graphic designers claim that the trouble and cost of organizing photographic shoots in India, as well as tight deadlines, lead them to download imagery on the Internet rather than create their own. While they complain that international agencies offer little Indian stock imagery, they also acknowledge that images of white people convey prestige. One explained,

> We try not to shoot too many white skins, but still it helps you communicate more international feel, especially with the NRIs. People relate. In India there is one major problem, is that anything which is white people, it's bound to be good. That's a misconception we have.

Such images certainly create an "international feel"; they *are* international, indexing non-Indian places and contexts that likely will not correspond to the completed building or its inhabitants.

Similarly, architects and developers often copy three-dimensionally modeled

A view of Central Park II

images from Chinese collections of computer imagery. Madhuri, the director of a company that creates both still and animated 3D computer renderings for real estate developers explained,

> Normally what happens is, these [Chinese] renderings are made in the market for very, very low price so what the guy does is, he makes your building as per the plan in 3D, OK, then he'll take this Chinese file of landscape and people included in it and put them lower in Photoshop so you will see all those Chinese characters [people] also.

Like stock photography, these 3D images often depict landscapes and inhabitants that are unlikely to correspond to the completed building.

Moreover, Madhuri complained that often, when she does a 3D rendering from the architect's CAD (Computer Aided Design) drawings, the resulting image does not match the concept drawing that the architect initially showed the developer. As a result, her renderings often disappoint the developer. She described a conversation from earlier that morning with a developer who wanted a 3D image for advertising that corresponded to the initial concept sketch—not to the CAD drawings that will be used to construct the building. She showed me the two images from her morning dispute, both of an aluminum and glass ship of a building with a space-needle turret at one end. Her 3D image based on the CAD files depicted a taller, boxier building with an entirely different glass grid, parking, and landscaping. Pointing to her own drawing, she said, "This is how the building will look. He says, 'No, you just give me that,'" referring to the architect's initial rendering. She called the latter "unrealistic," commenting, "I mean the building will never look like, you know, it will never look like this." In the end, however, Madhuri capitulated to the developer's demand, as she normally does. Even the architects agree, she said, "The architect is normally has always said that 'do as he [developer] says because what you are doing is just marketing,' so that's the stand. 'What I have to make as an architect and develop, I will make, so whatever he wants you to show, you show.'" Perceived as "just marketing" neither the developer nor the architect mind that the building will never approximate the advertising images.

Architects, graphic designers, and computer modelers complained to me about "unclear briefs" from developers, tight deadlines, and little coordination between consultants. One graphic designer told me about creating a twenty-four-page brochure from a few floor plans and two sketches. Another claimed that all she was told about one project was "we are doing a mall in Ludhiana, make a brochure." They described a production process in which professional roles are not well defined. The 3D imaging director Madhuri, for example, complained that her staff decides the decor of the interior images they produce rather than having it specified by the developer's interior designer, as international clients do.[13]

As we can see, the political economy of image production, the idea that this work is "just marketing," and the feeling that light skinned models convey prestige together result in poor correspondence between different representations of the building or representations and the final, finished building. Different images (brochures, print advertisements, and architectural construction documents) for the same project are often not well-calibrated to one another, hinting at a semiotic ideology and a production process that differs from those EuroFund is used to. As "forward-looking statements," these images of not-yet-constructed buildings do not lie, exactly (Sunder Rajan 2006, 132–33), but they are often interpreted as "fakery."

Bureaucrats, for example, sometimes find this lack of correspondence troubling. A member of the national environmental impact assessment committee that gives environmental clearance to real estate projects complained that some developers

> have the audacity to show us [the committee] promotional material as presentations that are outrageously different from what they are building. They show a big thick forest, but it's impossible because the whole site is a two-story basement car park! Or impossible water bodies. . . . it's all completely fake.

In this committee member's view, the mismatch between different representations of the same (as of yet nonexistent) building amounts to "fakery," making a mockery of a review process that treats drawings as binding promises of future action, legal documents to which future construction activities must adhere.[14]

Foreign developers share the committee member's expectation of the truth function of images. Donald Trump, Jr., for example, speaking of emerging markets in general, complained "I mean a floor could be humped, it could be sloped, it could be level. But because you call it five star, it all of a sudden is. Great marketing, lack of product to follow it" (Knowledge@Wharton 2008b). Similarly, the graphic designers I spoke with complained that developers' lack of "clarity" and "consistency" of vision contributed to inaccurate marketing materials, something which bothered them greatly. One graphic designer told me, "So you know we try and be honest. Sometimes we met clients who say it doesn't matter to us, I mean for them it is just selling, but for us, it's not really that thing, because we really want the real true thing of that development to come out." His partner added, "We can enhance, but we can't lie about anything you know."

A lack of consistency between advertising imagery and construction plans means that imagery, like language, provides a tricky terrain for proving claims about quality and construction capabilities. Moreover, the wide circulation of "photoreal" 3D architectural renderings and lush stock photography makes it difficult for EuroFund to prove its expertise merely by showing potential partners a corporate brochure with photographs of finished buildings. Just as the terms "quality" and "premium" have become watered down through overuse, the production and circulation of sophisticated imagery has produced a graphically saturated real estate market.

Perhaps in order to side-step this noisy semiotic environment rich with competing representations, EuroFund employees insisted that once they have completed a building in India, people will want to work with them. Jeremy said, "I absolutely believe that once the first building is built, once people can see, then the floodgates will open." According to EuroFund employees, one might be able to mimic "quality" with various representations, but one identifies true "quality" through un-mediated experience, not description. Nick explained, "Unless somebody has experienced it, it's hard to say or hard to explain the difference between a quality building and what they're in right now. . . . And it's only until you start building something that people can experience and then say, wow that is different."

Commensuration Work: Finding Partners

For Nick, charged with overseeing the construction of EuroFund's Indian projects, the indeterminacy of quality-related terms poses a challenge. In order to replicate the "quality" for which EuroFund is known, he must make sure the joint venture hires capable contractors, subcontractors, material suppliers, and consultants. He explained that he cannot just ask, "who are the best contractors? Because the best of anything isn't necessarily the same between people or between cultures or even between companies." Even in talking to potential contractors, ambiguous and overused terms like "world class" make determining skill level or experience problematic: "when somebody says, 'We've done world-class projects before' or 'We've had experience with world-class architects,' you really have to start saying, OK, who was that and where was it and what was the project and how was it done?"

Often, he finds that the consultants with whom he meets "have such a completely different experience that you can't just talk to them with generalities." Instead, he tries to define terms very specifically:

You've got to get deeper down into what that really means. You know to the point where you say, this is a Class A office building, *which means,* thirty to forty-five seconds wait time for an elevator is the most you'll ever have. They'll go, "Wow, never had that before." So if you just say, "We want a Class A office building with great elevator service," they're thinking, "Yeah a couple of elevators, that's great elevator service, one breaks down and you'll have the other one," instead of two banks of eight elevators each. That's unheard of.

Defining terms in such detail helps Nick to communicate the difference between Indian and international buildings to his interlocutors. By devaluing Indian definitions of "quality" and substituting his own, he establishes a common ground for reference in future discussions and a set of normative criteria for judging Indian construction.

Wary of miscommunication and variable interpretation, Nick has spent much of his time since arriving in India seeing for himself: visiting construction sites and finished buildings and meeting with contractors and manufacturers. Nick advocates,

> You have to go out and look, you have to go out and meet the people and see what they're doing, not just the end result but the process and how good they are at quality control and how good they are at understanding what your concept of quality is versus their concept of quality.

When someone tells him of a good facade subcontractor or local HVAC manufacturer, he visits them himself. As we have seen, he believes quality is a material condition best judged by the eye of an expert; only by *seeing* production processes and final products can Nick differentiate and compare— commensurate—"quality." By claiming that quality cannot be represented but must be experienced and judged by a professional like himself, Nick bolsters the importance of his own expertise. Implicitly, he is arguing that quality is a question of discernment and individual training; its production requires someone like himself.

Critique, then, is a central tool in EuroFund's quality project. Like Nick, the New York architects critiqued Indian buildings in order to distinguish Euro-Fund quality from Indian quality. By differentiating close look-alikes from "the real thing," the architects cast doubt on their Indian competitors' ability to produce the register and bolstered their own claims to it. One architect dismissed the buildings in Gurgaon as "flip and ill-considered . . . a pile of facile clichés"—suggesting he viewed Indian attempts at building global buildings as derivative, at best. Another critiqued the practice of architectural sampling:

> And then everywhere you look, it's pure visual chaos. Every building has at least four or five ideas tacked on to it—you know, one per side or something. It's like they're all competing—they're all *screaming* for attention, none of

them is worthy of the attention they're getting. And so, you know, the visual environment is just a mess.

Rather than producing international quality buildings, Indian developers have succeeded only in producing "pure visual chaos," in her view. Similarly, EuroFund employees often pointed out poor details and inefficiencies in the office they rented and complained of local architects' ignorance about international materials like double-glazed curtain wall glass.

However, criticism of Indian "quality" penetrated more deeply than design elements, the number of elevators, or the function of HVAC machinery; EuroFund's employees and consultants were critiquing the very practice of real estate development in India, problematizing it in order to offer their expertise as the solution. For EuroFund employees, "poor quality" buildings indicated poor quality workmanship, labor control, and management practices—in short, all of the work processes that they would have to transform in order to build different buildings. As much as "quality" is an aesthetic register, it is also an index of real estate construction practices.

In the search for development partners, EuroFund employees and consultants read "poor quality" construction details and designs as indicators of the attitudes, capabilities, and interests of potential partners. For example, Jeremy recounted visiting a potential land-owning partner, a telecom firm that had recently gone public. Jeremy explained, "So, on paper at least, they are worth $1 billion." Despite the firm's worth, their office was "way on the West side of town" in a "shabby neighborhood," on a dirt road. Jeremy was surprised by the office's location and appearance: "If you had a company with that kind of money, the first thing you would do is buy a piece of land and put up a new office," Jeremy commented. "So how do you convince guys like that that it's worth spending more to build a better building?" Jeremy read the "quality" of their current office as an index of their interest in his own quality project.

Like the principal of another private equity firm with real estate investments in more than eighteen countries who boasted, "We always say we're more than capital. We bring the experience of people in the firm, whether it's negotiation or leasing, hiring architects, structuring the deal, development expertise," EuroFund claims to offer potential partners an education in real estate practice. As Jeremy explained, "I think that the ones [Indian developers] that perhaps have the sort of the self-confidence not to feel too threatened by it recognize that there is a value in joining forces with someone like us." He summarized EuroFund's extensive experience working with "some of the best most sophisticated architects in the world." In short, a few Indian developers realize that by partnering with us they can sort of compress their learning curve from how do we go from relatively primitive design and construction projects that represent even most of the better stuff that's been done in India today to something that's much more comparable to a true international quality building.

Jeremy suggests that working with EuroFund provides a shortcut from the "primitive" state of the Indian construction industry today to the capacity to produce "true international quality" buildings.

Through critique, EuroFund employees and consultants judge potential partners and create a discursive need for their own expertise. However, finding a development partner while critiquing his work as "primitive" or "substandard" is a delicate task. Jeremy admitted, "It's hard to have a thoughtful conversation about the need for better office buildings with an Indian." He noted that in social settings Indians often derided the state of Indian construction or expressed an interest in living in a EuroFund building. "They can talk," Jeremy said, "but you as a foreigner—you can't say 'Gee, it needs to improve.' They'll get defensive and say, 'Things are improving fast, India's a democracy, it takes time.'"

Ravi, one of EuroFund's directors, was also particularly attuned to the delicacy of negotiating with potential partners. Beyond the financial details of a deal, he carefully considers how to approach Indian developers, considering their age, position, and what he called "style," before addressing them. He asks himself,

> So do I want to be more respectful and a little bit more deferential, I guess is the word, or do I want to be more pal-y or chatty, because coming as a [European] firm, at least being perceived as a foreigner, and really like an eight-hundred-pound gorilla from outside the country, people are intimidated. And they would never accept—they would never own up to that, but they are.

Because they are sure of their own superiority, Ravi and Jeremy feel that potential partners must be "threatened" or "intimidated" by their presence and often take up a defensive attitude as a result. To diffuse negotiations, Ravi drops outright criticism in favor of modesty. You have to "almost downplay your importance and show yourself a little smaller than they are," he explained. He characterized the image he tries to project at meetings:

> Yeah, I'm very big where I am, but today here in India, I am nothing. You are the one who is big. And you're the one I'm going to learn from. And yes I bring enough to the table that I will benefit you as well, but in this power equation I'm clear that you are the one who is the boss, because you have an asset [land], I have a talent [real estate development expertise]. You have a proven

value-add, I have a potential value-add, which has yet to be proven. It's been proven in other markets. I'm very confident of proving it, but it's still potential.

Jeremy and Ravi have to walk a fine line between downplaying their expertise as merely potentially useful and making a strong case for it through criticism of existing Indian real estate practice.

In the end, the continuous task of finding Indian developers, landowners, and contractors with whom to work requires that EuroFund employees convince developers of the *value* of their expertise. Will a partnership with EuroFund really add value to an already lucrative development process? Will it result in higher rents? Anthropologist Jane Guyer explains that "because there is no meaningful 'zero' point with respect to quality, the pegging of quality to prices necessarily involves criteria of judgment and expertise, as well as political pressure" (2004, 83). EuroFund's value project hinges on pegging quality to price, on quantifying just how much better a EuroFund building will be. To do so, employees use their own judgment—and call on the expertise of the American architects—to cast aspersions on Indian real estate practices, to distinguish between Indian and EuroFund buildings, and to quantify the differences. This process is made all the more uncertain by the fact that the thing in question is not yet built. As Ravi explains, in negotiations he finds himself politely arguing for a "potential value-add, which has yet to be proven."

Neither the quality of the future building nor EuroFund employees' expertise is proven. As we have seen, Indian real estate developers also aim to produce buildings as part of the international quality register, resulting in a profusion of claims to "quality" and diluting EuroFund employees' authority. For Bourdieu (1993) both authority and its legitimation—value and belief in that value—are produced through struggles in the field of cultural production. However, in India there is no unified "field of production." Struggles for value and legitimation take place on a complex terrain: the intersection of the Indian field of real estate production, with its own history of practices and politics of prestige, and the international field of real estate production, with practices emanating from "world cities" such as New York and London.[15] Thus the existing practices, political economy, and culture of Indian real estate production militate against valuing EuroFund's expertise.

This complicates working relationships between EuroFund and its partners. While Jeremy and Ravi did form a partnership with BuildIndia, the deal took them more than eighteen months to secure. Jeremy complained, "We're the most trusted firm in [Europe]. We have a very good name. But here, we have to start from scratch." Similarly, other EuroFund employees felt that many of the Indian developers with whom they spoke were "arrogant" about their own capabilities and doubtful of the worth of partnering with Euro-Fund. In the face of such challenges, Jeremy can only hope that as his firm completes projects in India, others' judgment will concur with his own and grant EuroFund employees more authority: he believes that more and more Indian developers and landowners will "begin to say, well, these guys know how to develop a product that does actually create more value and therefore there is some value that is inherent to their knowledge." It is to the process of "developing a product"—constructing buildings—that we now turn.

Quality Projects II: Transforming Practices

Is Value Primarily in the Land or in the Building?

In the last chapter, I described "quality" as a semiotic register, a strategy for entering a new market, and a means of producing profit. In order to implement its "quality project," EuroFund must enroll allies—an Indian developer, architects, consultants, and contractors—and control their work (see Latour 1987). I now explain how EuroFund's attempts to construct a building in India pit the company against established Indian real estate practices. The conflicts that emerged enable us to see some of the differences between Indian and international fields of practice. Due to the particular history of real estate development in India and the current speculative boom in land, Indian developers had little incentive to spend on building construction and finishes—the material elements central to the execution of the quality register—and were concerned instead with proving to Indian consumers that they could "deliver" finished buildings at all. These disincentives complicated EuroFund's attempts to convince others that their practices were valuable, to control the construction process, and to construct a "quality building" in India. Euro-Fund's struggles exemplify the political nature of value making, the fact that "what kinds of differences are important" (Ferry 2013, 18) is also up for debate, and they indicate just how much work making an international real estate market in India is.

Jeremy explained that much of the time, he doesn't make a hard sell for EuroFund's expertise. Instead,

the way that gets discussed is a little bit indirectly in talking about if we form a venture, how will the profits be split. . . . That's where the rubber really meets the road in terms of how much of the profit they think they should get before we get to share and how much we get to share in.

Negotiations over profit-sharing agreements reveal that EuroFund's Indian counterparts have a different theory of where value lies in the development process, and thus, of the value of EuroFund's expertise.

Jeremy, as we have seen, focuses on "designing and constructing a very high quality building" because he believes that "the lion's share of the value creation is in the design and construction." In India, by contrast,

> because it is difficult to assemble it [land] and it is difficult to get approvals, so once you have actually succeeded in assembling some land and obtaining approvals, that's in India considered by far and away the most difficult part of the development process and therefore the part that deserves to be rewarded most richly with profits.

Indian developers value land and their own expertise in assembling it, not EuroFund's development expertise.

The importance placed on developers' land banks in the press, in developers' rhetoric, and in stock market valuation exercises corroborates Jeremy's hunch that Indians see value as residing in the process of land assembly (see *Times of India* 2007a). One securities firm, for example, writes in a note to investors about the upcoming initial public offer for the real estate developer Parsvnath:

> The foresight in identifying the right area of development and acquiring the approvals and the land at a relatively cheap level distinguishes a good player from an also ran in the industry. Acquisition of land at low rates is the key differentiator in the margins on the projects. (Batlivala and Karani Securities 2006)

According to the note's authors, the most important aspect of real estate development is the initial steps ("identification of potential areas of development; evaluation of applicable laws & obtaining requisite approvals; acquisition of title and/or development rights of land")—*not* the construction of the building. Other consultants agree. JP Morgan, for example, writes in a note to investors that the "ability to source land at cheaper-than-market rates is the key competitive advantage of a number of developers" (JP Morgan 2007, 34). The principle of a private equity firm commented that "the markets are rewarding developers with land banks now. They are getting more valuation." He criticized the validity of this approach: "The capital markets are evolving. They don't know how to value a [real estate] company. The investment banks just say, this is how much land you have. Then they discount it at some rate, and that's the valuation."[1]

The differential understanding of the value of the various steps of real estate development—land agglomeration versus building construction—constitutes a structural friction between Indian and foreign investors that colors debates over the value of partnerships. Indian developers are selling their local expertise in assembling land parcels. If they believe that the value is in their work and constructing buildings is but a minor detail, they will be hesitant to share profits with foreign firms. As a result, many of the foreign funds have had an uphill battle convincing potential partners that, as one private equity fund manager quipped, "just because you've got the land, it's not the end of the game."

Real Estate Practice and the Production of Quality

The widespread belief that constructing buildings is only a side activity to the main business of trading in land indicates that the field of real estate production operates differently in India than in the United States and Western Europe. Whereas foreign funds and investors conceptualize commercial buildings as revenue-producing units and their construction as a gamble on streams of future rents, many Indian real estate developers understand buildings as one-time sales opportunities that can "unlock the value" of land parcels. Whether a building is leased or sold has important implications for construction practices and "quality," understood as the level of material finish required to position buildings as "international" and attract wealthy global tenants. Many Indian developers are not interested in constructing buildings to the design and finish specifications that EuroFund employees believe are necessary to produce "quality buildings."

The practice of selling rather than leasing commercial space (both offices and malls) reflects a general preference in North India for owning property. Just as individuals prize land and gold as stable, prudent investments, many Indian companies prefer to own property, not lease it as multinationals routinely do. One broker with whom I spoke expressed skepticism that leasing would ever become widespread in India since "any guy who made a decision to own office ten years ago, today thinks he did the wisest thing. . . . because the intrinsic valuations have been only northward."

On the production side, selling rather than leasing property has been the market norm in India because developers had little access to formal funding for either land acquisition or construction before the late 1990s. Instead, together with the landowner, a developer would sell his unconstructed commercial building in small sections (anywhere between 500 and 2,000 square feet) to numerous investors. Pre-selling provided the developer with cash upfront and little incentive to finish construction. According to Ashish, a real estate consultant, "those buildings would take ten to fifteen years to come because the land owner has made some money, the developer has made a profit already before he even starts digging." A building might be pre-sold to numerous owners, creating too fragmented a group to fight the developer over building completion. Furthermore, investors often sold their share of the building, earning a profit before the building was completed. In the 1980s and 1990s, commercial buildings in India operated as financial instruments regardless of the construction quality, indeed, regardless of whether construction was even carried out.

The same speculative trading of unfinished buildings occurs in residential projects. The developer increases the price of the property over the course of construction, and investors buy and sell at just under the developer's price, turning a profit with each paper transaction. One developer told *The Economic Times*, "I sell pieces of paper that are traded many times over before the end user comes in at the stage where the property is nearing completion" (Kurup 2007). While pre-selling prior to the finalization of land ownership or approvals—a practice called "prelaunching"—is officially illegal, pre-sales continue; they may have even increased due to the real estate rush (*Realty Plus* 2006a). In 2004–6, according to Ashish, "the developer would announce a project and he may have a brochure, he may not, he may have the plans, he may not have the plans, but he will announce the project. Over the weekend, the whole project is sold." As the editor of a real estate magazine explained, "developers sell everything in thin air. Before even the first brick is laid, it is all sold."[2]

As the market for residential properties tightened in 2007, such frenzied sales became the stuff of industry lore. Developers sold their projects more slowly, offered more amenities, and constructed model flats and more informative brochures to lure potential clients. For the commercial sector, however, it remained "a different story; there is no space, demand is so high, rentals have doubled, and everything is flying off the shelf," according to Ashish. Consultants told me that in 2007, commercial buildings in markets like Gurgaon were pre-sold or pre-leased well before construction was finished.

These practices—pre-sales, pre-launches, selling rather than leasing—and the high demand for office space have had important ramifications for the production of property with the high level of material finish and high construction costs requisite for EuroFund's quality project. First, to capitalize on the booming office market, most developers begin construction without complete construction documents, compressing the design and construction time into a short twelve to eighteen months. One Indian architect explained,

The American way is to finish the design first. Here, we design as we go along. Developers are brokers-cum-developers. They've booked a piece of land, and they want a hole in the ground to start booking [tenants]. Even a DLF works that way today. They don't fully engineer before construction.

The managing director of a large construction company complained that Indian developers provide unclear architectural briefs and usually do not pay enough of the architectural fee in advance to obtain complete drawings: "The client [developer] is not paying a significant amount of the fee before starting the work. He is only paying twenty-thirty percent of the fee. How do you expect ninety percent [of the work] with twenty percent of the fee?"

Without advance planning and complete documents, contractors and developers make ad hoc changes to the building design during construction. I heard of projects that started as malls and became office buildings half way through construction and vice versa. One architect, for example, described a project he worked on for DLF. They worked only "up to the construction stage." By then "the market had changed. We designed an office, and they wanted to change it into a hotel or retail." While working without documents provides Indian developers with the flexibility to adapt to changing demand, EuroFund employees feel that last-minute changes threaten their quality project. As Nick explains,

> If they have to rip out a wall or cut a piece of concrete out or redo something, then that's a small price to pay for a quick turnaround. But what that gives you is horrible quality. You leave a lot of the design decisions up to the contractor, who has no motivation to do it right and every motivation to do it as cheaply and quickly as possible.

Second, EuroFund employees feel that pre-selling provides a disincentive to spend on construction. Jeremy reckons,

> If you are primarily a landowner and investor who as a necessary evil also builds buildings because that's part of the deal of how you get your money extracted from land. If you can show somebody a picture of a building you're going to build, get them to agree to buy at a price, and sign a contract and you've sold it. . . . therefore, by definition, from that point on, any penny you save on actually building the building goes directly into your pocket.

He concludes that since the developer fixes the sales price in advance, "the value of your land, which is what you own at the outset is, will be greatest if you spend the least you possibly can on . . . what you build." By contrast, Indian consultants noted that Indian developers *will* spend on construction—up to a point. Indian developers often increase spending on certain finishes in order to market a building as "luxury," for example by installing wooden flooring instead of tile. These are small cost additions compared to the fixed costs of excavation, concrete, and steel, and they can result in significantly higher sales prices on the finished building (see Muthukumar 2007).

Third, developers need not worry about building maintenance or wear if they sell it off quickly after constructing it. As a result, facilities maintenance is a new field in India, a service few developers use. A retail consultant for one of the largest real estate developers in the country commented that most mall developers "simply take up the land that they bought cheap five years ago, sell it for wherever the booming marketplace is and why worry about anything. Once I've sold it, I can forget about it." While his company has moved to a lease-maintenance model and a more long-term view of mall development, he spoke wistfully of his competitors' business model, which he thinks will continue to "work in lots of places and lots of areas."[3] He commented,

> Sometimes we look to say, are we are getting too long in this process and too worried about it and missing all the opportunities? Because once you've sold it, that's it, you move on and move on to the next one. . . . There is nothing particularly wrong in that model from a purely profitability model.

He wonders if the attention his company is now paying to construction and building maintenance makes sense in a market where moving quickly from project to project remains profitable.

The build-and-sell model remains profitable in part because the rush for office space among IT firms, Business Process Outsourcing (BPO) firms, and multinational companies provides a ready market for whatever Indian real estate developers build and offers little incentive to change. As Nick asked,

> people have been building buildings that just are mediocre, but they get filled up immediately, they get sold for huge profits immediately, and so why would anybody spend any more time or any more effort or any more money making a better product when they can get mediocrity, get a huge profit, flip it quickly, and nobody complains?

Moreover, high land costs—driven by speculation, politicians' fees, and multinational corporate demand—add a further disincentive to spending on construction. In order to maintain large profit margins in the face of land costs which amount in some cases to 50 to 70 percent of project costs, developers do not increase construction budgets.[4]

Some who do business with Indian real estate developers interpret these practices as shortsighted and miserly. A graphic designer who works on real estate brochures complained, "Today the thing is, the builder's objective is very short term. He is launching a property, he wants to sell the property and get out." An architect explained that developers have a "two-faced approach. What is visible, dress it up. But what's not visible, just punch windows and paint it." Alexander, the managing director of a European kitchen fitting and architectural hardware firm, finds selling architectural hardware to Indian developers trying:

> If you sit in front of them as a professional company, trying to sell them a quality product, they are really not that interested. You know there's always— our conversation goes always, "give me your lowest price, give me your lowest price." You know, "your competition is quoting me thirty percent less than you, give me the lowest price." So it's something that can really tear at your nerves.

As I have shown here, this characterization of Indian real estate developers as interested in the lowest possible costs, the highest possible margins, and the quickest possible turn-around times on projects is a function of the field of real estate practice in India and its history—as well as developers' new role as intermediaries to global capitalists. These characterizations also result from foreign investors' attempts to distinguish themselves as international experts. As I show in the section "Conflicting Temporalities" later in this chapter, however, there are other elements of this field of practice that reward developers' long-term value projects at scales larger than individual buildings.

At the scale of individual projects, the field tilts so much in favor of low-cost construction that EuroFund has found limited support for its proposals to spend considerably more on construction than other developers, even from real estate consultants and other non-developer industry members. I accompanied two EuroFund employees to an interview with a property consultant who told them skeptically, "If you want to break even in nine or eleven years, not the standard six—if that's what you want to do, that's a business call." Another developer I spoke with also felt that EuroFund "might just break even" with construction costs of Rs. 3,500 per square foot. He felt he could do the same job for Rs. 2,000 per square foot, and that the difference lay in the high salaries EuroFund pays its expatriate employees, rather than in the level of construction finish. A retail consultant, familiar with the EuroFund/ BuildIndia deal, commented, that since "the marketplace here is not crying out for that top end," EuroFund's strategy is "a leading edge over everything else that is happening." EuroFund's strategy places it ahead of accepted local practice and perceived demand.

Indian Real Estate Developers' Other Quality Project

The field of Indian real estate practice discourages developers from investing in the expensive construction materials that EuroFund employees feel are necessary to attract a particular clientele and to uphold their reputation internationally. However, Indian developers hoping to distinguish themselves from their competitors do invest in a different quality project: the delivery of finished buildings to buyers. One consultant told me that when he was working with a developer, "if we produced 85 percent of what we showed [advertised], it used to be good enough." In a field of practice marked by such an attitude, as well as by outright fraudulence, "quality" means trustworthiness.

The public furor over the 1997 Uphaar fire, in which 59 people died at a Delhi cinema due to the negligence of developers, managers, and government inspectors, indicates that the Indian public cares deeply about the physical soundness of buildings, as does the pervasive advertising promise that buildings are "earthquake resistant" (Hussain and Nayak 2007; *Times of India* 2007d). Substandard materials, admixtures, and illegal practices cannot necessarily be seen in a finished building, rendering every leak or crack a potential indicator of something more dangerous than unsightly. Stories about crumbling walls, "seepage," construction accidents, and improper inspections abound, creating a discursive setting in which "quality" carries tremendous moral force (e.g., Thakurta 2007). In this context, "good quality" implies more than physical soundness; it connotes opposition to corruption, greed, and negligence. It is exactly this moral force that gives the critique of "poor quality" its teeth and which explains why Indian developers appeal to "quality" as they attempt to construct a trustworthy corporate image.

More than just eschewing shoddy construction, "quality" for Indian developers means *finishing* buildings, because the Indian public worries about developers who take consumers' money and never deliver homes. By prebooking plots of land and prelaunching projects, developers have been able to sell land that they do not own outright and promise construction for which they have not received government sanction. A real estate consultant told me about a developer who sold 105 acres of land, of which he only owned 76 acres. Absconding with the profit, the developer neither had the money to buy the remaining land nor to pay for the license to develop the property. The consultant explained,

> Usually you ask people to pay 10 to 15 percent up front as registration. You announce a scheme and you sell. Then once you get all the licenses, then the balance money comes in and you can develop it. These guys took the entire

money up front and they've eaten it up. They've got no money for the licenses. It was 70 crore! Now who in their right mind will fund them? Where is the 70 crore going to come from?

It seems unlikely that the developer will be able to assemble the money, the remaining land, and the sanctions necessary to go ahead with the project, potentially leaving numerous buyers in the lurch.

In a similar case investigated by authorities in the Economic Offences Wing,[5] the government believes that Y. S. Rana, owner of PS&G Developers and Engineers, Ltd. defrauded nearly four hundred people who had bought into his "fake housing projects" across North India. Rana had no permissions for building townships or housing, yet he showed prospective buyers photographs of construction and convinced them to invest. When investors later raised questions, Rana allegedly issued bad checks as "refunds" and closed his office in a swanky Delhi hotel (Chauhan 2007a, 2007b).

Even if developers intend to develop their projects, they often use buyers' money to fund procurement of land rather than construction, causing delays. When developers launch projects without the necessary approvals they also incur delays and jeopardize buyers' legal claims to the land (Kurup 2007; Nandy 2007). Nevertheless, even well-known builders prelaunch projects, some fraudulently declaring that they have government approvals in place and others optimistically promising delivery of properties by a certain date (Kurup 2007; Jha 2007). Many fail to deliver what they promise. For example, in 2006 Parsvnath Developers had eleven cases pending before various consumer dispute redressal forums, primarily for not providing the facilities or the square footage that they promised or for "delay in delivery of possession" (Parsvnath Developers Ltd. 2006, 221–22).

Cases that have come before the National Consumer Disputes Redressal Commission, a national consumer court established in 1988,[6] reveal that developers often delay project delivery by years and dodge refunding investors' money when projects do not go as planned (see also Garg 2008; *Hindustan Times* 2006). Complainant Kunj Behari Mehta, for example, signed a purchase agreement for a home in Celebrity Homes, Palam Vihar, Gurgaon with Ansal Properties and Industries Ltd. in March 1995, with the expectation of gaining possession of the house in October 1998. Ansal Properties did not deliver the property until December 2007 (*Kunj Behari Mehta vs. Ansal Properties and Industries, Ltd*).[7] Shri Taranjit Singh booked a flat with Unitech in 1991 and paid for 95 percent of it in installments by 1995,[8] but Unitech did not turn the flat over to him until September 2001 (*Shri Taranjit Singh vs. M/s. Unitech, Ltd*). Such cases can take five to ten years to resolve through the commission, especially if either party appeals, leaving consumers with neither their apartments nor the money they invested in them. Buyers who bought an apartment years ago find that even if their money is refunded, they cannot afford a similar apartment in the same location today due to the spike in housing prices (*Ms. Veena Khanna vs. M/s. Ansal Properties and Industries, Ltd*).

In the absence of clear national guidelines or specific language in the Indian penal code regarding false advertisement,[9] the Consumer Disputes Redressal Commission decisions delineate new parameters of culpability, representation, and intention as the Commission navigates complaints from property buyers. In *Shri Taranjit Singh vs. M/s. Unitech, Ltd*, the New Delhi Municipal Committee (NDMC) canceled Unitech's building sanction in 1993, a ruling which Unitech challenged in the Delhi High Court. The builders claimed that regulatory authorities held up construction, and the National Consumer Disputes Redressal Commission agreed, citing "unexpected judicial proceedings" rather than "deficiency of service" on the part of the builder as the reason for delay.

However, the commission faults builders who do not "diligently seek" government permissions. For example, DLF sold flats in a proposed complex to buyers in 1993 but did not receive approval for its building plans until 1995. DLF delayed delivery of the flats to buyers by three years yet attempted to charge them escalation fees to cover the increased costs of construction. The commission came down in favor of the buyer in a 2007 appeal ruling on the case, concluding that,

> in our view, before obtaining statutory clearances, such as, sanction for construction and approval of Site Plan and other relevant documents, if the builder issues tempting advertisement or promises to deliver the possession of the constructed flat within 2½ years to 3 years, then the fault lies with the builder.

Moreover, "it would be unfair trade practice, if the builder, without any planning and without obtaining any effective permission to construct building/ apartments, invites offers and collects money from the buyers" (*Brig. (Retd.) Kamal Sood vs. M/s. DLF Universal Ltd*). This decision also treats the brochure as part of the developer's contract with the buyer. In the case of *M/s. Madan Builders vs. R. K. Saxena*, the commission also came out strongly against the builder's use of advertisements, arguing that "it is evident from the record that the OP [Opposite Party] at the time of booking pointed a very rosy picture so as to lure gullible persons to invest their hard earned money in the project in question." Because the builder failed to get prior permissions for the features advertised in his brochure (for example, "glass capsule" elevators), the court felt that the advertisements were "false representations."

Despite the strong stance taken by the commission against late delivery of projects and developers' selling properties before they have government approvals, these cases reveal both to be common practices in the industry.[10] These practices also constitute the terrain of Indian developers' brand building campaigns. Clearly, Indian property buyers face fundamental uncertainty about whether buildings will ever materialize and confusion as to whether advertisements are to be trusted.[11] Developers (themselves not in control of an onerous government approval process) may never, or only belatedly, construct the building in which consumers have sunk lakhs of rupees, and buyers have only limited recourse through a court system that will take years to deliver restitution. In such an environment, developers build their reputations on delivery; those that can point to finished projects as indexes of their integrity and construction capacity have an advantage in this market.

I asked Rajesh, the vice president of an Indian real estate development firm that operates in the National Capital Region, about the importance of interior finishes and amenities on residential projects, and he answered instead, "Delivery makes the difference. That's how you get known in the market." He saw the successful delivery of finished projects—rather than design or amenities—as key to building a brand name. The ability to deliver

> impacts on the word of mouth publicity that you can go talk about that every time, all the time, we make projects on time, and we deliver the quality we promised we would do so. You know, there's a certain amount of integrity: I did what I did by when I said I would do it. . . . You walk the talk. So you know, so that credibility starts building up in the market and over a period of time it acquires a certain critical mass.

Rajesh's young company had yet to acquire a "critical mass" of credibility. Its promoter began acquiring land in Gurgaon only in 2006, and so Rajesh was anxious about completing the firm's first project: "we are very keen that this first project which is getting completed next year in NCR [National Capital Region], that will set the standard for this company for the future."[12]

By contrast, established firms like Unitech or DLF have delivered countless projects, and as a result, according to Rajesh, "they launch anything, everything sells." Gold-standard real estate brands, their reputations derive not from the structural integrity of their constructions (something about which residents griped), but from their record of constructing buildings. One broker told me, DLF's "reputation is to a large extent built on credibility of delivering. They have developed and built half of Delhi. They have done a lot of work here, so it's a great credit. And that trust is over fifty years or sixty years of work." In fact, their brand name is so strong, the broker asserted, that "they get away without showing any papers [licenses, approvals]. They get away without making a sample apartment. They could even get away without the brochure being ready." Because the urban landscape of South Delhi and Gurgaon testifies to DLF's construction capability, the firm is able to maintain a good reputation despite engaging in the same activities (prelaunches, lack of approvals, delayed delivery, etc.) as other developers.[13]

Indeed, DLF rarely adheres to the market norm of advertising through lavish brochures and impressive sample apartments. Strikingly, DLF is selling its most expensive residential properties, the Magnolias and Aralias, without interior fittings. Residents purchase bare concrete shells and build out the interiors themselves. Clearly, delivering a building matters in Indian real estate much more than the level of construction finish—or rather, producing a high end "international quality" building has little to do with producing a building with a high level of construction finish.[14] As one of the marketing agents for Silverglades, another high-end development company that maintains an excellent reputation yet foregoes sample apartments and detailed specification lists, quipped, "A guy will not buy a house because the marble is looking nice, or because the lights are put nicely."

Rather than nice lights or marble, Indian consumers are looking for a developer that will deliver buildings—that is, one they can trust, which explains the proliferation of company taglines like "Building Trust" or "Built on Trust." Claims to delivery are also common: for example, "At Alpha G:Corp, we don't just make promises. We deliver them." Indian developers publicize construction progress, showing up-to-date construction photographs on their websites or in newsletters distributed to buyers. Taneja Developers and Infrastructure (TDI) ran a bright red advertisement in the *Hindustan Times* with the banner headline "TDI fulfills its promise! Handing over possession of plots in Block A, B, & C" of the TDI City township in Sonepat. The firm claimed that construction on other sections of the project were proceeding "in full swing" and "at a fast pace."

Many developers appeal to international quality standards to position themselves as trustworthy. They often place ISO certifications right beneath the name of the company in print advertisements and on roadside hoardings (e.g., "Royal Palms: Leisure & Lifestyle ISO 9001 & ISO 14001 certified" or "JMD: Defining Quality, An ISO 19001:2000 Certified Company") (fig. 8.1). Roughly a third of the thirty-one real estate developers featured in the 2007 *Today Real Estate Buyer's Guide—Delhi and NCR* boasted of ISO or other certifications. Parsvnath, for example, claimed "ICRA DR 2-rating, ISO 9001, 14001 and OHSAS 18001 certification, Pan Indian Presence Award and Corporate Excellence awards in addition to personal acknowledgements from

FIGURE 8.1. Indian developers use international certifications to make claims about "quality," as on this sign for developer JMD. The child probably lives in the worker housing visible in the middle ground. Source: Photo by author.

some more recognized agencies."[15] Such standards do not define what a quality product is; rather, they "are intended to guarantee that production has been organized according to a number of structural elements which reflect certain minimum requirements" (ISO in Brunsson et al. 2000, 114). These are certifications of a real estate developer's business systems—not his products.

Such management certifications, then, certify Indian development companies as "quality" or trustworthy organizations. Short of pointing to completed projects, developers use them to build credibility in a market characterized by large sums of money, long investment periods, and limited accountability. Developers try to overcome these uncertainties through various credibility-building exercises (brand names, advertising, certifications, awards, etc.). This second quality project remains somewhat divorced from the production of quality qua a high level of construction finish, something that EuroFund hopes to change.

Conflicting Temporalities

EuroFund must *construct* a "quality building" in order to reap profits. As one of EuroFund's consulting architects commented, EuroFund "is really concerned that they want to be able to execute a quality building, not just design it, but execute it." As we have seen, when Indian real estate developers talk about quality, they mean a firm's status as a trustworthy company capable of delivering a building. Real estate practice and a market climate of high demand, speculation, and rapid construction militate against "quality construction," understood as high construction values and elaborate workmanship. These are important elements of EuroFund's goal of constructing a building in the quality register: buildings for multinational corporate clients and their employees need to be designed and made to certain parameters. In order for EuroFund to capitalize on their architects' expert knowledge of the quality register, they must make the constructed building conform to architects' specifications, and in order for the building to be profitable, it also has to conform to EuroFund's financial models. I now turn to EuroFund's attempts to control construction practices in order to achieve this conformity and construct a "quality building." Their difficulties asserting control highlight the conflicting temporalities of Indian and international real estate practices.

EuroFund employees believed that BuildIndia's management wanted to learn international real estate development methods, motivating their joint venture partnership. However, EuroFund employees still harbored doubts about BuildIndia's operating methods and goals—particularly their timeliness. Paul, the senior architect on the project, admitted to me that he was "not convinced that they [BuildIndia] really feel the same kind of pressures to bring a project to closure that EuroFund does." Nick and Paul were nervous about what they perceived as BuildIndia's laissez-faire attitude toward time because EuroFund faced distinct time pressures. Because EuroFund manages an investment fund, it has "to invest money at a certain pace, and they have to turn it around and bring it to revenue generation at a certain pace, and when they bring it to revenue generation, they've actually got thresholds that they have to meet, or else they pay penalties," Paul explained.

EuroFund employees are particularly concerned about time because the fund's land and construction costs are borne upfront, while revenues do not accrue until construction is completed. EuroFund's employees attempt to sustain those costs and create returns by using Excel spreadsheets to conjure not-yet-constructed buildings as flows of money over time. EuroFund's financial analyst, Samiksha, works backward from what she thinks the sale price (or rent) will be minus construction and other costs and the "developer's management fee" to get a floor square index cost. These costs and possible returns are calculated per financial quarter, taking into account the varying rates at which money will need to be spent, the time gap between expenditures and rents, the different costs of money from different sources (equity investments vs. debt), and the time value of money. (As Samiksha explained, "The later the money comes in, the less it is worth to me.") Samiksha and her colleagues attempt to foresee risks (lease values falling, the cost of debt rising, construction slowdowns, etc.) and build them into the model. These careful quarter-by-quarter projections rest on a fragile cascade of assumptions about time and money, but once established, they guide the project. To make money, EuroFund must make the construction project resemble the spreadsheet as much as possible. Thus, EuroFund operates in the space created by contracts between the past and the future; its employees attempt to fulfill obligations it has made to investors by making the present unfold in accordance to representations of the future made in the past.

By contrast, Indian developers make little pretense of controlling the future based on representations made in the past. Rather, they deal with risk by remaining open to emerging possibilities and flexible in the face of an unpredictable regulatory regime and a volatile market. As one Indian architect commented, "Owners keep something up their sleeve. They want to take advantage of new projects, a better market." Vague briefs to consultants, a piecemeal approach to construction, and flexible construction labor enable Indian developers to adopt "course corrections"—to change a mall into an office, mothball a project, or substitute building materials to take advantage of price fluctuations.

This flexibility is enabled, in part, by the fact that Indian developers start getting money back early in the development process as small-scale investors, brokers, and end users buy portions of buildings before they are constructed. For EuroFund, construction delays cost money. But Indian developers, cushioned with income during the construction process, sometimes *slow down* construction in order to preserve profits: they can transfer income to more profitable endeavors, or they can delay launching phases of the project until prices have appreciated. They respond in real time to their perception of market movements, carefully orchestrating construction with price appreciation, rather than estimating everything in advance.

As we saw at the beginning of this chapter, EuroFund employees point to their quality project as evidence of long-term thinking and code Indian practices as "short-sighted." However, given the large land banks that many Indian developers had amassed, it is clear that many had long-term visions that far exceeded EuroFund's seven year investment horizon or focus on a single building.[16] Many developers planned ambitious "integrated" townships extending over hundreds of acres that would take years to develop. This kind of large-scale strategizing is evidenced some of Indian developers' ongoing projects, for example, Hiranandani's 250-acre township at Powai, Mumbai, developed since the 1980s, and DLF's work in Gurgaon.

In Gurgaon, DLF has patiently developed approximately three thousand acres of land since the early 1980s, raising the values of its own properties over time by effecting large-scale changes in the built environment. One such manufactured "situational advantage" (see Lamarche 1976, 103) is the DLF Golf Course, which the company began constructing in 1996 (Singh 2011, 204–5). Creating an open green space dedicated to an elite sport raised the land values of DLF's adjacent landholdings and established Golf Course Road as a sought-after address.[17] DLF has profited from that resource by slowly developing properties around it. For example, the land for the Magnolias project adjacent to the golf course was purchased over the course of twenty-five years, from numerous individual landowners; DLF got land use conversions for the land in the mid-1990s, but it did not launch the project until 2005–6 (Sharma 2012).

Developers' ability to transform the built environment on such a grand scale over long time periods requires influencing the state. A small-scale developer in Pune showed me zoning maps on his laptop for the twenty-three municipalities surrounding Pune. He explained that these recently published zoning maps gave preferential treatment to prominent developers' landholdings because they had paid in advance to keep restrictions from their land. This is common practice across India.

Developers also pressure the state to build or sanction infrastructure projects that advantage their properties, particularly roads and increasingly, rapid transit. For example, the Haryana Urban Development Authority (HUDA) doubled the size of the Gurgaon Metro project to serve DLF's 26 million square foot office complex, Cyber City, and a number of its residential high-rises.[18] DLF has also partnered with HUDA to build an 8.3 kilometer 16-lane express-way to connect Golf Course Road with the NH-8 (*Business Standard* 2012).

This influence requires the long-term cultivation of relationships with powerful people. K. P. Singh's autobiography recounts years of negotiations with four Haryana chief ministers (particularly his attempts to win over Bansi Lal, who thwarted his development efforts), as well as his frequent use of powerful intermediaries—businessmen, government ministers, army officials, and others—to intercede on his behalf. Property development, in this account, is a matter of deftly navigating personal relationships (Singh 2011).

In particular, Singh's close ties with the Gandhi family over the last thirty years have made possible his transformation of Gurgaon. In the 1980s, Rajiv Gandhi (Prime Minister 1984–89 and son of Indira Gandhi) interceded with Haryana's Chief Minister Bhajan Lal on K. P. Singh's behalf first, to get him a license to develop land privately under the Haryana Urban Development Act of 1975, and then to attempt to restore the license after Bansi Lal's administration canceled it (Namburu 2007, 43, 45–46; Singh 2011, 127–28, 180–87).

These close relationships between DLF's promoters and Congress Party leadership continue. Between 2008 and 2012, DLF gave Rajiv Gandhi's son-in-law Robert Vadra crores of rupees, brought him in as a partner on a Hilton hotel project in Delhi, and sold him a 10,000 square foot penthouse and seven other apartments at DLF's most expensive properties in Gurgaon for considerably less than their market value (Singh 2012; Anand and Roy 2014).[19] Because of Robert Vadra's ties to the Congress Party (he is the son-in-law of Sonia Gandhi, Congress Party President and head of the ruling United Progressive Alliance at the time), anticorruption activist Arvind Kejriwal alleged that these property transactions were payment for political favors. In particular, Kejriwal claimed Vadra helped DLF to secure a 350-acre land deal with the Haryana State Industrial and Imports Development Corporation (*Hindu* 2012).[20]

When such allegations come to light they hint at the power that successful developers have been able to wield as well as the means that they use to transform large swaths of the built environment over time and thus create their own profitable "situational advantages." They suggest that while EuroFund was focused on one commercial building, the fund's Indian partner may have had his eye on wider panoramas, including other properties and people. These connections and concerns constitute uncertainties about which Samiksha was probably unaware and could not estimate, and they constituted a risk to EuroFund's attempts to make the building conform to its spreadsheets.

Quality Control

As they attempted to close the gap between spreadsheet and reality in order to construct a "quality building," EuroFund employees faced many sources of uncertainty and delay, from the shifting regulatory environment to the rising costs of basic building materials. Below I examine three basic sources of uncertainty in more detail: BuildIndia's decision-making style, local regulations, and labor. EuroFund employees attempted to manage the first through internal meetings and timelines; the second through hiring a knowledgeable, yet controllable, Indian associate architect; and the third through complete construction drawings and the sequencing of work.

MANAGING THE RELATIONSHIP WITH BUILDINDIA

EuroFund and its architects found working with BuildIndia challenging. EuroFund employees described BuildIndia as a disorganized and inefficient organization, slow to make decisions. They complained about numerous meetings and decisions deferred; about a complex organizational hierarchy; and about their hunch that the chairman himself was the only person at BuildIndia with the authority to decide even the most trivial things. EuroFund employees complained about difficulties scheduling meetings and establishing basic facts about the project—the location of the project's property line, for example—and they worried that BuildIndia might change direction or "lose focus," as it did when it tried to change the Floor Space Index on the project midstream. They felt the organization lacked "clarity." The senior architect Paul commented, "I don't think that they [BuildIndia] have the kind of rational and structured decision making process that [EuroFund] has." Such complaints are, of course, clear indications that the two firms have divergent modes of working and that EuroFund employees did not have the control they wanted over the project. As joint venture partners, EuroFund nevertheless needed BuildIndia's consent on design issues. As one of the architects explained, "[EuroFund] needs assurances that [BuildIndia] is on board with what we're doing because they don't want to proceed at risk, if [BuildIndia] has an objection to what we're doing."

To manage this risk, EuroFund devised a detailed project schedule, including lists of questions about important issues and deadlines for decisions. They also asked a BuildIndia representative to sit in on the design meetings. However, Linda, one of the architects, complained that "the person who sits at the meetings from [BuildIndia] is a messenger, and not empowered to make any decisions and the turnaround time from them, from [BuildIndia], does not correspond to our project schedule right now." To remedy this, the architects and EuroFund now schedule separate meetings with the BuildIndia chairman. Paul said, "The solution has to be to try to give him [the chairman] a presentation at the really key points to make sure that we get his sign-off . . . we try and [EuroFund] tries to be very clear about what it is that needs to be decided."

In desperation, they have even tried presenting design ideas directly to the associate architect, who has a close relationship with the BuildIndia chairman, in the hope that he will "pave the way" to the chairman's assent. As Linda explained, this is a risky approach:

> This is kind of an experiment this time with [the associate architect] to see if . . . by getting his buy-in and some sense, you know, by helping him to feel some sense of ownership on the decisions that have been made so far, that maybe he can be an ally in smoothing the way for the chairman. But, he may have his own agenda, who knows.

Linda was unsure if this strategy would work. Perhaps they could sway the associate architect to their side by providing a "sense of ownership," or perhaps the associate architect has "his own agenda," complicating the decision-making process further.

Control is at the heart of these negotiations and micro-political maneuverings. The architects seemed more concerned about leaving the decision-making process "wide open" than they did about particular aesthetic issues. In fact, Paul and Linda concluded that BuildIndia has, in the end, agreed with their design suggestions. Perhaps this is because Paul, Linda, Jeremy, Nick, and others at EuroFund have spent a long time preparing for meetings with the chairman, anticipating his concerns and troubleshooting solutions. Linda explained that they tried to "make sure that these meetings are really kind of a confirmation rather than a wide open forum." She explained further,

> What we've tried to do . . . is to lead them sort of to a conclusion that seems really inevitable by going through the history of how we got there because what's a little scary to us is to have a wide open forum where there are three or four options all of which are—have pros and cons—and to throw it open to a wide open discussion with them. Because that seems to be a little counterproductive and it seems hard to focus that kind of a discussion then, based on our interaction with them. Because they're not used to thinking in that way and working in that way and making decisions quickly or in a reasonable fashion with a lot of choices on the table.

Rather than have "wide open forums" for discussion, EuroFund and the architects try to narrow the choices to expedite the decision-making process.

They have tried to control the risk of an "undisciplined" partner through carefully managing interactions and the flow of information.

MANAGING THE LOCAL REGULATORY PROCESS: PART 1

As part of their efforts to negotiate the local regulatory process, EuroFund sought out an Indian associate architect to act as a local liaison.[21] In a conference room at a five-star hotel, the architects from New York and several EuroFund employees interviewed five firms for the position of associate architect on the project.[22] Even before the first candidate, Gaurav, sauntered into the room, the architects had remarked on the brevity of his proposal: three pages compared to other firms' bound booklets. Gaurav arrived in a plain white shirt and black jeans, carrying sunglasses and his mobile phone. Unlike the other candidates, he had no files, papers, or drawings, nor did he bring images of his work. The senior architect told him that they were looking for "fit, chemistry, personality, and skills" from the associate architect. He asked, do you think you'll be the "proper fit"?

Gaurav insisted that while he was "excited" about the project, he was not interested in "becoming a back office" to a New York company, referencing the common division of labor between design and associate architect using a term commonly used in other outsourcing contexts. He launched into a long monologue about the prestigious history of his firm. He distanced himself from Indian developers—"quality was not their aspiration"—and yet boasted of working with "every North Indian developer, and we're moving with them pan-India." He dropped the names of multinational corporate clients and boasted of the millions of square feet he was designing. He asked rhetorically, "So can we do large scale projects? Yes. Can we do them in a reasonable period of time? Yes. Do we have a culture to work with international design firms? Yes." At the same time, he insisted that his local expertise did not relegate him to "back office" status:

> [The New York architectural firm] must have design sensibilities, but we have local sensibilities. We are not the drivers of design, but we work with mutual respect. We can offer local knowledge that is of immense value. Things you cannot learn in a third country. Strong personalities? No problem. But we are not a back office. That's the key point I'm underlining.

After his monologue, Gaurav admitted that he had not read the request for proposals. He claimed that his firm was so busy, he could not say now who would be on the project team. Before he left, he commented, "At the end of the day, it's another building with another international architect. There's not much more to say."

The bravado with which Gaurav asserted his own professional expertise played disastrously with his audience. While knowledgeable about industry trends and the India-specific challenges EuroFund would face, his monologue about his own firm's size and history as well as his refusal of the role of "back office" signaled "arrogance" rather than competence to the architects. Nick had scratched him from the list of candidates before the interview was over. The architects made a few critical remarks about Gaurav over lunch, and Paul repeated Gaurav's last statement ("another building and another international architect")—with a chuckle—to Jeremy when he joined us at the end of the day.

The remaining interviewees demonstrated their local knowledge in a less threatening manner. However, all of the associate architect candidates came to the meeting with their own opinions and warnings. Presenting nuggets of information about the Indian construction industry and how to engage it, they displayed their qualifications for the job. The candidates warned of contractors and consultants so swamped with work that they would be unlikely to focus on the EuroFund project, produce drawings on time, or move "proactively" beyond the bounds of their usual practice. They discussed unreliable facade contractors, inadequate shop drawings, and difficulties obtaining vital building components like elevators. They advised that most consultants used Auto-Cad, not the newer computer program Revit. They offered advice on the proposed project schedule. They recommended particular firms for mechanical, electrical, and plumbing, structural, civil, traffic, and landscape engineering services, thus demonstrating their knowledge of the local professional landscape.

The American architects were curious about zoning regulations and the approval process. One candidate responded with suggestions for what the Ministry of Environment and Forests (MOEF) would look for in the project; another commented that environmental clearance would take six months. One firm promised to organize workshops to orient the New York designers to the bylaws, and its head architect claimed that the authorities were open to informal pre-authorization reviews as well as to "influence" on basic zoning regulations. Warning, "You need a great effort with the authorities," he was positioning his firm as the liaison capable of providing that "influence."

The architects from New York were clearly looking for local expertise and assistance in negotiating local authorities. In the architects' discussions of the merits of each candidate—and in their dismissal of Gaurav—it was also clear that they were looking for alignment of interests with EuroFund's quality project and tractability. While someone commented about one of the firms, "I didn't think they'd defend the quality level we want, the level of discipline, proactive thinking this would take," the winning firm demonstrated "a concern for quality, even if they haven't built it." As Nick explained, "We need someone who can push the envelope, not just tell us what can be done in India but how we get to the next level." Not only did the winning firm convey that "they've been thinking about how to apply international standards here," they seemed "eager" and showed "humility." EuroFund and the New York architects were not merely looking for local expertise, but for *manageable* local expertise.

MANAGING THE LOCAL REGULATORY PROCESS: PART 2

By the end of the interviews, the architects and EuroFund employees had decided on one firm, AssocArch. A visit to the AssocArch's studio the following day confirmed the verdict. However, even months later, EuroFund/BuildIndia had not formally hired the firm. I heard hints of a controversy in the EuroFund office; a year after the associate architect interview session, the lead architects on the project in New York told me the story.[23]

Apparently, after the interview process, BuildIndia raised small objections about AssocArch, little "roadblocks" around which the architects tried to maneuver. This went on for three or four months until it became clear that BuildIndia did not want to work with AssocArch. They offered the excuse—never well explained—that they had worked with AssocArch once in the past and the project had ended in a lawsuit. Paul did not understand why BuildIndia did not strike AssocArch from the list of candidates they had reviewed before the interviews took place. Nevertheless, BuildIndia then suggested that the New York office work either with Gaurav or with a candidate who had not been considered in the interview process, an old friend of BuildIndia's chairman. Paul returned to India for what he called a "sham" interview with the old friend, Aziz, who they eventually hired.

Not only were Paul and Linda furious over the time and money wasted in the interview process, Linda commented that the close relationship between BuildIndia's chairman and Aziz complicated her job. She had been reluctant to involve Aziz as closely as she might in the design process because EuroFund is worried that Aziz will take her ideas directly to the chairman, bypassing the process they want to have in place for decision making. Linda explained that she has been cautious about showing Aziz things without first gaining EuroFund's approval.

She also complained that Aziz's office had not been helpful in its role as regulatory intermediary. While BuildIndia had billed Aziz as an architect conversant with local regulations and promised their involvement would "speed up" the design process, Linda exclaimed,

> They don't know *anything* about [the site locality]—I mean, they don't know any more than we do as far as I can tell. You know, and *EuroFund* has been the one, *their* team, their construction management team has been the ones who, with, sometimes with Aziz but sometimes just because they're pushing it, have been more successful in getting to the bottom of some of these issues. And we also find that Aziz's office, depending on who's sitting at the table in a meeting, they give conflicting answers to the same question every week.

While she acknowledged that some of this inconsistency might be due to the nature of the local planning bureaucracy, she insisted, "but have they [Aziz's office] been helpful in negotiating that? Not terribly. It's been really tricky."

Linda felt that they could have had more support from Aziz's office in determining the height of the building, an example of a simple regulatory issue that turned into a risky uncertainty. While Paul and Linda think they now know how tall the building can be, Paul quipped, "it took us a hundred and fifty days to get a clear explanation of that interpretation" of the bylaws. Any day, they felt, the height might change:

LINDA: And even now, there seem to be late-breaking pieces of news, like four weeks ago, when [Jeremy] was on the phone saying, "Oh, we've got more height on the tower." And

PAUL: Nope, only joking.

LINDA: And then a week later, "Oh, that was a misunderstanding." I mean, to try to get an answer to the simplest things. That's a perfect example.

This inconsistency in interpreting the bylaws complicates her work designing the building and EuroFund's work calculating Floor Space Index, rental values, and construction costs. What might be a simple regulatory determination elsewhere, in India remains a flexible limit well into the project design phase. Linda added, in exasperation, that she thought the rules might change again:

> Probably, once the building is under construction, then they'll find out, "Oh, the law just changed. They just switched over to a new code. We can have more height, so let's just add twenty more stories or ten more stories, OK guys?" You know. Wouldn't surprise me.

Paul explained that every project faces uncertainties, "but working with this group, it's just been . . . amplified, extraordinarily." Paul and Linda compared the project to one they had done in another "emerging market." Although there were "a lot of code issues and antiquated fire protection issues that we weren't able to get around," Linda felt that the process was smoother there because of a "terrific" associate architect:

> We had to solve issues differently than we might have wanted to in the US, but we didn't have this much trouble getting information and sorting through it. It was a much more straightforward process and we had much better expertise I think guiding us in what would fly and what wouldn't fly. Whereas here, it seems to be—so many more issues seem to be so much more wide open and kind of unclear.

Linda had hoped the associate architect would be able to control the "wide open" nature of the regulatory process. Like BuildIndia's slow decision making, the lack of "clarity" about basic regulations undermined EuroFund's efforts to plan everything in advance.

MANAGING LABOR

Early on, Nick identified labor as a significant issue in the pursuit of a quality building. He worried that the "migratory" nature of construction labor in India would compromise the consistency of workmanship. Fresh from interviews with building contractors, Nick reported, "They say that almost every six to nine months you get an entirely new crew on site because people go back to the village or people decide they don't want to do this anymore." The result from this "churn rate," he worried, would be a "constant learning curve" and an inconsistent product; the crew laying tile on the third floor would not be the crew laying tile on the tenth. "I mean, we've talked to a lot of contractors and they've said the same thing: 'How are you going to ensure quality when you can't have a stable work crew that you can train and get their level of work up to standards and then carry them through the entire process?'" From what Nick had heard, the problem was the "transitory" nature of construction work:

> [A] laborer doesn't have any sort of concept of loyalty to a company. I mean, they are being paid a certain amount for a certain piece of work and you know, if somebody down the street is going to pay five rupees more, then they're going to go down the street and get that. If it's, you know, harvest time in the village, then they are gone for three months. . . . It's just not considered a real, stable kind of a job. It's a very transient job.

To counter the problem of a transient workforce, he thought he might pro-vide incentives for labor to stay on his site: schools or crèches for laborers' children, better on-site housing and facilities, and/or training programs. Jer-emy suggested that this approach would be in keeping with the company's social goals.

Certainly EuroFund could improve the living conditions of construction laborers, most of whom are currently housed on construction sites in brick or asbestos shacks, often without clean water or proper sanitation. However, the image of the fickle migrant laborer that contractors have painted for Nick obscures the usefulness of "transience" to Indian developers and contractors. Construction labor is a "transient job" because contractors profit from a flex-ible workforce, not because laborers view it as an irregular occupation.

A long chain of subcontractors separates the developer or main contractor from his labor. A survey by Mobile Crèches, an NGO that provides childcare on construction sites, of 425 migrant households from fifteen construction sites in the National Capital Region, found that only 14 percent of respon-dents (adult men and women in those households) were hired directly by a contractor; most were hired through middlemen known as *thekedars* or *ja-madars* (Mobile Crèches 2008, 21). Construction laborers do move frequently, staying on one site for less than a year, on average. However, contrary to the image of laborers moving in search of higher pay, construction laborers move with their *jamadar* from job to job. At each site they are paid a piece rate to do only a discrete portion of the construction work, and then they move to the next job. Although 69 percent had changed employer (i.e., *jamadar*) at least once, they cited lack of payment, lack of continuous work, cheating, and other exploitative practices as the reason for switching (Mobile Crèches 2008, 22–23).

While in the past, construction laborers may have returned to their vil-lages to work in agriculture, only 3 percent of the respondents in the Mobile Crèches study reported return visits for agricultural work. One third of mi-grants had not returned to their village since migrating, and those that had stayed for an average of one month to visit their families or attend family functions (Mobile Crèches 2008, 21). These statistics are consonant with the personal experience of labor activists. Subhash Bhatnagar, who has worked with construction and other unorganized workers for thirty years through the Nirman Mazdoor Panchayat Sangam, commented to me that in contrast to older scholarship on "seasonal" construction workers that do agricultural labor for part of the year, he's found that "construction workers are construc-tion workers," even when they only get ten to twenty days of work a month.

The supposed seasonality of the workforce provides the construction sector with a justification for not providing benefits and a means for skirting labor laws. The managing director of one of India's largest construction firms told me frankly,

> To take on labor on our rolls is a no-no because removing them is difficult. They become pretty much permanent. Removing them is possible, now it's a little easier. But it's not easy. Our workload is highly variable. Each region has a fluctuation. Bangalore, one year ago was the largest, but maybe now it's Delhi.

Large construction firms are unwilling to maintain a permanent labor force. This construction firm retains only approximately 5 percent of its employees (mainly engineering, management, and administrative staff) directly; they hire thousands of people "off the rolls" through subcontractors and thus avoid having to provide them with regular work. Since laborers hired through strings of contractors do not appear "on the books," large construction firms beg off responsibility for wages, benefits, and safety. Although laws such as the Contract Labor Act (1970), the Inter-State Migrant Workers Act (1979), and the Building and Other Construction Workers' Act (1996) clearly legislate provisions for migrant and construction labor, developers and construction firms routinely flout this legislation, and government agencies rarely enforce it.[24]

A flexible labor force drawn from all over the country is a pliant one, unlikely to unionize or even to demand legal entitlements. Indeed, the Mobile Crèches study found that few of their respondents had heard of the Construction Workers' Welfare Board, a government program for providing pensions, insurance, and loans to construction workers, and less than 1 percent had registered with it (Mobile Crèches 2008, 30). In addition, the flexible, undocumented workforce provides ample opportunity for contractors to hide black money from tax and other authorities by fudging worker rolls. Perhaps Indian buildings are poorly made because it suits powerful construction and development companies to move construction workers from site to site and deny them minimum wages, government benefits, health care, training, and decent living conditions. Whether EuroFund will be able to transform this entrenched system remains to be seen.

Perhaps Nick doubted his ability to transform hiring practices, for he also thought of ways to manage what he feared would be a "transient," largely unskilled, and illiterate labor force. He planned to build mock-ups of building details and construction finishes for new workers to copy. He also contemplated videotaping the construction of these models to demonstrate techniques to new foreman and workers. He figured, "We're going to have to be creative on how to keep the knowledge base of how things were done and why things were done somehow recorded and somehow transferable to the new regime that comes in every three to six months."

A New Representational Ideology?

Buildings result from the combined effort of hundreds of people, from architects and engineers to masons, plasterers, and painters. Even at the early stages of planning the project, EuroFund employees had ideas about coordinating these efforts. First, EuroFund planned to hire specialty subcontractors for different tasks, going against the industry norm of hiring one big firm and letting it subcontract the work or parcel it out to various in-house divisions. Nick felt that by informing contractors about this before the project had started and paying the main contractor a coordination fee, he would be able to accomplish this reorganization of construction work.

Second, Nick believed that sequencing work would help produce quality by minimizing damage to delicate finishes. He was appalled that Indian construction companies did not do this already. He recounted,

> I went to an office building when I first got here . . . and they were putting the wall fabric up in offices and ten feet away they were chipping out concrete and pouring concrete to do electrical runs. So here you've got a cloud of concrete dust while they're putting up finished silk fabric.

Instead, he will instruct his contractors to do demolition, concrete work, and tile setting before beginning finish work such as painting and fabrics.

Third, EuroFund insisted that the design for the building be completed *before* construction started. Nick saw this as essential to the production of "quality." Even with clear, finished construction drawings, he argued, it is difficult to control contractors on the construction site. He provided a hypothetical example:

> [The contractor] will say to the owner, "I know you showed stone on that wall, but I thought that was just concrete, so I don't have stone on that wall, so we're just going to put a plaster finish on that, and I won't charge you any more money." And the owner says, "Fine, do it, just get it done."

According to Nick, such compromises result in poor buildings. He explained that, without drawings, "they just don't have that quality because it's constantly being diluted by a contractor's assumptions of what he thought was going to be installed versus what the architect thought was going to be installed." For Nick, "quality" is produced through a clear chain of communication between architect and construction worker, with minimal negotiations, transformations, or "dilutions" along the way. Construction drawings constitute that chain of communication.

Scholars have theorized the importance of "graphic artifacts" (Hull 2008) or "inscriptions" (Latour 1986) such as maps, graphs, diagrams, and lists to the exercise of power, emphasizing their role in creating order and bureaucratic legibility (e.g., Scott 1998), as well as their susceptibility to mishap and malfeasance (Hull 2008). For Latour, the immutability, mobility, and combine-ability of graphic artifacts enables scientists and rulers to "muster, align, and win over new and unexpected allies, far away," to exercise power over distance (Latour 1986, 6). Latour writes that "the accumulation of drawings in an optically consistent space is . . . the 'universal exchanger' that allows work to be planned, dispatched, realized, and responsibility to be attributed" (Latour 1986, 28).

Of course, what counts is not just the graphic artifact, but how it is used. As we have seen, images abound in the production of Indian real estate, yet the quick pace of real estate development in India, the practice of pre-selling apartments, the common dismissal of images as "just marketing," a lack of clearly defined professional roles in image production, and other elements of Indian real estate practice contribute to a lack of consistency between representations and finished buildings and often, a disregard for them in the construction process. While this lack of consistency provides Indian developers with flexibility, it threatens EuroFund's quality project. In order to ensure a clear chain of command from architect to laborer, EuroFund is in the difficult position of attempting to change a "graphic ideology," the practices that govern drawings' production, circulation, use, interpretation, and authority (Hull 2008, 505; see also Keane 2003).

Changing the production and use of construction drawings is vital to EuroFund's quality project. First, drawings provide a means to hedge against "execution risk" by ensuring a correspondence between spreadsheet calculations and a future building. In short, they are financial tools. EuroFund employees believe that construction drawings help control costs by enabling them to be estimated in advance: "When we tell our investors, this is going to cost fifty million dollars, it really will cost fifty million dollars because we know that it is defined and the specifications are clear," Nick explained. Providing the contractor with "a complete road map" for construction, drawings should eliminate site problems and costly delays.

Second, EuroFund employees believed that their promise to control production through construction drawings helped to attract world-renowned architects who can produce the quality register. Nick claimed that the Indian practice of building from conceptual sketches rather than completed construction drawings is "why you don't see a Norman Foster or an I. M. Pei or a Caesar Pelli project in India." He felt that such "world-class architects" refuse to work in India because "if the architect doesn't have control over the entire process, their name is associated with a project that's of horrible quality." EuroFund, by promising "a process that guarantees the end result," hopes to serve as a mediator between Indian real estate development and international architectural practices. Indeed, Paul and Linda explained that they took the job in India because EuroFund's involvement in the project allayed their fears about working in an unfamiliar environment.

EuroFund's insistence on using complete construction drawings in its attempts to control costs, enroll partners, and build a "quality building" in India is just one practice that sets it apart from its Indian partners. In conclusion, the differences in practice between EuroFund and its partners are significant. EuroFund employees believe that representations of buildings should correspond as closely to possible to their future form; that risks can be mitigated through careful planning; that buildings should be leased for a period after construction; that construction costs should be high to attract international tenants able to pay high rents; and that value resides in their own expertise in building development. By contrast, Indian real estate developers have a loose interpretation of the truth value of images; attempt to remain flexible in the face of an uncertain future; sell buildings as quickly as possible and sometimes to a number of different owners; distinguish themselves by "delivering" buildings in the face of incentives to slow or stop construction; keep construction costs down to maximize profits; and believe that value resides in the process of agglomerating land. The latter activities often require long-term strategizing beyond the bounds of individual projects, as developers foster relationships with powerful people in order to influence the state.

These differences constitute two conflicting modes of spectacular accumulation, highlighting the variations in capitalist practices that shape landscapes and markets. Such variations provide the context for EuroFund's quality project—both its risks and its potential profitability—for EuroFund employees hope that distinguishing their practices from industry norms will produce profits. And yet, in order to do so, they must rely on Indian partners with other goals, putting EuroFund employees in the position of trying to redefine what differences matter and change industry practices. Doing so entails advertising their authority without alienating potential partners; en-rolling tractable local consultants; and creatively managing partners, labor, and project timing. Constructing globally standard buildings in India—while key to real estate producers' attempts to extend Indian real estate markets abroad—is thus an extremely uncertain gamble, dependent on power as much as on expertise. Contradicting popular narratives about the inevitable victory of global capital, aesthetics, and norms, EuroFund's struggles demon-strate that the authority needed to make markets is hard won, if won at all.

Conclusion

The "India Story" Revisited

Returning to Gurgaon in January 2014, it seemed that the landscapes of accumulation that had been under construction in 2006 had been built and that the vibrant future of industry discourse was still under construction. Rather than stand in a bus caught in traffic on the Mehrauli-Gurgaon road, as I had in 2008, I took the sleek, modern Delhi metro all the way to Gurgaon. Riding comfortably elevated above the scrubland south of Merauli, I looked down into the spacious grounds of "farmhouses" and out across an undulating acacia canopy. In Gurgaon, I disembarked at an expansive station with security lines and escalators. Below, in the hazy cold, autorickshaws awaited passengers, and a string of pushcarts sold *chai*, *paan*, *parathas*, belts, and socks, reminders of the Gurgaon that the metro had not obliterated. Signaling continued transformation, construction abutted the station: behind barbed wire fencing, there were piles of rebar, pipes, and workers' unmortared brick shacks.

As I rode further south in an auto on Golf Course Road, I was overwhelmed by how much had been built in Gurgaon since I was there in 2008. Empty lots were now high-rises whose windows and balconies suggested multitudes. Banks, car dealerships, and office complexes lined the road. Construction continued, especially at Gurgaon's far edges. I visited towers under construction south of what the Gurgaon Masterplan anachronistically called the Southern Periphery Road. Cranes swung overhead, punctuating a vast terrain of rutted dirt.

Despite the sheer scale of ongoing change, however, these were not the landscapes of accumulation many had envisioned in 2006.

I realized this as soon as I visited some of my informants. Sanjeev, a broker in Gurgaon, complained to me that while new buildings lined Golf Course

Road, not a single project there had met its delivery deadline; indeed, many that I had seen launched in 2006–2008 had just been finished in 2013, two to four years late. Sanjeev estimated that about five thousand luxury apartments were completed all at once in 2013. In the past, he said, only about five hundred luxury apartments would "hit" the market in a year. This sudden influx collapsed rental markets. Sanjeev, who in 2007 had insisted that property prices could *never* depreciate and that multinational corporations would inundate Gurgaon with thousands of high-net worth housing consumers, came close to admitting that there was an overproduction of luxury housing: "Where do you get five thousand people to rent or move in?" he asked rhetorically. "That's what you need . . . and five thousand houses is equal to maybe four towns in Australia!" As he marveled at the unlikeliness of filling Gurgaon's apartments, the anxieties that the "India story" had kept at bay in 2007—that price appreciation augured a crash, not long-term growth—infused his talk. His habit of comparing India to places abroad now served to highlight economic malaise, not promise.

The global financial crisis of 2008 and its aftermath created plot twists that the "India story" never hinted at. Despite ebullient descriptions of billions in foreign investments transforming Indian realty, foreign investors turned out not to be the source of capital that Indian developers had counted on. In the fall of 2008, Lehman Brothers—which had $375 million invested in DLF and Unitech (as well as smaller investments in six other firms)—went bankrupt. Panicking investors sold off shares in Indian real estate development companies, dragging real estate stocks down 20 percent between September 15th and October 1st, 2008 (Knowledge@Wharton 2008a).

This initial exodus of capital did not bring Indian real estate to a standstill. Many private equity funds were required by government regulation to keep their capital in India for three years, so money continued to flow to projects. After an initial decline, property prices continued to rise steeply, matching trends in Indian GDP growth. However, the crisis upset the *timing* of real estate and thus its profitability.

Because they took so long to build, many of the buildings I saw in 2014 did not make money the way that investors and developers had planned: as buildings, they existed, but as investments, they were a bust. For example, the crisis upset EuroFund's carefully orchestrated accumulation strategy. The project the fund had begun with BuildIndia in 2007 was still not finished in 2014. Difficulties raising debt funding in the wake of the global credit crisis delayed the start of construction. Once started, the partnership encountered problems with government approvals: the authorities changed the basement fire codes and the height of the building, incurring expenses and delays. As the project floundered, inflation and the devaluation of the rupee wreaked havoc with the construction budget, and the building process diverged from the fund's spreadsheets. The fund also had trouble finding competent subcontractors and managing their work, as its employees foresaw in 2008.

Eurofund's losses exemplify investors' difficulty turning Indian buildings into financial tools. Private equity investments in Indian real estate did not accumulate capital. Indeed, a McKinsey report titled "Private Equity in India: Once Overestimated, Now Underserved" (a title unthinkable in 2006) claimed that of a total of $9.8 billion private equity investments in Indian real estate companies and projects between 2000 and 2008, "only 14% (by value)" had exited by 2013, with a gross internal rate of return of only 2 percent (Pandit 2015, 5–6)—far from the 20% or higher returns of which investors dreamed. To put this low return in perspective, it is significantly less than the average inflation in India over the period, which was 5.185 percent.[1] Moreover, this data suggests that some firms lost considerable amounts of money, since 86 percent of investments did not make any returns or lost money, even with an average holding period of 5.3 years. Indian real estate investments proved disastrous gambles.

Manit, the managing director of an international property consultancy, recounted his version of what happened:

> They [private equity funds] invested in projects where—I mean, it's very sensitive to time, so if you don't get the returns [and waste] time, so. They invested at very heady heavy valuations, so they *had* to make money. If you don't make money, you cut your losses and get out. And they basically tried to cut their losses, and they got out. So they sold to another fund or they sold out back to the developer. They basically, wherever they could, they could, but they lost money.

The high valuations at the peak of the market intensified investors' concerns about time. Having put so much money in, they needed to start getting returns fast. The crisis upset this delicate choreography, causing an exodus of funds from India. The *Wall Street Journal* reported that "of about 35 foreign funds that invested in India between 2005 and 2007, only four or five [were] left" in 2012 (Anand 2012). Some funds successfully demanded that their Indian partners buy them out, but many found "exiting" harder than entering the market.[2] Fund managers who planned to exit by taking their Indian partners public found that poor stock market performance made initial public offers untenable. Where they could not extract their money, investors took developers to court—in Delhi, London, the Cayman Islands, depending on the structure of the investment—or, as Manit said, they simply incurred losses.

While foreign funds sweated construction delays, many of their Indian partners manufactured them. Continuing to focus on amassing land banks, many Indian developers diverted investor money and pre-sales payments away from construction. Instead, they bought more land. The head of valuations for another international property consultant told me:

> So you would find fair amount of projects—and I won't name any developers—where perhaps the project needs last 5 percent, 10 percent of the installment, however, the amount of work that remains in making it deliverable, it won't get covered by that last 5 percent, 10 percent because the money has gone out in acquiring other land and so on and so forth.

Stuck with projects they did not have the money to complete, developers stopped construction, exacerbating the delays that vexed their partners. The financial crisis, then, magnified differences in practice between investors and developers—particularly about timing. Indian developers were playing a long game, sure that their land would hold value regardless of construction. Foreign investors, however, were interested in near term profits. Despite considerable efforts to make Indian real estate development conform to international practices, these two different modes of speculative capitalism—marked by two different temporal strategies of accumulation—persisted rather than merged.

If the foreign investor model was troubled by construction delays and stock market devaluation, the developer model was dissolved when the consumers they had described so confidently to each other proved illusory. The "genuine residents" who guaranteed demand in 2006 stopped buying properties in 2013, after the unstoppable Indian economy slowed. The head of valuations told me, "People who are supposed to buy them [apartments] for their own use—they are not in the market. Not significantly. Not in significant numbers." Another broker I spoke to in Gurgaon had not sold a property in six months.

Without enough consumers, developers faced a dire situation. Right after the crisis they had stopped building office space and focused on residential projects, some of which they relabeled as "middle-income" rather than "luxury" properties. But when residential consumers and small-scale investor-brokers (many of whom, like international investors, were angered by slow construction), stopped buying, developers could no longer launch new projects to generate funds. Finding themselves in a bind, developers borrowed money to complete construction. This only compounded the debt they had already accrued by buying land at the height of the market (Nandy 2009). By

2014, many Indian developers were heavily indebted at high interest rates. For example, in March 2014, DLF had a debt of US$3 billion, with an average rate of interest of 12.08 percent and the lowest cash flows in four years (Shah and Sharma 2014). Debt payments equaled 30 percent of revenue between April and June 2014 (Kaul 2014).

In short, this was not the real estate market that many envisioned in 2006. The companies that had expected to go public did not; the consumers everyone imagined had disappeared; the foreign fund activity that was expected to keep growing had shrunk; and Indian developers' ever-expanding plans had halted.

Faced with unexpected situations, industry members were generating new stories and accepted truths in 2014. With accusations of developer fraud in the headlines and concerns about delayed construction mounting, developers' goal of improving their reputation proved elusive. As the broker who faced a lull in sales told me,

> Builders—as an industry or as a group of businesses, is not well looked up to. There might be a few—Sobha Builders, for example, is very well regarded, and you can have some people in the South as well who are bona fide good builders. And, ah, they have a reputation and they also attract a premium. . . . So there a few of the builders are getting out of this now bad reputation type of thing, and becoming bona fide solid builders. So it's happening in Maharashtra, it's happening in the South. Unfortunately, it hasn't happened very much in the North but I suppose at some point it will fall into place.

Even in painting this negative picture of the industry, the broker switches to positive statements, as though he feels more comfortable recounting Southern builders' achievements than Northern builders' problems. Reputation is a matter of profit; "bona fide builders" can charge a "premium." Reputation also has its own value as a matter of pride and self-worth, as I showed in chapter 6. The geography of reputation has changed in this account: rather than foreign developers having a good reputation and Indian developers a bad one, the dividing line has been recast inside India such that the North lags behind the South. Although there has been "progress," there is always more work to be done, as the frontiers of change push inward. Yet the broker ends on an uncertain note. Although he offers a nod toward improvement at the end of this statement, it sounds feeble, resigned, as though his faith has been shaken.

In 2006, the promise of global capital was taken as both sign and agent of industry transformation. In 2014, I heard stories about its impotence. For example, Manit told me,

I think lot of PE [private equity] funds who came in here and came in hoards, they threw in money. Most of them are out of business because they lost money. They transacted at high valuations. They bought the developers' story. Because they didn't have their own experience, so they bought the developers' story. And they pumped in a lot of money, too early without doing too much of analysis. You know, they took a pretty—they punted pretty high. And, ah, that, once they did that, ahm, I think within from 2009 to 11, most of them shut offices, shut shop, they lost money, they left.

In this account, the "India story" described in this book has become only the "developers' story"—a tale told to cheat unsuspecting outsiders. Foreign fund managers didn't buy property so much as they bought a story—not a prediction of probable futures (as it seemed in 2006) but a fantasy. Investors "bought" developers' claims about how much Indian land, buildings, and companies were worth; they "transacted at high valuations." As a result, many investors "shut offices, shut shop, they lost money, they left." According to Manit, the story was now a fable.

Contradictions of Mediation

Manit looked backward in 2014 and saw only dupes, wrongly placed bets, and losses. But back in 2006, other futures were possible. *Landscapes of Accumulation* has recorded what those futures looked like from that time. It thus provides a rare look at practices and uncertainties that often are lost in hindsight. Looking back, markets look self-evident instead of painstakingly, falteringly built. "Correct" predictions look like accurate prophecies rather than self-fulfilling ones. Buildings look like the outcome of social changes instead of hope-fueled forerunners. Failures make the "India story" look ephemeral rather than productive, epiphenomenal rather than central. We need to grasp the "India story's" productivity and centrality, however, to understand the contradictions in the activities that the story helped to foster, contradictions which led to the failed value projects I witnessed in 2014.

What we might be tempted to write off as an insular world of stories or as the hypocritical rationalizations of a group greedy for profit cannot be discounted so easily. Because the "India story" is a moral narrative that maps capital increase onto personal, industrial, and national improvement, it shapes aspirations and motivates people. EuroFund's financial analyst Samiksha, for example, was extremely proud of working for a European fund. She believed in EuroFund's quality project and the idea of bringing "better" construction to Indians. Like the editors of the *Economic Times* celebrating India's victories with their "Global Indian Takeover" campaign (chapter 2), Samiksha wanted progress, glory, and success for her nation, not just for herself. Stories provide not just thin rationalizations for greed (as critics are wont to think of them), but also positive sources of aspiration. Therein lies their power.

The "India story" inspired because it was never just about profit. My informants' attempts to make Indian land and buildings internationally tradable were not just financial projects, but moral projects that hinged on ideals of personhood. Value projects are about money, of course. But they are also about expertise, credibility, transparency, respectability, professionalism, and taste. These qualities are valuable in their own right as sources of self-worth and social esteem, but here they also intermingle with wealth, which comes to stand for these other values. When capital accumulation is a sign of improvement, money-making projects come to have new life—to inspire in ways that money alone does not.

The "India story" inspired actions which did not have the effects that people envisioned—but they had effects nonetheless. Developers bought farmland and municipalities demolished slums. Buildings went up along Golf Course Road and beyond, pushing the frontiers of urbanization out toward Manesar, Bhiwadi, and Sohna. The metro was built.

In addition to new landscapes, the "India story" moved money. The chief minister of Haryana, whose administration licensed 21,000 acres of land for development between 2004 and 2012 (Singh 2013), and private developers raked in crores of cash while farmers lost livelihoods in forced land sales. People invested their life savings in properties that appreciated at an exciting pace while others lost them in buildings that were never completed. Partnerships between investors and developers were forged—and broken. New companies were formed, bank accounts filled, masterplans filed, regulations changed, and elections won and lost.

Though they might look like failures of capitalism, the value projects described in this book have created the conditions for others to advance new value projects. As some foreign funds "shut shop," other fund managers eyed the devalued buildings created by speculation in 2006. Blackstone, a private equity fund based in New York City, bought commercial properties in India worth $900 million between 2011 and 2014, creating a portfolio of Indian assets larger than DLF's (Nandy 2014). This acquisition was made possible because others had created instruments for investment that Blackstone could recognize. In 2006, foreign investors thought that there were no assets to buy and certainly no portfolios to acquire, but by 2011 Blackstone could start buying completed buildings. Moreover, they did so on the assumption that long-standing efforts to make Real Estate Improvement Trusts (another financial structure) legal would finally bear fruit, suggesting that in the future they would be able to exit from these investments. Thus, activities at the height of the market—investing, lobbying, and constructing—created new routes of accumulation that connected Indian land and property to international markets.

Creating those routes of accumulation required a lot of work; capital does not just move on its own. Rather than exchange something already abstracted into strings of numbers, like currency or futures, or something small and light, like ballpoint pens, my informants worked hard to accumulate capital by moving objects that would never budge an inch: land and buildings. Constructed of concrete, rebar, steel, and glass, and anchored in Indian soil, the buildings themselves could not be moved to London or Singapore. But many people wanted them to circulate through those places.

Only by transforming the status of land—changing ownership, agglomerating small parcels of it, and transforming its legal status as agricultural land; and by constructing buildings from scratch, with new designs, techniques, and materials; and then transforming those buildings into shares owned by a cascade of companies and special purpose vehicles in different offshore tax havens, could investors, lawyers, accountants, and developers transform Indian buildings into assets that could be traded abroad. To do this, they also worked to transform the image of buildings, companies, and nations in an effort to garner the capital to move through the buildings they were constructing.

To understand contemporary capitalism, which operates through both spectacular accumulation and labor exploitation, we need to understand these acts of mediation: exchanges in which the thing being traded and the people doing the trading are transformed in the process. Constructing markets for trading Indian buildings required assembling chains of intermediaries who could do transformational work. By devising a proprietary fund structure, EuroFund transformed the individual contributions of many different investors into a pool of money that could be invested in India. BuildIndia served as an intermediary between EuroFund and the complex politics of Indian land agglomeration—a process of transformation which itself relied on BuildIndia's local networks of brokers, politicians, bureaucrats, and others. To draw up the paperwork to form their joint venture, the two companies hired lawyers, property consultants, and accountants. To construct the building, they assembled a chain of intermediaries that extended from an architectural team in the United States through Indian architects, engineers, contractors, subcontractors, *jamadars*, and laborers. Such chains of intermediaries have become a foundational organizational form in the era of globalization, as vertically integrated production has been distributed geographically through flexible chains of subcontractors linked together by cheap transportation and fast communication.[3]

These chains were not smooth; indeed they could not be. To build them, developers and investors amplified their differences, rather than erasing them.[4] Differentiating along lines of quality, transparency, and professionalism, industry members repurposed development discourses that defined Indian real estate practices and properties as inadequate. India's "backwardness" was key to advertising its profitability and enrolling intermediaries because Indians and non-Indians shared a faith in progress. Time's forward momentum would, they believed, repair the backwardness they emphasized. Businessmen would become professionals, rural areas would urbanize, Tier II cities would resemble the major metros, and Indian consumers would shop like global ones. This belief in modernization, in progress, in improvability is an old ideology given a new lease in the era of liberalization as a sign of profit. The mismatch between the present and a future shaped by improvement is what industry members hope to profit from as they transform discredited places (India, Tier II cities, rural areas) into global ones. By deferring standardization to the future and displacing it geographically "down" a hierarchy of places, industry members' stories create the frontiers of capitalist activity: the space-time of spectacular accumulation and market making.

Chains of capital thrived on stories of difference, but they also foundered on other, less immediately visible differences. *Landscapes of Accumulation* has described the power of global financiers to create new markets and landscapes, but it is also about the limits and contradictions of that very power—limits that are often obscured by triumphant globalist narratives, both popular and scholarly. To effect transformations, foreign investors needed to enroll and control Indian partners, but many of them found this quite difficult to do. They called on powerful normative discourses that made the acquisition of foreign capital and expertise attractive—to some extent conjuring a common ground for discriminating between companies and partners. And yet, they did not have the upper hand in negotiations with Indian real estate developers, not least of which because their Indian partners had their own value projects and used global discourses for their own ends. Lacking authority, investors' calls for transparency and quality were as much a complaint as a show of power.

Authority, credibility, and power in real estate are based on the ability to deliver land parcels, finished buildings, and returns. In India, in 2006, delivery was uncertain: what kind of capabilities would prove essential to accumulating capital? The ability to attract multinational tenants or to force farmers to sell land cheap? The ability to navigate the requirements of the London Stock Exchange or those of Indian bureaucracies? The process of transforming Indian land and buildings in order to circulate them required both sets of skills, complicating the differentiation of value. Indeed, the ability to effectively wield sociopolitical networks and navigate bureaucratic claims was now in high demand, making foreign investors' dismissal of this expertise ring hollow.

As much as they demanded conformity, foreign investors needed Indian partners with different practices, knowledge, and social capital. At the same time those differences threatened partnerships and profits, as when Build-India thwarted EuroFund's choice of an architect or developers turned to land brokering rather than construction. Indeed, there are central contradictions here, in that the very skills that developers cultivated in their role as intermediaries to global financiers enabled them to pursue their own accumulation strategies. The same stories that fueled investor interest in Indian buildings fueled the speculation in Indian land that made land agglomeration such a lucrative end in itself and perpetuated divergent interests, practices, and projects. Foreign investors' power to create markets, then, was limited by the very intermediaries on which it depended. Given these limits, assembling chains that can contain and profit from the contradictions of mediation—rather than splinter—is the precarious work of accumulation.

Notes

Introduction

1. The greater Delhi conurbation, now called the National Capital Region, includes nearby cities such as Faridabad, Ghaziabad, Noida, Greater Noida, and Gurgaon in the neighboring states of Haryana and Uttar Pradesh. Sometimes called "suburbs," these cities resemble neither American postwar suburbs nor Bombay's early twentieth-century suburbs (see Rao 2013).

2. According to one retail consultancy, there were only three malls in all of India in 1999, but by 2007, there were 104 (ICICI Property Services and Technopak Advisors 2007, 2–1). Another market research group reports that there were five malls in 2000, 179 in 2007, and an estimated 289 in 2008 (Images Multimedia 2007). According to this last report, there was one mall in the National Capital Region (NCR) around Delhi in 2000, forty in 2007, and an estimated sixty-four in 2008.

3. Mukhija 2003, 19–35; see also Nainan 2008; Nijman 2008.

4. Of course, anthropologists have been conducting "multisited" ethnographies since at least the 1990s (see Marcus 1995) in an attempt to track geographically attenuated cultural processes. For the framing of this book as the study of an "encounter," I am indebted to James Ferguson (1999, 21).

5. My fieldwork built on pre-dissertation research I conducted in Delhi, Pune, Mumbai, and Kolkata during the summer of 2005 and experience living in Jaipur for the 2004–5 academic year.

6. Many anthropologists have sought out examples of local resistance and hybridity to counter the idea that cultural practices are being homogenized through globalization (see Inda and Rosaldo 2008). By examining investors' attempts to standardize practices, I show by contrast that the project of producing similarities relies on reproducing hierarchies. That is, standardizing requires differentiation.

7. The term "neoliberal" is multivalent: scholars have used it variably to refer to a school of political and economic thought; reforms and policies; the ideologies that motivate those policies; a class project (Harvey 2003); forms of governmentality and subject formation; or an era (see Ganti 2014, 91). Thus the label "neoliberal" often obscures as much as it reveals. As Tejaswini Ganti suggests, "In many instances, neoliberalism appears as a linguistic gloss akin to 'globalization,' a placeholder to signal complex, abstract forces at work in the world that shape and constrain human action" (Ganti 2014, 98). In this book, rather than gloss the growth of Indian

real estate as "neoliberalism," I have explored those "complex, abstract forces" as tangible communicative moments, interactions, emblems, and buildings—things anthropologists can study in detail.

8. My fieldwork corresponded with the height of an international property bubble, a moment of frenetic capital expansion and speculative hubris. The Indian market showed signs of slowing in the second half of my fieldwork, as the US—and with it the rest of the world—slipped into financial crisis in the fall of 2007, but after an initial correction Indian real estate prices continued to rise for the next five or six years. The book focuses on the production of the speculative bubble, while the conclusion describes the economic downturn.

9. See also Hall and Hubbard 1998; Harvey 1989.

10. Banerjee-Guha 2002; Batra 2005; Goldman 2011.

11. Ajayan 2008; Chakravorty and Gupta 1996; Dasgupta 2007; *Economist* 2004; Krishnakumar 2007.

12. Anjaria 2009; Baviskar 2003, 2011; Fernandes 2004; Mehra 2009; Nair 2005; Rajagopal 2004; Srivastava 2009.

13. Adarkar and Menon 2004; D'Monte 2002, 2006; Hussain and Das 2007; Thomas 2007.

14. Aryad 2008; Bharati 2007; Philip 2008; Philip and Bharati 2008; Sanjai 2008; A. Singh 2007. Against the protests of environmentalists, the Delhi Development, for example, awarded developer Emaar MGF the contract to build thirty-four towers of athlete housing for the 2010 Commonwealth Games on twenty-seven acres of Yamuna riverbed; in the original agreement, Emaar MGF would be able to sell almost half the apartments as private housing (Pandit 2006; Emaar MGF Land Limited 2008).

15. According to official estimates, the Municipal Corporation of Delhi relocated more than 53,000 households living in *jhuggi-jhopri* ("slum") clusters between 1990 and 2005 (*Economic Survey of Delhi 2005–6*)—though nongovernmental organizations estimate that 79,000 households were evicted in slum demolitions in Delhi between 2000 and 2006, and that 27,000 households alone were evicted when the government razed the Yamuna Pushta settlement in 2004 (Menon-Sen and Bhan 2008, 12; Srivastava 2009, 341).

16. See Dasgupta 2003 for a discussion of evictions at Beleghata Canal and Tolly's Nala in Kolkata in the early 2000s.

17. See *Economic and Political Weekly* 2005. As Mahadevia and Narayanan (2008) show, the history of slum demolitions in modern Mumbai stretches back to the 1950s. In the latter half of the 1990s, the Municipal Corporation was removing slum dwellings at a rate between 50,000 and 100,000 each year.

18. At the time of my fieldwork, the Mumbai airport expansion project threated to dislocate 80,000 slum dwellers (*Mint* 2008), though the project later floundered (*Mint* 2013). The Maharashtra government was also eliciting bids from private developers to redevelop the 535 acres of the Dharavi slum into market-rate commercial and residential space; the project would affect close to 60,000 slum dwellers and net the government as much as Rs. 10,000 crore (Jacobson 2007; Jamwal 2007; Ramanathan 2007c, 2007d).

19. Other firms reported that they were buying land as well. Morgan Stanley Research estimated that as of February 2007, seventeen major Indian developers had acquired a total of 46,200 acres, much of it in the previous two to four years; the same companies planned to purchase another 99,164 acres (Baisiwala and Desa 2007). Of course, developers may not own all of the land they report as a "land bank" outright. DLF's land total, for example, includes land owned by the company; land to which the company has sole development rights; land which the

company plans to develop through a joint development agreement; land leased to the company by various government authorities; and land in respect to which the company has signed memorandum of understanding to purchase or develop (DLF Limited 2007, 3).

20. *Analytical Monthly Review* 2007; Handique 2007; Levien 2011.

21. For example, for its Maha Mumbai SEZ, Reliance Industries was paying the government Rs. 5–10 lakh per acre for land the government acquired from farmers on its behalf. However, concurrent transactions in the area suggest land was trading privately at Rs. 3–5 crore per acre (Kuber 2007; Manoi 2007). Similarly, Jha and Guha (2007a) report that farmers unable to obtain change in land use certificates were selling land to Reliance for its Haryana SEZ at Rs. 20 lakh an acre as against a market price of Rs. 28–30 lakh per acre; in Dadri and Greater Noida, Uttar Pradesh, farmers were selling at Rs. 10–12 lakh an acre, while the market price was Rs. 25 an acre. Jha and Guha point out that large companies setting up SEZs do not have to get change in land use certificates when they have tied up with state governments and that many state government also mandate that transactions take place at government-established circle rates that fall below market value. For a review of land compensation practices at Singur, West Bengal, see Chandra 2008.

22. The SEZ act was passed by Parliament in June 2005 and put into effect in February 2006. The SEZ rules were tweaked after protests over land acquisition in 2007.

23. As this book goes to press in 2016, the Government of India counts only 204 operational SEZs (Ministry of Commerce and Industry 2016), significantly fewer than the number proposed just after the Special Economic Zone Act of 2005 was passed. Yet SEZs account for a considerable swath of land appropriated from farmers, and they have captured the imagination of business elites, scholars, and the political Left. For a more nuanced discussion, see Cross 2014; Jenkins, Kennedy, and Mukhopadhyay 2014.

24. See Daniel 1984; Osella and Osella 1999; Selvaduri 1976.

25. See Agarwal 1994, 18n37. In a study of land transfers in Uttar Pradesh over a thirty year period (1952–53 to 1982–83), for example, Kripa Shankar (1990) found that only 0.13 percent of land was sold annually and that "marginalized farmers" with small holdings were the most likely to sell their land. Other studies report similar findings (for a review, see Rawal 2001, 617–19).

26. Both the Central Bureau of Investigation (although their report was never released to the public) and a three-member team from the Congress party concluded that CPI(M) militias and other cadres, some of them dressed as police, joined the police in the violence (*Economic Times* 2007b; *Economic Times* 2007c).

27. See R. Das 2007; Niyogi and Sen 2007. Eyewitness accounts suggest the death toll was much higher (see TASAM 2007). The attack followed months of sporadic violence between the CPI(M)—the majority party in the Left Front government that had ruled West Bengal since 1977—and the Bhumi Uchhed Pratirodh (Land Eviction Resistance), a group formed by local peasants and opposition parties (the Trinamul Congress, Jamait Ulema-i-Hind, and the Socialist Unity Centre of India) to resist the Left Front government's plans to acquire 14,000 acres. Clashes between the CPI(M) and Bhumi Uchhed Pratirodh continued throughout the summer and fall (A. Banerjee 2007; Chaudhuri, Rai, and Sivaraman 2007). In September, the government announced that the SEZ would be moved to Nayachar, a sparsely inhabited island (*Times of India* 2007c). After violence in Nandigram again made national headlines in November, the state called in the Central Reserve Police Force to pacify the area (Chattopadhyay 2007a, 2007b; Hossain and Chaudhuri 2007).

28. Government appropriation spurred real estate speculation in the vicinity of the project.

The price of land rose more than tenfold (from Rs. 3–5 lakh to Rs. 50–60 lakh) in some areas near Singur (Acharya and Gooptu 2008; Dutt and Pain 2007). As Majumder (2009) points out, there was "silent approval" of the car factory from some landowners interested in profiting from land sales and in gaining nonfarm employment. These landowners, he contends, were not "peasants" but middle-caste and middle-class *bandralok* who aligned themselves with state narratives of industrial progress and thus supported the project. His investigation reveals that the social realities in Singur were more complex than the narrative of peasant resistance that the national media circulated. Michael Levien (2012) and Aseem Shrivastava and Ashish Kothari (2012) have also added to our understanding of rural dispossession, highlighting the complexities of land acquisition and the ways in which it has exacerbated caste, age, gender, and class inequalities.

29. At the time of my fieldwork, protests had occurred at Manesar, Haryana; Wagholi and Raigad, Maharashtra; Nandagudi and Mangalore, Karnataka; Deganga and Chakchaka, West Bengal; and across Goa, Andhra Pradesh, Orissa, and Jharkhand, among other places (Balagopal 2007a, 2007b; *Business Standard* 2009; Dash 2007; *Economic Times* 2007e; India Knowledge@ Wharton 2008; Jones 2008; S. N. Kumar 2007; *South Asian* 2007). See also Shrivastava and Kothari (2012) for a discussion of land protests.

30. A number of scholars have described conflicts over land in India as accumulation by dispossession. See Basu 2007; Batra 2007; Chandrasekhar 2006; Whitehead 2003; cf. Weinstein 2013.

31. I think Harvey uses the term broadly because it is his way of explaining accumulation in a system now dominated by financial capital rather than industrial capital. Where once accumulation occurred through "an economy of labor exploitation in production" this is now overshadowed by the credit system. He writes that "the credit system, in short, becomes the main vehicle for that contemporary form of primitive accumulation that I call 'accumulation by dispossession.' How much of the wealth of today's financial aristocracy has been accumulated through the expropriation of the wealth of others (including other capitalists) through the machinations of the financial system?" (Harvey 2013, 235). If, as he suggests, accumulation by dispossession is the dominant form of accumulation today, then all the more reason to understand the mechanisms through which it works.

32. Batra and Mehra 2008; Dupont 2008; Doshi 2013. These authors continue a tradition within anthropology of considering the built environment in (Foucaultian) terms of state control and citizen resistance (Bourdieu 1979; Comaroff and Comaroff 1992; Foucault 1984; Ghannam 1998, 2002; Holston 1989; Mitchell 1988; Scott 1998; Wright 1991; Yeoh 1996). Similarly, historians of colonial Indian cities have described British attempts to govern and to transform colonial society through urban projects underpinned by modernist ideologies (Glover 2008; Hosagrahar 1999; Oldenberg 1984). These scholars have demonstrated the power of the built environment to reproduce inequalities and shape lives as well as the ways that resistance plays out in space. Notably, Ghertner has developed a persuasive argument about new techniques of governance through aesthetic norms and judgments, what he calls "aesthetic governmentality" (2008, 2011, 2015).

33. Levien (2012, 2015b), Majumdar (2009, 2012), Shrivastava and Kothari (2012).

34. Appel 2012; Callon 1998: 19; Kopytoff 1986; Stallybrass 1998; Weiner 1992. Humans have devised various mechanisms for "alienating, titling, standardizing, [and] utilizing" things that were initially difficult to exchange (Kockelman 2006, 88). Indeed, the current expansion of markets relies upon the quantification, standardization, commensuration, and privatization of what had been qualitative, unique, incommensurable, or commonly owned—for example, semiosis and sociality (Kockelman 2006), land (Verdery 2003), nature (Nevins and Peluso 2008), social

networks (Elyachar 2005), and "culture" itself (Brown 1998; Myers 2004). Scholars have shown that privatization and standardization are inherently sociocultural processes with unpredictable and varied outcomes (Burawoy and Verdery 1999; Espeland and Stevens 1998; Lampland and Starr 2009; Mandel and Humphrey 2002).

35. There is no one set of practices, technologies, and ideas that makes markets. Infrastructures are culturally variable and historically contingent. For a historical case study, see Cronon 1991.

36. This is not to detract from Sassen's powerful documentation of such "expulsions," only to point to another line of inquiry that needs to be taken to understand how such expulsions come about. Without such inquiry, it sometimes sounds as though Sassen sees technologies, not elites, as agents: "remarkable new tools at the disposal of powerful individuals and firms actually begin to constitute formations where these users are just one element, rather than masters of the domain, so to speak" (Sassen 2015, 179).

37. This phrase is from the title of an essay by Anne Haila (1997).

38. The "state" vs. the "private sector" is a useful heuristic for understanding the growing role of non-state actors in urban development in India in the 1990s and 2000s. I chose to study the private sector to capture these novelties and to open the "black box" of private development amid much scholarly focus on state transformations and policy. However the heuristic of state vs. private sector artificially divides a more seamless reality in which private individuals run urban redevelopment programs for municipal authorities (Weinstein 2014), management consultancies develop state policies, government-funded agencies do research for private firms, and public-private infrastructure projects abound. Moreover, scholarly literature on the Indian state has insisted on its porosity, particularly the social overlap between low-level functionaries and those they govern and the possibilities for negotiation this opens up (Anjaria 2011; Gupta 1995; Jauregui 2014; Ruud 2000). It is useful to note that the state-private sector distinction has slightly more traction in India than China, where the distinction between state-owned and private real estate developer companies is quite unclear (see Osburg 2013; Zhang 2010).

39. By examining the *production* of self-consciously "global" buildings in India, I contribute to a small, provocative literature on the globalization of architectural and real estate services (Cuff 1999; Fainstein 2001; Kanna 2011, 77–104; Ren 2011; Thrift 1986; Mitchell and Olds 2000; Olds 1997, 2001; Tombesi 2001; Tombesi, Dave, and Scriver 2003). Since my research began, geographers have made important contributions to our understanding of the political economy of the real estate industry. In India, the work of Ludovic Halbert, Hortense Rouanet, and Aurelie Varrel is exemplary.

40. Dupont 2005; Falzon 2004; King 2002; Waldrop 2004.

41. Caldeira 2000; Fraser 2000; Kuppinger 2004; Öncü 1997; Zhang 2010; Webster, Glasze, and Frantz 2002.

42. Applbaum 2004; Arvidsson 2000; Mazzarella 2003; Miller and Rose 1997.

43. Notable ethnographies which provide insight into producer strategies include Sylvia Yanagisako's study of Italian silk manufacturers (2002) and Tejaswini Ganti's study of Bollywood filmmakers (2012a).

44. Here I draw an analogy between real estate industry members and scientists, adapting Latour's conceptualization of science as an agonistic practice of enrolling allies and controlling their actions to real estate (Latour 1987).

45. Cf. Latour and Woolgar 1986:48–49. The amount of documentation varies among different members of the real estate industry and at different stages in a building project. Contrac-

tors, for example, often rely on verbal communications with workers; they strategically leave some work and workers undocumented in order to depress wages and avoid taxes. I discuss the ideologies of representation that inform the production of real estate documents in chapters 7 and 8.

46. The misrecognition that Marxist scholars identify in everyday discourses are often what makes discourses powerful in organizing people's perceptions of the social world. For example, Teresa Calderia (2000, 19–52) and Jane Hill (2008) provide analyses that show how narratives about race simplify social realities and thus provide coherent, generative symbolic frameworks that inform people's actions.

47. Jane Guyer compares West African economic systems, in which a lack of institutional structure provides "the opportunity, and even the need, for charismatic resolutions" in transactions, to Western markets, which are "finely structured, practically and ideological, to place price at the center of each transaction. Everything else is ideally decided in advance, so that there is a single point at which supply and demand intersect through the implicit bargaining embodied in market forces" (2004, 97). While India and West Africa are, of course, very different culturally and historically, I think there is something in the uncertainty of market making that does create the leeway for "charismatic resolutions"; where value is uncertain, real estate producers' value projects are all the more critical.

48. I am thankful to Aseem Shrivastava for this phrase.

49. See Abolafia 1998; Boyer 2008; Gusterson 1996, 1997; Traweek 1988.

50. Detailed research reports from international property consultants can cost upwards of Rs. 10 lakh. The 2004 report from the National Council of Applied Economic Research, *The Great Indian Middle Class*, which I tried to obtain for chapter 4, sells for Rs. 2.5 lakh (or $6,024).

51. Luckily, this conference's organizers waived the fee for me as an academic. Many conference organizers do not have such a policy, making corporate conferences inaccessible to ethnographers. This is a pity because conferences are excellent ethnographic resources. They provide an opportunity to observe formal presentations of industry concerns and rituals that communicate symbolic aspects of the community. As social events, they are excellent for meeting numerous industry members in one place, speaking with them informally, and getting a sense of industry politics.

52. In a most frustrating incident, the head of a small marketing agency allowed me to record an interview. Afterward, he had me play back what I had recorded, and then he asked me to erase it, citing concerns about the recording being digital, and thus easy to circulate. From what I could tell, there was absolutely nothing on the tape that was remotely confidential; he merely described his concept for a brochure for a Gurgaon office building (the brochure had already been printed, and I could have obtained it from the developer). After I unsuccessfully tried to convince him that I would never e-mail his interview to anyone nor let anyone else listen to it, I erased the file. Because of incidents like this, my fieldnotes are filled with complaints, concerns (did I do something wrong?), and frustrated rants.

53. Exciting new scholarship on corruption recognizes the ways in which it opens up avenues for action, as a kind of "provisional agency" (Jauregui 2014; also Anjaria 2011, Witsoe 2011). Corruption is not just top-down exploitation by elites but horizontal exchanges which provide opportunities for gains by street vendors, squatters, dalits, and others.

54. Industry members also claimed not to keep historical price data, old brochures, and the financials for constructed projects (of which, actually, there were relatively few).

55. Elyachar (2006) provides an excellent example of informants using research artifacts for their own projects. Miyazaki (2013) attends to the parallels between his informants' knowledge practices and his own, seeking collaboration with his informants in understanding arbitrage practices.

56. Here they, like other technocratic practices, "hide themselves not by their strangeness but by denying the anthropologist the cues or hooks that engage the analytical imagination" (Riles 2004, 401). Technocratic practices are difficult to analyze not because experts are that different from other groups of people but because anthropologists often share their expert informants' models of the world, research methods, and understanding of expertise itself.

Chapter One

1. As part of the attempts to open up new spaces for capital accumulation described in this book, the transportation routes to Gurgaon were being rebuilt during my fieldwork. Especially toward the end of 2007 and into 2008, the Mehrauli-Gurgaon Road was torn up to build the extension of the Delhi metro into Gurgaon. During fieldwork, the National Highway 8, the other main artery through Gurgaon was being widened (and was therefore partially closed), and the airport was also being enlarged and modernized.

2. Scholars debate how the transformations in media, commodities, and work wrought by liberalization have affected aspects of Indian social life. See Nakassis and Searle 2013.

3. The immediate catalyst for these reforms was a balance-of-payments crisis that had actually been brewing since the 1980s. Strapped with high central government debts, current account deficits, a sudden outflow of Non-Resident Indian investments, and a plunging international credit rating that limited borrowing options, the government neared default in early 1991. In July, the Government of India arranged a stand-by loan of $2.26 billion dollars from the International Monetary Fund (IMF) and began a series of policy reforms to "stabilize" the balance-of-payments situation and to liberalize the economy in line with IMF and World Bank orthodoxy. The government devalued the rupee; liberalized its industrial licensing program; dismantled import quotas and reduced tariffs; allowed foreign investment (including in portfolio investments) without prior government permissions in many sectors; partially deregulated the state-owned banking system, permitting private sector and foreign joint-venture banks; and sold off public sector industrial assets. The reforms that began in 1991 have been ongoing, with certain sectors (for example, retail) incrementally liberalized in the intervening years. For descriptions of the reforms see Bhaduri and Nayyar 1996; Ghosh 1992; Kumar 2000.

4. This view of the market that I provide here differs from that of my informants, who, couching specific local knowledge in international property jargon, see "Indian real estate" as a number of markets "segmented" by city, by grade of building (Class A, B, C), and by type of building (what my informants call "asset classes" or "verticals": hotels, retail, office, housing, etc.). For example, my informants would differentiate between the market for Class A office buildings in Kolkata and that in Bombay—or even between subareas within one city. They would consider the market for apartments in both cities different from that for office buildings. They reiterated that India is not "one market." While this is certainly true, I find dividing the market up instead into its subsidiary parts is a useful way to understand its history.

5. In fact, rather than think of these state representatives and employees as "the state," we might think of them as market participants, as my informants did. When I accompanied a young

developer, Vinay, to bribe planning officials (see chapter 5), he and his cousin joked as they toured me around the municipal corporation building:

> This hall is where the deputies, etc. sit—they do a volume business. Like the commodities market. Lots of little sums. But each take home Rs 100,000 to 150,000 a day, every day. . . . And that wing there is where the big transactions take place, where the mayor, the planning commissioner, and everyone is. There the turnover is small, but the amounts are huge.

For Vinay and his cousin, the municipal corporation *is* a market. By analogy, they cast bureaucrats as entrepreneurs selling commodities—but not much analogizing is needed. Developers like Vinay routinely "buy" land-use permits, exemptions, and services from bureaucrats and elected officials; they are just one more service to be purchased and coordinated by the developer. Of course, by labeling these exchanges "market exchanges" I do not mean to obscure the ways in which they depend on the deft manipulation of social networks and cultural expectations—that is, the ways in which they overlap with "gift economies."

6. The overwhelming majority of developers are men.

7. Commenting on the real estate industry in Ahmedabad in the mid-1990s, Patel writes, "Given the complexity of building construction and the ever present possibility of contractors producing substandard work, developers in Ahmedabad cannot, in effect, 'buy' well-constructed buildings by contracting the entire building construction work to a builder" (Patel 1995, 160).

8. Patel (1995) offers an extended comparison between these various modes of building. He sees three features of developer-organized capitalist property development which together differentiate it from government-produced, cooperative, or self-built construction: (1) Buildings are produced as commodities; (2) the goal of building is capital accumulation; and (3) producers compete with one another (Patel 1995, 100). His account also provides good examples of the difficulties an analyst might have in disentangling these three forms. He argues that in Ahmedabad (Gujarat), the first real estate developers emerged in the 1960s; many were builders who moved from construction to developing property after gaining experience with cooperative housing projects (Patel 1995, 60–61). He contends that by the 1970s, the cooperative housing movement (which had begun in the 1920s), was merely a facade for profit-oriented private development as developers created fake cooperative societies, complete with fictitious members, in order to avail of public financing (Patel 1995, 80; see also Wadhva 1989).

9. The act also established permissible building sizes for vacant urban lands, and it required sales of vacant urban land to be approved by the government. Passed by the central government, the act went into effect immediately in Andhra Pradesh, Gujarat, Haryana, Himachal Pradesh, Karnataka, Maharashtra, Orissa, Punja, Tripura, Uttar Pradesh, West Bengal, and all the Union Territories. Assam, Bihar, Madhya Pradesh, Manipur, Meghalaya, and Rajasthan adopted the act later, and Tamil Nadu already had similar legislation in place.

10. The DDA itself became a speculator in land—holding parcels until the price rose, selling through auctions to high bidders, etc.—in order to fund its building development costs. Its monopoly on land also squeezed supply and drove land prices up. It delivered only a fraction of housing and office space needed, and it catered predominantly to rich and middle-income groups (Kacker 2005).

11. By many accounts, the ULCRA failed to deliver a more equitable distribution of urban land (see Acharya 1987). The exemptions, in particular, crippled its effectiveness. By 1999, when

the government repealed the Act nationally, for example, municipal authorities had acquired only 8 percent of estimated surplus land (Batra 2007; Mahalingam 1998).

12. Cities and states across India have privatized urban development using diverse regulatory means. The city of Mumbai, for example, implemented a system of "transferrable development rights" beginning in the late 1960s which allowed builders to build more densely in return for handing land over to the state or carrying out public sector construction. This system was expanded dramatically through the 1991 Slum Redevelopment Program and the 1995 Slum Redevelopment Scheme, which opened land up for commercial redevelopment by allowing developers to build market rate high-rises on the site of slum tenements, provided they rehouse the slum dwellers in new buildings on site (see Björkman 2015 for a lucid explanation of this complex system).

13. According to the Haryana Development and Regulation of Urban Areas Act of 1975, "colonizers," as they are called, pay a fee for a license as well as a one-time external development charge for government construction of roads, electricity lines, sewerage, and water lines up to the boundary of the "colony." Developers are responsible for purchasing land directly from farmer-landowners; constructing infrastructure within the colony; maintaining it for five years; complying with planning regulations; and providing open space, schools, hospitals, etc., as well as a certain percentage of housing for the poor ("economically weaker sections"). Critics charge that the private sector has benefited unduly from this program, while the state has borne the burden of providing external infrastructure (Jamwal 2004). The one-time external development charges do not cover the cost of infrastructure provision or maintenance, which has fallen to Haryana's overwhelmed Urban Development Authority. However, developers do charge large maintenance fees to housing residents. Developers have also found ways to dodge the economically weaker section quotas by selling such housing through shell companies to nonpoor individuals. They have flouted land use regulations by allotting public uses to marginal lands, encroaching on public lands, and constructing buildings that do not comply with government-approved plans.

14. Delhi Land and Finance was the first to get a license under the Haryana Development and Regulation of Urban Areas Act in 1981. The Act was passed in 1975, but Delhi Land and Finance's K. P. Singh reports that Haryana Chief Minister Bansi Lal, who was staunchly against private development, put his own policy into place in 1976, preventing licenses from being granted under the Act (Singh 2011, 186). Singh, through his contacts with Prime Minister Indira Gandhi's son Rajiv Gandhi, convinced later Haryana Chief Minister Bhajan Lal to allow private township development in Haryana, beginning with Singh's own project in Gurgaon (Damodaran 2008, 285–86; Namburu 2007, 25–26; Singh 2011, 180–187; cf. Menon 2006). (I also heard rumors, which I was never able to substantiate, that Singh bribed Haryana authorities for his license by providing land for National Highway 8, which bisects Gurgaon.)

15. In Delhi, the firm Delhi Land and Finance (DLF), for example, used to operate on a "land-bank partnership model." Founded in 1946 to take advantage of the demand for housing after Partition, the firm developed approximately 5,800 acres of Delhi, selling plots of land in the neighborhoods (or colonies, as they are called) Hauz Kaus, Greater Kailash I and II, Kailash Colony, South Extension, Shivaji Park, and others before the Delhi Development Act came into effect. The firm acquired land on a profit-sharing model wherein farmers sold their land to DLF on credit. The company paid landowners back from the proceeds of plot sales, in installments with interest; many landowners redeposited the proceeds with DLF, in effect using the company as a bank (Damodaran 2008, 284–5; Namburu 2007, 11; Singh 2011, 174–5). The founder's son-in-

law, K. P. Singh, used the same strategy to finance his land acquisition in Gurgaon in the 1980s (Namburu 2007, 31).

16. The latter body develops regulations and provides funding for mortgage granting financial institutions. It attempts to expand the mortgage market through various schemes for expanding loan opportunities for rural populations, the poor, the elderly, and women, as well as by developing a secondary mortgage market, creating securitization processes, and devising other ways of involving the capital markets in housing finance (National Housing Bank 2006; interview with Shri Sridhar, Chairman and Managing Director of the National Housing Bank, December 24, 2006).

17. A rise in the total value of mortgages masks the fact that home prices were rising faster than new loan dispersals. A senior manager at ICICI bank told me that average loan sizes increased from Rs. 4.5 to 5 lakh in 2003–4 to 13–14 lakh in 2007. So while the mortgage industry grew at a compound annual growth rate of 40 percent CAGR between 2002 and 2007, the number of new mortgage loans only grew at a rate of 8–10 percent (interview with a senior manager at ICICI bank, October 26, 2007). A senior manager at HDFC bank corroborated this picture, explaining that while their total loan portfolio increased by 25 percent in 2006–7, the number of new accounts had only grown by 10–15 percent (interview with a senior manager at HDFC, February 23, 2007). The chairman and managing director of the National Housing Bank also explained that the overall growth of the real estate and mortgage industries might be due to the extraordinary rise in property values, masking an actual *increase* in the housing shortage (interview with Shri Sridhar, Chairman and Managing Director of the National Housing Bank, December 24, 2006).

18. One study of land markets in Lucknow conducted in the early 1990s found that 86 percent of 521 sampled households had paid for land (on which to build a house) in purchases dating back from the 1970s to the 1990s with a single payment, suggesting that families saved to buy land over a long period of time and did not avail of either developers' installment payment schemes or bank loans (Kundu 1997, 233). Today, the majority of loans fund home purchases, not self-construction, home improvement, or home equity (interview with a senior manager at HDFC, March 26, 2007).

19. For example, at the end of the 2005–2006 fiscal year, HDFC had cumulatively sold loans aggregating Rs. 2,043 crores as mortgage-backed securities, while in 2005–2006 alone, HDFC disbursed Rs. 20,679.20 crores in new loans (HDFC 2006).

20. The private Housing Development Finance Corporation (HDFC) began giving loans to real estate developers for construction in 1989, though it kept this lending at a very small scale (interview with a senior manager at HDFC, February 23, 2007). In a published interview from 1991, HDFC's managing director comments that banks do not fund developers in part because many set up their businesses as short-lived limited partnerships, producing "no track record for the financial institutions to consider." Also, he notes that he is careful that his loans go for construction, not land purchasing: "It is in the builder's interest to buy more land with our money, wait some 6–12 months, and sell the land to repay the loan and make a profit instead of investing it in actual construction" (Rao 1991, 51–52). Even with formal funding, published articles on the industry and my interviews with developers indicate that developers had a conservative attitude toward taking on formal debt. Unitech's Ramesh Chandra recounts Deepak Parekh, Chairman of HDFC Bank, "admonish[ing] Chandra for being a poor borrower" and promising to fund Rs. 500 crore of construction at a time when Unitech had only a total of Rs. 150 crore in debt. Chandra commented, "We were very conservative about borrowing but Parekh put ideas in our minds" (Surendar and Sinha 2008). By contrast, Patel found that the developers he interviewed

in Ahmedabad all found debt an essential aspect of their projects; what prevented them from taking on more projects at one time (and more debt) was their ability to supervise construction on more than one site (Patel 1995, 122–123).

21. The Reserve Bank of India sought to keep foreign capital in check as well. In 2007 it limited developers' ability to borrow money from abroad through External Commercial Borrowings (Unnikrishnan 2007).

22. The economist Arun Kumar defines "black" incomes narrowly as "factor incomes which should have been reported to the income-tax authorities but are not" (Kumar 2002, 9). Kumar defines black incomes narrowly so as not to double count bribes and other pay-offs in estimating the size of the black economy. Yet colloquially, Indians use the term "black money" quite widely: for cash transactions, unrecorded or untraceable transactions, and bribes or protection money (*hafta*) as well as counterfeit money, money not reported to the tax authorities, and money gained through illegal activities such as prostitution or smuggling. By contrast, "white" money includes checks, regular salaries, money on which tax has been paid, and money legally earned.

23. This is especially prevalent in the secondary market, where the ratio of black to white money can be the largest negotiation point between seller and buyer. From people who had recently bought apartments in Gurgaon, I heard of negotiations falling through because of disagreements over the black/white component of the sale. Salaried professionals whose entire earnings are white (declared and taxed) generally try to reduce the black proportion of the sale when purchasing property; many sellers (whether salaried or not) prefer a higher cash component to reduce stamp duty (a property transaction tax).

24. The 1973 Foreign Exchange and Regulation Act was amended in 1993 to allow NRIs and majority-NRI-owned businesses to buy real estate in India (see Nijman 2000).

25. Note the ad's use of the term "businessman." By the next decade, this term had gained a negative connotation in contrast with the term "professional," which is used in ads from the 2000s (see chapter 6).

26. This information on the inspiration for DLF's Corporate Park comes from an interview with a senior architect at the firm.

27. One study predicted 1,000 new architects and 5,000 civil engineers would be hired in 2007 (*Business Line* 2007). Anecdotally, all of the architects I interviewed said their firms were hiring. Srinivasa (2007) reports that the number of architecture graduates in India is not enough to keep pace with the demand, leading to rising salaries and stiff competition between companies to retain architectural staff.

28. Some are Indian productions (*Architecture + Design*; *Realty Plus*; *India Today Home*; *Ideal Home and Garden*) and others are international subsidiaries, with both Indian and foreign content (*Better Homes and Gardens*; *Good Housekeeping*; *Elle Décor*).

29. Of course, profits are merely a measure of how much a firm's promoter wants to take out of a company in a particular year, so alone, they are of limited usefulness in measuring company size or estimating future performance. Moreover, profits are often uneven in real estate as compared to other industries, fluctuating with completed projects (see Brett 1997, 128–145). Other issues can complicate profit reports. DLF's comparatively high profits in 2006–7 and 2007–8, for example, stem from sales the company made to DLF Assets Ltd, a sister concern that the promoters plan to list on the Singapore stock exchange. More than half of DLF's profit in the third quarter of 2007–8 derived from sales it made to DLF Assets Ltd, even though DLF had yet to receive full payment on those sales (Raja D. 2008b).

30. Cement company CEOs have also profited from the building boom. P. R. Ramasubrahmaneya Rajha, managing director of Madras Cements was the highest paid executive in India in 2006–7, earning Rs. 24.78 crore. By comparison, Ultratech Cement paid its director S. Mishra Rs. 3.36 crore; Yadupathi Singhania, managing director of JK Cement, earned Rs. 2.2 core; and Damia Cement's managing director earned Rs. 74 lakh (Raja D. et al. 2007).

31. Srinivasa (2007) provides an example of a twenty-five-year-old architect whose starting salary of Rs. 60,000 in 2004 had quadrupled to Rs. 240,000 (2.4 lakh) in 2007. By 2008, recent engineering graduates earned Rs. 12–15 lakh yearly at real estate firms (compared to Rs. 6 lakh in other industries), and vice presidents made approximately Rs. 50–60 lakh (Hussain 2008b). While the press made much of this apparent success, it often generalized in a misleading way. Hussain (2008b), for example, asserts, "It isn't just chief executives; everyone in the real estate business in earning more." She makes no mention of construction workers and their wages in her article. "Everyone in the real estate business" means, apparently, skilled, white collar employees.

32. Wadhva reports that for thirteen projects in Ahmedabad for which he was able to collect data in 1989, profit margins ranged between 18 and 195 percent of total project costs (Wadhva 1989, 136). Contemporary margins are probably equally variable; my informants estimated 20 to 100 percent. As one journalist explained to me, real estate development in India is "a high-margin business. Whereas most Indian businesses make an eight to 10 percent margin, in real estate it's 25 to 30 percent."

33. Developers can earn such high margins on luxury properties because the relative costs of fine finishes (marble instead of tile, for example) are small compared both to fixed construction costs (foundations, concrete and steel work) and to the final sales price, which is much higher for projects billed as "luxury."

34. A McKinsey Global Institute study reports that construction material costs are roughly the same between the US and India (30 percent and 28 percent of total project costs, respectively); land costs are higher in India (49 percent compared to 24 percent in the US); and labor costs are significantly lower in India (only 5 percent compared to 37 percent in the US) (McKinsey Global Institute 2001).

35. During my fieldwork, the minimum wage for unskilled labor was Rs. 101.47 per day in Delhi, Rs. 117 per day in Haryana, and Rs. 111.49 in Uttar Pradesh (see Mobile Crèches 2008, 27). According to a study of 425 construction worker households at ten sites in the National Capital Region, "Apart from one government site in Delhi, where 22% of the male workers received the minimum wages, almost no other employer pays the labour, and certainly not the women, the legal minimum. Women continue to do the head-loading, the most unskilled job at the site, and get paid less than the male workers" (Mobile Crèches 2008, 3). While all of the households in this survey were earning more in the Capital than they had in their villages, only nine had managed to save any money, and none had accumulated any assets. Fifty-five percent sent some money home to relatives, but the majority reported spending most of their income on food and medicine. Nevertheless, the study found that two out of three children in these families are malnourished (Mobile Crèches 2008, 5). Without permanent homes or identity cards, workers find themselves excluded from (and often ignorant of) government programs for the poor such as rations, schooling, and health care (Mobile Crèches 2008, 25–26).

36. Others came from Bihar, Uttar Pradesh, West Bengal, and Madhya Pradesh. Migrants from Bihar reported floods and those from Jhansi, Uttar Pradesh reported three years of drought (Mobile Crèches 2008, 13).

37. Other studies of construction laborers have also found that they migrate to survive. As David Mosse, Sanjeev Gupta, and Vidya Shah (2005) demonstrate, for example, *bhil adivasis* (tribals) in Madhya Pradesh, Gujarat, and Rajasthan are unable to sustain precarious rural livelihoods without seasonal migration to work on urban construction sites. The Second National Commission on Labour concludes that "workers in the construction industry are often rural migrants who were mostly landless labour and on the brink of starvation in villages" (2002, 100).

38. K. Das 2007; Ghosh 2004; Self Employed Women's Association 2000; Suryanarayan 2004.

39. *Asian Age* 2005; Dastidar and Krishnan 2008; *Hindu* 2008; Kumar 2005; Makkar 2007; Mukherjee 2003; *Times of India* 2002, 2008. Labor activists told me that most on-site accidents are never reported to the police or the press (the latter has difficulty accessing construction worker camps due to construction company security); that families rarely receive treatment or compensation from construction companies; and that sometimes injured workers are merely quietly shipped back to their villages. The Second National Commission on Labour also found that "contractors remove sick and injured workers from sites and pay rolls without giving them adequate compensation" (SNCL 2002, 634).

40. A number of laws apply to migrant construction workers but are rarely enforced: the Minimum Wages Act of 1948; the Contract Labour (Regulation and Abolition) Act of 1970; the Inter-State Migrant Workmen (Regulation of Employment and Conditions of Service) Act of 1979; and the Equal Remuneration Act of 1976.

41. These acts mandate that both contractors and construction workers register with the government and that each state establish a BOCW Welfare Board. They also require contractors to pay a cess (or tax) of 1 percent of construction costs (not including land) to the state Welfare Board, which oversees a fund from which accident assistance, pensions, insurance, scholarships, and maternity benefits are issued to registered workers (who are also required to contribute to the fund monthly). The BOCW Act mandates that state governments establish fixed hours of work and overtime wages, and that contractors provide drinking water, latrines, crèches, first aid, and canteens, as well as adequate accommodation, on site.

42. Kerala, Tamil Nadu, and Madhya Pradesh were among the few that had been successful in collecting the cess *and* distributing benefits to workers (CWG-CWC 2008). Madhya Pradesh's program has been comparatively successful, registering 3.5 lakh construction workers since 1996. 22,838 have received benefits under the scheme (CWG-CWC 2007). By contrast, the Delhi government has been among the laggards. It notified the BOCW rules and formed a Welfare Board six years after the legislation passed nationally, and it did not begin collecting the cess until 2006. The Haryana government published BOCW rules and put them into effect even later, in 2005; it established a Welfare Board in 2006 (Haryana Labour Department). As of 2008, Uttar Pradesh had yet to do so.

43. The High Court of Delhi, dismissing writ petitions filed by the Builders' Association of India and 97 contractors and developers against both acts, chided the government of Delhi for an "inexcusable delay" in enacting the legislation. "Given the fact that in the past decade Delhi has witnessed the execution of a large number of construction contracts involving hundreds of crores," High Court Justices Muralidhar and Mudgal write in their decision, the "loss of revenue" due to delayed implementation of the legislation is of "no small measure." They continue, "This failure on behalf of the State is questionable and should not be permitted to be perpetuated" (*Builders' Association vs. Union of India*). Here, bureaucratic delay and outright opposition from builders has hampered significant legislative reform. The High Court Justices themselves complain that they were unable to pry details from government officials about the cause of the delay.

They also failed to goad the Delhi government into action. By May 2007, the Delhi BOCW Welfare Board had collected Rs. 100 crore from contractors, but it had only registered approximately 2,250 workers (out of an estimated 800,000), none of whom had received any benefits (Sehgal 2007).

44. Other construction laborers (both recent migrants and long-time city residents) find work at the morning labor *mandis* that form at city intersections. *Mistris*, skilled masons or carpenters, often organize gangs of skilled and unskilled workers and negotiate for their employment with contractors scouting for workers at the *mandi*. Laborers at the *mandi* can sometimes negotiate higher wages than migrants contracted as groups through *jamadars* at the construction sites, but they have no guarantee of work and are not provided shelter; they often sleep on the sidewalk near the *mandi* at night (see Sethi 2005, 2012).

45. Gross internal rate of return is calculated before deducting management fees, interest, and disposal costs. One Trikona investment lost money, earning an internal rate of return of −38 percent. Some of these investments are at the project level and some at the company level.

46. Marx divides merchant's capital into "commercial" capital and "money-dealing" capital (see 1981, 379). The latter is what we would call finance capital today.

47. Because land is limited in supply and unique in its properties, buildings are nonstandard commodities, fundamentally different from mass-produced cars or blue jeans (Logan and Molotch 1987, 17–49). Property values depend in part on an owner's ability to extract ground rent, i.e. value that accrues through the owner's monopoly over a unique parcel with particular locational advantages. (Marxist scholars have debated the origins and role of rent in capitalist society and distinguished between different types of rent; for an excellent review see Patel 1995, 298–313). Marxist geographers assert that just as merchants create no surplus value of their own but extract some of the surplus value of the production of the commodities that they trade, so too are real estate developers parasitic on productive labor—particularly the labor that *will* take place in the commercial properties they construct (Harvey 1999; Lamarche 1976; cf. Fainstein 2001, 200–202). Buying land, "the money laid out is equivalent to an interest-bearing investment. The buyer acquires a claim upon anticipated future revenues, a claim upon the future fruits of labor" (Harvey 1999, 367). The *futurity* of this surplus value extraction opens it up to speculation. Rather than see speculation as inherently negative or "irrational," I argue that it enables us to study the politics of competing value projects and the semiotic work of creating and ranking differences. In what follows, instead of asking, "Where does value come from?" I consider "What work is being done to make speculative accumulation possible?"

48. The language Marx uses to describe these forms of capital are overwhelmingly negative: interest-bearing capital is "irrational," "capital mystification in the most flagrant form" (516), "lawless and arbitrary" (478). The "mystification" is the fetishism that obscures (in Marx's view) the fact that value does come from labor—and yet, he seems to have trouble showing that this is the case. In these passages of *Capital*, vol. 3, Marx "recognizes that he cannot accommodate the circulation of interest-bearing capital within the framework of assumptions that have hitherto guided his studies" (Harvey 2013, 187).

49. It should be clear from this discussion and from what follows (especially chapters 7 and 8), that I do not think Indian real estate developers are any less speculative in their operation than foreign investors. Both engage in spectacular accumulation; differences in practice between the two groups suggest different modes of speculative accumulation.

50. I understand that using the terms "labor" and "work" to describe the activities of financial analysts, lawyers, public relations executives, and others is fraught given the political and

historical weight accorded these categories in Marxist though. However, I think that to understand the forms of spectacular accumulation which have become so prevalent and powerful in contemporary capitalism, we cannot shy away from a reconsideration of concepts such as labor, work, and value.

51. When Nixon abrogated the Bretton Woods monetary system in the early 1970s, unpegging the dollar from its fixed rate of exchange and dismantling capital controls, he helped create a "new role for private finance in international monetary relations" by letting the markets decide exchange rates (Gowan 1999, 22). Deregulation, monetary reform, and the volatility of oil prices in the 1970s further increased international dependence on the financial markets for managing currencies, spurring the growth of private financial firms and the prominence of Wall Street (New York) and The City (London). For overviews of the effects of the development of these financial markets on the sociology and geography of New York and London, see Sassen 2001 and Massey 2007.

52. Gowan 1999; LiPuma and Lee 2005; Morris 2008; Partnoy 1997; Strange 1997, 112–115.

53. One might trace these trends back to the late 1960s. Several scholars describe the new role that financial firms played in the property boom in England during the late 1960s and early 1970s (Boddy 1981; Marriott 1967). Daly (1982) highlights the relationships between British capital and a concurrent property boom in Australia.

54. While economic sociologists often catalogue the social networks created by partnerships such as this (see Granovetter 1985, cf. Krippner 2001, Swedberg 1990) as a way to study business and investment sociologically, note that I am arguing that routes of accumulation encompass more than networks of people. They also include the objects being traded, mechanisms for doing so, representations of those objects, market actors, and markets themselves, as well as a range of practices and ideologies.

55. DLF, Unitech, and Hiranandani are large Indian real estate development firms.

56. By "portfolio," he means a collection of investments. In the world of finance, a building is an abstract entity, an asset that can be bought and sold along with other assets in a portfolio. One can diversify a portfolio by investing in a wide range of assets, and one's portfolio can gain or lose value as a whole, based on valuations of its components.

57. A special purpose vehicle (SPV) is a company set up for a specific purpose that limits the liability of the sponsoring company. In the US, the term is "special purpose entity" (see *Financial Times* 2005).

58. The example I've given here was as told to me by an informant who worked for a fund. The example in the figure explains a similar type of corporate structure for Unitech Corporate Parks, a subsidiary of Unitech (one of India's largest developers) that is incorporated in the Isle of Man and listed on the London Stock Exchange Alternative Investment Market (AIM). I think that industry members developed this type of structure after the Government of India declared that all foreign investment in the form of preference shares would be considered debt and thus be subject to the (more stringent) External Commercial Borrowing regulations (*Business Standard* 2007b; Ghosh 2007; Ghosh and Ramsurya 2006; Sikarwar 2007). This rule change sent numerous funds scrambling, as many had planned to invest in Indian real estate through the preference share route, which was now effectively shut down (*Economic Times* 2007f; Shah and Bagry 2007; Unnikrishnan 2007). A preference share is an instrument that has qualities of both debt and equity; it is technically share capital, but it provides a fixed dividend (usually less than prevailing interest rates). Often preference shares can be converted to ordinary shares on a set date (Brett 1997, 123–24).

59. Of course, as Patel (1995) points out, architects have historically been concerned with crafting unique building-images. He argues that under capitalist property development, image making is characterized by the profit motive (and thus the limitation of costs) and competition (241–42). His extended discussion of image making in the 1970s–1990s in Ahmedabad indicates that the brochures, model flats, and architectural motifs used today in India have roots several decades old and are not merely the result of foreign direct investment.

Chapter Two

1. The most expensive apartments in Gurgaon at this time were about Rs. 12,000 per square foot. My informants at EuroFund mulled over news of the same sale at lunch one day, debating whether the purchase was "rational" or not. The *Times of India* reported the story as well: a four-bedroom apartment on Marine Drive in Mumbai sold for 34 crore, or Rs. 97,842 per square foot, making it the largest recorded real estate transaction in India (Bharucha 2007). Another newspaper later reported the price as Rs. 63,000 per square foot (R. T. Sharma 2007). The variation in these reported prices on the same property indicates the difficulty one would have pinning down definitive price information. An apartment in the same building apparently sold for Rs. 73,000 per square foot in 2006 (Bharucha 2006).

2. Some scholars share this ebullient view. For example, geographer Sanjoy Chakravorty (2013a and 2013b) claims that the price of Indian land will never fall; Chakravorty maintains that "India is permanently in a new land regime" such that "there will be no return to the prices that prevailed a decade ago" (2013b, 52). Chakravorty ignores the reality of land speculation and merely recapitulates the view of people in the real estate industry when he argues that increased land prices in India result from constrained supply and increased demand due to economic growth, rising middle-class incomes, the expansion of mortgage markets, etc. I am arguing something quite different in this book, namely that "demand" is a shared story reinforced, in part, through books like Chakravorty's, such that land prices reflect collective imaginings about the future (see also chapter 3). Chakravorty's arguments are, as Preety Sampat succinctly puts it, "premised on capitalism's idealized tenets, liberal democracy with clear property rights; and well-functioning, transparent land markets with information symmetries" (Sampat 2014, 32). These tenets do not characterize India today; however, they are central to the neoliberal imagination that has fueled the speculation that has raised the price of Indian land to new heights.

3. Part 1 of this book builds on the work of sociologists of finance, who have shown that rather than merely describing markets, economic knowledge performatively produces effects in them (see Callon 1998; MacKenzie 2006; MacKenzie, Muniesa, and Siu 2007). While empirical demonstrations of the performativity of economics have been in financial markets such as derivative exchanges (see MacKenzie and Millo 2003), real estate markets are far less contained. It might be impossible to prove the performativity of speculative real estate discourses, since developers' claims to profitability rest on broad social trends that unfold through complex dynamics outside of the industry. However, in the next three chapters, I show that, to some extent, real estate industry discourses do bring about some of the effects that they describe, and moreover, that they are proleptic: they help to bring a projected future into being.

4. The National Housing Bank began a residential price index, the Residex, in July 2007. As of December 2008, however, the index had only been updated once and still covered only five cities (Delhi, Bangalore, Mumbai, Bhopal, and Kolkata). Given the number of unrecorded, cash property transactions, observers doubted the index's usefulness. Still, the index showed that

residential property rates increased by more than 20 percent between 2002 and 2007 in Delhi and Bangalore (18 percent in Mumbai, 17.5 percent in Bhopal, and 15.7 percent in Kolkata over the same period). These appreciation rates are the first official statistics available about real estate prices, and they are not particularly fine-grained (Verma and Chatterjee 2008). The index has been expanded and fine-tuned over time; in 2015 it included twenty-six cities (see http://nhb.org .in/Residex/About_Residex.php).

5. Apart from articles reporting specific deals and land auctions, some newspapers publish aggregate price data collected from the international property consultants for particular neighborhoods; the accuracy of this data is unknown. Official price data from transactions registered with the Land Registry offices usually underestimate prices because buyers registering properties often bribe land registry officials to record a price that reduces the Stamp Duty (property transaction tax) the buyer will owe (for a description of this process, see Kundu 1997, 150). Other official data sets often produce low price estimates. For example, Kundu reports that the minimum average price was Rs. 160 per square meter for land purchased in Lucknow public sector colonies in 1981–3 according to his questionnaire-based field data, while a government study based on data from state urban development institutions found the price to be Rs. 65 per square meter (Kundu 1997, 147).

6. Many consultancies—from international property consultants, to accountants, lawyers, and financial service firms—offer some kind of real estate advisory service to their clients. These same firms publish yearly or quarterly updates on the Indian real estate market, among others, as part of their efforts to attract clients to their services and to retain them. This motive is more or less clear depending on the report. For example, international consultancy Deloitte Touche Tohmatsu's 2007 report "Real Estate Investing in India: Why Now?" reads as dual advertisement for Indian real estate and Deloitte's services; it combines an optimistic market description with statements informing the reader about Deloitte's Construction Advisory Services practice and its foreign direct investment services (Deloitte Development LLC 2007).

7. As a foreign fund EuroFund would not have technically been able to buy the land outright. However, any deal concerning this parcel (either between the fund and the landowner or the fund and an Indian developer) would factor in a cost for land.

8. I am indebted to Constantine Nakassis for this insight.

9. In late 2000, the federal funds rate (the rate at which banks lend each other money, usually overnight, to meet their reserve requirements at the Federal Reserve) fell from 6.5 percent to 3.5 percent; it fell further to 1 percent in 2003, its lowest in fifty years. As Charles Morris explains, "for 31 consecutive months, the base inflation adjusted short-term interest rate was *negative*. For bankers, in other words, money was free" (Morris 2008, 59). This meant that government treasury bonds were not making money above inflation, pushing fund managers to look elsewhere for returns. Fund managers also borrowed heavily ("leveraged" their investments) at low interest rates to increase returns; this increased the total amount of money circulating, as well as the possibility of greater losses.

10. Hedge funds are "unregulated investment vehicles that cater to institutions and wealthy individuals and promise extraordinary returns" (Morris 2008, 109). Scholars have increasingly noted the power of hedge funds to change the markets in which they operate, to operate in concert, and to control the companies in which they have invested (see Gowan 1999, 95–97; MacKenzie 2003; Mollenkamp et al. 2007).

11. Private equity has been defined as investment in assets that are not publicly traded, though today private equity firms are also acquiring equity in listed assets through negotiated

buyouts. Most salient, private equity firms direct "their investments at acquiring a stake, often a controlling stake, with the aim of influencing the performance of companies rather than merely parking funds in financial assets incorporating varying degrees of risk and uncertainty." They combine the role of investor and advisor (Chandrasekhar 2007).

12. Wessel (2007) uses estimates made by the McKinsey Global Institute in its report "The New Power Brokers: How Oil, Asia, Hedge Funds, and Private Equity Are Shaping Global Capital Markets" from October 2007. McKinsey's estimates roughly correspond to the International Monetary Fund figures cited by Blumberg and Davidson (2008).

13. As investors and fund managers looked for returns, they sought out increasingly higher risk assets, but with so much money pouring into these assets, their profitability compared to safe investments like US Treasury notes plummeted. In financial lingo, the "risk premium" was low.

14. Blumberg and Davidson 2008; Morris 2008; Tett 2009, 94–98. The demand for mortgage-backed securities spurred the increase in sales of subprime mortgages that eventually precipitated the global credit crisis that began in 2007.

15. Banks and other financial services companies are also eager to expand to new markets. They aim to interest Western investors in investments in emerging economies as well as to set up offices abroad to service companies from those markets (*Economist* 2007).

16. Goldman Sachs 2007; O'Neill 2001; O'Neill and Poddar 2008; Wilson and Purushothaman 2003.

17. For examples of press summaries, see Balls 2003; Bogler 2003; *Economist* 2003; Zakaria 2006. The international consultancy PriceWaterhouseCoopers, for example, published a report titled "The World in 2050: How Big Will the Major Emerging Market Economies Get and How Can the OECD Compete?" in March 2006, with an argument along the same lines as the Goldman Sachs reports. To differentiate its analysis, PriceWaterhouseCoopers investigates the growth potential of the "E7," the BRIC countries plus Turkey, Indonesia, and Mexico. The report is available at http://www.pwc.com/gx/en/world-2050/growth-in-emerging-economies-oportunity-or -threat.html (accessed August 24, 2009).

18. For example, in 2006, the *Economist* declared that emerging economies like India and China "will provide the biggest boost to the world economy since the industrial revolution" (Woodall 2006).

19. MSCI had already established an Emerging Markets Index in 1987; it added India to the Emerging Markets Index in 1994. See MSCI Barra 2008 and the MSCI Barra webpage, "MSCI Indices: Overview," http://www.mscibarra.com/products/indices/index.jsp (accessed January 16, 2010).

20. Goldman Sachs has continued to move lock-step with investors' quest for new markets. In 2005 its researchers coined the acronym N11 to describe the "Next Eleven," i.e., "the next set of large-population countries beyond the BRICs" that Goldman Sachs researchers felt "could potentially have a BRIC-like impact in rivaling the G7" (Goldman Sachs 2007, 131). Similarly, enabling investors in their quest for returns on the "frontiers" of capitalism, MSCI Barra launched a Frontier Market Index covering nineteen "emerging markets" in 2007. HSBC also announced a frontier market fund in the same year (Assis 2007).

21. *Indian Express* 2004; Narayanan 2007; Roy 2003; Shukla 2003.

22. Some of the acquisitions which grabbed front-page headlines include: Mittal Steel's purchase of Arcelor; Tata's buyout of Tetley Tea; Tata Motors's purchase of Jaguar and Land Rover; Tata Steel's acquisition of Corus; Ranbaxy's buyout of Aventis; and VSNL's acquisition of Tyco

Global Network. There was a rash of these buyouts in 2006—115 foreign acquisitions, worth $7.4 billion, in the first nine months of 2006 alone—fueled perhaps by regulatory changes and Indian corporate confidence (India Knowledge@Wharton 2006). It is important to note that a lot of these buyouts are leveraged—i.e., funded through debt acquired from global financiers and institutional investors.

23. Twenty20 Cricket is a shortened form of the game introduced in 2003. Each team only bats for one inning, with a maximum of twenty overs. This form was designed to appeal to younger audiences and television viewers.

24. "Chak de India" refers to a 2007 Bollywood film by the same name, directed by Shimit Amin and staring Shah Rukh Khan as the coach of the (ultimately victorious) Indian women's field hockey team. *Chak de* means, roughly, "Go for it!"

25. This is exactly the logic propounded (and the language used) in the World Bank *World Development Report 1994* on infrastructure provision in the developing world. The Expert Committee cites examples from this World Bank report of "successful public provision of infrastructure services" (Department of Economic Affairs 1996, 218; Ghosh, Sen, and Chandrasekhar 1997; World Bank 1994).

26. The 1998 Budget also introduced a tax incentive for housing developers and an increase in the mortgage deductions for home buyers to jumpstart private sector housing provision (Ministry of Finance 1998).

27. The policy also suggested the repeal of the Urban Land (Ceiling and Regulation) Act (ULCRA) in order to make more land available for development. This had long been a demand of the real estate industry. The act was repealed by the Central Government in 1999 and many—though not all—states followed suit. As of 2005, Andhra Pradesh, Assam, Bihar, Kerala, Maharashtra, and West Bengal had not repealed the act (CREDAI 2005). Maharashtra repealed the ULCRA in November 2007, amid much fanfare. Stocks for Mumbai-based realty companies rose between two and 10 percent upon the announcement of the repeal, despite the fact that the estimated 15,000 acres land likely to open up in Mumbai as a result would probably not become available for development for two or more years (Bavdam 2008; *Economic Times* 2007i; Ramanathan 2007f).

28. As Lalit Batra writes,

the JNNURM is the culmination of a process of neoliberal urban reforms that has been going on since the late '90s. Its predecessors include the Urban Reforms Incentive Fund (URIF) and Model Municipal Law (MML), both of which were formulated on the basis of a set of policy postulates developed by the World Bank (WB), the Asian Development Bank (ADB), the USAID and the UNDP (Batra 2007).

The Urban Reforms Incentive Fund, begun in 2003, linked urban reforms to an annual allotment of Rs. 500 crore in central government funding; it was subsumed under the JNURRM in 2005 (Ministry of Housing and Urban Poverty Alleviation). Similarly, through the Model Municipal Law, the USAID Financial Institutions Reform and Expansion (FIRE-D) project and the Government of India provided a model of accounting norms, financial management, and reforms for urban bodies to emulate (Ministry of Urban Development).

29. The reforms include: lowering stamp duty; computerizing land registration records; introducing property title certification; streamlining the approval process for building construction; repealing the Urban Land (Ceiling Regulation) Act; and simplifying the procedures for converting agricultural land to nonagricultural uses.

30. These regulations enabled investment in construction projects rather than finished buildings; regulations about the conversion of agricultural land to other uses continue to prevent foreign investors from buying land directly.

31. For example, "India Advantage: A White Paper on the Indian Real Estate Opportunity," a pamphlet written by international property consultant Cushman & Wakefield and handed out at the Global Real Estate Institute conference in Mumbai in 2006, includes a section on expected returns. "The return potential of the Indian real estate market has been extremely attractive," its authors explain, with before-tax returns of 17 to 25 percent, depending on the type of project (Cushman & Wakefield 2006, 8). The report uses the term "cash-on-cash return," which is the ratio of before-tax earnings to the total amount invested. They estimate 17 to 22 percent returns for residential and township projects, 20 to 25 percent returns for IT parks, and 25 percent returns for hospitality, leisure, and entertainment projects. A year later, Deloitte's estimates are even more promising: "Annual return rates now exceed 20% for office, 25% for retail and 75% for existing and newly developed residential property" (Deloitte Development LLC 2007, 2). Other publications advertise the high cap rates (annual yields) of Indian commercial realty—"the highest in the region," according to one article (Basu 2004). Many presentations favorably compare the returns from investment in Indian real estate to those from other assets like stocks, bonds, or gold.

32. An approximation of the presentation was still available at the firm's website, which he directed me to look at. This website is what I have cited here.

33. Some of the companies investing included: Ascendas, SembCorp Engineers and Constructors, Lee Kim Tah Holdings, Singapore Housing Board, and Keppel Land, Evan Lim & Co. from Singapore; IJM Berhad and Kontur Bintang from Malaysia; Universal Success Enterprise from Indonesia; Emaar Group from Dubai; and Royal Indian Raj International from Canada.

34. The *Wall Street Journal* reported investors "flocking" to Indian real estate (Gangopadhyay 2006), as did reports by consultants such as Ernst & Young (2006), Knight Frank (2005), and the Associated Chambers of Commerce and Industry of India (2006), among others. Articles with titles like "Real Estate Funds Bullish on Sector's Growth" and "Foreign Investors Go into a Tizzy over Asian Real Estate" brought news of the foreign investment influx to Indian readers (Kilbinger 2007; M. Mehta 2007).

35. In general, firms raise money from institutional investors (insurance companies, pension funds, mutual funds, etc.), corporations, and high-net worth individuals around the world. They dedicate these investments to an India-specific fund, or they invest through existing multi-sector or regional funds (for example an India fund not dedicated to real estate or an Asian realty fund). A few funds are publicly listed; for example, investors can buy shares in Trikona Capital's Trinity Capital Fund on the London Stock Exchange Alternative Investment Market. Many of these firms invest through subsidiary companies officially incorporated in Mauritius, the Cayman Islands, or other tax havens. Whether floated by banks, private equity firms, or property investment firms, these various funds were created to invest in Indian real estate development companies directly or to form joint ventures with Indian companies to develop specific projects.

36. A broad range of reports, blogs, and articles cite the November 2006 ASSOCHAM report, "Study on Future of Real Estate Investment in India." For example, ASSOCHAM's foreign direct investment estimates appear in a report by international consultancy Deloitte Touche Tohmatsu (Deloitte Development LLC 2007) as well as in articles in the *Financial Express*, the *Hindustan Times*, and Chandigarh's *Tribune* (Satyanarayan 2006; Soni 2007; Uprety 2007). The real estate and financial websites Indian Real Estate Forum, Jab We Met Finance, and My Property India all quote from the report or its press release:

http://www.indianrealestateforum.com/real-estate-discussions/t-fdi-creating-a-competitive
-organised-real-estate-market-85.html (accessed August 13, 2009)

http://jabwemetfinance.blogspot.com/2008/08/fdi-guidelines_10.html (accessed August 13, 2009).

www.1888pressrelease.com/mypropertyindia-com-new-india-property-based-portal-from-re-pr
-0f0016d50j.html (accessed August 13, 2009).

37. Neither of these sets of figures corresponds with some of the real estate consultancy reports' calculations. For example, Jones Lange LaSalle reports: "Following relaxation of FDI [foreign direct investment] guidelines by the RBI in 2005, we have seen an exponential growth of FDI investment in the real estate sector. FDI inflows in real estate rose from about USD 0.2 billion in 2003–04 to about USD 10.0 billion in 2007–08" (Jones Lang LaSalle 2008, 5).

38. The DIPP, however, probably underestimates real estate foreign direct investment; according to an analyst I spoke with at an international property consultancy, the DIPP categorizes some real estate foreign direct investment as financial service sector investments.

39. Indeed, the *Financial Express* estimated that by the spring of 2007, only 10 to 15 percent of the foreign investment announced had actually been invested (Soni 2007). This crucial difference—between investments announced and actually made—was cited by industry members who took a cynical stance toward celebratory industry discourses. One journalist told me that "only 25 percent of projected FDI [foreign direct investment] is actually coming in. . . . the picture the industry projects is rosier than the real picture of the FDI scenario." In an interview, a representative of a foreign retail property developer pointed out that

getting a deal done and executing the deal, the two are very different things. In India, there are many deals which are happening. If you look at the newspaper for the last one year, two year, you'll find so many deals which are being covered in there. But please ask the media, how many of these deals are actually converted into successful structures? Not many.

40. R. Banerjee 2007, Chaudhary 2007, *Economic Times* 2007a. Ernst & Young published a table showing a total of $6.2 billion in September 2006, while Real Estate Intelligence, a Mumbai-based real estate "deal tracker" estimated $6.3 billion a year later (Ernst &Young 2006; Ramanathan 2007b). In 2007, Cushman & Wakefield, a property consultant, reported that foreign funds had actually raised $15 billion (P. Singh 2007).

41. The Confederation of Real Estate Developers Association in India predicted a "capital infusion" of $5 billion in foreign investment in 2005 (Basu 2004). Another report anticipated that the new foreign investment regulations would "inject more than US$1 billion annually into India's development and construction industry" (Srinivas 2006, 18). In 2006, the head of research at Knight Frank, an international property consultancy, estimated that foreign investment would grow "40–45% over last year's $1.2 billion" (Gangopadhyay 2006). By 2007, the estimates were even bolder: Indiareit Fund Advisors Pvt., Ltd. predicted that "India may get as much as $10 billion in overseas funds betting on real estate in the next two and a half years" (or roughly $4 billion a year) (Chaudhary 2007). ICICI Bank similarly estimated "FDI [foreign direct investment] in the Indian real estate market at US$4–5 billion annually for the next five years" (ICICI Securities 2007, 15).

Chapter Three

1. See also Chancellor 1999; Galbraith 1994; Kindleberger 2000.

2. While "anthropologists have generally found it difficult to say much about the future

and future-oriented cultural practices" (Holmes 2014: 30), this is beginning to change (see Appadurai 2013; Miyazaki 2013). In particular, recent scholarship on biotechnology has highlighted the ways in which future-orientations inflect profit making (Fortun 2008; Shapin 2008; Sunder Rajan 2006). For scholarship on development projects, see Ferguson 1994, 2005; Holston 1989; Li 2007; Scott 1998.

3. In this they resemble researchers who have studied Indian land markets. For example, in his study of land markets in Lucknow, Kundu relied on land price data he collected himself through household questionnaires. He specifically developed a good rapport with the *paan-wallas* and *chai-wallas* in the neighborhoods he investigated in order to gain residents' confidence, as well as introductions to important neighborhood figures and low-level government officials (1997, 127–30).

4. *Chappals* are slip-on sandals, often what Americans would call flip-flops.

5. These are potential project ideas that I heard EuroFund employees and others in the industry discuss.

6. Indian agriculture is in crisis: public investment has declined, new trade policies have left farmers vulnerable to volatile international commodity prices, and input costs have grown (exacerbated by the entrance of international agro-business into Indian markets). By 2007, food grain production had slipped back to 1970s levels, and an epidemic of farmer suicides made international headlines (Jeromi 2007; Planning Commission 2007; Reddy and Galab 2006; Suri 2006).

7. Liberalized in the mid-1980s, the object of favorable state policies, and (partially) funded by venture capitalists from the US, India's IT industry has grown tremendously fast, with a compound annual growth rate of 50 percent during the 1990s. As the practice of "body shopping," i.e., farming Indian software engineers out abroad, has declined, more and more multinational corporations have begun "off-shoring," i.e., establishing their own subsidiary software development units in India (see Dossani and Kenney 2002; Upadhya 2004; Xiang 2007). However, as Gordon and Gupta explain, while IT and IT-enabled services (including software development, call centers, and business process outsourcing) have been "the most visible and well-known dimension of the take-off in services," they make up only a small percentage of the growing service sector: "In fact, although IT exports have had a profound impact on the balance of payments, the sector remains a small component of GDP. As of 2003, business services (which includes IT) were only about 1.75 percent of GDP, accounting for just 3 percent of total services output" (Gordon and Gupta 2004, 4). Nevertheless, IT is a major consumer of Indian commercial real estate.

8. While developers publicly talk about filling the housing shortage and "shelter for all," some privately admit the discrepancy between the need for housing and what they build. For example, the marketing director for a Gurgaon-based developer told me, plainly: "These days, these high end apartments sell at about a crore—minimum, to start with—minimum a crore and upwards. But what about that 20 lakh guy or 25 lakh guy? Where the real demand is, when that real report comes in, that India Report, when they talking about housing shortfall of 28 million units, that is where the 28 million unit is. It is not there." Of course, a 20 lakh house would still be out of reach of most Indians.

9. Predictions of the total industry value of the real estate industry ranged from US$45–50 billion in 2010 to a staggering US$90 billion by 2015.

10. In August and September 2007, protesters concerned that organized retail would take business from small retailers attacked Indian retail chains such as Subiksha, Reliance Fresh, and Food Bazaar in Delhi, Ranchi, Kolkata, and Lucknow. The protests prompted the Uttar Pradesh

government to close Reliance Fresh stores in Lucknow and Varanasi and Reliance to reconsider a planned expansion into West Bengal (Bailey 2007; Das and Bailey 2007; Datta 2007; Rao 2007; Roy and Bailey 2008). The entrance of Wal-Mart into the Indian market through a joint venture with the Indian company Bharti Enterprises also raised the ire of the political Left, apprehensive that international retailers would displace Indian wholesalers, squeeze Indian farmers, and run small retailers out of business (*Economic Times* 2007g; Sridhar 2007).

11. I am indebted to Aseem Shrivastava for the term "gambling piece."

12. For information about these projects, see the developers' websites. Information about Raheja's SEZ can be found on the page, "Raheja engineering SEZ," http://www.rahejasez.com/re-sez-about.asp (accessed December 16, 2009). DLF touts its Emporio mall on the webpage "DLF Emporio," http://www.dlf.in/dlf/wcm/connect/dlf_malls/Retail/Retail/Projects/Operational+Projects/The+Emporio+Vasant+Vihar%2C+New+Delhi/ (accessed December 16, 2009). For information on "Aerotropolis," see Agrawal 2008 and *Express India* 2008.

13. Where the state has partnered with private firms to build urban infrastructure "for the masses," it is on model whereby users pay. Cost-recovery and user-fee schemes raise a number of issues in terms of equity, access, and implementation (see Ranganathan, Kamath, and Baindur 2009).

Chapter Four

1. The marketing director said "then, till the time he is 40–45, he's at a position where he can afford to buy a house" meaning, he wouldn't be able to afford a house until he is 40–45. I substituted "when" for "till" to make this clear.

2. For example, *Economic Times* 2008; R. Sharma 2007; Sharma and Sinha 2007; Singh and Sharma 2007; Subramanyam 2008.

3. For example, Binkley 2008; Chamikutty 2007; Somini Sengupta 2007.

4. The question of caste, in particular, distinguishes the new market-based social knowledge from earlier scholarship. While caste has fascinated scholars both as the signature difference between India and the West (Dumont 1970) and as a sociological construct to be historicized and deconstructed (Dirks 2001), Indian marketers today dismiss it entirely. Marketer Rama Bijapurkar writes that "caste influence[s] voting behavior but not consumption behavior" such that it "is impossible to tell a person's caste from a person's brand buying behavior or his or her home" (2007, 129). From the point of view of selling things, caste drops off the sociological map.

5. The NCAER has published the results of the MISH in *Consumer Market Demographics in India* (1994); the *Indian Market Demographics* reports (1996, 1998, 2003); and *The Great Indian Middle Class* (2004).

6. The NSS is a national household consumption survey that was developed originally by the statistician P. C. Mahalanobis at the Indian Statistical Institute in Kolkata and taken up by the Government of India when it established the National Sample Survey Organization (NSSO) in 1950. The survey is conducted in successive rounds, with a major survey every five years and smaller ones in between (see Deaton and Kozel 2005).

7. Although the Planning Commission and the Ministry of Industry initially funded the MISH, the NCAER's own budget, and thus report sales, now funds the survey (interview with Dr. R. K. Shukla, NCAER Senior Fellow, March 4, 2008). The NCAER also partners with multinational corporations that defray costs of the survey in return for access to the results and the right to run a concurrent survey on a topic of interest. For example, some of the 2004–2005

MISH data was published in *How India Earns, Spends, and Saves: Results from the Max New York Life—NCAER India Financial Protection Survey* which measures the Indian market for financial and insurance services.

8. For summaries of the NCAER's finding, see Beinhocker, Farrell, and Zainulbhai 2007; Daftari 2007; *Hindu Business Line* 2007; *Mint* 2007; Narayanswamy and Zainulbhai 2007; Nath 2008, 22; *Times of India* 2007b.

9. The MGI makes no mention of ongoing debates in India about poverty measurement (e.g., Deaton and Dreze 2002; Deaton and Kozel 2005, *Economic and Political Weekly* 2007). The MGI uses the NCAER income-based poverty level of Rs. 90,000 per year rather than the Planning Commission's poverty line based on caloric intake, producing an even more optimistic account of the decline of poverty since liberalization than the Planning Commission (see Ablett et al. 2007, 11n4). Ghertner (2015) demonstrates that even the Planning Commission has underestimated poverty in India, which has *increased* considerably since the 1990s. See his account for a detailed explanation of the "statistical conjuring" that the Planning Commission, NCAER, and McKinsey do, as well as the role poverty estimation plays in creating the myth that GDP growth automatically reduces poverty. The fact that we both analyze a similar set of documents speaks to their influence in Indian planning and real estate circles, as well as their power to shape "world-class city making" projects.

10. 1.13 billion is the estimated population for 2007 according to the Census of India, based on 2001 census data available online at http://www.censusindia.gov.in/Census_Data_2001 /Projected_Population/Projected_population.aspx (accessed October 27, 2008).

11. She did not indicate his total income, but even if we estimate that his disposable income was a generous half of his monthly income, her ideal consumer would make close to one million rupees a year, the cutoff for entry into McKinsey's "global" class.

12. To be more precise, he inhabits a high-rise condominium. Real estate developers have worked hard to associate their buildings with this high-earning consumer, as I describe elsewhere (Searle 2013).

13. This image also suggests Maslow's "hierarchy of needs," a psychological theory which suggests that people move from physiological needs through needs for safety, love, and esteem to the need for self-actualization (Maslow 1943). Applbaum (2000) finds First World marketers appealing to this hierarchy as they conceptualize Third World people being socialized into consumerism.

14. For other examples of producers' attempts to shape consumer desires, see Applbaum 2004; Arvidsson 2003; Mazzarella 2003.

15. For examples, see *Business Today* 2007; Hussain 2007c; Jones Lang LaSalle 2004; Roy 2007; Sharma and Pathak 2006.

16. While Mumbai, Delhi, and Bangalore are consistently referred to as Tier I cities, the rankings are malleable: which cities are considered which tier depends on whether you consult Knight Frank, Cushman & Wakefield, or DTZ. The international property consultant Jones Lang LaSalle Meghraj defined them in a 2007 report, *Accelerating Transformation*, as Tier I, "established metropolitan cities" (Delhi, Mumbai, Bangalore, Hyderabad and Chennai); Tier II: "upcoming cities" (Pune, Kolkata, Ahmedabad, and Chandigarh); and Tier III "including state capitals and district towns which are emerging as new IT and real estate destinations" (Jones Lang LaSalle Meghraj 2007). Others might have downgraded Hyderabad and Chennai to Tier II, and Ahmedabad and Chandigarh to Tier III.

17. Kolkata's progression in this ranking system from Tier III to Tier II is the result of con-

certed efforts on the part of its government to woo multinational companies and IT firms and to promote urban redevelopment (see *Economist* 2004).

18. In the meantime, there are some small cities which make good investment destinations, what MGI calls "Tier 3 niche cities with high average incomes and large numbers of middle-class and global households" (Ablett et al. 2007, 77). These are cities in wealthy states with a history of migration, like Punjab or Kerala. Another DLF employee discussed his firm's plans to construct a high-rise housing project in Kochi, a city in Kerala. He felt that the city's long history of migration to the Gulf made it a good place to do the project: "We don't envisage too much of problems because of acceptance. There's a higher level of exposure. Half the people there are going to Dubai. The lifestyle indicators are high." According to this logic, wealth and international exposure creates a market for real estate today in some Tier III cities.

19. According to these reports, the same logics that brought MNCs and IT firms to India in the first place—primarily the search for cheap labor and low overhead costs—have led them to search out new locations in India. As Tier I cities become saturated, their "rising real estate values, over-stretched infrastructure and high man-power costs" make them less competitive, and international firms move on, transforming Tier II cities into Tier I cities as they go (Cushman & Wakefield 2006, 2; see also Jones Lang LaSalle Meghraj 2007, 5).

20. By contrast many international firms work primarily in the Tier I metros because they are worried about "absorption problems," that is, having enough demand (either from corporate tenants or residents). Analogous to the McKinsey Global Institute's strategy of targeting the wealthy now and waiting for Indian society to change, international developers feel it is safer to execute projects today in the biggest cities, where there are consumers now.

21. Note that Gurdeep inflates the city's attractiveness by substituting Jaipur's total population for the smaller population of skilled workers in which foreign firms and BPOs would be interested.

Chapter Five

1. The US Foreign Corrupt Practices Act of 1977 and the OECD Convention on Combating Bribery of Foreign Public Officials in International Business Transactions, which has been ratified by thirty-seven countries, prohibit payments to foreign officials for the purpose of obtaining business (OECD; US Department of Justice). My informants referred to the US Foreign Corrupt Practices Act by name.

2. Chandra (2015) provides a detailed account of the complex bureaucratic process of converting agricultural land to other uses. Her account demonstrates how much government discretion there is in the process and thus how dependent it is on patronage relations.

3. Aggregating land also requires cultural competence. Delhi Land and Finance chairman K. P. Singh recalls negotiating with some 700-odd families in Haryana in order to purchase 3,500 acres of land in what is now Gurgaon. K. P. Singh needed the consent of all the adult members of these families, which was sometimes complicated by male relatives' refusal to share land sale proceeds with married sisters (Damodaran 2008, 286). His shared caste background (*jat*), as well as his ability to interact with "a sophisticated clientele simultaneous with drinking buffalo milk in the company of rustic farmers and *patwaris* (land record-keepers)" contributed to his success (Damodaran 2008, 286).

4. According to an article in the *Wall Street Journal*, fully one third of the twenty-six million cases pending before the Indian judiciary in 2002 were property disputes; cases often take

up to fifteen years to resolve (Slater 2002). D. C. Wadhwa (2002) describes numerous problems with India's land titling system. Beyond missing, outdated, and faulty records, he argues that the basic problem is that Indian land titles are presumptive, not conclusive; the government does not guarantee ownership, which is always open to challenge in court.

5. Of course, developers also sought domestic financing, either through domestic real estate funds (which operated very much like international funds but did not face many of the same legal restrictions) or informal sources (see chapters 1 and 6). The latter was impossible for me to track.

6. Often, when firms attract foreign private equity investment, the private equity investors help the firm list on the Bombay Stock Exchange, using the listing as a means to exit from the firm profitably.

7. After companies' own promoters, foreign institutional investors were the largest share-holders of the companies that made up the Bombay Stock Exchange SENSEX in 2005 (see Pal 2005).

8. In general, the investors and fund managers with whom I spoke said that deals took between five and nine months to complete, a long time by their standards.

9. I am overdrawing the difference between the two modes of working here in order to make a point. In actual practice, of course, members of large firms also operate through personal networks.

10. The proliferation of transparency discourses and projects from the early 1990s can be traced to the shareholder revolution (see Ho 2009, 122–212; Lazonick and O'Sullivan 2000), which coincided with corporate expansion into new markets in the wake of the Cold War (see Shleifer and Vishny 1997). Just as shareholders took a greater interest in corporate profits, they felt them threatened by foreign expansion:

> The transition of state socialist societies to market economies, and the spread of finan-cial markets to emerging economies around the globe, infused the puzzle of manage-rialism with enormous policy relevance. What mechanisms could be put in place to inspire the confidence of investors in businesses housed in distant and often unfamiliar cultures? (Davis and Useem 2002, 232–33)

Those mechanisms—a range of transparency projects usually glossed as "corporate governance"—are clearly about disciplining and controlling corporate behavior to ensure profits.

11. In her study of late colonial Indian business law, Ritu Birla traces British Colonial at-tempts to code indigenous capitalist practices as private, cultural, customary, and, in some cases, illegal. She argues that "colonial authorities regulated vernacular capitalism exactly by coding it as a rarefied cultural form," subject to Hindu personal law (Birla 2009, 5); and she demonstrates that Marwari merchants' attempts to legitimize themselves as Economic Men and modern sub-jects required them to use the very categories through which laws on market practice regulated them. We can find similar themes of subject formation, governance, and power in contemporary debates over the "transparency" of Indian real estate practices.

12. Recent anthropological and historical scholarship has highlighted the importance of con-ceptions of the self to business practices (Ho 2009; Sandage 2005; Zaloom 2006).

13. O'Malley notes that nineteenth-century economists and contemporary management gu-rus share the belief that profit stems from entrepreneurs' creative engagement with uncertainty (O'Malley 2000, 2003; see also Knight 1957). O'Malley points out that both Knight and con-temporary writers differentiate between risk (calculable, probable) and uncertainty (nonquanti-

fiable); engagement with the latter produces profit. As this section demonstrates, my informants believed that risk could produce profit. While I, and they, use the term "risk" here, the risks in real estate development are not entirely quantifiable and might more precisely be called "uncertainties," after Knight.

14. This informant had a habit of dropping the ends of his sentences. I have retained this quality of his speech in my transcription of the interview with my use of ellipsis (" . . . "), which in this context does not mean that I have left out words.

15. According to my informants, in 2006–8, after-tax returns of 9 to 15 percent might be expected in American real estate markets, with the lower returns for build-to-suit projects or construction in cities such as New York, where the risk of finding tenants is relatively low. For speculative buildings in suburban areas or expanding cities, returns might be as high as 15 percent.

16. The index has been compiled since 1999 by Jones Lang LaSalle, a real estate services and consultancy company, and its real estate asset management arm, LaSalle Investment Management, Inc. The 2008 report rated eighty-two countries.

17. In much of North India, the *patwari* is the village-level land record official, the officer of the Revenue Department responsible for keeping and updating land titles (records of rights). These land titles often include information about mortgages or encumbrances on the land. The *tehsildar* is the revenue official for a *tehsil*, a sub-sub district administrative unit that includes several villages. In addition, the Stamps and Registration Department maintains data on land transactions through the registrations of mortgages and sales. Sub-registries in this department provide encumbrance certificates that trace the transactions of a particular parcel over a period of years. For a description of these systems see World Bank 2007, 8–21; for an excellent treatment of their effects on women's rights to land, see Agarwal 1994.

18. When they complain about a lack of information, investors reveal as much about their own habits of working with statistical indicators and their belief that knowledge should be abstracted from social relations as they do about Indian deficiencies. For a nice discussion about the relationship between information, transparency, and the semiotic ideology that reduces language to its referential functions, see Hetherington 2011, 156–59.

19. While Indian developers today might be "unsophisticated" accountants by foreign standards, Indian businessmen have a long history of financial sophistication. Historically, Indian merchants from various communities have used bills of exchange (*hundis*) to finance far-flung trading activities and futures markets to hedge on crop prices; and Indian bankers set interest rates, developed a range of deposit and loan types, and kept detailed accounts (Bayly 1983; Birla 2009; Markovits 2000; Rudner 1994; Subrahmanyam and Bayly 1990).

20. Suraj also plans to develop intensive partnerships with a small number of developers, investing at the company level in order to work on numerous projects with each developer. (Similarly, Simon commented, "You know, I'd rather have half-a-dozen developers dotted around the country than twenty-five developers I can't control.") With this approach, he feels he can achieve more control over each project, as well as changes in the development firm's management structure.

21. Note how Govind describes his own way of working as "professional" and yet insists that he wants more independence. This hedging is key to Govind's self-presentation as both a professional and an Indian developer, as discussed in chapter 6.

22. In India, people tend to use the term "merchant banker" as the British do; in the US, they are referred to as "investment banks." Investment or merchant banks involved in Indian real estate IPOs include: Goldman Sachs, Citigroup, HSBC, JP Morgan Chase, Merrill Lynch, and

others (often through their Indian subsidiaries). Indian merchant banks involved in real estate IPOs include: Edelweiss Securities, Enam Financial Consultants, Kotak Mahindra Capital, and ICICI Securities.

23. The process of valuing that which has not been valued before is a contentious one. Since many consultants value real estate development firms based on their "land banks," the question of land value is tied up with the value of real estate firms. However, should the land be valued according to its purchase price, the likely return from development, or its current price? How does one value land that developers do not own outright (i.e., they own it through joint agreements with farmers), or land whose ownership is under litigation? Should the value of a company also reflect its development capacity and track record? What if it has no track record? Consultants, the SEBI, bankers, and others are answering these questions through daily decisions and valuations.

24. Tax authorities capitalize on the difference between the accounts reported to the Security and Exchange Board of India—which are also those reported to potential foreign shareholders—and those previously reported for tax purposes. Chetan explained:

> They [developers] can't show it suddenly that we are handling so much of money because then the tax fellows will go out. So we have crazy situation where, just before IPO [initial public offer] or during the IPO process, income tax raids. . . . That happened with *all* the companies, including DLF. Because you see, Indian tax system is such that people try to avoid tax, but then if you are going to the market, you need to put the best foot forward and you get good valuation, which means that your last two years have to be good and everything.

Chetan noted his public relations firm must then explain the tax authority investigations to the media: "Now that is one area where we step in and we have to tell to the media, look it's a routine check that they do with everybody. In this sector you have lot of black money, so you be careful with it and everything."

25. I am grateful to Constantine Nakassis for this insight.

26. At an exchange rate of Rs. 41.5 to the dollar (the average exchange rate from 2006–8), Rs. 550 crore is $132,500,000.00. At this exchange rate, DLF raised more than $2 billion, Purvankara raised approximately $301 million, and Parsvnath raised approximately $241 million from their respective initial public offers.

27. Citi Venture sold 4.7 million of its 11.69 million shares to D. E. Shaw for Rs. 325 crore, or approximately Rs. 691 per share. This is at the top end of the price band Emaar MGF set for the initial public offer, which was Rs. 610–690. Citi Venture bought 1.46 million shares for Rs. 1,558 per share in November 2006. They were diluted in a ratio of 7:1 in September 2007, making the effective cost for Citi Venture Rs. 195 per share. Thus the effective value of Citi Ventures shares rose from Rs. 195 to Rs. 691, or 3.5 times. Even at the lower end of the price band, the rise in their share values, from Rs. 195 to Rs. 530, would be 2.7 times, a considerable gain (see Raja D. 2008a, Raja D. 2008c).

28. Unfortunately for these investors, Emaar MGF's initial public offer was not a success. The Bombay Stock Exchange had fallen 18 percent since the beginning of the year, due in part to worries over the US financial crisis. Emaar reduced the price of the shares, from Rs. 610–690 to Rs. 540–630, and extended the offer, but institutional investors pulled out of the offer at the last minute, and retail investors under-subscribed to it. Emaar MGF eventually withdrew the offer, promising to "revisit the market only when the demand and sentiment are stable and better"

(Hussain 2008c). Since the Citi Venture sale of shares to D. E. Shaw was contractually dependent on the initial public offer, the sale was aborted (Raja D. 2008c).

29. As seen by the ultimate failure of the Emaar MGF listing, these investor sentiments were fickle.

Chapter Six

1. The title means "Khosla's little house," a reference to the dream house Khosla hopes to build on his plot of land.

2. By figures of personhood, I do not mean actual people but social types, ideals to which one might aspire or from which one might distance oneself. This discussion builds on work by linguistic anthropologists who have conceptualized identity in terms of enactable signs or emblems such as dress, speech, gesture, and conduct (see Agha 2007a, 234–7; Bucholtz and Hall 2004). Agha, in particular, has demonstrated that it is possible to trace historically the processes through which emblems come to be recognized as having particular social meanings, and how such processes of enregisterment are tied up in the circulation and advertising of commodities (see Agha 2007a, 190–232; Agha 2011).

3. For example, the Ansals (Ansal Buildwell, Ansal Properties and Infrastructure, and Ansal Housing and Construction), Pradeep Jain (Parsvnath Developers), Rohtas Goel (Omaxe), Pankaj Bajaj (Eldeco Infrastructure), and Mofatraj Munot (Kalpataru) are Bania/Marwari; Ashok Sarin (Anant Raj Industris) is a Khatri; the Rahejas (K. Raheja Corporation), Ramesh Chandra (Unitech), and Niranjan and Surendra Hiranandani (Hiranandani Developers) are Sindhis (see Damodaran 2008, 27, 272).

4. This close association between the personality of the owner and the company is common for American and European real estate companies as well (think of Donald Trump), reflecting the general industry wisdom that "personalities are more important in property than in many other types of businesses . . . it only takes one man to spot a site, visualize the development opportunity it presents, and negotiate a purchase (and possibly the finance for the scheme)" (Brett 2004).

5. For example, see Athale 2008; Kumar 2007; Menon 2006; Surendar and Sinha 2008. Namburu's recent book *Moguls of Indian Real Estate* (2007) expands the developer profile (a magazine article genre) to book length in its recording of the personal histories of prominent developers.

6. Patel (1995, 111–112) argues that the largest source of finance for housing developers in Ahmedabad in the 1960s and 1970s was government finance for registered cooperative housing societies. The developer would register a fictitious society, using his friends, relatives, and fictitious names as dummy members. He would purchase land using his own resources or money from the pre-sale of units, and then he would avail of government loans to the dummy members of the society in order to finance construction. Over time, the dummy members would "resign," and the real buyers who replaced them in the society membership would take on what remained of the government loans. I would assume that this kind of activity occurred in other Indian cities as well.

7. Of course, estimating the size of black economy requires a lot of guesswork. Other estimates range from 20 to 42 percent of GDP in 1980–81 to 47 percent in 1978–79 (see Kumar 2002, 55–75).

8. For example, Arun Kumar points out that people often confuse the "black economy" with the "unorganized" economy. The latter constitutes the noncorporate and often small-scale ac-

tivities that employ more than 90 percent of the Indian workforce. Many of the incomes in this sector do not meet the minimum thresholds for taxability (Kumar 2002, 19).

9. Not all developers agglomerate land. Those with "deep pockets" who can afford to purchase farmland and wait to develop it and those with the political connections to get approvals are more likely to be in the business of buying up small parcels of farmland and agglomerating them for large projects. Instead, some developers buy parcels directly from the government, work with landowners with large holdings, or work at a smaller scale on existing parcels.

10. Patel recounts a scandal in Ahmedabad in which a developer, Popular Constructions, signed nonbinding pre-sale agreements with farmers at a very low price. When the farmers learned of a state container facility planned for their land, they attempted to get out of the agreements because the government rate was higher than the rate the developer had offered to pay. Instead of honoring the farmers' rights, the state paid Popular Constructions directly for the farmers' land. Although the scandal made the newspapers, the chief minister supported Popular Constructions and allowed the farmers to be defrauded (Patel 1995, 143n44).

11. Some of these firms entered real estate during the mid-1990s boom, and others have joined only since the industry recovered from the late-1990s downturn, after 2000.

12. This is a common euphemism for large villas and private residences for the urban rich on Delhi's rural fringes. Many owners claim tax exemption and electricity subsidies as farms by growing a small number of crops on the property or running a plant nursery (see Soni 2000).

13. Concerns over the professional/businessman distinction do not map neatly onto class, understood as income level and educational achievement. Many Indian developers earn handsomely, and we might consider them elites. While some developers seemed comfortable performing "luxury" and flaunting their wealth, most seemed to share particularly middle-class anxieties over the decadence of wealth, instead investing in the performance of respectability (see Dickey 2013, Liechty 2003, Radhakrishnan 2009). Being a "professional" entails cultivating personal virtue as much as (or more than) accumulating wealth.

14. Smitha Radhakrishnan shows that information technology workers themselves also espouse the ideology of "professionalism," contrasting their own efficiency, hard work, and entrepreneurial striving with the assumed cronyism, bureaucracy, and corruption of government employees (Radhakrishnan 2011, 91–4).

15. The rating scheme is voluntary. As of November 2006, only thirty-eight companies had been rated.

16. In the pre-liberalization period, five-star hotels were some of the fanciest buildings in India, associated with international visitors, imported goods, and inaccessible luxury. They retain this prestige today.

17. Jones Lang LaSalle regards public listings as a sign of transparency. They report that "The number of listed companies in the real estate sector has increased multi-fold over the past 2 years, which has served to improve accounting standards, financial disclosure and corporate governance" (Jones Lang LaSalle 2008, 5).

18. Commentators felt that DLF's presence on the stock market would also change the image of Indian real estate in general. Akshay Kumar, head of the property consultant Colliers Jardine in India, is cited in the same article as saying, "The entry of DLF into capital markets would improve the stock of real estate sector in India. With its high ethical standards and huge size, it is poised to change the way the world looks at the realty sector" (Menon 2006).

19. DLF had previously been listed on the Delhi Stock Exchange until 2003. When it delisted, some minority shareholders remained with the company. Many of them, however, did not

receive offer letters from DLF when the firm later converted their debentures into equity shares. They filed against DLF with the Securities and Exchange Board of India (SEBI), which forced DLF to withdraw its public offer prospectus (Sinha 2006). DLF settled with its minority shareholders for Rs. 1,300 crore before refiling with SEBI in 2007 (Dalal 2007).

20. The Aam Aadmi Party ("Common Man's" Party), led by Arvind Kejriwal, is the political party that split from the anticorruption movement lead by Anna Hazare in 2012. It did surprisingly well in the 2013 Delhi elections, although it did not win a majority of the seats, and Arvind Kejriwal became Delhi's Chief Minister. He took to the streets in front of the Rail Bhavan in central New Delhi in January 2014 to protest the fact that the Delhi police are controlled by the Union government, not his own administration.

21. Bhiwadi is a city approximately 65 kilometers southwest of New Delhi in Rajasthan, on the Harayana-Rajasthan state line.

22. This case was in the headlines again in May 2007, when EuroFund employees pointed out the connection to Emaar MGF. Given the high profile of the case, its long run through the courts, and the fact that EuroFund employees knew all about it, I assumed that others in the industry also made this connection.

23. While the foreign developer might not pay for land directly, the structure of the deal usually factors in a cost for land that affects profit sharing between the parties.

24. State governance is often derailed by the material practices of legibility (Hull 2008). Government auditing programs flounder under layers of abstraction (Miller 2003). Programs designed to produce trust instead erode it (Strathern 2000, John 2011), while programs designed to "certify virtue" lead to "moral involution" (Brown 2010). Right-to-information activists "mimic" the state and thus reproduce the inefficiencies and inequalities they aim to subvert (Webb 2013).

Chapter Seven

1. While "quality" may be transformed into specific measures during the construction process—distances, heights, thicknesses, tensile strengths, and loads—due to the particularities of location, design, and construction, buildings are never uniform commodities. Never truly substitutable (Fanselow 1990), their quality and value are difficult to commensurate and are thus always in doubt.

2. Some of the differences include divergent semiotic ideologies, valuation techniques, and construction practices. In short, we might think of Indian real estate as a separate field of practice, in Bourdieu's sense. The architects' expertise is cultural competence, the embodied understanding of "implicit schemes of perception and appreciation" inculcated through upbringing, schooling, and participation in the elite field of global architectural production (Bourdieu 1984, 2; see also Olds 2001). Abroad, as masters of a highly valorized and institutionally sanctioned register, these architects wield symbolic power, "the power to constitute the given by stating it," the power to determine what is legitimate architectural taste (Bourdieu 1977, 117). Yet this power is not necessarily ratified in India.

3. One of EuroFund's employees estimated that the company makes a 20 percent premium over its competition in emerging markets.

4. I am grateful to Asif Agha for this insight.

5. Five-star hotels are the original "international quality" buildings in India. In the preliberalization era they gained prestige as places built to international specifications. They offered luxurious amenities (swimming pools, etc.), sold imported goods, and attracted foreign clien-

tele. Five-star hotels (and even hotels in general) retain a certain cachet today. For this reason, one consultant told me, "Every new developer wants to be a hotelier. They all *have* to become hoteliers." This is also why many developers hold meetings in five-star hotels.

6. Examples of housing complexes in the National Capital Region with British or American names include: Marble Arch, Wembly Estate, Trinity Towers, Hamilton Court, Victoria Gardens, Westend Heights, Malibu Town, Beverley Park, Central Park, Orange County, Park Place, The Palm Springs, and Aspen Greens. Other more generically "international" names include: Le Residency, Unitech Grande, Olive County, Uniworld City, Eldeco Riviera, Exotica, La Tropicana, and The Nile.

7. The advertising executive used the phrase "cracked our head" in English.

8. There is no simple metric for comparison between Indian real estate and international real estate, between two buildings, or between two conceptions of quality. Even the universal commensurator, money (here, rent), is of little help, first, because for EuroFund and others planning to construct buildings, rent is an uncertain, future possibility. Second, factors other than building quality—supply, demand, speculators exiting the market, regulations, etc.—affect rent. In fact, commercial rents in Mumbai, especially, have rivaled those in the world's major cities, in 1995–6 (Brauchli 1995; Nijman 2000) and again in 2007–2008 (Pathak 2007; Ramanathan 2007e; Sadovi 2007)—despite a paucity of "international quality" buildings. Third, successfully commanding high rents in the market requires that tenants recognize a building's value. As one international retail investor at a conference worried, "what bothers us is the guy across the road—we invest, our work conforms with all the due diligence . . . then some 'cowboy' comes across the road with a product that is built improperly, approved improperly, and they've got all your clients because he's cheaper."

9. Technological advances such as computer-based drafting and e-mail have enabled the geographic disarticulation of the design process. In the international division of architectural labor, some "design" firms in the global North now outsource routine drawing production tasks to "associate" firms in the global South with comparatively low wages (see Cuff 1992; Tombesi 2001; Tombesi, Dave, and Scriver 2003). As part of this trend, some Indian architects outsource their services as draftsmen or "architects of record" to architectural firms based elsewhere in the world, exacerbating the existing divisions between Indian architects with "a significant ideological commitment to the formal and theoretical autonomy of Indian architecture from the globalizing forces of the present world market" and a more commercially oriented group, "unencumbered by the weight of history" (Tombesi, Dave, and Scriver 2003, 84, 86).

10. Before I interviewed a 3D modeler, I assumed that these renderings were actual photographs spliced together and altered in a program like Photoshop; in fact, they are created entirely on the computer. The director of the 3D modeling firm I interviewed was pleased by my confusion. She measured success in terms of "photorealism": "Now when we say that we give the best 3D visualization in the country, we say it is more photorealistic. I mean if you can differentiate that yes this is 3D and this is not 3D, then that is where we have not done a good job."

11. 3D animation often takes only four to six weeks to produce and costs anywhere between Rs. 3 and Rs. 18 lakhs.

12. Asher Ghertner shows how idealized images of homes inspire even those who will never be able to afford them and whose own homes are being demolished to make way for elite construction (Ghertner 2011).

13. The 3D imaging company director Madhuri complained about this because she feels that she and her employees are often required to make decisions about architectural interiors beyond their professional-technical competence. She showed me an example of an interior that one of

her staff members designed that she did not think was appropriate. "It would be good for a twenty lakh apartment," she recalled telling him, "but he [the developer] is selling this for one point five crores, so that doesn't go with that look." The problem is that her staff come from a different class background than the proposed housing consumers, and they are not trained as interior designers. Madhuri explained, "He [her employee] has never seen a one-and-a-half crore villa, or he has not seen a three crores." She pointed out the cluttered look of the room he designed, with, she felt, too much molding work and overly busy walls. She commented that "that is the way it is in his [her employee's] house." Her employees understand the technical aspects of imaging, "but to really set standards as to what is good and what is not good becomes a little difficult. So that is why working with companies which are corporate interior *ka* firms and interior companies is so much easier."

14. While legally the drawings may have some standing, in practice, plans submitted for environmental approvals need not necessarily guide or constrain future construction activities. This reviewer commented that the environmental permitting board did not have the enforcement capabilities to follow-up and determine whether each developer builds his project according to the documents he submits for permitting. "There is no enforcement. Who is going to go check the effluent, the UV ratings on the glass, whether they are using the water they said they would? Who is going to do it?" he asked rhetorically.

15. The application of Bourdieu to this case demonstrates how limiting the idea of bounded, unitary fields is in the analysis of real world situations, for Indian and international fields of real estate practice overlap, intermingle, and mirror each other.

Chapter Eight

1. As this private equity firm principle's comment suggests, valuing real estate development companies based on their land holdings is controversial. A discussion on valuation at the 2007 Global Real Estate Institute conference in Delhi drew heated debate on this question from consultants who value properties and real estate firms for a living. In the discussion, a consultant asked if a real estate company was like a cotton spinning mill. Would the valuation of the mill change if the mill got in a new shipment of raw cotton? If not, he argued, why do we value land? While international practice might treat land as merely a "basic material," in India, "land banks" remain a "store of value" (as one fund manager at the conference put it) and a means of valuing companies with little else on their books.

2. Apartments are pre-sold in American and Western European markets, too, though not until ownership, approvals, and architectural plans are in place.

3. A few real estate companies have, in fact, advertised this new lease model as a boon. For example, DLF's website highlights the company's leasing strategy to create an aura of exclusivity and prestige for its new mall, the Emporio:

> "Emporio" has been designed by architect Mohit Gujral as a premium luxury shopping-cum-recreation center. Since all spaces are to be leased only, the "Emporio" management will have complete control of the tenant mix—thereby ensuring the highest levels of exclusivity for all its lessees. Other planned attractions include fine dining restaurants, a spa, a salon and a member's club; all designed to invite people to spend an entire day in five-star luxury.

Here, leasing is listed along with other amenities as a marker of "five-star luxury," indicating something of its rarity in the Indian market. This quote comes from the DLF retail website's page on "The Emporio": http://www.dlf.in/dlf/wcm/connect/dlf_malls/Retail/Retail/Projects/Operational+Projects/The+Emporio+Vasant+Vihar%2C+New+Delhi/ (accessed March 21, 2009).

4. In 2006–8, land costs in India were a significantly higher proportion of development costs than in Europe or the US.

5. I assume of the Delhi police, but Chauhan 2007a does not specify.

6. This is the apex body for a system of district and state commissions designed to redress consumer grievances. It hears cases appealed from the lower commissions, or where the compensation claim exceeds one crore.

7. Not only was Mr. Mehta denied possession of his flat, apparently, an Ansal Sales Manager "roughly and curtly" told Mr. Mehta, "Go to the Court and get its possession through the Court" when he came to ask why the adjoining flats had already been given over to buyers and his had not. The court fined Ansal Rs. 50,000 for this behavior (*Kunj Behari Mehta vs. Ansal Properties and Industries, Ltd*).

8. It is common practice to pay for the remaining 5 percent upon taking possession of the property.

9. The Supreme Court did issue a notice to the state, union territory, and central governments in 2007, asking them to reply to a public interest litigation by an NGO requesting national guidelines for real estate developers issuing advertisements and an amendment to the Indian Penal Code to make the publication of false advertisements punishable (*Hindu* 2007; T. Sharma 2007).

10. These practices continue today, as Praveen Donthi (2014) reports.

11. I do not mean to suggest, either here or in the earlier discussion of advertising images, that Indian housing consumers are gullible or entirely taken in by developers' promises. Consumers' readings of advertising materials (though not directly studied here) is undoubtedly complex, shaped by individual interests, backgrounds, etc. The point is that this is an environment where a) such advertising materials are finished with a high level of sophistication; and b) a long and uncertain development process and developer malfeasance combine to make advertising promises uncertain indicators of future construction and thus of the security of consumers' investments.

12. Note that both Rajesh and Jeremy hope that completed construction will contribute to their firms' reputations, indexing the uncertainties that plague their corporate value projects. For Rajesh, the completed building will index construction capacity—the ability to "deliver"—whereas Jeremy hopes that a finished building leased to global companies will attest to the income-generating potential of using international architects and spending more than competitors on construction costs.

13. In fact, as of May 2006, DLF had 82 complaints pending against it under Consumer Protection Act, 1986, including:

> failure to hand over possession of the properties after payment of minimum amount due, failure to allot property preferred by the consumers, selling properties at a particular price and consequent reduction of price of identical properties, alleged *mala fide* enhancement in external development charges and payment of escalation charges, charging additional sums for increase in area, deficiency in construction services and alleged *mala fide* cancellation of allotment and forfeiture of earnest money. (DLF Limited 2006, 358)

Numerous other criminal and civil suits were also pending against the company at the time of its initial public offer.

14. Other elements of these two towers identify them as "super-luxurious": their proximity to the DLF Golf Course (and the additional nine hole golf course at the Magnolias); the relatively low number of units per tower (250–300); their address on Golf Course Road; the large size of the apartments (5,800–10,000 square feet); the opulent finishes on the communal spaces, which several people told me in 2014 reminded them of five-star hotels; and their sale by invitation.

15. The ICRA DR 2-rating is the Indian Credit Rating Agency's rating for real estate developers. It means "strong project execution capability" according to their 2008 rating scale (www .icra.in). The most commonly cited certification, the ISO (International Standard Organization) 9000, is a set of "internationally agreed principles and requirements *for managing an enterprise* so as to earn the confidence of customers and markets" (Brunsson et al. 2000, 71, emphasis added). Similarly, the ISO 9001 is a "generic set of requirements for implementing a quality management system and ISO 14001 for an environmental management system" (http://www .iso.org/iso/about/discover-iso_whats-different-about-iso-9001-and-iso-14001.htm. Accessed April 9, 2009). OHSAS 18000 is an "international occupational health and safety management system specification" (see http://www.ohsas-18001-occupational-health-and-safety.com/. Accessed January 27, 2016). Note that all of these standards refer to the developer's business systems (quality management, environmental management, occupational health, or execution capability) not to the developer's products.

16. I am grateful to William Mazzarella, Meredith McGuire, Kaushik Sunder Rajan, and Adam Sargent for suggesting this point.

17. Singh boasts that the Aralias, built next to the golf course, were launched at Rs. 1,800 per square foot in 2004 but by 2011 were selling for Rs. 30,000 sq foot (Singh 2011, 204).

18. The project is being constructed privately, but the land is being provided on a 99 year lease by HUDA. HUDA tendered bids in 2008 for a 3.2 km metro line, which a consortium of DLF and a subsidiary of infrastructure company IL&FS won (they were the only bidders). But when the project was formally announced in July 2009, the proposed metro line was 6.1 km and served many key DLF properties, including Cyber City (*Times of India* 2009; Bijith and Gupta 2008; Gupta and Soni 2013). DLF pulled out of the project by 2013 (Gupta and Soni 2013), but phase two of the metro will run down Golf Course Road, again serving many DLF projects (Rapid MetroRail Gurgaon Ltd. 2012).

19. Vadra reported the Rs. 80 crore it received from DLF (and other real estate firms: Bedarwals Infra Projects, Nikhil International, and VRS Infrastructure) as "advances" against ongoing property transactions (Singh 2012). In one deal that received considerable press scrutiny, Vadra bought a 3.5 acre parcel in Gurgaon for Rs. 15 crore in 2008, received a change in land use permission from Haryana, and sold the parcel to DLF for Rs. 58 crore. DLF "advanced" Rs. 50 crore to Vadra in 2008 but did not take ownership until 2012 (*Hindu* 2012; Anand and Roy 2014). A 2015 Comptroller and Auditor General investigation reported that Vadra received "undue favors" in obtaining the land use permissions for the plot (*Financial Express* 2015). When land office official Ashok Khemaka tried to revoke the permissions, he was overruled by the Haryana Chief Minister, a Congress Party politician, and transferred (Anand and Roy 2014).

20. India Against Corruption, the anticorruption organization that Kejriwal led with Anna Hazare, published a statement that alleged that of three bids for the project, only DLF's bid was opened; that numerous environmental permissions were waived for the project; and that the project violates the mandates of the Haryana Urban Development Authority (from which some of the land for the project was sourced) to develop land for public purpose (*Hindu* 2012).

21. Clearly, working with the local planning and regulatory agencies was an ongoing process

(and one to which I did not have full access). It extended throughout the project's design and construction phases and beyond the period of my fieldwork with EuroFund. Hiring the associate architect was merely one step in this process.

22. The associate architectural firm was to provide local design expertise to the design architect during the design phases of the project; advise on the government approval process and produce the drawings necessary for it; help identify and select other local consultants; complete construction drawings; oversee the bidding process; carry out various construction administration tasks such as site visits and review of change orders; and provide documentation for the owners and lenders on the progress of the project and contractor performance.

23. At the very start of the interview, Paul asked me what I knew about the associate architect. Paul has an understated way of speaking and a dry sense of humor, but he purses his lips and his eyes light up indicating that whatever he's talking about is more important than his deadpan voice suggests. Since clearly this was an important issue for them, I suggested we start the interview with that.

24. The Building and Other Construction Workers' Act (1996), in particular, has been fully implemented in only a handful of states (see chapter 1).

Conclusion

1. Data averaged from the website Global-Rates: http://www.global-rates.com/economic -indicators/inflation/consumer-prices/cpi/india.aspx (accessed August 3, 2015).

2. For example, Lodha Developers bought out Deutsche Bank's stake of $515 million and DLF bought out investor D. E. Shaw for $500 million (Anand 2012).

3. I am grateful to the participants of the workshop "The Entrepreneur and the Broker: Mediating Transregional Flow, Scale, and Belonging" organized by the CETREN Transregional Research Network at the University of Göttingen, January 14–15, 2016, for lively discussions that helped me formulate this view. I'm particularly grateful to Lisa Björkman and Nellie Chu for organizing the workshop.

4. As sociologist Philip McMichael has observed, because of this patchwork form of industrial organization, "former categories like the Three Worlds, and 'core' and 'periphery,' lose their salience" (1996, 41). However, while the geography has changed, the hierarchies that structured those global social relations—hierarchies like core/periphery, developed/undeveloped, advanced/backward—are still being reproduced (alongside new ones like transparent/nontransparent), now in the service of new social relationships and institutions.

References

Abbreviations

ASSOCHAM	Associated Chambers of Commerce and Industry of India
BOMA	Building Owners and Managers Association International
CWFI	Construction Workers Federation of India
CWG-CWC	Commonwealth Games' Citizens for Women, Workers, and Children
DIPP	Department of Industrial Policy and Promotion
HDFC	Housing Development and Finance Corporation
JNNURM	Jawaharlal Nehru National Urban Renewal Mission
NASSCOM	National Association of Software and Services Companies
NCAER	National Council of Applied Economic Research
OECD	Organisation for Economic Co-Operation and Development
SNCL	Second National Commission on Labour

Sources

Ablett, Jonathan, et al. 2007. *The "Bird of Gold": The Rise of India's Consumer Market.* McKinsey Global Institute.

Abolafia, Mitchell Y. 1998. "Markets as Cultures: An Ethnographic Approach," in *The Laws of the Markets*, ed. M. Callon, 69–85. Oxford: Blackwell.

Abrahamsen, Rita. 2000. *Disciplining Democracy: Development Discourse and Good Governance in Africa.* London: Zed.

Acharya, Ballabh Prasad. 1987. "The Indian Urban Land Ceiling Act: A Critique of the 1979 Legislation." *Habitat International* 11 (3): 39–51.

Acharya, Namrata, and Pradeep Gooptu. 2008. "Singur Braces for Realty Freeze, Locals Fear Losses." *Business Standard*, online edition, September 26. http://www.business-standard.com /india/news/singur-braces-for-realty-freeze-locals-fear-losses/335546/. Accessed June 1, 2009.

Adarkar, Neera, and Meena Menon. 2004. *One Hundred Years, One Hundred Voices: The Mill-workers of Girangaon; An Oral History.* Calcutta: Seagull.

Agarwal, Bina. 1994. *A Field of One's Own: Gender and Land Rights in South Asia.* Cambridge: Cambridge University Press.

Agha, Asif. 2007a. *Language and Social Relations.* Cambridge: Cambridge University Press.

———. 2007b. Recombinant Selves in Mass Mediated Spacetime. *Language & Communication* 27: 320–35.

———. 2011. "Commodity Registers." *Journal of Linguistic Anthropology* 21 (1): 22–53.

Agrawal, Raj Shekhar. 2008. "Aerotropolis Comes to India." *Project Monitor*, May 19–25. http://www.projectsmonitor.com/detailnews.asp?newsid=16227. Accessed October 20, 2008.

Agtmael, Antoine van. 2007. *The Emerging Markets Century: How a New Breed of World-Class Companies Is Overtaking the World.* New York: Free Press.

Ahmed, Waquar. 2010. "Neoliberalism, Corporations, and Power: Enron in India." *Annals of the Association of American Geographers.* 100 (3): 621–39.

Aiyar, Swaminathan S. Anklesaria. 2004. "The Global Indian Takeover." *Times of India*, January 4, online edition. http://www.swaminomics.org/articles/20040104_globalindiantakeover.htm. Accessed September 2, 2009.

Ajayan. 2008. "IT Park Spurs Local Economy as Skills, Job Avenues Grow." *Mint*, February 2.

Analytical Monthly Review. 2007. "Land Grab and Development's Fraud in India." Online edition. http://mrzine.monthlyreview.org/amr210906.html. Accessed May 6, 2007.

Anand, Geeta, and Rajesh Roy. 2014. "Good Timing: Behind a Real-Estate Empire, Ties to India's Gandhi Dynasty." *Wall Street Journal*, April 18.

Anand, Shefali. 2012. "Global Investors Take Fresh Angle in India." *Wall Street Journal.* December 5.

Anjaria, Jonathan Shapiro. 2009. "Guardians of the Bourgeois city: Citizenship, Public Space and Middle Class Activism in Mumbai." *City and Community* 8 (4): 391–406.

———. 2011. "Ordinary States: Everyday Corruption and the Politics of Space in Mumbai." *American Ethnologist* 38 (1): 58–72.

Ansal API. 2007. *Annual Report 2006–2007.*

Appadurai, Arjun. 1996. *Modernity at Large: Cultural Dimensions of Globalization.* Minneapolis: University of Minnesota Press.

———. 2013. *The Future as Cultural Fact: Essays on the Global Condition.* London: Verso.

Appel, Hannah. 2012. "Offshore Work: Oil, Modularity, and the How of Capitalism in Equatorial Guinea." *American Ethnologist* 39(4): 692–709.

Applbaum, Kalman. 2000. "Crossing Borders: Globalization as Myth and Charter in American Transnational Consumer Marketing." *American Ethnologist* 27 (2): 257–82.

———. 2004. *The Marketing Era: From Professional Practice to Global Provisioning.* New York: Routledge.

Arvidsson, Adam. 2000. "The Therapy of Consumption: Motivation Research and the New Italian Housewife, 1958–62." *Journal of Material Culture* 5(3): 251–74.

———. 2003. *Marketing Modernity: Italian Advertising from Fascism to Postmodernity.* London: Routledge.

Aryad, Byju. 2008. "LIC to Invest in Real Estate." *Indian Express*, January 16, Trivandrum edition.

Asian Age. 2005. "12 Bengal Labourers Die in Delhi Collapse." December 25, online edition. http://www.asianage.com/printarticle.asp?newsid=199770. Accessed January 19, 2010.

Assis, Claudia. 2007. "Searching for Shelter on the 'Frontier': Slowdown Paves the Way for the Next Darlings in Emerging Markets." *Wall Street Journal*, November 29, Eastern edition.

Associated Chambers of Commerce and Industry of India. 2006. Press release on "Study on Future of Real Estate Investment in India" report. November 20. http://www.assocham.org/prels/printnews.php?id=792. Accessed August 13, 2009.

Athale, Gouri Agtey. 2008. "Sweet Smell of Success." *Economic Times*, February 4.

Austin, J. L. 1975. *How to Do Things with Words*. 2nd ed., ed. J. O. Urmson and Marina Sbisa. Cambridge, MA: Harvard University Press.

Bailey, Rasul. 2007. "Protest against Big Retail Comes to New Delhi Today." *Mint*, September 20, Delhi edition.

Baisiwala, Sameer, and Varun Desa. 2007. *India Property: India's New Landlords*. Morgan Stanley Research, Asia/Pacific. February 2.

Bakhtin, Mikhail M. 1981. *The Dialogic Imagination*, ed. M. Holquist. Austin: University of Texas Press.

Balagopal, K. 2007a. "Land Unrest in Andhra Pradesh I: Ceiling Surpluses and Public Lands." *Economic and Political Weekly* 42 (38): 3906–11.

———. 2007b. "Land Unrest in Andhra Pradesh II: Impact of Grants to Industries." *Economic and Political Weekly* 42 (39): 3829–33.

Balls, Andrew. 2003. "Why the G7 Must Soon Make Way for the 'Brics.'" *Financial Times*, October 7, London edition.

Banerjee, Aloke. 2007. "Fresh Violence Claims Two in Nandigram." *Hindustan Times*, April 30, Delhi edition.

Banerjee, Rumu. 2007. "A Foreign Lifeline for Realty." *Today*, April 23, Delhi edition.

Banerjee-Guha, Swapna. 2002. "Shifting Cities: Urban Restructuring in Mumbai." *Economic and Political Weekly* 37 (2): 121–28.

Banga, Rashmi. 2005. "Critical Issues in India's Service-Led Growth." Indian Council for Research on International Economic Relations, working paper no. 171, October.

Basu, Indrajit. 2004. "FDI Rush in Indian Real Estate." *Asian Times*, December 23, online edition. http://www.atimes.com/atimes/South_Asia/FL23Df02.html. Accessed December 7, 2007.

Basu, Pranab Kanti. 2007. "Political Economy of Land Grab." *Economic and Political Weekly* 42 (14): 1281–87.

Batlivala and Karani Securities. 2006. IPO note: Parsvnath Developers, Ltd.

Batra, Lalit. 2005. "Vanishing Livelihoods in a 'Global' Metropolis," in *Draft Delhi Master Plan 2021: Blueprint for an Apartheid City*, ed. Dunu Roy and Lalit Batra, 22–32. New Delhi: Hazards Centre.

———. 2007. *JNNURM: The Neo-Liberal Mission for Indian Cities*. http://cpiml.org/liberation /year_2007/July/jnnurm_neo_liberal_mission.html. Accessed September 25, 2007.

Batra, Lalit, and Diya Mehra. 2008. "Slum Demolitions and Production of Neo-Liberal Space, Delhi," in *Inside the Transforming Urban Asia: Processes, Policies, and Public Actions*, ed. Darshini Mahadevia, 391–414. New Delhi: Concept Publishing Company.

Bavdam, Lyla. 2008. "Hot Property." *Frontline*, January 4.

Baviskar, Amita. 2003. "Between Violence and Desire: Space, Power, and Identity in the Making of Metropolitan Delhi." *International Social Science Journal* 55 (1): 89–98.

———. 2011. "Cows, Cars and Cycle-Rickshaws: Bourgeois Environmentalists and the Battle for Delhi's Streets," in *Elite and Everyman: The Cultural Politics of the Indian Middle Classes*, ed. Amita Baviskar and Raka Ray, 391–418. New Delhi: Routledge.

Bayly, C. A. 1983. *Rulers, Townsmen and Bazaars: North Indian Society in the Age of British Expansion, 1770–1870*. Cambridge: Cambridge University Press.

Best, Jacqueline. 2005. *The Limits of Transparency: Ambiguity and the History of International Finance*. Ithaca, NY: Cornell University Press.

Beinhocker, Eric D., Diana Farrell, and Adil S. Zainulbhai. 2007. "Tracking the Growth of India's Middle Class." *McKinsey Quarterly* 3: 51–61.

Bery, Suman, and R. K. Shukla. 2003. "NCAER's Market Information Survey of Households: Statistical Properties and Applications for Policy Analysis." *Economic and Political Weekly* 38 (4): 350–54.

Bhaduri, Amit. 2007. "Development or Developmental Terrorism?" *Economic and Political Weekly* 42 (7): 552–53.

Bhaduri, Amit, and Deepak Nayyar. 1996. *The Intelligent Person's Guide to Liberalization.* New Delhi: Penguin India.

Bharati, Niranjan. 2007. "Land Sale May Help Cure Sick PSUs." *Economic Times*, September 10, Delhi edition.

Bharucha, Nauzer. 2006. "Mumbai Flat Sold for a Record Rs 73,000 sq. ft." *Times of India*, December 3.

———. 2007. "Mumbai Flat Sells for a Record Rs 34 Crore." *Times of India*, November 22, online edition. http://timesofindia.indiatimes.com/Business/India-Business/Mumbai-flat-sells-for-a-record-Rs-34-crore/articleshow/2560344.cms. Accessed July 8, 2009.

Bhatia, Gautam. 1994. *Punjabi Baroque and Other Memories of Architecture.* New Delhi: Penguin India.

Bhatia, Rahul, and Gouri Shah. 2007. "Realty Firms Take to Ads." *Mint*, February 6, Delhi edition.

Bijapurkar, Rama. 2007. *We Are Like That Only: Understanding the Logic of Consumer India.* New Delhi: Penguin India.

Bijith R., and Surajeet Das Gupta. 2008. "DLF-Led Consortium Sole Bidder for Gurgaon Metro Project." *Business Standard.* December 11. http://www.business-standard.com/article/economy-policy/dlf-led-consortium-sole-bidder-for-gurgaon-metro-project-108121101092_1.html. Accessed June 25, 2015.

Binkley, Christina. 2008. "Want to Be a CEO? Dress the Part." *Mint*, February 2, Lounge section.

Birla, Ritu. 2009. *Stages of Capital: Law, Culture, and Market Governance in Late Colonial India.* Durham, NC: Duke University Press.

Bisht, Mitu. 2007. "Pradeep Jain: Dreamer . . . Believer . . . Performer . . . Achiever . . . Owner . . . Parsvnath Developers." *Real Estate Observer*, May.

Björkman, Lisa. 2014. "'You Can't Buy a Vote': Meanings of Money in a Mumbai Election." *American Ethnologist* 41 (4): 617–34.

———. 2015. *Pipe Politics, Contested Waters: Embedded Infrastructures of Millennial Mumbai.* Durham, NC: Duke University Press.

Blumberg, Alex, and Adam Davidson. 2008. "The Giant Pool of Money," *This American Life* episode #355, WRNI, Providence, May 9.

Boddy, Martin. 1981. "The Property Sector in Late Capitalism: The Case of Britain," in *Urbanization and Urban Planning in Capitalist Society*, ed. Michael Dear and Allen J. Scott, 265–86. London: Methuen.

Bogler, Daniel. 2003. "Asia's Economies Moving into the Fast Lane." *Financial Times*, October 6, Asian edition.

Bourdieu, Pierre. 1977. "Symbolic Power," in *Identity and Structure: Issues in the Sociology of Education*, ed. Denis Gleeson, 112–19. Driffield: Studies in Education, Ltd.

———. 1979. "The Disenchantment of the World," in *Algeria 1960*, trans. R. Nice, 1–94. Cambridge: Cambridge University Press.

———. 1984. *Distinction: A Social Critique of the Judgement of Taste.* Translated by R. Nice. Cambridge, MA: Harvard University Press.

———. 1986. "The Forms of Capital," in *Handbook of Theory and Research for the Sociology of Education*, ed. J. G. Richardson, 241–58. New York: Greenwood.

———. 1993. *The Field of Cultural Production*. Edited by Randal Johnson. New York: Columbia University Press.

Boyer, Dominic. 2008. "Thinking through the Anthropology of Experts." *Anthropology in Action* 15 (2): 38–46.

Brauchli, Marcus W. 1995. "Bombay Is World Capital of High Rents—Rent-Control and Land-Use Laws Produce Bubble." *Wall Street Journal*, April 25, Eastern edition.

Brenner, Neil, and Nik Theodore, eds. 2002. *Spaces of Neoliberalism: Urban Restructuring in North America and Western Europe*. Oxford: Blackwell.

Brett, Michael. 1997. *Property and Money: A Simple Guide to Commercial Property Investment and Finance*. London: Estates Gazzette.

Brig. (Retd.) Kamal Sood vs. M/s. DLF Universal Ltd. National Consumer Disputes Redressal Committee, First Appeal No. 557 of 2003. April 20, 2007.

Brown, Michael. 1998. "Can Culture Be Copyrighted?" *Current Anthropology* 39 (2): 193–222.

———. 2010. "A Tale of Three Buildings: Certifying Virtue in the New Moral Economy." *American Ethnologist* 37 (4): 741–52.

Brunsson, Nils, Bengt Jacobsson, and associates. 2000. *A World of Standards*. Oxford: Oxford University Press.

Bucholtz, Mary and Kira Hall. 2004. "Language and Identity," in *A Companion to Linguistic Anthropology*, ed. Alessandro Duranti, 369–93. Malden, MA: Blackwell.

Budhiraja, Sudeep, Gita Piramal, and Sumantra Ghoshal. 2001. "Housing Development Finance Corporation: The Extraordinary-Ordinary Company," in *World Class in India: A Casebook of Companies in Transformation*, ed. Sudeep Budiraja, Gita Piramal, and Sumantra Ghoshal, 589–617. New Delhi: Penguin.

Builders' Association of India. N.d. "Real Estate Industry." Photocopy.

Builders' Association vs. Union of India. Delhi High Court. Writ Petition (C) No. 3620 of 2003. February 28, 2007.

Building Owners and Managers Association International. "Building Class Definitions." http://www.boma.org/Resources/classifications/Pages/default.aspx. Accessed January 17, 2010.

Burawoy, Michael, and Katherine Verdery, eds. 1999. *Uncertain Transitions: Ethnographies of Change in the Postsocialist World*. Lanham, MD: Rowman and Littlefield.

Business Line. 2007. "Market for Architects, Engineers May Grow 30%." May 15, Delhi edition.

Business Standard. 2007a. "Private Placement to Be Treated as FDI in Realty." April 23.

———. 2007b. "Raising Foreign Money Tougher." May 1, online edition. http://www.business-standard.com/common/storypage_c.php?leftnm=10&bKeyFlag=BO&autono=283024&chkFlg=. Accessed May 1, 2007.

———. 2009. "12 Zones Scrapped: Goa to Review Its SEZ Policy." February 3, online edition. http://www.business-standard.com/india/news/12-zones-scrapped-goa-to-review-its-sez-policy/54229/on. Accessed November 12, 2009.

———. 2012. "DLF, Huda to Invest up to Rs 600cr on 16-lane Road in Gurgaon." May 17, online edition. http://www.business-standard.com/article/companies/dlf-huda-to-invest-up-to-rs-600cr-on-16-lane-road-in-gurgaon-112051700141_1.html. Accessed June 25, 2015.

Business Today. 1996. "The New Marketplace: A Bonus Supplement," in *Indian Market Demographics*," S. L. Rao and I. Natarajan. Delhi: Global Business Press.

———. 2007. "Best Cities, or So We Say." August 26.

Caldeira, Teresa. 2000. *City of Walls: Crime, Segregation, and Citizenship in São Paulo*. Berkeley: University of California Press.

Çalişkan, Koray. 2010. *Market Threads: How Cotton Farmers and Traders Create a Global Commodity*. Princeton, NJ: Princeton University Press.

Callon, Michel. 1998. "Introduction: The Embeddedness of Economic Markets in Economics," in *The Laws of the Markets*, ed. Michel Callon, 1–57. Oxford: Blackwell.

Callon, Michel, and Vololona Rabeharisoa. 2003. "Research 'in the Wild' and the Shaping of New Social Identities." *Technology in Society* 25 (2): 193–204.

Carney, Scott. 2008. "The Godfather of Bangalore." *Wired Magazine* 16 (11), online edition. http://www.wired.com/techbiz/people/magazine/16-11/mf_mobgalore?currentPage=all. Accessed October 26, 2008.

Carvalho, Brian, and Anusha Subramanian. 2007. "Will It Trickle Down?" *Business Today*, January 14.

Chakravarti, Sudeep. 1995. "The Middle Class: Hurt but Hopeful." *India Today*, April 15.

Chakravorty, Sanjoy. 2013a. *The Price of Land: Acquisition, Conflict, Consequence*. New Delhi: Oxford University Press.

———. 2013b. "A New Price Regime: Land Markets in Urban and Rural India." *Economic and Political Weekly* 48 (17): 45–54.

Chakravorty, Sanjoy, and Gautam Gupta. 1996. "Let a Hundred Projects Bloom: Structural Reform and Urban Development in Calcutta." *Third World Planning Review* 18 (4): 415–31.

Challapalli, Sravanthi. 2004. "Going to Town." *Hindu Business Line*, March 18, online edition. http://www.thehindubusinessline.com/catalyst/2004/03/18/stories/2004031800160300.htm.

Chamikutty, Preethi. 2007. "Full House: Home Is Where the Cash Is." *Economic Times*, August 3, Brand Equity section.

Chancellor, Edward. 1999. *Devil Take the Hindmost: A History of Financial Speculation*. New York: Farrar, Straus, Giroux.

Chandler, Alfred D. 1977. *The Visible Hand: The Managerial Revolution in American Business*. Cambridge, MA: MIT Press.

Chandra, Kanchan. 2015. "The New Indian State: The Relocation of Patronage in the Post-Liberalization Economy." *Economic and Political Weekly* 50 (41): 46–58.

Chandra, Nirmal Kumar. 2008. "Tata Motors in Singur: A Step towards Industrialisation or Pauperisation?" *Economic and Political Weekly* 43 (50): 36–51.

Chandrasekhar, C. P. 2006. "Primitive Accumulation." *Frontline*, October 20.

———. 2007. "Private Equity: A New Role for Finance?" *Economic and Political Weekly* 42 (13): 1136–45.

Chatterjee, Saikat. 2007. "Wealth Splits Traditional Indian Homes as Sons Buy Their Own Space." *Mint*, May 17.

Chattopadhyay, Suhrid Sankar. 2007a. "Fanning the Flames." *Frontline*, November 16.

———. 2007b. "Return to Peace." *Frontline*, December 17.

Chaudhary, Deepti. 2007. "American Real Estate Firm Invests $100 mn in Shriram Properties." *Mint*, November 1.

Chaudhuri, Dipanjan Rai, and Satya Sivaraman. 2007. "Nandigram: Six Months Later." *Economic and Political Weekly* 42 (14): 4103–4106.

Chauhan, Neeraj. 2007a. "Delhi Police Train Another 'Multi-Crore' Housing Scam; Cops Say They Have Received Complaints from 40 Investors Already." *Indian Express*, August 7, Delhi edition.

———. 2007b. "Kingpin of Rs 500-cr Scam Caught." *Indian Express*, 13 October, online edition. http://www.expressindia.com/latest-news/kingpin-of-rs-500cr-scam-caught/227751/. Accessed January 17, 2010.

Chittum, Ryan. 2006. "Real-Estate Transparency Grows." *Wall Street Journal*, July 12, Eastern edition.

Citizens' Research Collective. 2008. "SEZs: Frequently Asked Questions." *Seminar*, no. 582, February.

Coggan, Philip. 2003. "The Attractions of the Four BRICs—Can They Be Ignored?" *Financial Times*, October 25.

Cohen, Lizabeth. 2003. *A Consumers' Republic: The Politics of Mass Consumption in Postwar America*. New York: Vintage.

Cohn, Bernard S. 1990. "Notes on the History of the Study of Indian Society and Culture," in *An Anthropologist among the Historians and Other Essays*, 136–71. New Delhi: Oxford University Press.

Comaroff, Jean, and John L. Comaroff. 1992. "Home-Made Hegemony: Modernity, Domesticity, and Colonialism in South Africa," in *African Encounters with Domesticity*, ed. K. T. Hansen, 37–74. New Brunswick: Rutgers University Press.

Commonwealth Games' Citizens for Women, Workers, and Children. 2007. "Welfare Provisions for M.P. Construction Workers." *CWG-CWC Newsletter*, no. 4, November–December.

———. 2008. "Implementation Status: Building and Other Construction Workers (Regulation of Employment and Conditions of Service) Act." May 12. PDF available at http://cwg2010cwc.org/laborActs.php. Accessed January 19, 2010.

Construction Workers Federation of India. 2008. "Memorandum to Labour Minister, Ministry of Labour & Employment, Government of India." September 26. http://www.cwfigs.org/events.htm. Accessed January 14, 2010.

CREDAI. 2005. "Urban Land Ceiling: The Last Few Bastions." *Real Estate Review*. July.

Cronon, William. 1991. *Nature's Metropolis: Chicago and the Great West*. New York: Norton.

Cross, Jamie. 2014. *Dream Zones: Anticipating Capitalism and Development in India*. London: Pluto Press.

Cuff, Dana. 1992. "Divisive Tactics: Design-Production Practices in Architecture." *Journal of Architectural Education* 54 (4): 204–12.

———. 1999. "The Political Paradoxes of Practice: Political Economy of Local and Global Architecture." *Architectural Review Quarterly* 3 (1): 77–88.

Cushman & Wakefield. 2006. *India Advantage: A White Paper on the Indian Real Estate Opportunity*. In association with the Global Real Estate Institute.

Daftari, Irshad. 2007. "India to Be 5th Largest Consumer by '25: McKinsey." *Economic Times*, May 4, Delhi edition.

Dagar, Shalini S. 2007. "Second Time Lucky? DLF's Revised Bid for an IPO Is High on Ambition." *Business Today*, February 11.

Dalal, Sucheta. 2007. "Coming Clean on the Real Deal." *Financial Express*, May 14, Delhi edition.

Daly, M. T. 1982. *Sydney Boom, Sydney Bust: The City and Its Property Market 1850–1981*. Sydney: George Allen & Unwin.

Damodaran, Harish. 2008. *India's New Capitalists: Caste, Business, and Industry in a Modern Nation*. Ranikhet, India: Permanent Black.

Daniel, E. Valentine. 1984. *Fluid Signs: Being a Person the Tamil Way*. Berkeley: University of California Press.

Das, Kalyan. 2007. *Construction Workers of Guwahati City: Employment, Employability and Social Security.* NLI Research Studies Series No. 081/2007. Noida: V. V. Giri National Labour Institute.

Das, Rahul. 2007. "Victims Wrest Lost Land from Red Brigade." *Hindustan Times*, March 17, Delhi edition.

Das, Sanchita, and Rasul Bailey. 2007. "Reliance Suspends Kolkata Roll-Out." *Mint*, August 27.

Dasgupta, Keya. 2003. "Evictions in Calcutta: Creating the Spaces of 'Modernity.'" *City: A Quarterly on Urban Society* 4:31–43.

———. 2007. "City Divided? Planning and Urban Sprawl in the Eastern Fringes of Calcutta," in *Indian Cities in Transition*, ed. Annapurna Shaw, 314–40. New Delhi: Concept Publishing Company.

Dash, Dipak Kumar. 2007. "SEZ Plan Runs into Irate Farmers." *Times of India*, May 14, Delhi edition.

Dastidar, Avishek G., and Vidya Krishnan. 2008. "Whispers of Death at 2010 Games Hub." *Hindustan Times*, March 4, online edition. http://www.hindustantimes.com/News-Feed/india/Whispers-of-death-at-2010-Games-hub/245064/Article1-279714.aspx. Accessed November 23, 2009.

Datta, Soumen. 2007. "Reliance Fresh Outlet Vandalized." *Hindustan Times*, August 19, Delhi edition.

Davis, Gerald F., and Michael Useem. 2002. "Top Management, Company Directors and Corporate Control," in *The Handbook of Strategy Management*, ed. Andrew Pettigrew, Howard Thomas, and Richard Whittington, 232–58. London: Sage.

Deaton, Angus, and Jean Dreze. 2002. "Poverty and Inequality in India: A Re-examination." *Economic and Political Weekly* 37 (36): 3729–48.

Deaton, Angus, and Valerie Kozel. 2005. Introduction to *The Great Indian Poverty Debate*, 1–22. Delhi: Macmillan India.

Deloitte Development LLC. 2007. "Real Estate Investing in India: Why Now?" www.deloitte.com/dtt/cda/doc/content/us_re_india-pov_010607.pdf. Accessed August 13, 2009.

Department of Economic Affairs. 1996. *The India Infrastructure Report: Policy Imperatives for Growth and Welfare.* Expert Group on the Commercialization of Infrastructure Projects, Ministry of Finance, Government of India. Delhi: J. M. Jaina & Brothers.

Department of Industrial Policy and Promotion. 2005. Ministry of Commerce and Industry, Government of India. SIA (FC Division). "Press Note 2," http://www.urbanindia.nic.in/moud/programme/ud/main.htm. Accessed November 23, 2006.

———. 2006. Ministry of Commerce and Industry, Government of India. "Fact Sheet on Foreign Direct Investment (FDI) from August 1991 to November 2006," http://dipp.nic.in/fdi_statistics/india_fdi_index.htm. Accessed August 17, 2009.

———. 2008. Ministry of Commerce and Industry, Government of India. "Fact Sheet on Foreign Direct Investment (FDI) from August 1991 to March 2008," http://dipp.nic.in/fdi_statistics/india_fdi_index.htm. Accessed August 17, 2009.

Dickey, Sara. 2013. "Apprehensions: On Gaining Recognition as Middle Class in Madurai." *Contributions to Indian Sociology* 47 (2): 217–43.

Dirks, Nicholas B. 2001. *Castes of Mind: Colonialism and the Making of Modern India.* Princeton, NJ: Princeton University Press.

DLF Limited. 2006. *Draft Red Herring Prospectus.* May 11.

———. 2007. *Draft Red Herring Prospectus.* January 2.

———. 2008. Q4 FY08 analyst presentation. Online at http://www.dlf.in/dlf/wcm/connect/dlf_common/DLF_SITE/HOME/TOP+LINK/Investors/Financial+Results/. Accessed January 3, 2010.

D'Monte, Darryl, 2002. *Ripping the Fabric: The Decline of Mumbai and Its Mills*. New Delhi: Oxford University Press.

———, ed. 2006. *Mills for Sale: The Way Ahead*. Mumbai: J. J. Bhabha and Marg.

Donthi, Praveen. 2014. "The Road to Gurgaon: How the Brokers of Land and Power Built the Millennium City." *Caravan* 6 (1): 24–38.

Doshi, Sapana. 2013. "The Politics of the Evicted: Redevelopment, Subjectivity, and Difference in Mumbai's Slum Frontier." *Antipode* 45 (3): 1–22.

Dossani, Rafiq, and Martin Kenney. 2002. "Creating an Environment for Venture Capital in India." *World Development* 30 (2): 227–53.

DTZ. 2007. "Norwegian Wood (This Bird Has Flown)." India commercial real estate report.

Dua, Aarti. 2006. "Charting the Change." *Telegraph*, June 3, online edition. http://www.telegraphindia.com/1060603/asp/weekend/story_6303201.asp#. Accessed August 7, 2009.

Dumont, Louis. 1970 [1966]. *Homo hierarchicus: The Caste System and Its Implications*. London: Weidenfeld and Nicolson.

Dunn, Elizabeth. 2004. *Privatizing Poland: Baby Food, Big Business, and the Remaking of Labor*. Ithaca, NY: Cornell University Press.

Dupont, Veronique. 2005. "The Idea of a New Chic Delhi through Publicity Hype," in *The Idea of Delhi*, ed. R. Khosla, 78–93. Mumbai: Marg.

———. 2008. "Slum Demolitions in Delhi since the 1990s: An Appraisal." *Economic and Political Weekly* 43 (28): 79–87.

Dutt, Ishita Ayan, and Tamajit Pain. 2007. "Realtors Make Hay as Singur Prices Zoom." *Business Standard*, May 2.

Economic and Political Weekly. 2005. "Housing: Demolition Drive." 40 (4): 260. January 22.

———. 2007. "On the New Poverty Estimates." 42 (13): 1067.

Economic Survey of Delhi, 2005–2006. Government of Delhi, Planning Department. http://delhiplanning.nic.in/ecosurvey.htm. Accessed November 5, 2009.

Economic Times. 2006. "It Is India's Time to Shine Fair and Square." December 29, online edition. http://articles.economictimes.indiatimes.com/2006-12-29/news/27419820_1_corruption-index-bric-countries-india-83rd. Accessed January 25, 2016.

———. 2007a. "Ex-Morgan Chief Unveils South India-Focused Realty Fund." March 17.

———. 2007b. "CPM Cadre Shot Villagers: Digvijay." March 20, Delhi edition.

———. 2007c. "CBI Team Seconds Digvijay Report." March 22, Delhi edition.

———. 2007d. "Building a New World." March 24, Delhi edition.

———. 2007e. "Videocon Faces Villagers' Ire over Proposed SEZ." May 13, Delhi edition.

———. 2007f. "ECB Norms Tightened—Foreign Debt Door Shut on Realty." May 19.

———. 2007g. "Bharti, Wal-Mart in Pact for Cash & Carry Biz." August 7, Delhi edition.

———. 2007h. "Trump Card: Donald Trump Jr. Is Taking His Real Estate Operations Global." August 17, Delhi edition, Corporate Dossier section.

———. 2007i. "Realty Stocks Soar as State Plans to Repeal Land Ceiling Act." November 30.

———. 2008. "Pay Cheques to Get Fatter." February 20, Delhi edition.

Economist. 2003. "Follow the Yellow BRIC Road." 369 (8345), October 11.

———. 2004. "West Bengal: The Thin Red Line." May 8.

———. 2005. "The Global Housing Boom: In Come the Waves." 375 (8431), June 16.

———. 2007. "Here, There, and Everywhere." 383 (8529), May 19.

———. Economics A-Z, s.v. "Transparency." http://www.economist.com/research/economics/alphabetic.cfm?letter=T#transparency. Accessed June 26, 2009.

Edelweiss Securities. 2006. *Real Estate: Realty Is for Real.* December 5.

Elyachar, Julia. 2005. *Markets of Dispossession: NGOs, Economic Development, and the State in Cairo.* Durham, NC: Duke University Press.

———. 2006. "Best Practices: Research, Finance, and NGOs in Cairo." *American Ethnologist* 33 (3): 413–26.

Emaar MGF Land Limited. 2008. *Draft Red Herring Prospectus.* January 17.

Ernst & Young. 2006. *Indian Real Estate: Opportunities and Returns.* September. Published with the Federation of Indian Chambers of Commerce and Industry.

Espeland, Wendy Nelson, and Mitchell L. Stevens. 1998. "Commensuration as a Social Process." *Annual Review of Sociology* 24: 313–43.

Express India. 2008. "State to Get Is First Aerotropolis." January 19, online edition. http://www.expressindia.com/latest-news/State-to-get-its-first-aerotropolis/263264/. Accessed October 6, 2009.

Fainstein, Susan S. 2001. *The City Builders: Property Development in New York and London, 1980–2000.* Lawrence, KS: University Press of Kansas.

Falzon, Mark-Anthony. 2004. "Paragons of Lifestyle: Gated Communities and the Politics of Space in Bombay." *City & Society* 16 (2): 145–67.

Fanselow, Frank. 1990. "The Bazaar Economy or How Bizarre Is the Bazaar Really?" *Man*, n.s., 25 (2): 250–65.

Ferguson, James. 1994. *The Anti-Politics Machine: "Development," Depoliticization, and Bureaucratic Power in Lesotho.* Minneapolis: University of Minnesota Press.

———. 1999. *Expectations of Modernity: Myths and Meanings of Urban Life on the Zambian Copperbelt.* Berkeley: University of California Press.

———. 2005. "Seeing Like an Oil Company: Space, Security, and Global Capital in Neoliberal Africa." *American Anthropologist* 107 (3): 377–82.

Fernandes, Leela. 2004. "The Politics of Forgetting: Class Politics, State Power and the Restructuring of Urban Space in India." *Urban Studies* 41 (12): 2415–30.

———. 2006. *India's New Middle Class: Democratic Politics in an Era of Economic Reform.* Minneapolis: University of Minnesota Press.

Ferry, Elizabeth Emma. 2013. *Minerals, Collecting, and Value across the U.S.-Mexico Border.* Bloomington: University of Indiana Press.

Financial Express. 2015. "Robert Vadra, Builders Received 'Favours' from Haryana Govt: CAG." March 26, online edition. http://www.financialexpress.com/article/economy/robert-vadra-builders-received-favours-from-previous-congress-led-haryana-govt-cag/57551/. Accessed June 28, 2015.

Financial Times. 2003. "India's Opportunity: The Economy Is Buoyant but Has Disappointed Before." November 5.

———. 2005. "What Is a Special Purpose Vehicle?" March 21, online edition. http://www.financialexpress.com/news/what-is-a-special-purpose-vehicle/129610/0. Accessed August 18, 2009.

Forbes. 2007. "The World's Billionaires: #754 PNC Menon." http://www.forbes.com/lists/2007/10/07billionaires_PNC-Menon_51LT.html. Accessed September 29, 2009.

Fortun, Mike. 2008. *Promising Genomics: Iceland and deCODE Genetics in a World of Speculation.* Berkeley: University of California Press.

Foucault, Michel. 1984. "Space, Knowledge, and Power," in *The Foucault Reader*, ed. P. Rabinow, 239–56. New York: Pantheon.

Fourcade, Marion, and Kieran Healy. 2007. "Moral Views of Market Society." *Annual Reviews of Sociology* 33 (14): 1–27.

Fraser, David. 2000. "Inventing Oasis: Luxury Housing Advertisements and Reconfiguring Domestic Space in Shanghai," in *The Consumer Revolution in Urban China*, ed. D. S. Davis, 25–53. Berkeley: University of California Press.

Galbraith, John K. 1994. *A Short History of Financial Euphoria*. New York: Penguin.

Gangopadhyay, Abhrajit. 2006. "India Attracts Real-Estate Investors." *Wall Street Journal*, February 8, Eastern edition.

Ganti, Tejaswini. 2012a. *Producing Bollywood: Inside the Contemporary Hindi Film Industry*. Durham, NC: Duke University Press.

———. 2012b. "Sentiments of Disdain and Practices of Distinction: Boundary-Work, Subjectivity, and Value in the Hindi Film Industry." *Anthropological Quarterly* 85 (1): 5–44.

———. 2014. "Neoliberalism." *Annual Review of Anthropology* 43: 89–104.

Garg, Abhinav. 2008. "Builders in a Spot for Not Sticking to Court Deadline; Did Not Refund Money for a Botched Housing Project." *Times of India*, February 10, Delhi edition.

Garsten, Christina, and Monica Lindh de Montoya, eds. 2008. *Transparency in a New Global Order: Unveiling Organizational Visions*. Cheltenham: Edward Elgar.

Gentleman, Amelia. 2006. "Letter from India: India Can't Wait to Put the 'Super' before 'Power.'" *International Herald Tribune*, November 23, online edition. http://www.nytimes.com/2006/11/23/world/asia/23iht-letter.3642086.html?_r=1&scp=1&sq=india%20can%27t%20wait%20to%20put%20the%20super%20before%20power&st=cse. Accessed September 2, 2009.

Ghannam, Farha. 1998. "The Visual Remaking of Urban Space: Relocation and the Use of Public Housing in 'Modern Cairo.'" *Visual Anthropology* 10 (2–3): 265–80.

———. 2002. *Remaking the Modern: Space, Relocation, and the Politics of Identity in a Global Cairo*. Berkeley: University of California Press.

Ghertner, D. Asher. 2008. "Analysis of New Legal Discourse behind Delhi's Slum Demolitions." *Economic and Political Weekly* 43 (20): 57–66.

———. 2011. "Rule by Aesthetics: World-Class City Making in Delhi," in *Worlding Cities: Asian Experiments and the Art of Being Global*, ed. Ananya Roy and Aihwa Ong, 279–306. Oxford: Blackwell.

———. 2015. *Rule by Aesthetics: World-Class City Making in Delhi*. Oxford: Oxford University Press.

Ghosh, Arun. 1992. "New Economic Policy: A Review." *Economic and Political Weekly* 27 (23): 1175–78.

Ghosh, Jayati, Abhijit Sen, and C. P. Chandrasekhar. 1997. "All Dressed Up and Nowhere to Go: India Infrastructure Report." *Economic and Political Weekly* 32 (16): 803–8.

Ghosh, Ruma. 2004. "Brick Kiln Workers: A Study of Migration, Labour process and Employment." NLI Research Studies Series No. 057/2004. Noida: V. V. Giri National Labour Institute.

Ghosh, Sugata. 2007. "With Fistful of Dollars, Cos. Outwit Realty Rules." *Economic Times*, May 21, Delhi edition.

Ghosh, Sugata, and M. V. Ramsurya. 2006. "Real Estate Cos. Building on Foreign Equity Hiding behind Debt Curtain." *Economic Times*, December 20, Delhi edition.

Gieryn, Thomas. 1983. "Boundary Work and the Demarcation of Science from Non-Science:

Strains and Interests in Professional Ideologies of Scientists." *American Sociological Review* 48: 781–95.

———. 2002. "What Do Buildings Do?" *Theory and Society* 31: 35–74.

Glover, William J. 2008. *Making Lahore Modern: Constructing and Imagining a Colonial City.* Minneapolis: University of Minnesota Press.

Goldman, Michael. 2011. "Speculative Urbanism and the Making of the Next World City." *International Journal of Urban and Regional Research* 35 (3): 555–81.

Goldman Sachs. 2007. *Brics and Beyond.* Goldman Sachs Global Economics Group, November. http://www2.goldmansachs.com/ideas/brics/BRICs-and-Beyond.html. Accessed January 17, 2010.

Gordon, James and Poonam Gupta. 2004. "Understanding India's Service Revolution." IMF Working Paper No. WP/04/171, Asia and Pacific Department, September.

Gowan, Peter. 1999. *The Global Gamble: Washington's Faustian Bid for World Dominance.* London: Verso.

Goyal, Malini. 2007. "Blue Shirt with a White Collar." *Economic Times,* August 31, Corporate Dossier section.

Granovetter, Mark. 1985. "Economic Action and Social Structure: The Problem of Embeddedness." *American Journal of Sociology* 91 (3): 481–510.

Guano, Emanuela. 2002. "Spectacles of Modernity: Transnational Imagination and Local Hegemonies in Neoliberal Buenos Aires." *Cultural Anthropology* 17 (2): 181–209.

Gupta, Abhishek Kiran. 2007. "Are Tier II Cities Taking the Glory Away from Tier I Cities?" *Asia Pacific Property Digest: India,* Second Quarter (Jones Lang LaSalle).

Gupta, Akhil. 1995. "Blurred Boundaries: The Discourse of Corruption, the Culture of Politics, and the Imagined State." *American Ethnologist* 22 (2): 375–402.

———. 1998. *Postcolonial Developments: Agriculture and the Making of Modern India.* Durham, NC: Duke University Press.

Gupta, Surajeet Das, and Anusha Soni. 2013. "Gurgaon Rapid Metro Blazes a New Trail." *Business Standard,* Novemer 25, online edition. http://www.business-standard.com/article/companies/gurgaon-rapid-metro-blazes-a-new-trail-113112501161_1.html. Accessed June 25, 2015.

GurgaonWorkersNews. "About Gurgaon." http://gurgaonworkersnews.wordpress.com/about-gurgaon/. Accessed November 11, 2009.

Gusterson, Hugh. 1996. *Nuclear Rites: A Weapons Laboratory at the End of the Cold War.* Berkeley: University of California Press.

———. 1997. "Studying Up Revisited." PoLAR 20 (1): 114–19.

Guyer, Jane I. 2004. *Marginal Gains: Monetary Transactions in Atlantic Africa.* Chicago: University of Chicago Press.

Haila, Anne. 1997. "The Neglected Builder of Global Cities," in *Cities in Transformation—Transformation in Cities: Social and Symbolic Change of Urban Space,* ed. O. Kalltorp et al., 51–64. Ashgate, Aldershot.

Halbert, Ludovic, and Hortense Rouanet. 2014. "Filtering Risk Away: Global Finance Capital, Transcalar Territorial Networks, and the (Un)making of City-Regions: An Analysis of Business Property Development in Bangalore, India." *Regional Studies* 48 (3): 471–84.

Hall, Tim, and Phil Hubbard, eds. 1998. *The Entrepreneurial City: Geographies of Politics, Regime and Representation.* Chinchester UK: Wiley.

Handique, Maitrevee. 2007. "Tata Plan Splits Chattisgarh Villagers." *Mint,* November 3, Delhi edition.

Harvey, David. 1989. "From Managerialism to Entrepreneurialism: The Transformation in Urban Governance in Late Capitalism." *Geografiska Annaler.* 71B: 3–17.

———. 1999 [1982]. *The Limits to Capital.* London: Verso.

———. 2003. *The New Imperialism.* Oxford: Oxford University Press.

———. 2013. *Companion to Marx's* Capital. Vol. 2. London: Verso.

Haryana Labour Department. "The Haryana Building and Other Construction Workers Welfare Board," http://hrlabour.org/page.php?module=boards&pid=5. Accessed January 14, 2010.

Hetherington, Kregg. 2011. *Guerilla Auditors: The Politics of Transparency in Neoliberal Paraguay.* Durham, NC: Duke University Press.

Hill, Jane H. 2008. *The Everyday Language of White Racism.* Malden, MA: Wiley-Blackwell.

Hindu. 2007. "Notice to Centre, States on PIL Petition Seeking Guidelines for Real Estates Ads." 26 March, online edition. http://www.hindu.com/2007/03/20/stories/2007032003751300.htm. Accessed January 17, 2010.

———. 2008. "Labourer Killed at Games Village in the Capital." December 15, online edition. http://www.thehindu.com/2008/12/15/stories/2008121560360300.htm. Accessed November 23, 2009.

———. 2012. "IAC and DLF: Point-Counterpoint on Vadra's Deals." October 10, online edition. http://www.thehindu.com/opinion/op-ed/iac-and-dlf-pointcounterpoint-on-vadras-deals/article3982064.ece. Accessed June 28, 2015.

Hindu Business Line. 2006. "Aerens Goldsouk to Expand." May 6, online edition. http://www.thehindubusinessline.com/2006/05/06/stories/2006050603380500.htm. Accessed January 16, 2010.

———. 2007. "India Set to Become World's Fifth Largest Consumer Market by 2025." May 4, online edition. http://www.thehindubusinessline.com/2007/05/04/stories/2007050403051300.htm. Accessed April 28, 2016.

Hindustan Times. 2006. "Erring Builders Cannot Forfeit Earnest Money." December 5, Delhi edition.

Hiscock, Geoff. 2008. *India's Global Wealth Club: The Stunning Rise of Its Billionaires and the Secrets of Their Success.* Singapore: Wiley.

Ho, Karen. 2009. *Liquidated: An Ethnography of Wall Street.* Durham, NC: Duke University Press.

Holmes, Douglas R. 2014. *Economy of Words: Communicative Imperatives in Central Banks.* Chicago: University of Chicago Press.

Holmes, Douglas R., and George E. Marcus. 2005. "Cultures of Expertise and the Management of Globalization: Toward the Re-functioning of Ethnography," in *Global Assemblages: Technology, Politics, and Ethics as Anthropological Problems,* ed. Aihwa Ong and Stephen J. Collier, 235–52. Malden, MA: Blackwell.

Holston, James. 1989. *The Modernist City: An Anthropological Critique of Brasilia.* Chicago: University of Chicago Press.

Hosagrahar, Jyoti. 1999. "Fractured Plans: Real Estate, Moral Reform, and the Politics of Housing in New Delhi, 1936–1941." *Traditional Dwellings and Settlements Review* 11 (1): 37–47.

Hossain, Rakeep, and Drimi Chaudhuri. 2007. "CPM Cadres Kill 3 in Nandigram." *Hindustan Times,* November 11, Delhi edition.

Housing Development and Finance Corporation. 2006. "Reports and Accounts of HDFC and Its Key Unlisted Subsidiaries and Associates, 2005–2006."

Hudson, Michael. 2006. "Goldman Sachs Adds a Fund to the BRIC collection." *Wall Street Journal*, July 22, Eastern edition.

Hull, Matthew S. 2008. "Ruled by Records: The Expropriation of Land and the Misappropriation of Lists in Islamabad." *American Ethnologist* 35 (4): 501–18.

Hussain, Shabana. 2007a. "Aerens Gold Souk Plans to List Abroad, Raise $400 Million." *Mint*, August 17, Delhi edition.

———. 2007b. "Speculators Exiting Real Estate Market." *Mint*, September 7.

———. 2007c. "India's Most Liveable Cities." *Mint*, September 28.

———. 2008a. "Rs3,000 Crore Uppal Public Offer This Year." *Mint*, January 8, Delhi edition.

———. 2008b. "Talent Crunch Sees Real Estate Salaries Touch Dizzying Heights." *Mint*, January 23, Delhi edition.

———. 2008c. "No Takers: Emaar MFG Yanks Rs6,400 Crore IPO." *Mint*, February 9.

Hussain, Shabana, and Sanchita Das. 2007. "Cos. Take Advantage All the Way to the Bank." *Mint*, September 21, Delhi edition.

Hussain, Shabana, and Malathi Nayak. 2007. "Uphaar Verdict: Ansals, 10 Others Held Guilty in Cinema Fire." *Mint*, November 21.

ICICI Property Services and Technopak Advisors. 2007. "Indian Retail Real Estate: The Road Ahead."

ICICI Securities. 2007. *Indian Real Estate Sector: Opportunities Unleashed.* May 21.

Images Multimedia. 2007. *Malls in India: Shopping Centre Developers and Development.* New Delhi.

Inda, Jonathan Xavier, and Renato Rosaldo, eds. 2008. *The Anthropology of Globalization: A Reader.* 2nd edition. Malden, MA: Blackwell.

India Knowledge@Wharton. 2006. "Indian Companies Are on an Acquisition Spree: Their Target? U.S. Firms." December 13, online edition. http://knowledge.wharton.upenn.edu/article.cfm?articleid=1627. Accessed September 3, 2009.

———. 2008. "Bumps in the Road: India's Industrial Growth Seeks Solid Ground." October 30, online edition. http://knowledge.wharton.upenn.edu/india/article.cfm?articleid=4329. Accessed November 13, 2008.

Indian Express. 2004. "India Could Overtake China in 15 Years." October 22, online edition. http://www.indianexpress.com/storyOld.php?storyId=57429. Accessed August 20, 2009.

———. 2008. "Welfare of Construction Workers: SC Seeks Report from States." May 13, online edition. http://www.indianexpress.com/news/welfare-of-construction-workers-sc-seeks-re/308644/. Accessed January 14, 2010.

Ip, Greg, and Mark Whitehouse. 2005. "Awash in Cash: Cheap Money, Growing Risks." *Wall Street Journal*, November 3, Eastern edition.

Jacobson, Marc. 2007. "Dharavi: Mumbai's Shadow City." *National Geographic*, May.

Jamwal, Nidhi. 2004. "Dhamaal Growth." *Down to Earth*, January 31, online edition. http://www.downtoearth.org.in/cover.asp?foldername=20040131&filename=anal&sid=1&page=1&sec_id=7&p=1. Accessed May 24, 2007.

———. 2007. "No Vacancy." *Down to Earth*, November 30.

Jauregui, Beatrice. 2014. "Provisional Agency in India: *Jugaad* and the Legitimation of Corruption." *American Ethnologist.* 41 (1): 76–91.

Jawaharlal Nehru National Urban Renewal Mission. 2007. "Checklist for the Urban Reforms Agenda under the JNNURM: Kochi." http://jnnurm.nic.in/MoA/Kochhi_MoA.pdf. Accessed December 2007.

Jayashankar, Mitu. 2007. "Companies Pay Lib Service to Women." *Economic Times*, March 8, Delhi edition.

Jenkins, Rob, Loraine Kennedy, and Partha Mukhopadhyay. 2014. *Power, Policy, and Protest: The Politics of India's Special Economic Zones.* Oxford: Oxford University Press.

Jeromi, P. D. 2007. "Farmers' Indebtedness and Suicides: Impact of Agricultural Trade Liberalisation in Kerala." *Economic and Political Weekly* 42 (31): 3241–47.

Jha, Mayur Shekhar. 2007. "Sahara Housing Faces Probe for Not Keeping Ad Promise." *Economic Times*, May 24, Delhi edition.

Jha, Mayur Shekhar, and Rajat Guha. 2007a. "Farmers with No CLU Selling Out to SEZ at Half the Price." *Economic Times*, February 5, Delhi edition.

———. 2007b. "Ansal API Lines Up Rs 1,000-Cr Follow-On Issue, $250m PE Deal." *Economic Times*, September 3.

John, Gemma. 2011. "Freedom of Information and Transparency in Scotland: Disclosing Persons as Things and Vice Versa." *Anthropology Today* 27 (3): 22–25.

Jones, Jonathan. 2008. "India's Democracy Has a Heartbeat." *Seminar*, no. 582 (February).

Jones Lang LaSalle. 2004. *Global Offshoring Index: Deciding Where to Offshore.* January 2.

———. 2006a. *India: The Next IT Offshoring Locations, Tier III Cities.* World Winning Cities Series, Emerging City Winners.

———. 2006b. *Real Estate Transparency Index.*

———. 2008. *Transparency Comes of Age: Real Estate Transparency in India.* Real Estate Transparency Index, Global Foresight Series.

Jones Lang LaSalle Meghraj. 2007. *Accelerating Transformation: Investments in Indian Real Estate.* Knowledge Centre White Paper Series. 2 (2).

JP Morgan. 2007. *Indian Realty: Super Build Up.* Asia Pacific Equities Research, August 1.

Kacker, Suneetha Dasappa. 2005. "The DDA and the Idea of Delhi," in *The Idea of Delhi*, ed. R. Khosla, 68–77. Mumbai: Marg.

Kalpataru Group. "Corporate Information: About Us." http://www.kalpataru.com/corporate -information/default.asp. Accessed September 29, 2009.

Kanna, Ahmed. 2011. *Dubai: The City as Corporation.* Minneapolis: University of Minnesota Press.

Kar, Sohini. 2013. "Recovering Debts: Microfinance Loan Officers and the Work of 'Proxy-Creditors' in India." *American Ethnologist* 40 (3):480–93.

Karmin, Craig. 2006a. "Going for BRIC: Emerging Fund Lures Investors." *Wall Street Journal*, March 6, Eastern edition.

———. 2006b. "Templeton to Launch BRIC Fund." *Wall Street Journal*, April 4, Eastern edition.

Kaul, Vivek. 2014. "DLF Shares in Debt Spiral: Decoding Why the Stock Fell 28% after Sebi Ban." Blog post. October 15. https://teekhapan.wordpress.com/2014/10/15/dlf-shares-in-debt -spiral-decoding-why-the-stock-fell-28-after-sebi-ban/. Accessed October 15, 2014.

Keane, Webb. 2003. "Semiotics and the Social Analysis of Material Things." *Language and Communication* 23: 409–25.

Keynes, John Maynard. 1936. *The General Theory of Employment, Interest, and Money.* New York: Harcourt, Brace, and Company.

Kilbinger, Sara Seddon. 2007. "Foreign Investors Go into a Tizzy over Asian Real Estate." *Mint*, February 7.

Kindleberger, Charles Poor. 2000. *Manias, Panics, and Crashes: A History of Financial Crises.* 4th ed. New York: Wiley.

King, Anthony. 2002. "Speaking from the Margins: 'Postmodernism,' Transnationalism, and the Imagining of Contemporary Indian Urbanity," in *Globalization and the Margins*, ed. R. Grant and J. Rennie, 72–90. New York: Palgrave Macmillan.

Knight Frank. 2005. *India Property Investment Review, Quarter 4 2005*.

Knight, Frank H. 1957 [1921]. *Risk, Uncertainty, and Profit*. 8th ed. New York: Kelley & Millman, Inc.

Knorr Cetina, Karin, and Urs Bruegger. 2002. "Global Microstructures: The Virtual Societies of Financial Markets." *American Journal of Sociology* 107 (4): 905–50.

Knowledge@Wharton. 2008a. "Indian Real Estate Firms Face a Reality Check." October 2, online edition. http://knowledge.wharton.upenn.edu/article/indian-real-estate-firms-face-a-reality-check/#. Accessed August 3, 2015.

———. 2008b. "The Son Also Rises: Donald Trump, Jr., on Real Estate Opportunities in Emerging Markets." December 10, online edition. http://knowledge.wharton.upenn.edu/article.cfm?articleid=2113. Accessed January 10, 2009.

Kockelman, Paul. 2006. "A Semiotic Ontology of the Commodity." *Journal of Linguistic Anthropology* 16 (1): 76–102.

Kopytoff, Igor. 1986. "The Cultural Biography of Things: Commoditization as Process," in *The Social Life of Things: Commodities in Cultural Perspective*, ed. Arjun Appadurai, 64–94. Cambridge: Cambridge University Press.

Krippner, Greta R. 2001. "The Elusive Market: Embeddedness and the Paradigm of Economic Sociology." *Theory and Society* 30 (6): 775–810.

———. 2005. "The Financialization of the American Economy." *Socio-Economic Review* 3: 173–208.

Krishnakumar, R. 2007. "A Deal in Kerala." *Frontline*, June 1.

Kuber, Girish. 2007. "Farmers Won't Buy Reliance SEZ Package." *Economic Times*, March 15, Delhi edition.

Kulkarni, Rajesh. 2006. "GenX Rides Realty Boom." *Realty Plus*, May.

Kumar, Arun. 1982. "Real Estate as Business." *Economic and Political Weekly* 17 (50): 1984.

———. 2002. *The Black Economy in India*. New Delhi: Penguin.

Kumar, Arun. 2007. "Hot Property: Unassuming Real Estate Baron Ramesh Chandra Is the New Face on Forbes' List of Indian Billionaires." *Hindustan Times*, March 17, Delhi edition.

Kumar, Ashok. 2008. "Sanjeev Nanda Held Guilty in BMW Hit-and-Run Case." *Hindu*, September 3, online edition. http://www.thehindu.com/todays-paper/tp-national/tp-newdelhi/sanjeev-nanda-held-guilty-in-bmw-hitandrun-case/article1331692.ece. Accessed January 20, 2015.

Kumar, Lalit. 2005. "15 Workers Injured in G Noida Building Collapse." *Times of India*, April 3.

Kumar, Nagesh. 2000. "Economic Reforms and Their Macro-economic Impact." *Economic and Political Weekly* 35 (10): 803–12.

Kumar, S. Nagesh. 2007. "Under Fire." *Frontline*, August 24.

Kundu, Amitabh. 1997. *Urban Land Markets and Land Price Changes: A Study in the Third World Context*. Aldershot, UK: Ashgate.

Kunj Behari Mehta vs. Ansal Properties and Industries, Ltd. National Consumer Disputes Redressal Committee, Original Petition No. 190 of 2000. May 12, 2008.

Kuppinger, Petra. 2004. "Exclusive Greenery: New Gated Communities in Cairo." *City & Society* 16 (2): 35–62.

Kurup, E. Jayashree. 2007. "Believe It or Not." *Economic Times*, March 25, Delhi edition.

Lal, Deepak, Rakesh Mohan, and I. Natarajan. 2001. "Economic Reforms and Poverty Allevia-tion: A Tale of Two Surveys." *Economic and Political Weekly* 36 (12): 1017–28.

Lamarche, Francois. 1976. "Property Development and the Economic Foundations of the Urban Question," in *Urban Sociology: Critical Essays*, ed. C. G. Pickvance, 85–118. New York: St. Martin's.

Lampland, Martha, and Susan Leigh Star, eds. 2009. *Standards and Their Stories: How Quantify-ing, Classifying, and Formalizing Practices Shape Everyday Life.* Ithaca, NY: Cornell Univer-sity Press.

Larson, Magali Sarfatti. 1993. *Behind the Postmodern Façade: Architectural Change in Late Twen-tieth Century America.* Berkeley: University of California Press.

Latour, Bruno. 1986. "Visualization and Cognition: Thinking with Eyes and Hands," in *Knowl-edge and Society: Studies in the Sociology of Culture Past and Present*, vol. 6, ed. H. Kuklick and E. Long, 1–40. Greenwich, CT: JAI Press, Inc.

———. 1987. *Science in Action: How to Follow Scientists and Engineers through Society.* Cam-bridge, MA: Harvard University Press.

Latour, Bruno, and Steve Woolgar. 1986. *Laboratory Life: The Construction of Scientific Facts.* Princeton, NJ: Princeton University Press.

Lazonick, William, and Mary O'Sullivan. 2000. "Maximizing Shareholder Value: A New Ide-ology for Corporate Governance." *Economy and Society* 29 (1): 13–35.

Levien, Michael. 2011. "Rationalising Dispossession: The Land Acquisition and Resettlement Bills." *Economic & Political Weekly.* 46 (11): 66–71.

———. 2012. "The Land Question: Special Economic Zones and the Political Economy of Dis-possession in India." *Journal of Peasant Studies* 39 (3–4): 933–69.

———. 2015a. "From Primitive Accumulation to Regimes of Dispossession: Six Theses on India's Land Question." *Economic and Political Weekly* 50 (22): 146–57.

———. 2015b. "Social Capital as Obstacle to Development: Brokering Land, Norms, and Trust in Rural India." *World Development* 74: 77–92.

Li, Tania Murray. 2007. *The Will to Improve: Governmentality, Development, and the Practice of Politics.* Durham, NC: Duke University Press.

Liechty, Mark. 2003. *Suitably Modern: Making Middle-Class Culture in a New Consumer Society.* Princeton, NJ: Princeton University Press.

LiPuma, Edward, and Benjamin Lee. 2005. *Financial Derivatives and the Globalization of Risk.* Durham, NC: Duke University Press.

Logan, John. 1993. "Cycles and Trends in the Globalization of Real Estate," in *The Restless Urban Landscape*, ed. Paul L. Knox, 34–54. Englewood Cliffs, NJ: Prentice Hall.

Logan, John, and Harvey L. Molotch. 1987. *Urban Fortunes: The Political Economy of Place.* Berkeley: University of California Press.

M/s. Madan Builders vs. R. K. Saxena. National Consumer Disputes Redressal Committee, First Appeal No. 411 of 2004, December 5, 2008.

Mackay, Charles. 1980 [1841]. *Extraordinary Popular Delusions and the Madness of Crowds.* New York: Three Rivers Press.

MacKenzie, Donald. 2003. "Long-Term Capital Management and the Sociology of Arbitrage." *Economy and Society* 32 (3): 349–80.

———. 2006. *An Engine Not a Camera: How Financial Models Shape Markets.* Cambridge, MA: MIT Press.

MacKenzie, Donald, and Yuval Millo. 2003. "Constructing a Market, Performing Theory: The Historical Sociology of a Financial Derivatives Exchange." *American Journal of Sociology* 109 (1): 107–45.

MacKenzie, Donald, Fabian Muniesa, and Lucia Siu, eds. 2007. *Do Economists Make Markets? On the Performativity of Economics.* Princeton, NJ: Princeton University Press.

Mahadevia, Darshini, and Harini Narayanan. 2008. "Shanghaing Mumbai: Politics of Evictions and Resistance in Slum Settlements," in *Inside the Transforming Urban Asia: Processes, Policies, and Public Actions*, ed. Mahadevia, Darshini, 549–89. New Delhi: Concept Publishing Company.

Mahalingam, Sudha. 1998. "The False Ceiling." *Frontline*, August 1–14.

Mahmud, Lilith. 2014. *The Brotherhood of Freemason Sisters: Gender, Secrecy, and Fraternity in Italian Masonic Lodges.* Chicago: University of Chicago Press.

Majumder, Sarasij. 2009. "'Peasants' against the Nano? Neoliberal Industrialization and the Land Question in Marxist West Bengal, India." American Anthropological Association annual meeting, Philadelphia PA, December 2–6.

———. 2012. "'Who Wants to Marry a Farmer?' Neoliberal Industrialization and the Politics of Land and Work in Rural West Bengal." *Focaal* 64: 85–98.

Makkar, Sahil. 2007. "Workers Building New Airport Terminal Face Health Hazards." Indo-Asian News Service, October 31, online edition. http://www.indiaenews.com/print/?id=78084. Accessed November 23, 2009.

Mandel, Ruth, and Caroline Humphrey, eds. 2002. *Markets and Moralities: Ethnographies of Postsocialism.* Oxford: Berg.

Manoi, P. 2007. "Rs10 Lakh per Acre Is Offer Price for Farm Land in Maharashtra." *Mint*, February 20, Delhi edition.

Marcus, George E. 1995. "Ethnography in/of the World System: The Emergence of Multi-Sited Ethnography." *Annual Review of Anthropology* 24: 95–117.

Markovits, Claude. 2000. *The Global World of Indian Merchants, 1750–1947: Traders of Sind from Bukhara to Panama.* Cambridge: Cambridge University Press.

Marriott, Oliver. 1967. *The Property Boom.* London: H. Hamilton.

Marx, Karl. 1981 [1894]. *Capital: A Critique of Political Economy.* Vol. 3. Trans. David Fernbach. London: Penguin, in association with *New Left Review.*

Maslow, A. H. 1943. "A Theory of Human Motivation." *Psychological Review* 50 (4): 370–96.

Massey, Doreen. 2007. *World City.* Cambridge, UK: Polity.

Mazzarella, William. 2003. *Shoveling Smoke: Advertising and Globalization in Contemporary India.* Durham, NC: Duke University Press.

———. 2006. "Internet X-Ray: E-Governance, Transparency, and the Politics of Immediation in India." *Public Culture* 18 (3): 473–505.

McKinsey Global Institute. 2001. *India: The Growth Imperative.* September.

McMichael, Philip. 1996. "Globalization: Myths and Realities." *Rural Sociology* 61 (6): 25–55.

Mehra, Diya. 2009. "Redefining Neighborhoods, Redefining Self: Urban Middle Class Activism in 'New' World Class Delhi." American Anthropological Association annual meeting, Philadelphia PA, December 2–6.

Mehta, Mona. 2007. "Real Estate Funds Bullish on Sector's Growth." *Financial Express*, February 6.

Mehta, Sumeet. 2007. "Is There a Bubble? With Land Being a Scarce Resource, Property Prices Follow the Basic Economics of Demand-Supply." *Economic Times*, April 13, Delhi edition.

Menon, P. Sreevalsan. 2006. "The Rs. 90,000 Crore Man." *The Week*, May 14.

Menon-Sen, Kalyani, and Gautam Bhan. 2008. *Swept Off the Map: Surviving Eviction and Re-settlement in Delhi*. New Delhi: Yoda Press.

Michael, A. C. 2007. "Need of the Hour: A Regulatory Body for Real Estate." *Hindustan Times*, May 12.

Miller, Daniel. 2003. "The Virtual Moment." *Journal of the Royal Anthropological Institute* 9 (1): 57–75.

Miller, Peter, and Nicholas Rose. 1997. "Mobilizing the Consumer: Assembling the Subject of Consumption." *Theory, Culture, Society* 14: 1–36.

Ministry of Commerce and Industry. 2016. "Updated Factsheet on SEZs." Government of India. http://www.sezindia.nic.in/writereaddata/pdf/factsheet.pdf. Accessed January 24, 2016.

Ministry of Finance. 1998. *Union Budget 1998–99*. Government of India. http://indiabudget.nic .in/ub1998–99/welcome.html. Accessed January 1, 2009.

———. 2007. *Mumbai—An International Financial Centre: Report of the High Powered Expert Committee on Making Mumbai an International Financial Centre*. New Delhi: Sage.

Ministry of Housing and Urban Poverty Alleviation. 2006. "Brief Note on Urban Reforms Incentive Fund (URIF)." Government of India. http://www.mhupa.gov.in/programs/housing /urifII.htm. Accessed October 1, 2007.

Ministry of Urban Affairs and Employment. 1998. *National Housing and Habitat Policy*. Government of India.

Ministry of Urban Development. 2006. "Jawaharlal Nehru National Urban Renewal Mission: Overview." Ministry of Urban Employment and Poverty Alleviation. Government of India. http://jnnurm.nic.in/nurmudweb/defaultud.aspx. Accessed September 1, 2009.

———. n.d. "Model Municipal Law." Government of India. http://www.urbanindia.nic.in/moud /legislations/li_by_min/Model_Municipal_Law.html. Accessed September 2, 2009.

Mint. 2007. "Indian Consumer to Spend Rs. 200 a Day by 2025: Study." May 4, online edition. http://www.livemint.com/2007/11/04145027/Indian-consumer-to-spend-Rs200.html.

———. 2008. "HDIL to Raise Rs1,000 cr for Slum Land Swap." August 27, online edition. http:// www.livemint.com/Articles/2007/04/20001413/2008/08/27002142/HDIL-to-raise-Rs1000 -cr-for-s.html?d=2. Accessed August 30, 2008.

———. 2013. "Mumbai Airport Terminates HDIL Contract." May 29, online edition. http://www .livemint.com/Companies/LdaQdkOW90CI40Xc81HGcO/Mumbai-airport-terminates -HDIL-contract.html. Accessed August 1, 2013.

Mishra, Pankaj. 2006. "The Myth of the New India." *New York Times*, July 6, online edition. http:// www.nytimes.com/2006/07/06/opinion/06mishra.html?ei=5090&en=63b065e1403c4316 &ex=1309838400&partner=rssuserland&emc=rss&pagewanted=print. Accessed September 2, 2009.

Mitchell, Katharyne, and Kris Olds. 2000. "Chinese Business Networks and the Globalization of Property Markets in the Pacific Rim," in *Globalization of Chinese Business Firms*, ed. Henry Wai-chung Yeung and Kris Olds, 195–219. New York: St. Martin's.

Mitchell, Timothy. 1988. *Colonising Egypt*. Cambridge: Cambridge University Press.

———. 2002. *Rule of Experts: Egypt, Techno-Politics, Modernity*. Berkeley: University of California Press.

Miyazaki, Hirokazu. 2013. *Arbitraging Japan: Dreams of Capitalism at the End of Finance*. Berkeley: University of California Press.

Mobile Crèches. 2008. "Distress Migration: Identity and Entitlements: A Study on Migrant Construction Workers and the Health Status of Their Children in the National Capital Region, 2007–2008." New Delhi: Mobile Crèches.

Mollenkamp, Carrick, Jason Singer, Alistair MacDonald, and Edward Taylor. 2007. "For Most Hedge Funds, Hunting in Packs Pays High Dividends." *Mint*, September 20.

Morris, Charles R. 2008. *The Trillion Dollar Meltdown: Easy Money, High Rollers, and the Great Credit Crash*. New York: Public Affairs.

Mosse, David, Sanjeev Gupta, and Vidya Shah. 2005. "On the Margins in the City: Adivasi Seasonal Labour Migration in Western India." *Economic and Political Weekly* 40 (28): 3025–38.

MPD-2021. 2007. *Delhi Master Plan*. W.e.f. 7 February. (as published in Gazette of India, Part 2 of Section 3, Sub-section [2] Extraordinary, Notification No. S. O. 141[E] dated 7.2.2007). Delhi: Akalank.

MRUC—Hansa Research. 2006. *Guide to Indian Markets*. Mumbai: MRUC & Hansa Research.

Ms. Veena Khanna vs. M/s. Ansal Properties and Industries, Ltd. National Consumer Disputes Redressal Committee, First Appeal No. 155 of 2006. July 9, 2007.

MSCI Barra. 2008. *Emerging Markets: A 20-Year Perspective*.

Mukherjee, Anuradha. 2003. "Metro Sets Up Labourers' Fund." *Times of India*, March 27, online edition. http://timesofindia.indiatimes.com/cms.dll/html/uncomp/articleshow?msid =41498600. Accessed January 19, 2010.

Mukhija, Vinit. 2003. *Squatters as Developers? Slum Demolition and Redevelopment in Mumbai, India*. Ashgate, London.

Muthukumar, K. 2007. "So What If It's a Clubhouse?" *Economic Times*, November 15.

Myers, Fred. 2004. "Ontologies of the Image and Economies of Exchange." *American Ethnologist* 31 (1): 1–16.

Nader, Laura. 1969. "Up the Anthropologist—Perspectives Gained from Studying Up," in *Reinventing Anthropology*, ed. Dell Hymes, 284–311. New York: Pantheon.

Nainan, Navtej. 2008. "Building Boomers and Fragmentation of Space in Mumbai." *Economic and Political Weekly* 43 (21): 29–34.

Nair, Janaki. 2005. *The Promise of the Metropolis: Bangalore's Twentieth Century*. New Delhi: Oxford University Press.

Nakassis, Constantine V. 2016. *Doing Style: Youth and Mass Mediation in South India*. Chicago: University of Chicago Press.

Nakassis, Constantine V., and Llerena Guiu Searle. 2013. "Introduction: Social Value Projects in Post-Liberalisation India." *Contributions to Indian Sociology* 47 (2): 169–83.

Namburu, Manoj. 2007. *Moguls of Real Estate*. New Delhi: Roli.

Nandy, Madhurima. 2007. "Misleading Ads Are a Way of Life." *Hindustan Times*, March 24, Delhi edition.

———. 2009. "DLF, Unitech Show Path to Beat Real Estate Downturn." *Mint*, June 24, online edition. http://www.livemint.com/2009/06/24005439/DLF-Unitech-show-path-to-beat.html. Accessed July 8, 2009.

———. 2014. "Blackstone Set to Become India's Largest Office Assets Owner." *Mint*, October 8, online edition. http://www.livemint.com/Companies/Rjyyr13vYtTGf33YOZm9mK /Blackstone-set-to-become-Indias-largest-office-assets-owner.html. Accessed March 26, 2015.

Narayanan, Dinesh. 2007. "India to Overtake US by 2050." *Times of India*, January 24, online edition. http://timesofindia.indiatimes.com/NEWS/India/India-to-overtake-United-States -by-2050-Report/articleshow/1411052.cms. Accessed August 20, 2009.

Narayanswamy, Subbu, and Adil Zainulbhai. 2007. "India's Consumption Evolution." *Business*

Standard, May 5, online edition. http://www.business-standard.com/common/storypage.php?autono=283444.

Nath, Kamal. 2008. *India's Century: The Age of Entrepreneurship in the World's Biggest Democracy*. New Delhi: Tata McGraw-Hill.

National Association of Software and Services Companies. 2008. "IT Industry Factsheet—Aug 2008.doc." http://www.nasscom.in/Nasscom/templates/NormalPage.aspx?id=53615. Accessed November 3, 2008.

National Building Organisation. 2008. "Housing Data Table." http://nbo.nic.in. Accessed November 10, 2008.

National Council of Applied Economic Research. 2003. *India Market Demographics Report 2002*. New Delhi: NCAER.

National Housing Bank. 2006. *Report on Trend and Progress of Housing in India 2005*. New Delhi.

Nevins, Joseph, and Nancy Lee Peluso, eds. 2008. *Taking Southeast Asia to Market: Commodities, Nature and People in the Neoliberal Age*. Ithaca, NY: Cornell University Press.

Nijman, Jan. 2000. "Mumbai's Real Estate Market in 1990s: De-regulation, Global Money and Casino Capitalism." *Economic and Political Weekly* 35 (7): 575–82.

———. 2008. "Against the Odds: Slum Rehabilitation in Neoliberal Mumbai." *Cities* 25: 73–85.

Niyogi, Subhro, and Saibal Sen. 2007. "The Killing Fields." *Times of India*, March 25, Delhi edition.

Oldenberg, Veena Talwar. 1984. *The Making of Colonial Lucknow, 1856–1877*. Princeton, NJ: Princeton University Press.

Olds, Kris. 1997. "Globalizing Shanghai: The Global Intelligence Corps and the Buildings of Pudong." *Cities* 14 (2): 109–23.

———. 2001. *Globalization and Urban Change: Capital, Culture, and Pacific Rim Megaprojects*. Oxford: Oxford University Press.

O'Malley, Pat. 2000. "Uncertain Subjects: Risks, Liberalism and Contract." *Economy and Society* 29 (4): 460–84.

———. 2003. "Moral Uncertainties: Contract Law and Distinctions between Speculation, Gambling, and Insurance," in *Risk and Morality*, ed. Richard V. Ericson and Aaron Doyle, 231–57. Toronto: University of Toronto Press.

Omaxe Limited. 2007. *Draft Red Herring Prospectus*. July 24.

Öncü, Ayşe. 1997. "The Myth of the 'Ideal Home' Travels across Cultural Borders to Istanbul," in *Space, Culture, and Power: New Identities in Global Cities*, ed. A. Öncü and P. Weyland, 56–72. London: Zed.

O'Neill, Jim. 2001. "Building Better Global Economic BRICs." Goldman Sachs Global Economics Paper No. 66. November 30.

O'Neill, Jim, and Tushar Poddar. 2008. "Ten Things for India to Achieve Its 2050 Potential." Goldman Sachs Global Economics Paper No. 169. June 16.

Organisation for Economic Co-Operation and Development. "Convention on Combating Bribery of Foreign Public Officials in International Business Transactions." http://www.oecd.org/document/21/0,3343,en_2649_34859_2017813_1_1_1_1,00.html. Accessed December 29, 2008.

Osburg, John. 2013. "Global Capitalisms in Asia: Beyond State and Market in China." *Journal of Asian Studies* 72 (4): 813–30.

Osella, Filippo, and Caroline Osella. 1999. "From Transience to Immanence: Consumption, Life-Cycle, and Social Mobility in Kerala, South India." *Modern Asian Studies* 33 (4): 989–1020.

Pal, Parthapratim. 2005. "Volatility in the Stock Market in India and Foreign Institutional Investors: A Study of the Post-Election Crash." *Economic and Political Weekly* 40 (8): 765–72.

Pandit, Ambika. 2006. "DDA Kicks Off Games Village Housing Plan." *Times of India*, December 16, Delhi edition.

Pandit, Vivek. 2015. "Private Equity in India: Once Overestimated, Now Underserved." McKinsey & Company. February. http://www.mckinsey.com/insights/financial_services/private_equity_in_india. Accessed July 18, 2015.

Parsvnath Developers Ltd. 2006. *Draft Red Herring Prospectus*. August 29.

———. 2007. "Corporate Presentation." Powerpoint presentation. September.

———. 2008. *Annual Report 2007–08*.

Partnoy, Frank. 1997. *F.I.A.S.C.O.: Blood in the Water on Wall Street*. New York: Norton.

Patel, Bimal Hasmukh. 1995. "The Space of Property Capital: Property Development and Architecture in Ahmedabad." PhD diss., University of California at Berkeley.

Pathak, Maulik. 2007. "Go Manhattan, Nariman Point Space Will Cost 1.5 Times More." *Economic Times*, September 12.

Pawley, Emily. 2011. "Coining Foliage into Gold: Speculation, Value, and the Mulberry Bubble, 1828–1839." Unpublished paper.

Philip, Joji Thomas. 2008. "DoT Set to Auction Rs10k-cr VSNL Land." *Economic Times*, February 11, Delhi edition.

Philip, Joji Thomas, and Niranjan Bharati. 2008. "Post Office Addresses May Get Swish after Invite to Bit Realty." *Economic Times*, February 7, Delhi edition.

Pinney, Christopher. 1997. "Stern Fidelity" and "Penetrating Certainty," in *Camera Indica: The Social Life of Indian Photographs*, 17–71. Chicago: University of Chicago Press.

Planning Commission. 2007. "Agricultural Strategy for Eleventh Plan: Some Critical Issues." Government of India, May.

Porter, Theodore M. 1995. *Trust in Numbers: The Pursuit of Objectivity in Science and Public Life*. Princeton, NJ: Princeton University Press.

Prahalad, C.K. 2006. *The Fortune at the Bottom of the Pyramid: Eradicating Poverty through Profits*. Upper Saddle River, NJ: Wharton School Publications.

Preda, Alex. 2008. "Technology, Agency, and Financial Price Data," in *Living in a Material World: Economic Sociology Meets Science and Technology Studies*, ed. T. Pinch and R. Swedberg, 217–52. Cambridge, MA: MIT Press.

Primary Real Estate Advisors, website. http://www.primaryindia.com. Accessed November 5, 2007.

Radhakrishnan, Smitha. 2009. "Professional Women, Good Families: Respectable Femininity and the Cultural Politics of a 'New' India." *Qualitative Sociology* 32 (2): 195–212.

———. 2011. *Appropriately Indian: Gender and Culture in a New Transnational Class*. Durham, NC: Duke University Press.

Rai, Nayantara. 2007. "Private Developers to Get 27,000 h Bonanza." *Business Standard*, January 25.

Rai, Nayantara, and Siddharth Zarabi. 2007. "DLF Will Always Be Family-Owned but Professionally Run: KP Singh." *Business Standard*, June 18, Delhi edition.

Raja D., John Samuel. 2008a. "Hedging Strategy: Citi Arm Cashes Out Part of Its Stake in Emaar ahead of IPO." *Mint*, January 22.

———. 2008b. "Assets Sale to Promoter Firm Boosts DLF Profit." *Mint*, January 31.

———. 2008c. "Emaar MGF's Aborted IPO Costs Citi Dear." *Mint*, February 22.

Raja D., John Samuel; and Shabana Hussain. 2007. "Omaxe Ltd Renting 'Omaxe' Name from Goel." *Mint*, July 4, online edition. http://www.livemint.com/articles/2007/07/04003517 /Omaxe-Ltd-renting-Omaxe-name.html. Accessed January 9, 2010.

Raja D., John Samuel, et al. 2007. "Madras Cement's Rajha Is Highest Paid Executive." *Mint*, Delhi edition, September 4.

Rajagopal, Arvind. 2004. "The Menace of Hawkers: Property Forms and the Politics of Market Liberalization in Mumbai," in *Property in Question: Value Transformation in the Global Economy*, ed. Katherine Verdery and Caroline Humphrey, 227–48. Oxford: Berg.

Raman, Bhuvaneswari. 2012. "The Rhetoric and Reality of Transparency Initiatives: Transparent Cities, Opaque Power and Urban Poor's Claims to Land." *Journal of Community Informatics.* 8 (2): 866–909.

Ramanathan, Gayatri. 2007a. "High Net Worth NRIs Go Long on Realty." *Business Standard*, February 1.

———. 2007b. "Overseas Investors Look at Varied Fund Options in Real Estate." *Mint*, August 22.

———. 2007c. "Dharavi Redevelopment Plan Is Robbing Us of Space: Residents." *Mint*, September 5, Delhi edition.

———. 2007d. "State in for Rs10,000 cr Dharavi Bonus." *Mint*, October 5, Delhi edition.

———. 2007e. "Office Space Rentals in Mumbai, Delhi Soar, B'lore Holds Steady." *Mint*, November 15.

———. 2007f. "Mumbai Set to Gain from Land Ceiling Act Repeal." *Mint*, November 30.

Ranganathan, Malini, Lalita Kamath, and Vinay Baindur. 2009. "Piped Water Supply to Greater Bangalore: Putting the Cart Before the Horse?" *Economic and Political Weekly* 44 (33): 53–62.

Rao, G. V. L. Narasimha. 2007. "UP's Stand on Reliance Smacks of Vendetta." *Mint*, August 27.

Rao, Nikhil. 2013. *House but No Garden: Apartment Living in Bombay's Suburbs, 1898–1964*. Minneapolis: University of Minnesota Press.

Rao, Prakash. 1991. "HDFC: A Bank, and Yet Not a Bank. Deepak Parekh, Managing Director, in Conversation with Prakash Rao." *Indian Architect & Builder* 4 (6): 50–54.

Rao, S. L., and I. Natarajan. 1996. *Indian Market Demographics: The Consumer Classes*. Delhi: Global Business Press.

Rapid MetroRail Gurgaon Ltd. 2012. "The Project" webpage. http://www.rapidmetrogurgaon .com/theProject.aspx. Accessed June 28, 2015.

Rawal, Vikas. 2001. "Agrarian Reform and Land Markets: A Study of Land Transactions in Two Villages of West Bengal, 1977–1995." *Economic Development and Cultural Change* 49 (3): 611–29.

Realty Plus. 2006a. "Exposed: Property Pre-Launches." April, online edition. http://www .realtyplusmag.com/cover_fullstory.asp?cover_id=18. Accessed June 24, 2009.

———. 2006b. "Indian Real Estate Gaining Greater Transparency." September.

———. 2006c. "Developer Speak: Price Correction Augurs Well for Real Estate." October.

———. 2006d. "We Want Indian Public to Be Part of Our Growth Story." December.

———. 2007. "Hot Emerging Destinations of 2007: Places to Go, Money to Make." January.

———. 2008. "Hot Emerging Destinations of 2008." January.

Reddy, V. Ratna, and S. Galab. 2006. "Agrarian Crisis: Looking beyond the Debt Trap." *Economic and Political Weekly* 41 (19): 1838–41.

Reddy, V. Ratna, and B. Suresh Reddy. 2007. "Land Alienation and Local Communities: Case Studies in Hyderabad-Secunderabad." *Economic and Political Weekly* 42 (31): 3233–40.

Ren, Xufei. 2011. *Building Globalization: Transnational Architectural Production in Urban China*. Chicago: University of Chicago Press.

Riles, Annelise. 2004. "Real Time: Unwinding Technocratic and Anthropological Knowledge." *American Ethnologist* 31 (3): 392–405.

Robertson, Roland. 1994. "Globalisation or Glocalisation?" *Journal of International Communication* 1(1): 33–52.

Robinson, William I., and Jerry Harris. 2000. "Towards a Global Ruling Class? Globalization and the Transnational Capitalist Class." *Science & Society* 64 (1): 11–54.

Roy, Abhijit. 2003. "India Set to Rank Third by 2040." *Hindu*, December 29, online edition. http://www.thehindu.com/thehindu/biz/2003/12/29/stories/2003122900341600.htm. Accessed August 20, 2009.

Roy, Prithwiraj. 2007. "Boom Towns: The Magnificent Seven in Residential March." *Realty Plus*, September.

Roy, Saumya, and Rasul Bailey. 2008. "Chemists' Groups, Hawkers and Traders Join Hands for Nationwide Stir Today." *Mint*, February 23.

Rudner, David West. 1994. *Caste and Capitalism in Colonial India: The Nattukottai Chettiars*. Berkeley: University of California Press.

Rutland, Ted. 2010. "The Financialization of Urban Redevelopment." *Geography Compass* 4 (8): 1167–78.

Ruud, Arlid Engelsen. 2000. "Corruption as Everyday Practice: The Public-Private Divide in Local Indian Society." *Forum for Development Studies* 27 (2): 271–94.

Sabharwal, Binny. 2007. "Real-Estate Finance: New Delhi Builds Ambitions; Housing Expansion Attracts Foreign Investment, Developers; Infrastructure Poses Challenge." *Wall Street Journal*, May 9, Eastern edition.

Sadovi, Maura Webber. 2007. "Rising Values Spur Concern about Overheating." *Wall Street Journal*, March 28, Eastern edition.

Sampat, Preeti. 2014. "On the Land Question in 21st Century India." *Economic and Political Weekly* 49 (10): 30–33.

Sandage, Scott A. 2005. *Born Losers: A History of Failure in America*. Cambridge, MA: Harvard University Press.

Sanjai, P. R. 2008. "Tatas, Ambanis, DLF Interested in Modernizing Railway Stations." *Mint*, January 4, Delhi edition.

Sassen, Saskia. 2001. *The Global City: New York, London, Tokyo*. 2nd ed. Princeton, NJ: Princeton University Press.

———. 2014. *Expulsions: Brutality and Complexity in the Global Economy*. Cambridge, MA: Harvard University Press.

———. 2015. "At the Systemic Edge." *Cultural Dynamics* 27 (1): 173–81.

Satyanarayan, S. 2006. "Foreign Investors Eyeing Realty Market, Says Assocham Study." *Tribune* (Chandigarh), November 25, online edition. http://www.tribuneindia.com/2006/20061125/rea11.htm. Accessed Auguat 13, 2009.

Scott, James. 1998. *Seeing Like a State: How Certain Schemes to Improve the Human Condition Have Failed*. New Haven, CT: Yale University Press.

Searle, Llerena Guiu. 2013. "Constructing Prestige and Elaborating the 'Professional': Elite Residential Complexes in the National Capital Region, India." *Contributions to Indian Sociology* 47 (2): 271–302.

Second National Commission on Labour. 2002. *Report*. Ministry of Labour and Employment,

Government of India. http://labour.nic.in/lcomm2/nlc_report.html. Accessed February 3, 2008.

Sehgal, Rashme. 2007. "Give Labour Force Stake in Games, Say NGOs." *Asian Age*, October 5, online edition. http://www.asianage.com/archive/htmlfiles/Top%20Story/Give%20labour%20force%20stake%20in%20Games%20%20say%20NGOs.html. Accessed January 14, 2010.

Self Employed Women's Association. 2000. "Labouring Brick by Brick: A Study of Construction Workers." Ahmedabad. June.

Selvaduri. A. J. 1976. "Land, Personhood, and Sorcery in a Sinhalese Village," in *Religion and Social Conflict in South Asia*, ed. Bardwell L. Smith, 82–96. Leiden: Brill.

Seminar. 2008. "SEZ: Expressway or Cul-de-Sac?" No. 582, February.

Sengupta, Snighda. 2007. "It Is Only Worth Investing in the Top 20–25% of Funds Here." *Mint*, August 27.

Sengupta, Somini. 2007. "The Traditional Whiskey-Drinker Develops a Taste for Fine Wine." *Mint*, August 13.

Sethi, Aman. 2005. "In a Buyer's Market." *Frontline*, November 19, online edition. http://www.flonnet.com/fl2224/stories/20051202001408800.htm. Accessed February 10, 2008.

———. 2012. *A Free Man: A True Story of Life and Death in Delhi*. New York: Norton.

SG Estates. "The Company: Profile." http://www.sgestates.in/profile.html. Accessed May 8, 2009.

Shah, Aditi, and Himank Sharma. 2014. "DLF, India's Most Indebted Property Firm, Faces Tough Choices after Fund-raising Ban." Reuters, October 14. http://in.reuters.com/article/2014/10/14/india-dlf-debt-idINKCN0I31KP20141014. Accessed October 15, 2014.

Shankar, Kripa. 1990. *Land Transfers: A Case Study*. New Delhi: Gian.

Shapin, Steven. 2008. *The Scientific Life: A Moral History of a Late Modern Vocation*. Chicago: University of Chicago Press.

Sharma, Harish, and Gaurav Pathak. 2006. *Real Estate: Realty Is for Real*. Edelweiss Securities, Dec. 5.

Sharma, Rajeshwari. 2007. "Salary Hikes in India Were Second Highest in Asia-Pacific Region." *Mint*, November 22.

Sharma, Ravi Teja. 2007. "For a Few Crores More." *Business Standard*, January 20, online edition. http://www.business-standard.com/india/news/forfew-crores-more/272001/. Accessed October 6, 2009.

———. 2012. "DLF Denies Charges Made by Kejriwal, Says Has Given No Unsecured Loans to Vadra or His Companies." *Economic Times*, October 6, online edition. http://articles.economictimes.indiatimes.com/2012-10-06/news/34293860_1_dlf-robert-vadra-unsecured-loans. Accessed June 28, 2015.

Sharma, Samidha, and Vivek Sinha. 2007. "Rewards Are All Caught in the Middle." *Economic Times*, May 18, Delhi edition.

Sharma, Tanu. 2007. "Ads by Builders under Supreme Court Scanner." *Indian Express*, March 26, online edition. http://www.indianexpress.com/story/26117.html. Accessed January 17, 2010.

Shah, Amrish, and Rehka Bagry. 2007. "FDI vs ECB: A Clutch of Unanswered Questions." *Economic Times*, May 23, Delhi edition.

Shastri, Paromita. 2007. "Computerization Will Do Land Market More Good than Reforms." *Mint*, May 1, Delhi edition.

Sheth, Alpa. 1993. "Corporate Builders: Godrej Properties, Tata Housing, a Profile." *Indian Architect & Builder* 6:6–7: 126–30.

Shiller, Robert J. 2000. *Irrational Exuberance*. New York: Broadway Books.

Shleifer, Andrei, and Robert W. Vishny. 1997. "A Survey of Corporate Governance." *Journal of Finance* 52 (2): 737–83.

Shore, Cris, and Susan Wright. 2000. "Coercive Accountability: The Rise of Audit Culture in Higher Education," in *Audit Cultures: Anthropological Studies in Accountability, Ethics and the Academy*, ed. M. Strathern, 57–89. London: Routledge.

Shri Taranjit Singh vs. M/s. Unitech, Ltd. National Consumer Disputes Redressal Committee, Original Petition No. 36 of 2001. September 3, 2005.

Shrivastava, Aseem, and Ashish Kothari. 2012. *Churning the Earth: The Making of Global India*. New Delhi: Penguin Viking.

Shukla, Archna. 2007. "The Market Makers: How India's Middle Class of 300 Million Became Not Just One of the Largest Markets, but a Global Phenomenon." *Business Today*, January 14.

Shukla, Seema. 2003. "No Kidding, by '50 India May Be No 3 Economy." *Economic Times*, October 10.

Sikarwar, Deepshikha. 2007. "DIPP Faces Finmin Roadblock over Lock-In for FIIs in Real Estate Cos." *Economic Times*, November 6.

Singh, Abhay, and Subramaniam Sharma. 2007. "Skilled Workers Exploit Talent Crunch, Impede Growth Story." *Mint*, August 22.

Singh, Animesh. 2007. "Railway Land on Sale May Not Impress Bidders." *Business Standard*, October 12., Delhi edition.

Singh, K. P. 2011. *Whatever the Odds: The Incredible Story behind DLF*. With Ramesh Menon and Raman Swamy. New Delhi: Harper Collins India.

Singh, Piya. 2007. "Foreign Institutions Queuing Up to Invest in Indian Real Estate." *Mint*, April 10.

Singh, Shalini. 2012. "Behind Robert Vadra's Fortune, a Maze of Questions." *Hindu*, October 8, online edition. http://www.thehindu.com/news/national/behind-robert-vadras-fortune-a -maze-of-questions/article3975214.ece. Accessed June 28, 2015.

———. 2013. "Behind Realty Rush in Haryana, a Gilt-Edged Licence Raj." *Hindu*, February 4, online edition. http://www.thehindu.com/news/national/behind-realty-rush-in-haryana-a -giltedged-licence-raj/article4375630.ece?ref=relatedNews. Accessed June 15, 2015.

Sinha, Partha. 2006. "DLF Revives Plan for IPO." *Times of India*, November 6, Delhi edition.

Sklair, Leslie. 2005. "The Transnational Capitalist Class and Contemporary Architecture in Globalizing Cities." *International Journal of Urban and Regional Research* 29 (3): 485–500.

Slater, Joanna. 2002. "India's Land Market Impedes Growth: Murky Records, Litigation Entangle Real-Estate Deals, but Change Comes Slowly." *Wall Street Journal*, May 15, Eastern edition.

Smart, Graham. 1999. "Storytelling in a Central Bank: The Role of Narrative in the Creation and Use of Specialized Economic Knowledge." *Journal of Business and Technical Communication* 13 (3): 249–73.

———. 2006. *Writing the Economy: Activity, Genre and Technology in the World of Banking*. London: Equinox.

Smith, Neil. 2002. "New Globalism, New Urbanism: Gentrification as Global Urban Strategy." *Antipode* 34 (3): 427–50.

Smith, Ray A. 2004. "Developers Enter India Market—Indirectly; Ownership Restrictions Force Foreign Companies to Settle for Side Roles." *Wall Street Journal*, June 30, Eastern edition.

Sobha Developers. "About Us: Our Profile." http://www.sobhadevelopers.com/about/index.html. Accessed June 10, 2009.

Soni, Anita. 2000. "Urban Conquest of outer Delhi: Beneficiaries, Intermediaries and Victims," in *Delhi: Urban Space and Human Destinies*, ed. V. Dupont, E. Tarlo, and D. Vidal, 75–96. New Delhi: Manohar.

Soni, Varun. 2007. "Global Funds Elude Indian Realty." *Financial Express*, April 13, Delhi edition.

South Asian. 2007. "Women Farmers Protest Reliance SEZ." July 23, online edition. http://www .thesouthasian.org/archives/2007/women_farmers_protest_reliance.html. Accessed August 5, 2007.

Sridhar, V. 2007. "Wal-Mart Walks In." *Frontline*, January 12.

Srinivas, B. 2006. "Currying Favor Again with Global Investors." *Global Dateline*, ed. Cushman & Wakefield (winter), 17–20. http://www.execcouncil.org/ExecutiveCouncil/Member /ECWhitePapers/WhitePapers/indiagd06.pdf. Accessed, December 16, 2007.

Srinivasa, Kavitha. 2007. "Growth Pangs: Too Many Firms, Not Enough Architects Around." *Mint*, November 30, Delhi edition.

Srivastava, Sadhana. 2003. "What Is the True Level of FDI Flows to India?" *Economic and Political Weekly* 38 (7): 608–10.

Srivastava, Sanjay. 2009. "Urban Spaces, Disney-Divinity and Moral Middle Classes in Delhi." *Economic and Political Weekly* 44 (26–27): 338–45.

Stallybrass, Peter. 1998. "Marx's Coat," in *Border Fetishisms: Material Objects in Unstable Spaces*, ed. P. Spyer, 183–207. New York, Routledge.

Strange, Susan. 1997 [1986]. *Casino Capitalism*. Manchester, UK: Manchester University Press.

Strathern, Marilyn, ed. 2000. *Audit Cultures: Anthropological Studies in Accountability, Ethics and the Academy*. London: Routledge.

Subrahmanyam, Sanjay, and C. A. Bayly. 1990. "Portfolio Capitalists and the Political Economy of Early Modern India," in *Merchants, Markets and the State in early Modern India*, ed. Sanjay Sibrahmanyam, 242–65. Delhi: Oxford University Press.

Subramaniam, Ganapathy. 2007. "Realty Check for FII Portfolio." *Economic Times*, Delhi edition, March 22.

Subramanyam, Chitra. 2008. "Cracked Up." *India Today Woman*. February.

Sukumar, C. R. 2007. "Ramky Group Mulls IPOs for Three Firms." *Mint*, December 13, Delhi edition.

Sunder Rajan, Kaushik. 2006. *Biocapital: The Constitution of Postgenomic Life*. Durham, NC: Duke University Press.

Surendar, T., and Prabhakar Sinha. 2008. "An Unlikely Real Estate Tycoon." *Times of India*, February 9, Delhi edition.

Suri, K. C. 2006. "Political Economy of Agrarian Distress." *Economic and Political Weekly* 41 (16): 1523–29.

Suryanarayan, S. S. 2004. "Labour Laws, Contractural Parameters and Conditions of Construction Workers: A Study in Chennai." NLI Research Studies Series No. 050/2004. Noida: V. V. Giri National Labour Institute.

Swedberg, Richard. 1990. "International Financial Networks and Institutions." *Current Sociology* 38 (2): 259–81.

TASAM. 2007. "A Brief Report on Nandigram." http://sanhati.com/news/257/. Accessed August 4, 2007.

TDI. "Taneja Developers & Infrastructure Ltd: Group Profile." http://72.3.191.201/grp_profile.
htm. Accessed May 8, 2009.

Tett, Gillian. 2009. *Fool's Gold: How the Bold Dream of a Small Tribe at J. P. Morgan Was Corrupted by Wall Street Greed and Unleashed a Catastrophe.* New York: Free Press.

Thakurta, Indrani. 2007. "Home Groan." *Today Real Estate Buyer's Guide—Delhi and NCR.*

Thomas, Shibu. 2007. "HC Nod to Close Mumbai Mill Units." *Times of India,* June 17, online
edition. http://timesofindia.indiatimes.com/articleshow/2128701.cms. Accessed October 29, 2009.

Thrift, Nigel. 1986. "The Internationalization of Producer Services and the Integration of the Pacific Basin Property Market," in *Multinationals and the Restructuring of the World Economy,*
ed. M. Taylor and N. Thrift, 142–92. London: Croom Helm.

Times of India. 2002. "Six Killed, 20 Hurt in Building Collapse." January 16.

———. 2006. "Average Delhiite Earns 54K." July 22, online edition. http://timesofindia.indiatimes
.com/articleshow/1789927.cms. Accessed January 17, 2010.

———. 2007a. "Landbanking." February 11, Ahmedabad edition.

———. 2007b. "Country of Consumers." May 27, Delhi edition.

———. 2007c. "Nandigram's Chemical Hub Shifted to Nayachar." September 4, online edition. http://timesofindia.indiatimes.com/India/Nandigrams_chemical_hub_shifted_to
_Nayachar/rssarticleshow/2335936.cms. Accessed May 31, 2009.

———. 2007d. "DVB Staff Held 'Directly Responsible' for Tragedy." November 24, Delhi edition.

———. 2008. "Another Metro Site Mishap Kills Worker." December 29, online edition. http://
timesofindia.indiatimes.com/Cities/Labourer_dies_at_a_Delhi_metro_site/articleshow
/3905430.cms. Accessed November 23, 2009.

———. 2009. "Gurgaon Metro Link to Be Completed in 30 Months." July 16, online edition.
http://timesofindia.indiatimes.com/city/delhi/Gurgaon-metro-link-to-be-completed-in-30
-months/articleshow/4781644.cms. Accessed June 28, 2015.

Tombesi, Paolo. 2001. "A True South for Design? The New International Division of Labour in
Architecture." *Architectural Research Quarterly* 5 (2):171–80.

Tombesi, Paolo, Bharat Dave, and Peter Scriver. 2003. "Routine Production or Symbolic Analysis? India and the Globalization of Architectural Services." *Journal of Architecture* 8: 63–94.

TrammellCrowMeghraj. 2006. "Information Technology (IT) and Information Technology Enabled Services (ITeS) Hubs in India," Quarter 4.

———. 2007. *Accelerating Transformation: Investments in Indian Real Estate.* Knowledge Centre
Strategy Paper Series 2 (1).

Traweek, Sharon. 1988. *Beamtimes and Lifetimes: The World of High Energy Physicists.* Cambridge, MA: Harvard University Press.

Trikona Trinity Capital PLC. 2008. *Reports & Accounts for the Year Ended 31 March 2008.*

Tsing, Anna Lowenhaupt. 2005. *Friction: An Ethnography of Global Connection.* Princeton, NJ:
Princeton University Press.

Turow, Joseph. 1997. *Breaking Up America: Advertisers and the New Media World.* Chicago: University of Chicago Press.

Unitech. 2007. *Annual Report, 2006–2007.* http://www.unitechgroup.com/investors/financials
.shtml. Accessed January 3, 2010.

———. 2008. "CIG Realty Fund IV." Powerpoint presentation. March.

———. 2009. *Annual Report, 2008–2009.* http://www.unitechgroup.com/investors/financials
.shtml. Accessed January 3, 2010.

Unitech Corporate Parks, Plc. 2006. *AIM Admission Document.*

Unnikrishnan, Rajesh. 2007. "Global Realtors on Retreat, $1b in Limbo." *Economic Times*, May 11.

Unnikrishnan, Rajesh, and Piyush Pandey. 2007. "Tatas Map Realty Foray, to Develop Land of Group Cos." *Economic Times*, May 25, online edition. http://economictimes.indiatimes .com/Tatas_map_realty_foray_to_develop_land_of_group_cos/articleshow/2072846.cms. Accessed May 22, 2009.

Upadhya, Carol. 2004. "A New Transnational Capitalist Class? Capital Flows, Business Networks and Entrepreneurs in the Indian Software Industry." *Economic and Political Weekly* 39 (48): 5141–51.

———. 2007. "Employment, Exclusion and 'Merit' in the Indian IT Industry." *Economic and Political Weekly* 42 (20): 1863–68.

Uprety, Pushpendra. 2007. "Real Estate Funds." *Hindustan Times*, April 27, Delhi edition.

US Department of Justice. Foreign Corrupt Practices Act. http://www.usdoj.gov/criminal/fraud /fcpa/. Accessed December 29, 2008.

Varrel, Aurelie. 2015. "Tapping the Diaspora Money: The Dynamics of the Indian Real Estate Corporate Sector through the Transnational Lens." American Association of Geographers annual meeting, April 23, Chicago, IL.

Verdery, Katherine. 2003. *The Vanishing Hectare: Property and Value in Postsocialist Transylvania.* Ithaca, NY: Cornell University Press.

Verma, Sunny, and Kakoly Chatterjee. 2008. "17 Months on, Residex Fails to House Real Data." *Financial Express*, December 16, online edition. http://www.financialexpress.com/news/17 -months-on-residex-fails-to-house-real-data/398798/. Accessed July 8, 2009.

Vinayak, Ramesh. 2006. "Land of Paradoxes." *India Today*, October 9.

Wadhwa, D. C. 2002. "Guaranteeing Title to Land: The Only Solution." November 22. http:// siteresources.worldbank.org/INTINDIA/Resources/dc_wadhwa_paper.pdf. Accessed July 31, 2008.

Wadhva, Kiran. 1989. *Role of Private Sector in Urban Housing—Case Study of Ahmedabad.* New Delhi: Human Settlement Management Institute (HUDCO).

Waldrop, Anne. 2004. "Gating and Class Relations: The Case of a New Delhi 'Colony'." *City & Society* 16 (2): 93–116.

Wall Street Journal. 2006. "Dow Jones BRIC-50 Index to Track Markets of Brazil, Russia, India and China." June 8, Eastern edition.

Webb, Martin. 2013. "Disciplining the Everyday State and Society? Anti-Corruption and Right to Information Activism in Delhi." *Contributions to Indian Sociology* 47 (3): 363–93.

Webster, Chris, Georg Glasze, and Klaus Frantz. 2002. "The Global Spread of Gated Communities." *Environment and Planning B: Planning and Design* 29: 315–20.

Weiner, Annette B. 1992. *Inalienable Possessions: The Paradox of Keeping-while-Giving.* Berkeley: University of California Press.

Weinstein, Liza. 2008. "Mumbai's Development Mafias: Globalization, Organized Crime and Land Development." *International Journal of Urban and Regional Research* 32 (1):22–39.

———. 2013. "Demolition and Dispossession: Toward an Understanding of State Violence in Millennial Mumbai." *Studies in Comparative International Development* 48 (3): 285–307.

———. 2014. "'One-Man Handled': Fragmented Power and Political Entrepreneurship in Globalizing Mumbai." *International Journal of Urban and Regional Research* 38 (1): 14–35.

Weiss, Robert S. 1994. *Learning from Strangers: The Art and Method of Qualitative Interview Studies.* New York: Free Press.

Wessel, David. 2007. "Financial Globalization's New Sources of Power." *Mint*, October 5.

Whitehead, Judy. 2003. "Space, Place and Primitive Accumulation in Narmada Valley and Beyond." *Economic and Political Weekly* 38 (40): 4224–30.

Whiting, Dominic. 2007. "India's Realty Boom Losing Steam?" *Hindustan Times*, April 26, Delhi edition.

Wilson, David. 2007. "Investors Have Reason to Cheer on Bric's Fourth Anniversary." *Mint*, October 3.

Wilson, Dominic, and Roopa Purushothaman. 2003. "Dreaming with BRICs: The Path to 2050." Goldman Sachs Global Economics Paper No. 99. October 1.

Witsoe, Jeffrey. 2011. "Corruption as Power: Caste and the Political Imagination of the Postcolonial State." *American Ethnography* 38 (1): 73–85.

Woodall, Pam. 2006. "The New Titans." *Economist* 380 (8495), September 16.

World Bank. 1994. *World Development Report 1994*. New York: Oxford University Press.

———. 2000. *India: Reducing Poverty, Accelerating Development*. New Delhi: Oxford University Press.

———. 2007. *Land Policies for Growth and Poverty Reduction*. Agriculture and Rural Development Sector Unit, South Asia Region. New Delhi: Oxford University Press.

Wright, Gwendolyn. 1991. *The Politics of Design in French Colonial Urbanism*. Chicago: University of Chicago Press.

Xiang, Biao. 2007. *Global 'Body Shopping': An Indian Labor System in the Information Technology Industry*. Princeton, NJ: Princeton University Press.

Yanagisako, Sylvia. 2002. *Producing Culture and Capital: Family Firms in Italy*. Princeton, NJ: Princeton University Press.

Yates, JoAnne. 1989. *Control through Communication: The Rise of System in American Management*. Baltimore: Johns Hopkins University Press.

Yeoh, Brenda S. A. 1996. *Contesting Space in Colonial Singapore: Power Relations in the Urban Built Environment*. Oxford: Oxford University Press.

Zachariah, Reena, and Rajesh Abraham. 2007. "Hedge Funds Make a Beeline for Real Estate Sector." *Business Standard*, October 8.

Zakaria, Fareed. 2006. "India Rising." *Newsweek*, March 6.

Zaloom, Caitlin. 2006. *Out of the Pits: Traders and Technology from Chicago to London*. Chicago: University of Chicago Press.

Zhang, Li. 2010. *In Search of Paradise: Middle-Class Living in a Chinese Metropolis*. Ithaca, NY: Cornell University Press.

Index